Art: Rick Griffin

**In Memory of
Rick Griffin**
(1944 – 1991)

pages i-ii, 199-200:
Tapa cloth from Western Samoa

THE Surfin'ARY

A DICTIONARY OF SURFING TERMS AND SURFSPEAK

Art: The Pizz

COMPILED AND EDITED BY TREVOR CRALLE

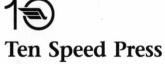

Ten Speed Press
Berkeley, California

This book is dedicated to my parents, Bob and Judy Cralle.

Ten Speed Press
P. O. Box 7123
Berkeley, CA 94707

Cover and text design/production by Fifth Street Design, Berkeley, California
Front cover photo of Ray Chapman at San Quintin, Baja by Aaron Chang
Back cover photo of Trevor Cralle at Myth Beach, California by Bill Schwob
Edited by Carol Henderson

Library of Congress Cataloging-in-Publication Data

Cralle, Trevor.
    The Surfin'ary / Trevor Cralle
       p.   cm.
    Includes bibliographical references.
    ISBN 0-89815-422-7
    1. Surfing—Dictionaries.   I. Title.
GV840.S8C66   1991   90-28517
797.32'03—dc20   CIP

Printed in the United States of America

   2 3 4 5 – 95 94 93 92

Table Of Contents

Art: Jen Delyth

Backdoor Pipeline
North Shore, Oahu, Hawaii
Photo: Bill Romerhaus

FOREWORD

The Surfin'ary is much more than a dictionary. It is a walk down the memory lane of surfing, a time machine that will transport you anywhere in the history of surfing. Sometime in the early sixties I bought my first book on surfing. Since then I have acquired more than 180 books about the culture of surfing. I have been the director of the surfing program at the University of California, Santa Cruz, for seventeen years, and I am on the board of directors of the Surfrider Foundation. I write a regular surfing column for a surfing magazine and consider myself a surfing bibliographer. I am very concerned about preserving and recording the history of surfing, and it is exactly this service that Trevor Cralle has admirably performed for all surfers as well as for the rest of the world. *The Surfin'ary* is an invaluable contribution to the history of surfing.

I rode my first wave (actually the *soup*) sometime in the latter part of 1961. Almost overnight I became a surf junkie. It wasn't long before my entire lifestyle metamorphosed, and surfing became the focal point of my existence. My vocabulary began to change, also. I began to use words like *bitchin', Cowabunga!, hang ten, walkin', wipeout, surfari.* I began having trouble communicating with my parents and nonsurfing friends; for that matter I still do. Enter Trevor Cralle. His epic work, six years in the making, defines not only my childhood verbiage from the sixties but also surfing terms from the seventies, eighties, and nineties, as well as ancient Hawaiian terms. This book will be an essential aid in helping surfers and nonsurfers communicate with each other. It will even help *surfers* communicate with each other. This book could be a college text for a cultural anthropology class!

The wonderful thing about language is that it is always changing. The climate of the nineties and beyond will definitely affect surf talk, creating more new words, words that the surfers of today won't be able to comprehend. Trevor says this is only the first edition and he will continue to record the language of surfers in future editions.

Put this book by your waterbed or beach chair and read ten or twenty pages a day. You can't help but learn something new and entertaining on every page. Get stoked!

Ward Smith
Santa Cruz, California
March 1991

PADDLING OUT: A PREFACE

The Surfin'ary is the first serious attempt at a complete vocabulary of the surfer and the sport of surfing. Surfing and the ocean have always fascinated me. From the time I was born, my parents took me to different beaches up and down the California coast. We rented a house in Newport Beach every summer, where I first saw hip-looking kids hanging out with their surfboards at the beach. Like many surfers, I began wave riding with bodysurfing, and later I graduated to a surf mat. In 1975, at age fourteen, I bought my first surfboard in Santa Cruz — a heavy old nine foot, eleven inch Holden longboard with a laminated wooden skeg. I'll never forget the first time that same summer when I stood up at La Jolla Shores and rode a wave straight into the beach. That feeling of stoke lit a spiritual fire inside me which every surfer can relate to.

I've always enjoyed describing waves and rides and talking surf with my friends. The idea for a surfing dictionary evolved from reading glossaries that have appeared over the years in books about surfing. In the summer of 1984, I began entering those glossaries on a computer in the hope of creating the ultimate surfing glossary. Soon I had around five hundred terms — the seeds of *The Surfin'ary.*

Next I combed through hundreds of back issues of surfing magazines. Another source — an especially entertaining one — was the glossaries on the backs of old sixties surf music albums (not always known for their high degree of accuracy).

I also conducted extensive field research for this book, primarily in California, Hawaii, and Australia. I did additional work in Mexico, the Caribbean, the South Pacific, and Indonesia. Wherever I was — on the beach, at surf shops, out in the lineup waiting for waves with fellow surfers — I carried out interviews.

In 1990, the Australian magazine *Tracks* and Southern California's *Surfer* Magazine featured pieces on *The Surfin'ary.* These articles, and flyers I distributed to surf shops, asked surfers to send me their favorite words. This request elicited many strange and wonderful responses. For example, I got a call from a bank teller in Sherman Oaks, California (the San Fernando Valley), whose friend was an undercover cop posing as a surfer. She wanted to give him a copy of *The Surfin'ary* so he would know what to say and sound hip. I also received numerous letters from surfers around the world who sent in their local terms.

The need for a surfing dictionary was brought home to me in New Zealand in the fall of 1988. Some kiwi friends, who didn't surf, tried to mimic California surfer talk with sayings such as "Oh, woe, wipe me out — I'm out the backdoor" to mean "No way, you're kidding."

"That's old-style Beach Boys talk," they said, and continued to use expressions like "Wipe me out the backdoor" or "Blow me out the backdoor" to say "See ya later" or "Good-bye."

Along the same lines, an editor at a major East Coast newspaper with international distribution, unsure whether to run a front-page article on *The Surfin'ary,* asked, "Do people in California still surf after Labor Day?" Although some surfers may feel that such ignorance is its own punishment, this editor's misperception made me realize that *The Surfin'ary* might help the media, and other terrestrial professions, understand our surf reality a little better.

Because surfspeak is so totally dynamic and culture specific (or culture bound, as some linguists prefer), its varied meanings and usages can never be fully conveyed to an outsider who hasn't ridden the big one. This kind of action-based knowledge is intimately understood and masterfully used by those who surf. Outside of the surf context, something gets lost in translation and delivery.

The Surfin'ary is intended for all those interested in surfing, including the novice and the nonsurfer who may want to learn about the sport. It is also for the experienced surfer, well-versed in surf talk, who is curious to find out what surfers are saying in different parts of the world. Anyone interested in or involved with the ocean should find this a wealth of information. *The Surfin'ary* collects and preserves our rich and diverse global surfing culture. Although there are many great books on surfing, none has focused in such detail on the language of the surfer. This book attempts to chronicle how surfers communicate with each other. Surf's up!

The author with his first surf-board at La Jolla (1975) and today in Baja.
Photos: Nina Aldrich-Wolfe (left), Judith Cralle (right)

Trevor Cralle
Surf City, California
April 1991

ACKNOWLEDGMENTS

This book is the result of a collaboration between many individuals, including hundreds of surfers past and present, renowned and unknown. Also, without the many books and magazines on surfing, and other published materials, this project would have been virtually impossible. I am deeply indebted to all of the interviewees for their contributions. As much as feasible, I have tried to give credit throughout this book to the various surfers, scientists, writers, and other individuals who made this project a reality. Please consult the sources and credits at the back of the book for a complete listing, including all the photographers and illustrators who have brought the text to life.

First and foremost, I wish to thank my parents, Robert Kenner Cralle and Judith Ann Schuyler Cralle, for all of their love, encouragement, and support, which has allowed me the freedom to follow my bliss. Thanks to my dear sister, Heather Stover; my niece, Cassandra Marie; and my brother-in-law, Rick Stover. Thanks to my granny, Margaret Cralle, who used to bodysurf at Redondo Beach even before George Freeth!

I wish to thank my very special friends Ellen Nachtigall and Michelle Anne Stevens, who each lived with me for about a year and a half while I was working on the manuscript. Their encouragement, patience, ideas, and enthusiasm were constant sources of strength. Michelle, you were in it since day one. Thanks, El, for being a great travel buddy, for all the great concepts, and for coming up with the title *The Surfin'ary*.

Invaluable advice, comments, and criticism came from the following special consultants and contributing editors: Dan Jenkin ("Paco"), Drew Steele, Amy Agigian, Ben Marcus at *Surfer* Magazine, and Pizz. Significant contributions also came from Lisa Hybarger, Mac Reed, Ken Seino, and Ward Smith.

My thanks are also due to the following individuals: Paul McEntyre, Michael Fletcher, Laura Agigian, Greg Histed, Rebecca Fish, Kini Harvey, Jan Thorell, Sherry Carlson, Lulie Haddad, Jawara, Karen Delgadillo, Tom Dodd, Laura Platt, Ken Regalia, Kirk Steers, Dr. James D. Rawls, Mike Peterson, Dan Bush, Valerie Jones, Ira Miller, and The Geneva Brothers — especially Tony Misner and Brian Plotkin.

I wish to thank the students, staff, and alumni of Maybeck High School, especially the class of '79. Thanks to Dave "The Wave" Kinstle, my high school teacher, mentor, travel partner, best buddy, guiding light. Thanks to Kathleen Aldrich, whose English classes I struggled through; she twisted the thumbscrews so tight that I eventually had to write a complete sentence, which made me a better writer.

Special thanks to Professor Barney Q. Nietschmann and Doug Powell at the University of California, Berkeley, for introducing me to the wonderful world of geography. Thanks to Lloyd Austin and all the U.C. Divers, especially Scott Cameron and Henry Kaiser.

Many thanks to the California Coastal Commission staff, and especially to Gary Holloway for his boundless enthusiasm and wealth of information. Thanks to Mary Travis and Jo Ginsberg for all the "little lifts." Thanks also to Victoria Randlet, Marty Frum, Lee Micheaux, and Briggs Nisbet.

Lucky Roberts, a hep cat, my publishing consultant and total pal, brought me luck and publication. I also want to thank J. T. O'Hara ("The Queen of Mental Health"), who earned her other title, "The Finder." Thanks to Jim Herron Zamora, whose front-page *Wall Street Journal* article about *The Surfin'ary* set off a wave of media attention and inquiries.

Thanks to Fifth Street Design, first and foremost to Brent Beck, who designed the book and was completely dialed in to the vision, and to Judy Hicks, whose contributions were many. Thanks also to his partner, Jerry Meek, the resident expert in converting a computer-generated manuscript, such as mine, into a typeset book. I also want to acknowledge the efforts of all the people working behind the scenes during the book's production, especially the proofreaders.

I would like to extend a very special thanks to my editor, Carol Henderson. I was a bit skeptical at first when I walked into her home and saw a Mexican Christmas tree ornament in the form of a wooden blue shark dangling in front of her computer screen, with pink legs protruding from the shark's jaws. Did she not like surfers? It turned out to be a very good omen. Thank you, Carol, for all your concentrated energy and wonderful input into this project.

Finally, the crew at Ten Speed, including David Hinds, Phil Wood, George Young, and Sal Glynn, are simply great. Six years ago when I began working on this book, I dreamed that one day Ten Speed Press would publish it. Now this dream has come true.

Photo: Bill Romerhaus

OFF-THE-LIP:
AN INTRODUCTION
TO SURFSPEAK

stoked: To catch a wave was (and is) to stoke the fires of the heart and soul; hence the terms: to be stoked, the stoked life, degrees of stoke, and pure stoke.

— **John Grissim**, *Pure Stoke* (1982)

"Hey, bro, Topanga is going off! Yeah, it's pumping, hair balls, man. Totally macking; six feet and offshore." Translation: Yo, dude, a specific surfing location is producing exceptionally large, six-foot-high waves that are big and powerful, like a Mack truck; also, the wind is blowing favorably from the land out to sea — the surf's up!

Ever since the 1959 Hollywood movie *Gidget* made the bohemian life of the Malibu surfer look and sound alluring, surfing terms have trickled into the American mainstream. And since 1961, the songs of The Beach Boys (for instance, "California Girls") have fueled the land-locked dreams of those people who, never having seen the ocean, can only imagine what it's like to "catch a wave" and view the world from a different perspective. Yet the complex language of the surfer has been around for a long time, dating back to ancient Polynesia, where the sport of surfing originated centuries ago.

Surfers have developed a language with a colorful vocabulary of words and expressions. Many of the terms and phrases used by surfers are international in scope, yet they are relatively unknown to people outside the sport.

Why is everyone so fascinated by surfspeak? The sun, sand, and surf combine to form a wonderful fantasy of relaxed pace and gentle sensuality that has captivated people for ages. The popular image of the surfer as a bleached-blonde, blue-eyed, suntanned male with salt caked on his eyelids, is held attractive. The romance and mystery of the ocean, with all the potential dangers, such as large sharks (yipes!), that a surfer may encounter, have always been captivating. Big-wave surf pioneer Phil Edwards likened the act of surfing to mountain climbing — only in this case the mountain chases after you. Surf lingo sounds hip. It's free-flowing and often humorous.

Surfers don't conform to any particular set of rules. So why should their language? The surfer speaks from the heart with a playful, lazily articulated slang that reflects a laid-back, unhurried life. Standard

English does not cover the nuances that surfspeak embraces, such as the term *tube chip* (any tortilla chip that resembles a curling wave).

Surfers have found a way of embracing nature and harmonizing with its flow that is lacking in late twentieth-century pedestrian life. Whereas many individuals are estranged from the natural world, surfers are immersed in it.

The majority of surfing terms spring from California, Hawaii, and Australia, the major wave centers of the world. Modern Hawaiian surfing terms are a mixture of words from the Hawaiian language and Hawaiian Pidgin English. In Hawaiian, bad sores on the feet caused by stepping on coral are called *kakios.* Australian surfers call hammerhead sharks *formula ones* — like the racing car.

Surfing Meets the Valley

If you can't surf, at least you can try to talk like a surfer or attempt to dress the part. In 1982, surfing slang moved inland and burst into national — even international — prominence with the hit song "Valley Girl" by Frank Zappa. The tune contained lyrics made up of dialogue overheard by his daughter, Moon Unit, at the Sherman Oaks Galleria shopping mall in the San Fernando Valley, just north of Los Angeles. But as a special language confined to the San Fernando Valley, "Valspeak" is a media myth. The particular accent and slang words associated with Valspeak can be heard among many middle-class teenagers in other suburban areas.

> Surfing's been a real trendsetter — surf music, fashion, even the lingo. You know, terms that were developed on the beach to describe waves and rides and other surfers you end up hearing on sitcoms a year later, like "dweeb." I've heard that word a hundred times on TV, but I made it up a buncha years ago. Or that so-called Valley Girl slang, which is really beach talk that moved a few miles east 'cause the Vals were hangin' out on the beach. "Gnarly," "rad," "radical to the max," it was all beach talk. But now you can walk into a school in Boise, Idaho, and hear kids talking like that.
>
> — **Corky Carroll (1989)**

Surfing spin-off sports, such as skateboarding, windsurfing, and snowboarding, have appropriated surf terms for their specific argots. Surf talk also draws on the icons of popular culture, especially those of TV and film, which everyone can relate to. A *casper,* as in "the Friendly Ghost," is a fair-skinned tourist who comes out to the beach.

The 1989 movie *Fast Times at Ridgemont High* was the single most important event propelling surf terms such as *dude* and *gnarly* into the mainstream. The film *Under the Boardwalk* introduced *bro* to the moviegoing masses. More recent creations, like the Teenage Mutant Ninja Turtles and Bart Simpson have adopted words such as *radical* and *Cow-*

1962

Moondoggie: *Didja see that kuk, man? He cut me off just as I was about to hang ten. I was so stoked. It was a bitchin wave.*
Tubesteak: *Yeah, well, that hot dog never takes gas, even on the die. But listen, man, it's gettin' cold, anyway. Wish I had my beavertail. Let's split and get some burgers. We can check out Motherbu on the way.*

abunga! (a surfer's exultant cry). Still, the surf slang presented by the media represents only a few grains of sand from the vast beaches of surf lingo.

Terms from the suit-'n'-tie workaday world brought into an atmosphere of salt air evoke a sense of whimsy. Witness the variation called *surf crimes* (legalese applied to surfing): "Guy got 'prosecuted' on that wave" (wiped out to the fullest extent).

The ultimate surfing experience — a *tube ride,* where the surfer gets *covered up* by a *barreling* wave — is akin to a religious vision, sometimes described as a *whirling cathedral, going to church,* or being *in the Pope's living room.*

Surfers can be very territorial and their lexicon is full of derogatory terms aimed at people who aren't lucky enough to live near the beach: *nonlocals, valleys, inland squids, flatlanders, smog monsters,* etc.

Over the years, surfing terminology has evolved. For example, a *pipeline* (a fifties term) became a *tube* in the sixties, which became a *barrel* in the seventies and eighties. Terms have also been adjusted to follow changing surfboard technology, which now enables surfers to execute moves never before attempted, let alone named. The hot surf moves of the fifties and sixties were *drop-knee cutbacks, quasimotos, hanging ten, cover-ups, head dips,* and *soul arches.* In the seventies, along with radically shorter boards, came *roundhouses, reentries, backdoors, off-the-lips,* and *snapbacks.* Now we're dealing with *floaters, aerials,* and *slashes.* Waves have gone from *steep* to *hollow* to *square* and from *rolling* to *tubing* to *dredging* to *grinding.*

Surfers are keen on abbreviations, as illustrated by the following names for surf spots: *J-Bay* for Jeffrey's Bay, a famous right pointbreak in South Africa; *V-Land* for Velzyland in Hawaii, named after the famous surfboard manufacturer, Dale Velzy; *K35, K38,* and *K39,* roadside kilometer markings where the surf is good in Baja. Other abbreviations include *TK* for totally killer, *nar* for gnarly, *reo* for reentry, and *tri,* a three-finned surfboard. In Santa Cruz, surfers are breaking new ground in lazy surf talk with minimal-effort expressions like *"Zup"* (for "What's up"), to which the reply would be *"Nuch"* ("Not much"); Orange County surfers say *"S'later"* for "See you later" and *"Latronic"* for "Later on, dude," which has been shortened even further to *"Lonic."*

Why are so many surf terms so funny? This may seem like an obvious question. Living at the beach, frolicking under the sun, surfing in the saltwater playground is a totally healthy and positive experience, which breeds true endorphin-induced happiness.

Surfing terms are continually being created afresh. While words like *stoke, ripping,* and *barrel* are constants throughout the surfing world, regional conditions and attitudes lead to hundreds of specially encoded

1981

Shaun: *The break was way zooed out, man. I shoulda said later for that. But it was really pumping, hair balls, man. Totally gnarly. Soon as I caught my wave, some goob, probly a valley, cut me off. I sliced his board.*
Scott: *I was watchin', man. The dude's a gyro goon. His board got real dung up. Way rad. I heard tomorrow'll be all mush doggies. Blown out totally.*

"Beach Banter" cartoon
Art: Rick Griffin

sublingos, which don't always spread throughout the global surfing community. Local surfers are the only ones completely immersed in their own indigenous lingo, and they often use slang specifically to keep outsiders at bay.

In Santa Cruz, a group of "East Side" surfers invented a surfing sub-language in the late 1980s that stems from their word *haken,* which means "to go surfing." From that one word they have created a seemingly endless vocabulary that includes terms like *hakenvesmo* (to surf — with a meal afterwards) and *haken visuals* (getting good barrels). These terms can probably never be fully appreciated by outsiders. The language of the surfer can metamorphose within a sentence. Surfers fool around with different combinations of words and if the result sounds good, they keep it.

Although surf talk may sound simplistic, it has been shaped by a vast and varied set of influences. The earliest known surfing terms came from the Hawaiians, who had words for every aspect of the sport. *Nuumehalani* referred to a surf site on Oahu meaning "the heavenly site where you are alone." *Ahua* was a place close to shore where a broken wave rose and broke again.

A Breakfast Note before Kicking Out

Just as Eskimos have fifty-two different terms to describe various kinds of snow, and desert nomads in the Sahara have numerous terms for all the types of sand, surfers have countless words for waves, from *micro* to *gnarlatious* to *sucky* to *burgery.* A good rule of thumb for the true surf linguist is that any adjective used to describe your breakfast food can also be used to describe a wave: *crispy, crunchy, hearty, tasty, sweet, unreal,* and so on.

Misguided dweeby types who perceive surf lingo as juvenile do so, perhaps, because of their own ambivalent feelings. Like any normal human, they yearn for sun, fun, and fancy-free existence to the beat of nature's rhythms. But, due to career pursuit, the work ethic, or whatever, they belittle surfing because it doesn't produce wealth and hence is deemed unworthy of adult activity.

True surfers realize how spiritually wealthy the ocean, waves, and they — the riders of ocean and waves — really are. They place their love for this wealth above the desire to make money. These values are seen in expressions like *soul surfing,* to describe noncompetitive surfing for the fun of it, and *the Big Mama,* for the ocean. The surfer's life is attractive to much of the world because it embodies that unbridled, raw, uncontrollable lust for life that so many people who live only to make money have become numb to. It's exactly this joyous youthfulness that keeps surfers, both young and old, in the water and near the ocean.

All of these influences make surfspeak a textured, richly layered language that requires the experience of surfing for its meaning to be fully understood. At the same time, its free-flowing multitextuality makes it universally appealing and enthralling to all. *Fer sure.*

Art: Rick Stover

Paul Gebauer, Sunset Beach,
Hawaii
Photo: John Severson / Surfer
Magazine

WHAT IS SURFING?

surfing: (sur'fing) *n*. A water sport, in which the participant stands on a floating slab of wood resembling an ironing board in both size and shape, and attempts to remain perpendicular while being hurtled toward the shore at a rather frightening rate of speed on the crest of a huge wave. (Especially recommended for teenagers and all others without the slightest regard for either life or limb.)

— The Beach Boys, *Surfin' U.S.A.* album liner notes (1963)

Surfing is a thrilling water sport for persons of all ages that has been practiced for centuries. The act itself involves riding across the face of a wave toward the shore while standing on a special board, called a surfboard. Modern surfboards are made of foam and fiberglass and come in various shapes and sizes, from shortboards to longboards and everything in between.

Although the above definition describes surfing at its purest, the sport takes several forms: *bodysurfing,* the simplest variation, with just a body and a wave (some people wear fins or use a hand-planing device, such as a swimmer's kickboard); *bellyboarding,* with a small wooden or plastic board; *bodyboarding* (also called *boogie boarding*), with a flexible foam board; *mat surfing,* with inflated rubber surf mats; and *kneeboarding,* using a smaller, specialized surfboard. Surfers also ride the waves on *wave skis, surf skis,* and *paddleboards* and do *boat surfing* with dories, canoes, sea kayaks, and catamarans. Out on the open ocean, sailboats "surf" down unbroken swells. Surfing spin-off sports include *snowboarding* on mountain ski slopes, *sandboarding* on sand dunes, *skimboarding* along the shoreline, and *windsurfing (sailboarding)* on a modified surfboard with a sail. Even *skateboarding* has its roots in surfing.

Regardless of the type of surfing, the basic principles are the same. The surfer strokes with the arms, or paddles, toward the shore just ahead of an incoming, unbroken wave. As the wave moves forward and catches up to the surfer, the surfboard (or body, raft, bodyboard, etc.) starts to slide down the face of the wave. At this point the surfer has caught the wave and must stay just ahead of the breaking portion of the wave to maintain the ride; this is done by shifting body weight to maneuver the board in the appropriate direction.

Surfing takes place along all of the coastlines of the world, but California, Hawaii, and Australia are the best-known areas because of their many high-quality surf spots, large surfing populations, and local knowledge combined with advanced design and equipment technology. The most highly regarded surfing spots are usually locations where waves either approach the shore at an angle, break over an offshore

Art: Deano

Art: The Pizz

reef, or are refracted around a protruding landform, such as a rocky point or a headland.

Surfing is a sport, an art form, a subculture, a social phenomenon, an existential attitude, and a way of life that is worldwide. The popular image of the surfer has changed over the years. The hip but clean-cut surfers in the movie *Gidget* (1959) became the long-haired, pot-smoking Spicoli types in *Fast Times at Ridgemont High* (1982). Today's professional surfer is once again clean-cut, and the advertisements in surfing magazines reflect fashion consciousness. Regardless of the image portrayed by the media, however, surfers are a diverse group of individuals who do not conform to any set type.

Surfers feel a special connection to the ocean environment because they are in tune with the rhythms of the sea. It is no wonder humans feel such an attraction to our mother ocean when 98 percent of our bodily fluids are made up of saltwater. The amazing truth is that the sound of the waves crashing and receding is a direct reproduction of the sound of the blood flow heard by a baby in its mother's womb. This rhythm creates a feeling of tranquility for all of us, as it does for the unborn child.

In surfing, we have found a way to use an untapped energy source. As George Leonard notes in *The Ultimate Athlete* (1974), "A surfer takes only the barest minimum of equipment into the sea and prevails — not by opposing but by joining a wave." Surfing is a unique activity because each wave is always changing, so that each ride is a new experience.

Brian Wilson of The Beach Boys probably said it best in 1962 with the line, "Catch a wave and you're sittin' on top of the world." The surfer views the world from a different perspective — from a place high above everyone else:

> . . . and for one quick second up there I could see all of Dana Point, Capistrano Beach, the beige hills off inland Omaha, Nebraska, and everything.
>
> **— Phil Edwards (1967), on catching a wave**

Surfing embodies a multitude of senses and sensations, including the sound of a wave crashing; the thrill of watching someone else get a hot ride; the intoxicating smell of surf wax, neoprene wetsuits, and fiberglass surfboards in a surf shop; and the euphoric feeling of tapping the pure source of an ocean wave.

There are risks involved when taking off on a big, powerful ocean wave, where one false move can get you pounded into a razor-sharp coral reef or held down beneath the surface for what may seem like an eternity. There are also moments of elation: the rush of adrenaline that you feel when dropping down the steep face of a towering wave —

making the drop — and shooting back up to the top of the wave and continuing on a hot ride; and the ultimate in surfing — a tube ride, when the breaking wave that is being ridden curls overhead and engulfs you in a churning liquid cylinder. All of these elements combine to give the surfer that stoked feeling that gives rise to endless hours of storytelling.

> Surfing attracts dedicated cultists who build their lives around their sport — but so does golf. The important distinction between the two is that no one ever stays up late to catch a great golf flick on the late show. No one cruises down Pacific Coast Highway with the radio blasting out a bitchin' golf tune. Indeed . . . there is something very nearly mystical about the lone surfer who spends hours bobbing atop powerful ocean swells just for the chance to thrust himself into the curl of a breaking wave for a few heart-stopping moments. "Surfing is a dance form, and the ocean is like a liquid stage," says one veteran surfer.
> — **Jonathan Kirsch, "Still Surfin' After All These Years,"** *New West* **(May 1981)**

Surfers all over the world share a reverence for the sensations that surfing evokes. Through this common love of the ocean and the sport of surfing, surfers are able to communicate with one another. Truly, this love is so intense that it crosses borders and bridges cultural gaps that language and governments are unable to span. Reduced to instinctual survival in the surf, we are united with each other at the most fundamental level.

But why do we continually subject ourselves to the potential dangers of the waves? Being out in the ocean stimulates a sensation of extreme vitality that is druglike and addictive. As any surfer will tell you, there's no feeling in the world comparable to gliding on water, bringing us closer to the gods of the ocean and satisfying the soul through a form of art and play as pure as the ocean itself.

Art: The Pizz

THE HISTORY OF SURFING!

A BRIEF HISTORY OF SURFING

Long before humans began using surfboards for surfing on waves, marine mammals such as dolphins and sea lions were taking energy out of waves to propel themselves along the front of an advancing wave. The sport and art of surfing originated centuries ago (some claim A.D. 400) somewhere in the Pacific islands, most likely Polynesia. This wave-riding activity was started, perhaps accidentally, by fisherfolk who had to get their ocean-going crafts out and back through the surf. In 1777, British explorer Captain James Cook observed islanders surfing at Matavai Point in Tahiti. Cook also noticed people surfing when he visited the Sandwich (Hawaiian) Islands in 1778.

Beginning in 1821, surfing was almost completely eliminated by European Christian missionaries, who considered it an immoral form of amusement and suppressed it along with much else in the Hawaiian culture. By the time surfing was revived around the turn of the century, there were only a handful of Hawaiian surfers left.

Surfing was "officially" introduced to California in 1907 when the Irish-Hawaiian surfer George Freeth visited from Hawaii to put on some surfing exhibitions at Redondo Beach in Southern California. However, evidence suggests that Hawaiian Prince David Kawonanaokoa surfed Santa Cruz in Northern California in 1885 and was probably the first

Hawaiian man with his family and surfboard by a beach shelter, 1890s
Photo: T. Severin / Bishop Museum

person ever to surf in California. Hawaiian Olympic swimmer Duke Kahanamoku popularized the sport in California beginning in 1911 and introduced surfing to Australia at Freshwater Beach, Sydney, in 1915.

At first the sport attracted only a limited following, one reason being that early surfboards were 14 to 18 feet long and each was constructed of a solid redwood plank weighing up to 150 pounds. Tom Blake invented the "hollow" surfboard in 1928 at Waikiki, reducing the weight to 75–100 pounds. He later contributed another important design feature when he attached a fin (also called a *skeg*) to the underside of a paddleboard in 1935. The birth of modern surfing came with the introduction of lightweight balsa boards in the 1940s and the development of polyurethane foam boards in the 1950s, the latter of which changed the sport forever.

The 1959 film *Gidget* set the stage for a string of Hollywood beach movies in the 1960s, which planted a very strong suggestion that the bohemian life of the surfer was just the sort of romantic world a teenager would like to escape to. In the early 1960s came a wave of instrumental surf music that was shortly joined by vocal groups, led by The Beach Boys, whose anthems spread inland and, fueling the surfing dreams of landlocked people who had never seen the ocean, turned into a national craze that touched the world. Bruce Brown's *The Endless Summer* (1964), a real-life adventure documentary film about two California surfers who traveled around the world in search of "the perfect wave," generated another positive image for surfing.

The wetsuit — a snug-fitting neoprene rubber garment invented in the early 1960s — kept surfers warm and made surfing a year-round activity in temperate waters. The Shortboard Revolution, in the mid- to late sixties, sparked a period of innovative surfboard design that has continued to the present.

The surf leash, or leg rope, a flexible cord that tethers the surfboard to the surfer's ankle, was experimented with in the late sixties and became standard equipment in the 1970s. The leash made the sport a little safer and accessible to a greater number of individuals; it also opened up many new surf spots where previously a lost board would have been smashed on the rocks. Professional surfing was born in the late 1970s and dominated by the Australians.

The growth of surfing was marked by the commercialism of the 1980s. Surf fashion, which has always set trends, grew into a $2-billion-a-year industry. The bright, often fluorescent, multicolored wetsuits, surf trunks, and T-shirts became the uniform for youth in America. Surf music and longboarding experienced tremendous revivals, and surfing museums began to appear.

The average surfboard weighed about eight pounds and was around six feet in length. In 1981, with the advent of Australian Simon Anderson's revolutionary design for the three-fin surfboard, called the *thruster*, surfing was well on its way into the ultramodern era.

Until the 1980s, surfers were never really known for their social, political, or environmental activism, but that has changed dramatically. The Surfrider Foundation, a California-based environmental watchdog group dedicated to saving waves, monitoring coastal development, stopping ocean pollution, and preserving coastal access, has experienced phenomenal membership growth among surfers since its inception in 1984. Surfers Against Apartheid is a group of professional wave riders who have boycotted surfing competitions in South Africa since 1985. The San Francisco–based Surfer's Medical Association was formed in 1985. Australian organizations, also formed during the 1980s, include Surfers for Rainforests and Surfers Against Nuclear Destruction.

Surf-O-Rama poster, 1961
Dave Kinstle Collection

left:
Surfers catching a wave, Waikiki, 1925
Photo: Honolulu Advertiser / Bishop Museum

below:
Tom Blake with his surfboard, Waikiki
Photo: Bishop Museum

overleaf :
Art: Bob Penuelas

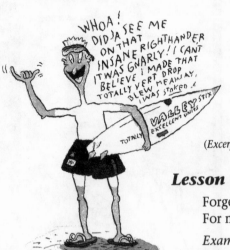

Art: Peter Spacek

SURFISH AS A SECOND LANGUAGE

Dr. John Cohen, Ph.S. (Doctor of Surfish)
(*Excerpted with permission from* Surfer Magazine, *"Getting Air," September 1984*)

Lesson #1

Forget every rule you've ever learned about English.
For most of you, this will create no problem at all.

Examples: See Lessons 2–10

Lesson #2

Use one adjective as a complete sentence whenever possible.

Examples: Crucial. Random. Critical. Treacherous. Solid. Unreal.
Insane. Bizarre. Cool. Hot. Awesome.

Lesson #3

Add "dude" or "bro" to the end of each sentence that begins with
an adjective.

Examples: Crucial, dude. Critical, bro. Insane, dude. Unreal, bro.

Lesson #4

Modify nouns, verbs and modifiers whenever possible.
Modifiers include: entirely, so, too, totally, super, heavily
and sorta.

Examples: Don't say: It was happening at Eleventh Street. Say: It
was so happening at Eleventh Street. Don't say: That flick was
cool. Say: That flick was totally cool. Don't say: It was crowded.
Say: It was super crowded.

Lesson #5

ALWAYS use "way" instead of "very."

Examples: Don't say: These waves are very good. Say: These waves
are way good. Don't say: The tide was very low. Say: The tide was
way low. Don't say: It was very hard when I broke my arm and
couldn't surf. Say: It was way hard when I broke my arm and
couldn't surf.

Lesson #6

Describe waves in terms of cereal.

Examples: The inside was crunchy. It was insanely crispy yesterday. I just got the tastiest wave! The outside's pretty chewy. It gets tres mushy when the tide goes in. Tomorrow's gonna be fully scrumptious.

Lesson #7

To save time, abbreviate whenever possible.

Examples: We can hit DT's in the Whaler. Let's cruise the cycles down to HB. Fresh heiny's in the fridge, bro. Note: Save more time by calling both the ocean and the waves "it." (e.g., "Howz it look?", "How was it?", "Let's check it out.")

Lesson #8

Use aggressive verbs whenever possible. Excellent examples of aggressive verbs include: dominate, capitalize, blow out, blow away, shred, destroy, crank, whip, rip and zip.

Examples: We dominated the peak all morning. You entirely capitalized on that right. I cranked this screaming bottom turn, destroyed the lip by cranking a hard cutback, and then I totally blew everyone out by shredding the inside section and zipping off a reentry before ripping off a part of my foot on the reef.

Lesson #9

Only talk about subjects you're way familiar with. Safe topics include: the tide, yesterday's waves, tomorrow's swell, the opposite sex, parties, concerts, racks, and pressure systems.

Lesson #10

To finish off our class, you should be warned not to use Olde Surfish as it will definitely brand you a geek. Words to avoid include: baggies, gremmies, combers, breakers, tubular, ho-dads, nay (instead of no), chicks (try wahinis or ladies), da kine, far out, primo and man.

AN ILLUSTRATED GLOSSARY OF SURFING TERMS

Before going any further with this article, it will be necessary for the reader to familiarize himself with the Surfer's private language. There is a definite purpose in this language. It was not created for any of the square reasons that many Clubs or Fraternal Organizations have for their mumbo-jumbo. It was not created just to have a silly secret language. The reason for Hip Surfer Talk is more serious and meaningful than that. It's to show off!

"GREMMIE"

A beginning Surfer. Easily recognized because they're the ones who mostly use the idiotic words on this page.

"HO-DAD"

A refugee from the drop-out motorcycle set who takes up Surfing. Easily recognized because they can only dig the pictures on this page.

"DING"

What happens when your surf-board hits something hard.

"BING"

What happens when the some-thing hard your surfboard hits hits you right back.

"ALL-TIME"

A great surf! For example, Hawaii's surf is always all-time! California's surf is often all-time! Arizona's surf is never all-time!

"TAKING GAS"

Losing control and going down — not to be confused with stealing fuel from a parked car to get to beach.

"DOWN"

What happens to a Surfer after "taking gas." He is underwater and is expected to reappear momentarily.

"DROWN"

What happens to a Surfer after "taking gas." He is underwater — not expected to reappear momentarily.

"SAND"

Found in every orifice and pore of a Surfer's body, it makes a gritting sound when he chews or blinks his eyes.

"BULLY"

A big bronze-skinned Surfer who carelessly kicks sand when he walks on the beach.

"SKINNY"

A weak pale-skinned Surfer who usually gets all of the sand kicked by the Bully.

"VAVAVOOM"

A beach bunny who goes off with the Bully, leaving the Skinny — while everyone else wonders what she saw in the Skinny in the first place.

"PUKA"

This is not what a Surfer becomes when the waves go down and up and down and — It's a break in the surface of the board. Not serious.

"COMPOUND FRACTURE"

A break in the body of the Surfer. Also not serious. Unless it's a break in the body of the board. Then it is serious. Only then, it is called a compound puka.

"BIG MAN"

A Surfer who carries his board around during non-surfing weather to give the impression he's hardy.

"WIPE OUT"

To lose a wave. Also what Surfers will probably do to the MAD Magazine office when they see this article!

MAD Magazine, 1965
Text: Al Jaffee
Art: George Woodbridge

A GUIDE TO THE DICTIONARY

Anyone opening this book and expecting to find a standard dictionary is in for a surprise. *The Surfin'ary* is really a combination word reference, encyclopedia, and glossary. Even if a single term or phrase could be narrowly defined, I often chose to include several definitions if each gave an intriguing nuance or perspective or drew attention to a different cultural or geographical twist. I also felt free to supplement definitions with "interesting information" — a story or quote or background material to give a term more of a context. In this way I hoped to present a broad picture of the current worldwide surfing subculture, interwoven with some historical notes.

Art: The Pizz

Another unusual feature of *The Surfin'ary* is its fluid form, a reflection of the language itself. You won't find in these pages the rigid constructions — the unrelenting consistency — and the sometimes bewildering complexities of most dictionaries. The emphasis is on usage, not theory, semantics, or etymology. The choice of main-entry words is very much rooted in the fact that surfspeak is primarily a spoken language. Consequently the word defined in the dictionary won't necessarily be the "base" form (for instance, an infinitive) but instead may be the form most frequently heard (for instance, an inflection of a verb). So, for instance, you will find *getting a place wired* (a participial form) instead of *get a place wired* (the infinitive form). A further potentially disconcerting aspect is surfers' irreverent attitude toward so-called standard English. Surfers tend to be as free and easy in their use of the language as they are in every other respect. They play with words, constantly experimenting and improvising, and they don't feel obliged to be constrained by rules of grammar or usage. I hope that the many usage examples will clarify the meaning of terms applied in nonstandard ways.

With the reader's convenience in mind, I did try to maintain a minimum of consistency in editing the dictionary entries. Basically each entry consists of the term being defined (called the main entry); a part of speech (except for proper names); and one or more definitions. For example:

crank a turn: *v.* To lean into a turn at a radical angle.

A term that is a synonym or a shortened form of a term defined elsewhere may simply refer the reader to the other term. For example:

crossover: *n.* CROSS STEP.

To find the meaning of *crossover,* look up *cross step*.

The main entry may include more than a single term or phrase. Alternative spellings are separated by *or,* as in the entry "**beach break** or **beach-break** or **beachbreak**." Variant terms are separated by commas: "**geek, geekster, geek-a-mo**."

For terms with possibly questionable pronunciation, I included a phonetic spelling, as in *tsunami,* below.

The abbreviations for parts of speech are explained in the list following this section. Many words can be used as more than one part of speech. This is especially true of a surfing maneuver, which can be thought of as both a noun — the maneuver itself — and a verb — the action of performing the maneuver. Sometimes both (or all) possibilities are given in the usual position, immediately following the main entry. For example:

walking the dog: *v., n.* Moving back and forth on a surfboard to alter speed.

If the different part of speech requires a separate definition, it will be given as a numbered item, usually at the end of the entry, as in *slide.*

slide: *n.* **1**) A long track down a large wave from which a safe deviation is usually not possible without wiping out. **2**) A diagonal descent on a wave. **3**) **sliding** Movement across the face of a wave, as opposed to going straight in with the wave. **4**) *v.* To ride either left or right, on a track somewhat parallel to shore.

Note that item #3 defines *sliding,* a variant of *slide,* but no part of speech is given because it's the same as that of the main entry.

In many entries, a usage example is included, preceded by the word "Usage." For example:

beached *adj.* Totally stuffed from eating. Usage: "I'm so beached, I can't move."

Synonyms are given as "Also called," "Also known," or "Same as" cross-references. A "See" cross-reference indicates that additional or related information can be found at another entry. Some entries, for example *tsunami,* contain both types of cross-reference.

tsunami (sue-NAW-me): *n.* A series of waves (not a single wave) caused by a sudden movement along a large portion of the ocean floor. Means "tidal wave" in Japanese, although the waves it describes have nothing to do with tides. They should also not be confused with storm-surge waves. Same as SEISMIC SEA WAVE. See TIDAL WAVE.

The source of a term or definition may be indicated, sometimes together with the place where the term originated and the date the term entered the surfing lexicon. This kind of information always appears in parentheses. Sources are given as abbreviations, keyed to the list that follows this section.

abb: *n.* An abnormal person; same as KOOK. See GO-ABB. (San Diego; MVA)

The last element in the definitions portion of an entry may be a frequently encountered variant of the main entry (for instance, an inflected form) or a closely related term not requiring a separate definition. Following the definitions may be a separate paragraph or paragraphs of additional material; this is the encyclopedic part of *The Surfin'ary*. The entry for *wave,* for example, includes variants and an interesting observation quoted from another book.

wave: *n.* **1**) Undulating or rippling water, the three main natural causes of which are wind, earthquakes, and the gravitational pull of the moon and the sun. (WB) **2**) A moving pulse of energy; a horizontally moving ridge of water the particles of which move in closed curves. **3**) A requisite for surfing. (JRW) —**permanent wave, new wave, ultimate wave**

. . . .
"Waves are an endless source of fascination for everyone, from scientists to surfers. Who, in watching, is not mesmerized by the ongoing cycles of surge and rush, flow and ebb, storm and calm?" —Drew Kampion, *The Book of Waves* (1989)
. . . .

(The full publishing information for *The Book of Waves* may be obtained by looking up the book in the bibliography.)

Sometimes, instead of giving several separate entries and defining each, I lumped together closely related terms under a single main entry. I did this partly to save space, partly because it made finding the variant terms easier, and partly because I just thought it was interesting to see all the variations in one place. For example, item #2 under the main entry *evening glass-off* is *evening glass.* Under the main entry *stoked* you will also find *stoke* (noun and verb) and *stoker,* each listed as separate numbered items and defined.

The main typographic distinctions observed in the dictionary are these: **boldface** is used for the main entry, for variants, and for related terms; SMALL CAPS are used for all cross-references (indicating that the term is defined elsewhere in the dictionary); and *italic* is used for emphasis (mainly in usage examples, to try to give the flavor of the spoken phrase), for synonyms that aren't defined elsewhere, for "words

Art: The Pizz

as words," and for various formal ways of treating particular groups of words (for example, book titles).

A word about offensiveness. Some of the terms and definitions in *The Surfin'ary* may offend some people, but, as Sidney Landau stated in *Dictionaries: The Art and Craft of Lexicography* (Cambridge University Press, 1989), "The lexicographer can only claim to be objectively reporting usage." I compiled the terms and phrases contained in *The Surfin'ary* in a strictly lexicological manner. The inclusion of offensive terms or ideas is by no means an endorsement. Rather, in this age of increasing censorship of artists, musicians, writers, and thinkers, *The Surfin'ary* attempts to present all that is out there and let the reader decide.

I want to make it clear that I do not endorse any localism, sexism, or other shallowness that may exist in the world and therefore be documented in this dictionary. Personally, I want to see a world where all living beings, including kneeboarders, women, boogie boarders, and vals are respected in the ocean and on the earth.

Art: Deano

ABBREVIATIONS USED IN THIS WORK

Parts of Speech

adj.	adjective
adv.	adverb
n.	noun
pl.	plural
prep.	preposition
v.	verb

Sources

(For complete references, please consult the bibliography and the credits lists at the end of this book.)

A&B	Rick Abbott and Mike Baker	BP	Bob Penuelas
A&M	Dennis Aaberg and John Milius	BTV	Bob Travis
		C&M	Richard Chester & McCall
AC	Aqua Culture Surf Shop	CC	Corky Carroll
ADW	Lorrin Andrews	CCRG	*California Coastal Resource Guide*
AHD2	*The American Heritage Dictionary,* Second College Edition	CGL	Chris Gallagher
AHK	Arthur H. Klein	CSD	Ted Cassidy
AJM	Anthony James Misner	CVG	Carlos Vidal Greth
ALN	Matt Allen	DD	Dr. Dume
ASKC	Australian Surfing Kit Co.	DDN	Dennis Dragon
ASL	*Australia's Surfing Life* magazine	DBF	Dick Banfield
ATRL	Ad the Rad Lad	DPL	Denny Plyer
B	*Breakout* magazine	DWK	Dave Kinstle
B&F	Reginald Bragonier, Jr., and David Fisher	DKM	Drew Kampion
		DM	Desmond Muirhead
BB	*Body Boarding* magazine	DS	Drew Steele
BBD	Brian Baird	DSM	Deanne Stillman
BBR	Bernie Baker	DSN	Douglas Simonson
BC	*Beach Culture* magazine	DSHJ	D. S. Halacy, Jr.
BH	Bob Hasier and Co.	ECN	Ellen Nachtigall
BHP	Katherine Bishop	EF	Eric Fairbanks
BHT	Bob Hightower	ELK	Elkins
BLT	Brock Little	ELN	Erik Larson
BMS	Ben Marcus	EPG	Eric Partridge
BNJ	Benjah	EPZ	Eric Penzower
BSM	Brad Smith	ESM	*The Endless Summer* movie

EWY	Ernest Weekley
F&H	Ben Finney and James D. Houston
FLD	Paul Feldman
GCD	George Colendich
GFF	Gary Fairmont R. Filosa II
GN	Greg Noll
GS	*Groundswell* magazine
GSM	*Golden Summer* record album
GTM	Grady Timmons
GTV	Greg Travers
GVS	Don Groves
H&R	Harold Hawkins and Tony Ramarez
HJP	Hal Jepsen
IBN	I. B. Nelson
IDSM	*The Illustrated Discography of Surf Music*
J	Gerry Chalmers
JARR	Phil Jarratt
JB	Jennifer Blowdryer
JDH	James D. Hart
JGD	Jay Gould
JGM	John Grissim
JHM	Jared Hermann
JJV	John Javna
JKMJ	John M. Kelly, Jr.
JMZ	Julie Moniz
JP	Jon Pine
JPD	Jack Pollard
JRN	Joe Ryan
JRW	James R. Walker
JWN	Jos Walton
KAH	Kevin Ascher
KH	Keith Hunter
KSO	Ken Seino
KTD	Karen T. Delgadillo
L&L	Brian J. Lowdon and Margaret Lowdon
LH	Lisa Hybarger
LJE	Lawrence J. England
LMY	Lemay
LMZ	*Local* magazine
LP	Laura Platt
LRI	Lisa Roselli
LWK	Tony Litwak
MBR	Mark Barbour

MCR	Mac Reed
MDF	Mary Duffy
MF	Midget Farrelly
MFM	Marcy Fleming
MGE	Matt George
MHG	Paul McHugh
MLI	Mike Locatelli
MM	Mitch McKissick
MMN	Michael Martin
MNL	Margaret Nicholson
MON	Margot O'Neill
MPN	Mike Peterson
MPZ	M. Paskowitz
MSO	Marcel Soros
MVA	Michael V. Anderson
MW	Mark Warren
MWV	*Making Waves* newsletter
NAT	Nat Young
NHF	Noah Franzblau
NHMLA	Natural History Museum of Los Angeles County
NTS	Non Travis
NWT	*New West* magazine
OA	*Ocean Almanac*
OED	*Oxford English Dictionary*
P	Paco
P&E	Mary Kawena Pukui and Samuel Elbert
PDX	Peter Dixon
PHL	Phil Hellsten
PJN	Paul Johnson
PMO	Pamela Munro
PPJ	P. J.
PT	Peter Townend
PZ	The Pizz
R&D	Rich & Dunc
R&F	Riche Maile and Felix Alfaro
RA	Rick Abbott
RBQ	Robbie Quine
RBS	Rich Bass
RC	R. C.
RDTW	Ric D. T. Wilson
RG	Rob Gilley
RHD	*Random House Dictionary*
RJS	R. Jones

RMN	Runman		THR	*Thrasher* magazine
RMYN	Dave Romyn		TJ	Todd Jacobs
RO	Ron Ortron		TLH	Tex and Lynn Haines
RPD	Rusty Preisendorfer		TMA	Tamara Lipper
RPM	Rosemary Prem		TMN	Thomson
RSM	Richard Schmidt		TRKS	*Tracks* magazine
S&C	David H. Stern and William S. Cleary		TRN	Tim Ryan
			TDW	Todd Wolf
S&S	Ken Suiso and Rell Sunn		UTB	*Under The Boardwalk* movie
SAB	Sunny Abberton		VAB	Victor Abubo
SBT	Steve Barilotti		W	*Waves* magazine
SCSM	Santa Cruz Surfing Museum		W9	*Webster's Ninth New Collegiate Dictionary*
SFR	*Surfer* magazine		WA	*World Almanac*
SFG	*Surfing* magazine		W&B	Tom Wegener and Bill Burke
SGE	Sam George		WB	Willard Bascom
SLS	Dennis Salles		WCH	Will Church
SHS	Steven H. Scheuer		WLK	Richard Wolkomir
SJN	Dr. Scott Jenkins		WS	Ward Smith
SMH	Lynn Smith		WSF	*Wind Surf* magazine
SP	Surf Punks		WW	Woody Woodworth
STM	Shaun Tomson		WWK	Wayne Warwick
SW	*Surfing World* magazine			
SWH	Steven White			
TBB	The Beach Boys			

Art: Deano

Liam McNamara
Rocky Point, Oahu, Hawaii
Photo: Bill Romerhaus

aaaaahooo! or **ahoooooo!** or **AWOOO! 1**) A surfer's hoot or scream when up and riding on a wave. **2**) A yell of encouragement when watching another surfer get a hot ride. (CC) **3**) A call to signal others that an outside wave or set of waves is approaching. **4**) **aawh wooo!** A scream of appreciation; a mating call of sorts. (MVA)

abb *n.* An abnormal person; same as KOOK. See GO-ABB. (San Diego; MVA)

above the peak *adv.* A position along the line of the swell, with the breaking wave in front of you. Usage: "I took off above the peak."

accelerate (out of a turn) *v.* To gain maximum speed off a bottom turn in order to climb up the wave face. **—acceleration** *n.*

accelerator *n.* In surfboard construction, a material used in conjunction with a catalyst to produce and hasten the internal heat reaction in the liquid resin; part of the curing process. The accelerator used in most polyester resins for fiberglass work is cobalt napthanate, usually referred to as "cobalt." Almost all resins sold today already contain the required amount of accelerator. (ORB)

acetone *n.* A highly flammable and extremely toxic cleaning solvent most commonly used to dissolve uncured or uncatalyzed resin from tools and clothing. (ORB)

ache, aching *v.* How you feel after you've been hammered by a wave.

acid drop *n.* Dropping into a wave and having the bottom suddenly fall out, followed by a sense of weightlessness and helplessness. (MVA)

action *n.* Activity. *Action* is almost always used together with another word to form a unified phrase, as in "Check out the swell action."

activator *n.* ACCELERATOR.

aerial *n.* **1**) Any maneuver during which the surfer and surfboard leave the water and return intact; exiting and reentering a wave. **2**) A reentry in which the entire board extends above the lip. (L&L) **3**) The process by which board and rider use parts of a wave as a launching pad to become airborne. (MVA) See COVER-SHOT SURFING.

aerial
Christian Fletcher
Photo: Robert Brown

"I think that aerials are the biggest hoax ever perpetrated on modern surfing. . . . They're just trying for aerials on every wave and they don't realize that 99.9% of the photos that they see in the magazines are flying kick-outs." —Shaun Tomson (L&L)

aeriollo *n.* A bodyboarding maneuver similar to an EL ROLLO, but executed in a tube.

A-frame barrel *n.* The peeling peak of a wave that pitches out in front of itself, offering left and right tube rides — a wave that goes both ways.

afteredge *n.* The trailing edge of a fin.

aggressive *adj.* Said of a surfer who displays a forceful riding style. Usage: "He's really aggressive in the water."

aggro *adj.* **1**) Australian slang for aggressive behavior, usually aggression in the water. (NAT, 1985) **2**) A cross between aggressive and aggravated. Usage: "That guy looks pretty aggro out there." (JP)

aggrobatics *n*. An aggressive surfing style linked with aerials.

aided forward 360 *n*. A bodyboarding maneuver where the rider spins the board around a full 360 degrees on the wave. The move is initiated by digging a hand into the water. (BB, 12/90)

aided reverse 360 *n*. A bodyboarding maneuver where the rider spins the board 360 degrees back into the advancing wave. (BB, 12/90)

air *n*. **1**) As in "getting air" or "catching air" on a surfboard or bodyboard. See AERIAL. **2**) The vibes in the air. See BAD AIR, GOOD AIR.

airbrush *n*. An artist's tool for applying detailed color to a surfboard — be it fade, graphic, or mural — to create airbrushed art. (MVA)

air-inhibited resin *n*. A resin that will not completely cure, or set up, in the presence of air. Polyester resin that does not contain wax is classed as "air inhibited." (ORB)

alaia board *n*. An ancient Hawaiian board for bodysurfing. (DM)

all-time *adj., adv*. Great, fantastic, the most, exceptional, the best, primo, first-quality, without equal. Usage: "That was an all-time classic ride."

all-time-hooter *n*. An exceptionally good surfer party. (A&M)

all-timer's disease *n*. An affliction that causes surfers to overstate the quality of the surf or overemphasize the radicalness of their surfing ability. Symptoms of all-timer's are wide eyes, arms held far apart, a constantly nodding head, a protruding, wagging tongue, and overuse of the word *full-on*. (Santa Cruz & Hawaii; SFR, 3/90)

aloha The Hawaiian word that extends the warmth, friendliness, and pride of the Hawaiian people to their islands' visitors. It has several meanings: **1**) Hello. **2**) Welcome. **3**) Good-bye. Usage: "If I'd hit my head on that reef it would have been aloha." **4**) Love. **5**) A salutation used by surfers everywhere. (GFF) **6**) A feeling toward something, an attitude that reflects the generous feelings implicit in the word *aloha,* as in "the spirit of aloha" or "the aloha spirit."

aloha print *n*. Fabric used in the production of aloha (Hawaiian) shirts, dresses, etc. Patterns traditionally include such elements as hibiscus flowers, coconut palm trees, outrigger canoes, hula dancers, volcanos, surfers, waves, drums, parrots, pineapples, islands, or abstract images. Also called HAWAIIAN PRINT.

aloha shirt *n*. The uniform of many surfers. See HAWAIIAN SHIRT.

amp, amper *n*. Someone who's too stoked to surf.

amped, over-amped, amped out *adj., adv*. Overdoing it, overenergetic, making loud or sudden movements. Usage: "This spot is totally amped out."

amped up *adv*. Excited; STOKED. Of all the *amp* words, this is the only one with a positive connotation. Usage: "I was so amped up after that ride."

angle, angling *v*. To ride to the right or left across the face of a wave or toward the shoulder of a wave, rather than straight toward the beach. The term *angling* was very popular in the 1940s and 1950s and is still used occasionally.

angle off *v*. To gradually descend the face of a wave toward the right or left. (ORB)

angular 757 fin *n*. A fin with straight, rather than curved, edges and corners, which cause the water to break away cleanly. Same as STRAIGHT-EDGE FIN.

animal *n*. Someone with an aggressive approach to surfing. In the 1960s Nat Young gained the nickname "The Animal."

ankle slapper *n*. A wave that is barely ridable.

ankle strap *n*. A Velcro fastener that secures the surf leash to the ankle.

Anybody home? What you say when paddling out, meaning, "Are there any sharks in the water?" (Derived from a Greg Noll story in Hawaii)

aqua boot *v*. Vomiting into the ocean; same as TALKING TO THE SEALS. (LWK)

arc 1) *v*. To turn in an arc-shaped line on a wave. (NAT) **2)** *n*. The line of a turn on a wave.

arch *n*. A back bend used mainly in turns. Also called SOUL ARCH.

arctic *adj*. Used to describe water that is so cold your fingers curl shut and you can't paddle. (P)

arm-dance *n*. The waving of the arms out the car windows on the way to the surf in order to conjure the waves. (South Australia; R&D)

artificial blonde *n*. A male or female with unnaturally blonde hair from bleach, lemon juice, etc. See PEROXIDE.

artificial reef, artificial surfing reef *n*. An underwater structure, such as a pile of cement blocks, used to create waves.

The world's first permanent artificial surfing reef is planned to be constructed off the Ventura County coast at Emma Wood State Beach. When surfing areas are in danger of being spoiled by coastal developers, a reef project can sometimes serve as a bargaining chip to compensate displaced surfers. (FLD)

artificial wave pool *n*. WAVE POOL.

ASP Association of Surfing Professionals, the international organization that oversees surf competitions in the World Tour.

Begun in 1982, the ASP's founding members, led by Ian Cairns, saw the need for standardized criteria that would give consistency to the World Tour. They put together a brief but comprehensive statement: "The surfer who executes the most radical maneuvers in the most critical section of the biggest waves for the longest distance shall be deemed the winner." Note: this rule was amended prior to the 1985/86 season. (L&L) See SURFING CRITERIA.

asphalt surfer *n*. Another name for SKATEBOARDER. The phrase appeared in The Beach Boys' song "It's a Beautiful Day" in the movie *Americathon* (1979). See SKATEBOARDING.

asshole *n*. Everyone else in the water.

Association of Surfing Professionals See ASP.

asymmetrical tail *n*. A surfboard having two different tail shapes to allow for changes in wave conditions; essentially, two boards in one.

ate it *v*. See EAT IT.

atoll *n*. A coral island or group of islands encircling or nearly encircling a lagoon; common throughout the South Pacific. Also called CORAL ATOLL.

Aussie *n*. Someone from Australia; an Australian.

Australia A continent southeast of Asia, between the Indian and Pacific oceans, with a major surfing population. Also called DOWN UNDER or OZ.

Surfing was introduced to Australia at Freshwater Beach, Sydney, in 1915 by Hawaiian Duke Kahanamoku. In 1956 Greg Noll and a few others visited Australia from the United States, taking along some surfing films and boards; their trip became the basis for the modern surfboard movement in Australia. (GN) The Australians are generally cred-

animal
Nat Young, "The Animal"
Photo: John Witzig / Surfer Magazine

ited with the development of the Shortboard Revolution.

. . . .

avalanche *n.* **1)** What the white water looks like pouring down the face of a wave. **2) Avalanche** An outer reef surf spot on Oahu, Hawaii.

awesome *adj.* **1)** Great, fantastic, as in "totally awesome." **2)** Implying great respect for a given situation or physical achievement. (MVA)

axe *n.* The lip of a wave. "To be given the axe" is to get smacked in the face by a wave.

axed *v.* To be knocked off the surfboard by the wave's lip; a hatchet job. (MVA)

Aye Carumba! (eye-ka-RUM-bah) **1)** A Spanish exclamation meaning "Wow!" or "Shit!" **2)** What you say when you see a really good-looking person. **3)** What TV cartoon character Bart Simpson utters when he's upside down on a wave.

baby gun or **baby-gun** *n.* A miniboard with big-gun shape characteristics.

back *n.* The backside of a wave.

back attack *n.* A bodysurfing take-off lying on one's back.

back down *v.* To withdraw from a position or commitment, for instance to decide not to take off on a wave. This choice was illustrated in the song "Don't Back Down" by The Beach Boys, which featured the lyrics "Don't back down from that wave."

back off *v.* **1)** When a wave breaks once and then becomes unbroken green water again. **2)** When a wave breaks and then reforms, the white water having "backed off." **3)** When a wave abruptly subsides ("backs off") as it moves into a deep-water trough after crossing an offshore bar or reef. See RE-FORM. **4)** To change one's mind just prior to take-off and hold back.

back out, backing out 1) *v.* To pull back rather than continue into

backside
Kim Mearig
Photo: Rob Gilley

a wave that could have been caught; to sit back on the board. **2) back-out** *n.* The act of terminating an attempted takeoff by sitting up.

backdoor *n.* **1)** A maneuver in which the surfer takes off to one side of or behind the peak in order to traverse the section of the wave where the lip will throw first; **2) going backdoor** *v.* An expression used to describe situations where a surfer is forced to pull into an already pitching barrel from behind the peak. (MW) **3) Backdoor** *n.* A surf spot on the North Shore of Oahu, Hawaii.

backhand turn *n.* A turn made with one's back to the wave; the opposite of a forehand turn.

backing off *n.* **1)** The sudden flattening of waves as they move over deeper water, for example over a channel between sandbars. (A&B) **2)** A wave action that occurs when a large wave decreases quickly in size. (MM) **3)** The way a wave will flatten out when water depth increases, and then break again inshore. (RA) See BACK OFF, HUNTINGTON HOP.

backlash *n.* A wave action occurring in areas where the depth is uniform.

backpaddle or **back-paddle** *v.* When a surfer decides not to take off and backstrokes with the arms to keep from being sucked over the falls.

backpedal or **back-pedal** *v.* To walk backward, foot over foot, from the nose toward the rear of the surfboard. (A&M)

backside *adv.* **1)** Riding with one's back to the wave. (ORB) **2)** To be positioned on a board so that one is turned away from the wave face when riding. **3)** From the surfer's standpoint (while facing the beach), going right with the right foot forward or going left with the left foot forward. (MVA) Usage: "I saw you went backside on that last ride."

backside layback *n.* Leaning backwards while surfing with one's back to the wave; sometimes performed in the tube.

backside off the top, backside off the lip *adv.* Turning a surfboard off the lip of a wave with one's back to the sea.

backside rail grab *n.* Holding the outside rail while going backside in order to keep riding in the mid-face of the wave.

backside snap *n.* An intermediate bodyboarding maneuver. (BB) See SNAP.

backsiders *n.* Surfers who put their right foot forward. See GOOFY FOOT, SCREW FOOT.

backspray *n.* Spray picked up from a breaking wave and blown back over the wave by offshore winds; sometimes stings your face.

backup waves *n.* The term competitive surfers use for lower-quality waves that may come at the beginning or end of a set or merely at ran-

dom intervals on days when the sets are not well defined; as distinct from SET WAVES. (L&L)

backwash *n.* **1)** Water running rapidly off the beach from a broken wave and frequently colliding in the shallows with incoming water; generally happens on a steep beach. **2)** A wave bounced back out to sea from a steep shoreline. (A&B, ORB) **3)** A wave returning to the ocean after crashing on the beach. (MM)

. . . .

A backwash may cause a current to run out from the beach; when timed properly it can be used to carry a surfer out into the lineup. It normally occurs at high tide. (MVA)

. . . .

bad air *n.* The atmosphere created by people who invade your space or burst your bubble. See VIBE. (MVA)

bad-o *adj.* **1)** Describes a surfer with a hipper-than-thou attitude. (CVG) **2)** Really cool. (PZ)

bag, bag it *v.* To quit doing something, get lazy, or take a break. Usage: "I was surfing almost every day last month, but this week I bagged." (SFG, 12/81)

baggies or **baggys** *n.* Large, oversized, loose-fitting, boxer-type swim trunks that are considerably longer in the legs than regular surf shorts and are worn by surfers for a show or comfort; usually made of Hawaiian print. (IDSM)

baguio (bah-GHEE-o) *n.* A typhoon or tropical cyclone in the Philippines. See HURRICANE.

bail *v.* **1)** To abandon a ride, usually by diving or jumping off the board. Usage: "I fully bailed." **2)** To leave a place. Usage: "I'm bailing." "Let's bail." **3)** To get out of a current spot or situation. Usage: "How bay. Let's bail this place." (MVA)

bail out 1) *v.* To intentionally get away from, jump off, or dive off the surfboard in the face of a coming

backside layback
Photo: Rob Gilley

bailout
Photo: Robert Brown

wipeout in order to avoid getting creamed by a section. **2) bailing out** *n.* When a surfer decides it's time to abandon ship; a survival tactic. (IDSM, A&M) —**bailout** *n.*

Baja (BAH-ha) Baja (lower) California, Mexico, a major surf destination for California surfers. See MEXICO.

Baja Bug *n.* A Volkswagen Beetle modified into a surf vehicle; fully equipped for driving off-road on surf trips.

bake *n.* **1)** Someone from Bakersfield in California's Central Valley. Usage: "What a bake." **2) full bake** Said of a bake — there's no hope for change. (San Luis Obispo; SWH)

balls to the wall Surfing up against the wall of a huge wave. (CSD)

balsa board, balsa-wood board *n.* A surfboard made of balsa wood.

Balsa wood was first used in surfboards by Lorrin Thurston of Hawaii in 1926. The balsa-wood surfboard built in the early 1930s was laminated with spruce or redwood and weighed sixty pounds. In the early 1940s the all-balsa board was developed, weighing about forty pounds; balsa strips were added to the mold for reinforcement. Surfboards were constructed primarily of balsa wood from 1949 until 1957. Because boards made of balsa wood were lighter, more people were able to get into surfing.

balsa wood (*Ochroma lagopus*) *n.* A soft, lightweight, porous wood found mainly in Ecuador and parts of tropical South America. Balsa wood is designated "male" or "female" depending on weight, the female being lighter.

banana *n.* ROCKER.

bananabender *n.* A surfboard shape with exaggerated rocker. (Australia; W#8)

bank 1) *n.* An Australian term for SANDBANK. **2)** *v.* To use white water as a pivot point for directional changes. (MVA) —**banking** *n.*

bank turn *n.* A carving turn, rolling the board along on one rail or edge. (A&M) —**bank a turn** *v.*

Banzai! 1) A Japanese cheer or war cry adopted by surfers in the early 1960s. **2)** A gung-ho type of yell given by surfers as they shoot the curl. (IDSM)

Banzai Pipeline A surf spot on the North Shore of Oahu, Hawaii. See PIPELINE.

Barbie, Barbie doll *n.* A plastic doll with an hourglass figure, produced by Mattel Toys in Southern California since 1959. The term is applied to girls with figures or intellects like the doll's. See MALIBU BARBIE.

bare back *adv.* Surfing without a wetsuit; same as TRUNK IT or SKIN IT. Usage: "I went out bare back today."

barge *n.* An extremely heavy or large surfboard.

barn *n.* A California term for BARNEY.

barnacle *n.* **1)** Someone who is better off sticking to the rocks; same as KOOK or GEEK. (Florida; TDW) **2)** A sharp, rock-encrusting marine organism, which surfers have to negotiate while climbing around rocky coastlines.

barney 1) *n.* Someone who doesn't surf very well. The term was derived from the Hanna-Barbera cartoon character Barney Rubble on "The Flintstones." Usage: "Get out of my way, ya barney." (SFG, 1989) **2)** GEEK. **3)** *v.* To act like a barney. Usage: "Look at that guy barneying all over the place." (PZ) See FRED.

"The '60s 'ho-dad' turned into the '70s 'geek,' who evolved into the '80s 'dweeb.' Today, the put-down of choice is 'barney.' The tourist with the farmer tan and the plastic Party Animal sun visor? Barney. The overzealous kid who cut you off on the best wave of the morning? Little barney. The frat boy who errantly winged a Frisbee off the back of your head, interrupting your nap and spilling half your Miller Genu-

Baja Bug
Art: I. B. Nelson

Banzai Pipeline
Gerry Lopez
Photo: Bill Romerhaus

ine Draft over the neck and shoulders of your new girlfriend? A complete, unreconstructed, spazmodic, full-on barney!" —Matt Warshaw, *Outside* magazine (1990)

barnyard *n.* A derivation of BARNEY — an unskilled or uncool surfer. (Central Florida) Usage: "Why does the swell always come up on weekends? The Inlet was just crawling with barnyards yesterday" —Matt Kechele. (SFR)

barometer *n.* An instrument for determining the pressure of the atmosphere; used for judging how the weather and wind will be on any particular day. A change of one-tenth of one degree can mean that a high or a low is moving in, accompanied by a major change in weather. (W&B)

barrel 1) *n.* A 1980s term used to describe the breaking motion of a perfect wave; same as PIPE (1960s) and TUBE (1970s). (MW) **2)** A hollow channel formed inside a good wave when it breaks and curls over, as in "wide-open barrel," "pitching barrel," or "sun-lit barrel." Surfers crouch down and ride inside the barrel. (JP) **3) get barreled** *v.* To GET TUBED.

barrel roll *n.* An inverted maneuver made with a bodyboard (or boogie board), using the curling wave to roll with. See EL ROLLO.

barrier beach *n.* A long, narrow beach created by wave action and separated from the mainland by a lagoon, bay, or river mouth. (CCRG)

bash, bashing *v.* To slam into a wave. See LIP BASH.

basic drop-in rule *n.* See DROP-IN RULE.

bay 1) *n.* A partially enclosed inlet of the ocean. (CCRG) **2)** *adj.* A term applied to the ocean itself when surfers are not satisfied with wave size; indicates a lack of action. Usage: "How bay." (San Diego; MVA)

beach *n.* **1)** The spiritual center of the universe, according to surfers. (JARR) **2)** The spot where terrestrial activities take place. **3)** Where surfers like to hang out. **4)** An accumulation of rock fragments subject to movement by ordinary wave action. **5)** Dynamic landform altered by wind and waves in a continual process of creation and erosion. See SANDBAR.

The beach extends seaward as far as ordinary waves move sand particles, or about thirty feet below the low tide level; it extends landward to the edge of the permanent coast, which can be a cliff, sand dunes, or an artificial structure. (WB)

Seasonal cycles of sand deposition and loss dramatically affect the appearance of beaches from summer to winter (the beach profile). Wide and gently sloping in summer, they become steep-fronted and narrow in winter and can vanish overnight, stripped of sand by violent storm waves; most of the sand removed from winter beaches is deposited in offshore sandbars and is returned to the beach by gentle swells during the mild summer months. (CCRG)

beach berm *n.* BERM.

beach bomber *n.* A bicycle with fat balloon tires and wide handlebars. Also called BEACH CRUISER or RAY.

beachboy or **beach boy** *n.* **1)** Historically, someone whose livelihood is derived from surfing instruction and outrigger-canoe rides. **2)** Someone who spends time at the beach. **3)** In general, a boy or a man who works at the beach. **4)** A male beach attendant (as at a club or hotel). (W9, 1939)

The first beachboy is thought to have appeared at Waikiki on Oahu, Hawaii, soon after the first major resort hotel was completed in 1901. At that time, surfing and outrigger canoeing were in great decline, and the beachboys were largely responsible for reviving these

barrel
Art: Rick Stover

beachboys
Betty Compson with beach boys, c. 1920
Photo: Bishop Museum

two Hawaiian watersports. (GTM)

"John ('Hawkshaw') Paia could take a ukulele, a chair, and a surfboard, catch a wave, set up the chair, and play the ukulele as he rode in toward the beach." —Grady Timmons (*Waikiki Beachboy*, 1989)

beach party
Beach conga in session,
Northern California
Photo: Don Balch

Beach Boys, The A popular rock music group from Southern California led by Brian Wilson, which, since 1961, has been instrumental in the spread of surfing culture to the rest of the world. Through their song lyrics, they have popularized the California Myth as well as the geography of Californian and Hawaiian surf spots ("All over La Jolla and Waimea Bay . . . Everybody's going surfing!"). Drummer Dennis Wilson was the only member of the group who actually surfed.

beach break or **beach-break** or **beachbreak** *n*. **1)** Waves breaking on a sand bottom or sandbank in close to the beach, rather than out on the reefs. Same as SHORE BREAK. **2)** A wide, hot-dog-shaped board designed for small fast waves breaking near the beach.

beach bum *n*. A derogatory term for someone who hangs around the beach.

beach bunny or **beach bunnie** *n*. A girl who goes to the beach to watch surfing, usually a nonsurfer or a beginner. Also called SURF BUNNY.

beach coat *n*. GREMMIE COAT.

beach cruiser or **beach cruizer** *n*. A balloon-tired bicycle. Same as BEACH BOMBER or RAY.

beach dog *n*. A special breed of dog, able to fetch a Frisbee or a driftwood stick from the shallows of foamy broken surf; usually an Irish setter or golden retriever with a red bandana tied around its neck and answering to a name like "Storm" or "Sandy." Same as SURF DOG. See SOGNAR.

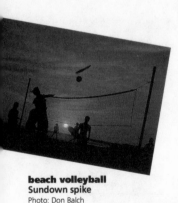

beach volleyball
Sundown spike
Photo: Don Balch

beach girl *n*. Used to describe an attractive female who clearly lives at or near the beach.

beach grem *n*. GROMMET. See GREMMIE.

beach party *n*. **1)** A nighttime gathering on the sand, usually with a fire, maybe with somebody playing guitar, a little drinking and dancing, etc. Popularized in Hollywood surfing movies in the sixties. **2)** **"Beach Party"** The title song from the first American International Pictures (AIP) beach party flick featuring the former Mousketeer, Annette Funicello, who was Frankie Avalon's girlfriend in the series. (GSM)

beach party films *n*. A genre of motion pictures made in the sixties. The title of the first such movie, *Beach Party* (1963), was given to numerous other films produced by several companies. All featured teenage romances on Southern California beaches, where the protagonists were untroubled by parents, schools, and most of the realities of life. (JDH)

beach profile *n*. The distribution of sand on a beach and its slope relative to the water. The amount of sand deposited and stripped away changes with the seasons. See BEACH.

beach volleyball *n*. A team sport usually played with double partners on a sand court.

beach wagon *n*. A station wagon. (W9, 1935) See WOODY.

beachcomber *n*. **1)** Someone who searches the beach for shells and driftwood and other goodies washed up by the sea. **2)** A person who lives on what can be found on beaches or in wharf areas. **3)** A long wave rolling in toward the beach. (AHD2)

beached *adj*. Totally stuffed from eating. Usage: "I'm so beached, I can't move."

beached whale *n*. A derogatory term for an obese male or female. Also called WHALE.

beachhead *n*. Anyone who hangs around the beach.

beachwear *n*. **1)** Casual clothes. **2)** Boardshorts, bikinis, etc.

beachy *adj*. **1**.) Used to describe anything pertaining to the beach environment, as in "beachy feeling." Usage: "That girl has really beachy hair."

beads up *v*. What surf wax does when it is rubbed evenly on the deck of a surfboard. The "beads" refer to the small scabs formed by the wax, which give good traction.

beard *n*. **1)** An older surfer. **2)** Someone with ten-year-old surf equipment, a beard, and a hood. (San Luis Obispo; SWH)

beat *adj*. **1)** Used to describe undesirable waves. Usage: "The water's really beat today." (JP) **2)** Feeling worn, not too good. Usage: "Man, I'm feeling mighty beat today." (MVA)

beat a section 1) *v*. To cut ahead of a breaking section of a wave. **2) beating a section** *n*. A scoring move in a surfing contest; same as MAKING A SECTION. Usage: "She received extra points for beating a section."

beaver tail or **beavertail, beavertail wetsuit** *n*. A wetsuit that features a snap-on crotch, the shape of which resembles a beaver's tail. Worn unsnapped — as surfers always wear it — it hangs down like a beaver tail, hence the name. Popular in the 1960s to mid-1970s and now completely out of style.

beef *n*. What happens when you eat it really bad. Usage (while watching a surf video): "Dude, check out these hot beefs." (LH)

beer *n*. The ever-present alcoholic beverage. Löwenbrau is called a LOWIE; Heinieken is a HEINI or, in Australia, a GREENIE IN A BOTTLE. (PZ) See PRIMO BEER.

behemoth wave *n*. HUGE MONOLITH.

behind the peak *adv*. ABOVE THE PEAK.

belloomer *n*. A type of bellyboard popular in Australia.

belly *n*. A convex bottom contour of a surfboard. (ORB)

belly surfing, belly womping *n*. BODYSURFING.

bellyboard or **belly board** *n*. A small surfboard used primarily to ride the waves on your stomach, but it can also be ridden kneeling or standing. (MF) Same as PAIPO BOARD.

bellyboarding *n*. Bodysurfing with the aid of a planing device, such as a small hand-held kickboard or surfboard.

bend *v*. The motion characteristic of a wave as it wraps around a point. Usage: "Look at the swell bend."

benny *n*. A person who dresses in the latest surf fashions and is hip on all the local surf lingo, but neither owns a surfboard nor knows how to surf. (New Jersey; NHF, 1985)

berm *n*. The steep part of the beach near the water's edge. (A&M) Same as BEACH BERM.

betty *n*. An attractive female. Derived from Betty Rubble, a character on "The Flintstones." —**bettys** *pl*.

bicycle *n*. A stance on a surfboard with legs wide apart as though riding a bicycle. (MF)

bicycle surfboard rack *n*. A framework mounted on the rear of a bike for holding a surfboard in an upright position.

biff *v*. Falling and hitting; to get smacked by a wave. (PZ) Usage: "I got biffed on that last wave."

big air *n*. Getting some major altitude above the water. Usage: "I saw you got some big air on that last ride."

beating a section
Art: I. B. Nelson

beaver tail
Art: Peter Spacek

big gun
Derek Ho
Photo: John S. Callahan

big board *n.* LONGBOARD. "On a small board, you make the board perform. On a big board, *you* perform" —Buffalo Keaulana.

big gun or **big-gun** *n.* A surfboard specially designed for large waves; originally an eleven-footer or longer.

big-headed surfer *n.* Someone who thinks he's great. (San Clemente)

Big Mama, the *n.* The ocean. (CVG)

big open face *n.* A large wall to surf across. See WAVE FACE.

big sea *n.* Large, breaking surf; high seas.

big smoker *n.* Jack London's term for a big wave at Waikiki. (1907) He also used the terms *white-headed combers, smoking combers,* and *bull-mouthed monsters.*

big south *n.* A large SOUTH SWELL.

big surf *n.* **1**) Extremely large waves. **2**) Waves that create a thunderous sound. See ROAR OF THE OCEAN. **3**) **Big Surf** The first artificial wave machine, built in Tempe, Arizona, in 1969. Also known as *The Flush.* See WAVE POOL.

big time *adv.* An intensifier roughly meaning anything in high proportions, as in "to eat it big time." (P)

big-wave board design *n.* A design incorporating elongated rail lines and a narrow pointy nose.

big-wave pioneers *n.* The first individuals brave enough to ride the really big waves in Hawaii in the 1950s. George Downing was the first of the modern big-wave riders. Other veterans include José Angel, Peter Cole, Pat Curren, Ricky Grigg, Greg Noll, Mike Stange, and Buzzy Trent.

big-wave rider *n.* Someone who rides the giant surf on the North Shore of Oahu, Hawaii.

big-wave stability stance, big-wave survival stance *n.* A board position with feet spread apart but toes facing the nose of the board instead of the rail.

Big Wednesday 1) Originally a 1961 surf film by John Severson. **2**) A 1978 Hollywood movie by John Milius. **3**) A specific day in Hawaii in the 1960s when the surf was unusually large.

biggest waves *n.* Of waves that have been ridden, generally defined as reaching at least the thirty-foot mark.

Of all the records and achievements in the surfing world, none sparks as much controversy as the question of who has ridden the biggest wave. Ace Cool rode a record-breaking thirty-five-foot wave at Outer Pipeline (two miles offshore) on January 5, 1985. The most well-documented big-wave nominees having reached the coveted thirty-foot mark are Buzzy Trent at Makaha, 1958; Greg Noll at Makaha, the epic swell of 1969; and Mark Foo at Waimea, in winter 1986. Only a handful of others are also in contention, among them Peter Cole and the late Eddie Aikau, who bagged thirty-footers in 1969. (SFG, 4/87)

biker *n.* Someone who wears full leathers when it's eighty degrees out. (MVA)

bikini *n.* A woman's skimpy two-piece swimsuit, introduced by France's Louis Reard on July 5, 1946 at a Paris fashion show; named after the Marshall Islands atoll, Bikini, where the first announced atomic bomb was tested. Over the years bikinis became smaller, and enterprising girls went topless and created the monokini. (SFG, 11/89) See BUTT THONG, FIO DENTAL, FLOSS.

bikini-bimbo *n.* A derogatory term for a beach girl. See DEBBIE.

bikini contest *n.* Females modeling swimsuits; sometimes featured at surf contests.

billow *n.* A large wave or ocean swell. (AHD2)

bitchin' or **bitchin** *adj.* **1)** A fifties and sixties term for *cool* adopted by surfers; very good, tops, excellent. Usage: "That's a bitchin' surfboard." (PMO) **2)** Anything that is cherry, boss, or neat. (A&M) *Bitchin'* has now been replaced by *rad*. (MVA)

. . . .

The word *bitchin'*, derived from *bitching* — as in, "Quit your bitching" — may have been coined by Dale Velzy in 1949. While surfing with the Manhattan Beach Surf Club, Velzy was overjoyed after a ride and said, "That was a bitchin' wave," giving the word new meaning and a positive connotation. *Bitchin'* is an example of adolescents' tendency to reverse the meaning of a word so that "bad" means "good" and so on.

. . . .

bite *n.* The way in which a surfboard grabs the wave when turning.

black ball flag *n.* A flag with a yellow background and a solid black ball in the center, which means "no surfing" in many areas of Southern California, for instance Newport Beach. Some spots allow boogie boards and swimmers to share the same water space but not hardboards, such as a surfboard.

black tide *n.* An oil slick, such as the big Santa Barbara Channel oil spill in 1969, which contaminated more than thirty miles of beaches, and the Huntington Beach spill of 1989.

. . . .

"EXXON DON'T SURF"
—1990 California bumper sticker

. . . .

blank *n.* The polyester-based urethane foam core of a surfboard that the shaper starts out with when making a surfboard. (ORB) Same as FOAM BLANK.

blast 1) *v.* To come off the top of a wave with a powerful maneuver, as in "to blast off the top." **2) blast air** To CATCH AIR. **3)** *n.* A helluva good time.

blend, blended lines *n.* The functional unifying of the lines of a surfboard; the FAIRING.

blind *adj.* Riding backward on a surfboard. Usage: "I rode that last one blind."

blisty (BLICE-tee) *adj.* Used to describe terrible surfing conditions — windy, cold, choppy, gray, real big or real small waves. (Marin County, California; BH)

blocky rails *n.* Surfboard rails that have straight, rather than rounded, edges.

blondecease *n.* That moment when the last of the summer's bleached-blonde hair hits the barbershop floor. (SFG, 1990)

blow off *v.* **1)** To quit doing something, to abandon it. **2)** To bail on doing something; to flake. (P)

blow-out *n.* A descriptive term for the water surface when it's so badly chopped up by local winds that the approaching ground swells are impossible to ride or are not worth riding. (DSHJ) See BLOWN OUT.

blowhole surf *n.* Waves breaking over holes in a lava bottom, which creates a boiling surface. (MF)

blowing *v.* Said of conditions when the wind is strong. Usage: "It was really blowing today." Same as HOWLING.

blown off *v.* What happens to surfers who are lifted by the wind right out of the wave they were riding or attempting to catch — they are literally blown off the wave.

blown out *adj.* Describes conditions when very high onshore winds are ruining the surf, causing waves to be misshaped or rippled and virtually unridable. Usage: "The surf was

black tide
Art: Glenn Bering

blanks
T&C factory, Hawaii
Photo: John S. Callahan

blown out totally." "Today it was all blown-out surf." See MUSHY.

blue bottle *n.* PORTUGESE MAN-OF-WAR. (Australia and New Zealand)

blue juice *n.* A big wave with a lot of energy. (PZ) See JUICE.

blue room *n.* GREEN ROOM.

. . . .

"Blue is for water
Water is for waves
Waves are for surfers
and surfers are babes!"
—Anonymous

. . . .

bluebird *n.* **1)** An extra-big set wave. (SFR, 6/89) **2) bluebirds** An old-time surfers' term for a set of blue waves on the horizon.

bluff *n.* **1)** A steep headland or cliff along the coast. **2) blufftop** A good vantage point for SURF CHECKS.

board *n.* **1)** SURFBOARD. **2)** A North San Diego County term for a burrito. (LH)

board bag or **boardbag, board cover** *n.* A carrying case for a surfboard to protect it while traveling by car, airplane, camel, etc.

board rash *n.* What you get from lying on a surfboard for long periods of time. (P)

board shape *n.* A design feature of a surfboard that can vary widely. Among the different shapes are — BULLET, SPEED, STINGER, etc.

board speed *n.* The rate at which a surfboard travels over the waves. Can be affected by a number of factors, such as board design (shape and weight) and the position of the board on the wave being ridden.

board-to-wave angle *n.* The angle of the surfboard relative to the steepness of the wave.

board wax *n.* SURF WAX.

boardhead *n.* Someone who's really into surfing.

boardies *n.* An Australian term for BOARDSHORTS.

boardman *n.* A surfer; same as SURF-MAN.

boardshorts *n.* A 1980s term for SURF SHORTS.

boat surfing *n.* Riding the waves or a swell with such ocean crafts as kayaks, canoes, dories, and catamarans.

boat wake, boat wake surfing *n.* Using the wake of a boat to surf. The hull of a fast-moving boat can displace enough water to create ridable waves, with no towline required. All it takes is plenty of horsepower and a delicate sense of TRIM. Hobie Alter once trimmed twenty-six miles to Catalina Island behind a boat. (SFG, 4/87)

body wompers *n.* Refers to huge, closed-out waves ridden by bodysurfers intent on getting worked. (P)

body wompin' *n.* Riding waves with the body and usually a pair of fins. Same as BODYSURFING and BELLY SURFING.

bodyboard *n.* Originally a BOOGIE BOARD, but now includes soft foam boards with a hard plastic or fiberglass covering.

bodyboarder *n.* Someone who surfs using a bodyboard.

bodyboarding *n.* Riding a bodyboard in the surf. Bodyboarders originally rode lying down, but now they occasionally stand up. See BOOGIE BOARD.

bodyroll *n.* A bodysurfing maneuver first done by Buffalo Keaulana in Hawaii in the 1950s. (GN)

bodysurfer *n.* **1)** A surfer who rides the waves with the body alone; swim fins are sometimes used to help propel the bodysurfer through the wave. **2)** Someone who uses the body as a wave vehicle.

bodysurfing or **body surfing** or **body-surfing** *n.* The art of riding the waves without a surfboard, using the body as a planing surface.

board bag
Art: I. B. Nelson

bodyboarding
Photo: Woody Woodworth

Bodysurfing is considered by some to be the purest form of surfing. The sport was invented by marine mammals such as dolphins, seals, and sea lions. Unlike their marine counterparts, however, humans occasionally need to wear swim fins to help them generate enough speed to catch a wave. Three famous bodysurfing spots are Sandy Beach and Makapuu on Oahu's southeast shore in Hawaii and the Wedge at Newport Beach, California.

bog down, bogging down *v.* To be unable to maneuver or accelerate because of equipment design, lack of skill, or wave quality. Usage: "I was bogged down by the kelp."

bogger *n.* Someone who ends up in a spot on a wave where he or she shouldn't be.

bogulate *v.* To surf poorly. (East Side, Santa Cruz; R&F) Usage: "I saw you bogulating on that last wave."

bogus 1) *adj.* Describing lame action, a false idea or concept.   **2)** Ridiculous, unfair, unbelievable. Usage: "That's completely bogus." "Bogus swell, brah."   **3) bogosity** *n.* Usage: "The utter bogosity of that guy taking off on my wave!"

boil *n.* **1)** A turbulent patch of water on a developing wave face, usually a couple of feet in diameter, caused by water flowing over an underwater coral or rock outcropping; looks like a pot of boiling water and indicates very shallow water or an underwater hazard.   **2)** Circular turbulence caused by tidal surges over shallow reefs. (MVA)

bollockhead *n.* A British term for an individual performing meritorious surfing acts with total disregard for personal safety. (LJE)

bomb out, bombed out 1) *v.* To WIPE OUT.   **2) bombout** *n.* Early elimination in a surfing contest. (L&L)

bomber *n.* A hard-breaking wave, usually TOP-TO-BOTTOM.

bombora *n.* **1)** An Australian term for an outside break — a large wave breaking beyond the normal lineup.   **2)** A huge wave breaking over submerged reefs or rock shelves. (IDSM)   **3)** Offshore reef surf, usually big and powerful. (MF) Also called BOMMIE, CLOUD BREAKS, CLOUD BURST.   **4)** A deep-water reef well offshore. (NAT, 1985)

bommie *n.* Short for BOMBORA. (Australia, MW)

bone crusher *n.* A big wave that breaks with extreme force. Usage (from the movie *Big Wednesday*): "Gerry Lopez thunders down another Pipeline bone crusher."

bone yard *n.* The area where the waves break. Also known as GRAVEYARD, IMPACT ZONE, SOUP BOWL. (P)

bonzer *n.* A type of surfboard with double concaves shaped into the tail area that can be used in conjunction with a multitude of templates and bottom contours. The design also features two short, angled ventral fins and a short-raked center fin placed at the outside edge of the concave.

boogie board *n.* A soft, flexible foam bodyboard, which can be used in flagged areas. (MW) The original Boogie Board (a brand name) was invented by Tom Morey in the 1970s. A boogie board is ridden in a prone position. (NAT, 1985)

". . . ain't nothing but a speed bump to a longboarder." —Longboard Larry

boogie flapper *n.* A derogatory term for a BODYBOARDER. (Santa Cruz)

boomer *n.* A large, heavy-breaking wave, usually unridable. —**booming surf**

boomerang fin *n.* A narrow-based fin shape which Bobby Owens is credited with adapting from a windsurfer to a surfboard.

bone yard
Art: The Pizz

boomerang fin
Bobby Owens, 1984
Photo: Bob Barbour

bowl
North Peak, Blacks Beach
Photo: Rob Gilley

bowl cut
Art: Rick Stover

bottom turn
Robbie Burns, Pipeline
Photo: Bill Romerhaus

booties *n*. Neoprene rubber surf shoes worn for warmth and grip. (MM) —**hard-soled booties**

born-again surfer *n*. Someone who surfed, then quit (got married, got a job, had a family), but started again in his mid-thirties, thus being "saved" by surfing. The term was coined in the early 1980s by Ward Smith, the coauthor of a cartoon strip of the same name.

boss *adj*. Outstanding, the greatest or best, totally bitchin'.

bottom *n*. **1**) The underside of a surfboard. **2**) The bottom of a wave. **3**) The ocean floor.

bottom contour *n*. **1**) The particular shape of a surfboard's underside, or planing surface. Bottom contours are designed to direct water flow; the various shapes include flat, vee, slight vee, concave, channel concave, channel hull, tri plane hull, hydro hull, belly, chine hull, and hydrofoil stepped. **2**) The shape of the ocean floor, including its reef configuration. (W&B) Also called BOTTOM PROFILE.

bottom out *v*. To come to the end of a drop down the face of a wave from a straight-off position at high speed.

bottom profile *n*. **1**) The contour plan for the bottom of a surfboard. See BOTTOM CONTOUR. **2**) The configuration of the ocean bottom or floor.

bottom turn *n*. **1**) A turning maneuver executed following the takeoff and the drop to bring the rider back onto the wave face. **2**) A turn at the bottom or out in front of the wave, well below the crest of the wave; a turn at the bottom of the wall. **3**) A banking turn off the bottom of the wave used to generate vertical momentum. (L&L) **4**) The initial turn after completing the drop.

bounce, bounce straight in *v*. To shift one's weight up and down on the front of the surfboard in order

to keep forward momentum going, as in "bouncing straight into shore." Same as HOPPING.

bouncing off the white water *v*. To rebound off the incoming foam.

bowl *n*. **1**) A marked, bowl-like concavity on a wave face, a condition often associated with breaking waves that bend or wrap as they move toward shore; sometimes caused by a shallow place in the ocean bottom where a wave breaks with more than usual suddenness and force and is often bigger as well. Two well-known bowls are located at Makaha and Ala Moana on Oahu, Hawaii. **2**) A particular wave shape, caused by reef contour, which is likely to have a close-out section. (L&L) **3**) A wave that, viewed from above, forms a crescent shape. (A&B) Also known as HOOK. **4**) The convex bottom of the forward section of a big-gun surfboard. (MF)

bowl cut *n*. A sixties type of haircut that still looks hip on a surfer; originally created by placing a bowl upside down on someone's head and cutting around it. Also called BOWLY or SURFCUT.

bowleous *adj*. Used to describe a bowly wave or a bowl cut. Usage: "You got bowleous, dude." (San Diego)

bowly 1) *adj*. Used to describe a wave that exhibits bowl characteristics. **2**) *n*. BOWL CUT.

box seat *n*. An Australian term for the hottest spot at the takeoff site.

boxy *adj*. Refers to sharp, well-defined edges on the sides of a surfboard, as opposed to smooth, rounded rails. —**boxy rails**

boys, the or **the boyz** *n*. A group of male surfers who are friends and surf together. Usage: "The boys head out for an early-morning surf check." Also called CREW.

brah or **bra, brudda** or **bruddah** *n*. Hawaiian Pidgin English for brother. Usage: "Howzit brah?" "Howzit goin', brah?" Same as BRO in California.

BRATS Acronym for Boca Residents Against Tourists. (Florida; TDW)

break *n.* **1**) The place where waves tumble over and break in shallow water. A wave breaks when the water depth becomes less than one-seventh of the distance between wave crests. (OA) **2**) The action of a wave as the top spills forward down its face. **3**) The area in the surf where the waves are breaking. (MF) See SURF BREAKS. —**break** *v.*

break through a section *v.* **1**) To beat or negotiate a wave that breaks in front of you when you are already riding it. See BEAT A SECTION.
2) **breaking a section** *n.* A scoring move in a surf contest.

breakaway edge or **break-away edge** *n.* **1**) The trailing edge(s) of a surfboard. **2**) Where the surfboard separates from the water (at its rails, tail, or the afteredge of the skeg).

breaker *n.* Any wave that breaks on its journey to the beach. See PLUNGING BREAKER, SPILLING BREAKER.

breaking *v., adj.* Used to describe a surf spot if it looks good to ride. Usage: "I heard that the point was breaking yesterday."

breaking right, breaking left *adv.* The direction a wave is breaking, as viewed from the water facing the shore.

breaking section *n.* On a wave, any place that's curling over.

breakwater *n.* A protective device for shorelines that may create a new surf spot or totally ruin an existing one; made with large boulders or steel. See JETTY.

brisk *adj.* Freezing-cold air or water.

bro *n.* Short for brother; a mid-1980s substitute for DUDE. The term was popularized in the Hollywood movie *Under the Boardwalk* (1989).

Usage: "Hey, bro." "What up, bro?" "Later, bro." (Southern California) See BRAH.

broadie *n.* A South African term for SLIDE.

brodad *n.* Someone who overuses the term *bro,* even to the point of calling his mom "bro." A derivative of HODAD. Usage: "Morning, bro. Hey, bro, what's for breakfast, bro?" (P) "My grandma and grandbro are taking me to Hawaii this summer."

broken board, busted board *n.* A surfboard broken into two pieces, usually as a result of getting pounded in the surf during a wipeout. Same as SNAPPED BOARD.

"It used to be a big deal if you broke a board in half — a black mark against the surfboard designer — but nowadays, guys go to the Islands and break two, three boards or more riding the winter surf because modern surfboards are lighter and slimmer." —Greg Noll, *Da Bull* (1989)

broken wave *n.* A wave that has reached water shallow enough to cause it to curl over from crest to trough and break. As it continues its journey to the beach, it is termed a "broken wave."

broly *adj.* Being cool, nice, or cooperative. Usage (if someone lets you grab a wave): "That was completely broly of you." Or (if someone is uncool): "You're being fully **nonbroly**." (Newport Beach; J)

Bronzed Aussies An Australian group of professional surfers formed in 1976 by Peter Townend, Ian Cairns, and Mark Warren, who thereby introduced the idea of surfers as bankable media superstars.

brown boardshorts material *n.* A really huge wave. (Australia; MW)

brush in, brushing in *v.* To work resin well into fiberglass cloth with a brush and spreader made from a stiff piece of plastic. (ASKC; 1965)

broken board
Tom Curren
Photo: John S. Callahan

BSA British Surfing Association.

BTO (basic takeover) Sending everyone home with a frown (East Side, Santa Cruz; R&F); the situation when surfers take over a surf spot and hog all the waves.

Bu, the Bu Abbreviation for MALIBU. Also called MOTHER BU.

buck *v.* To fight one's way out through the surf.

bucket o' nugs Lots of waves. (East Side, Santa Cruz; R&F)

bucket toss *n.* Hitting the lip. (East Side, Santa Cruz; R&F)

bugged *v.* **1**) To be annoyed or disquieted. **2**) To be pestered by flies or people at the beach. (MCR)

BUI "Biking Under the Influence" — Isla Vista, California, vehicle traffic infraction. (P)

build *v.* To get stronger. Usage: "Hey, look at that wave build." "The sets are building."

bull nose *n.* A 1960s surfboard shape featuring a nose more rounded and wider than the tail. (ASKC)

bullet *n.* A shortboard with a well-rounded nose, as opposed to a pointy nose.

bum *v.* **1**) To mooch, as in "to bum off one's friends" or "to bum wax." (The question is, if surfers are always bumming wax from each other, who buys it?) **2**) To be down on someone, to be angry with them. Usage: "My girlfriend bummed on me for missing our anniversary to go surf in Mex." See HARSH.

bummer *n.* A total drag; too bad; an unfortunate occurrence. Usage: "Bummer, dude."

bump, bump on the water *n.* An approaching swell or set of waves. Usage: "Here comes a couple of bumps."

bump wing, bump *n.* A marked inward shift of the rail toward the stringer in the tail half of a surfboard, making that half slightly nar-

burly
Art: Peter Spacek

rower than the front half. Same as WING.

bumper surfing *n.* Riding on the rear bumper of an automobile in a standing position while trying to keep your balance as the car zooms around the streets. (Fresno; AJM)

bumps *n.* A colloquialism for the calloused skin on the instep or knees that results from surfing. Also called SURF BUMPS.

bumpy *adj.* **1**) Very choppy water, as in "bumpy waves." A ride over choppy water would be described as a "bumpy ride." **2**) An ocean condition somewhere between glassy and blown out. (MVA)

buoy *n.* **1**) Someone who floats around, never takes a wave, and is often in the way. Same as DUCK, SOAKER, MALLARD. **2**) A sophisticated weather station that floats around in the ocean. (WS) **3**) A float moored in water as a warning of danger or as a marker for a channel. (AHD2) See BUI.

buoy reports *n.* Valuable information gleaned from floating weather stations, including wind direction, wind speed, and visibility (meaning the amount of fog or haze in the atmosphere). Buoy reports are broadcast over the RADIO WEATHER CHANNEL. (WS)

burger *n.* **1**) A mushy (shapeless), uneven, bumpy wave. See MUSH-BURGER. **2**) **burgers** A series of such waves. —**burgery** *adj.*

Burleigh Heads A famous right point in Australia, which has been the site of the annual Stubbies professional surfing competition since 1977.

burly *adj.* **1**) Used to describe freezing cold water. Usage: "It's burly out there." (Laguna Beach) **2**) Sometimes used as a substitute for GNARLY. (Santa Monica; JB)

burn, burn up the wave *v.* To do some really hot moves on a wave.

(BP) Usage: "You were really burning it up out there."

burn off *v.* Refers to coastal fog that usually dissipates, or "burns off," in the morning or mid- to late afternoon on days that are really socked in.

bust a few *v.* To go surfing. (East Side, Santa Cruz; R&F)

bust through the lip *v.* To pierce through the wave lip as it curls over and then to continue with a reentry or floater, etc.

butt thong, butt floss *n.* A California term for a G-string bikini. Same as FIO DENTAL, FLOSS, BUN FLOSS.

butter *n.* Girls. (Florida; TDW)

butterfly *n.* A stance on a longboard where the surfer forms a V position by squatting down on the nose of the board with head down, arms straight back and out, and fingers outstretched.

butterfly stomp patch *n.* DECK PATCH.

Butthole Surfers A punk–acid rock group from Texas, formed in the 1980s, that has nothing to do with surfing except having a cool name for a band.

butt thong
Bahia, Brazil
Photo: John S. Callahan

cafard (ka-FAR) *n.* A French term for cockroach, said of a surfer who is badly positioned on the shoulder of a wave and is blocking the passage of others. (WSF; 1989)

Cajon (ka-HONE) **Zone** *n.* A derogatory term for inland surfers from El Cajon — San Diego's "valley." *Cajón* is Spanish for large box, bin, drawer, or locker (not to be confused with *cojón*, meaning testicle). (RO, P)

caked on *adj.* Refers to surf-wax buildup on a surfboard deck.

Cali CALIFORNIA.

California 1) The home of a major surfing population.   **2**) An endless summer vacation spot in the eyes of the rest of the world.

. . . .

The name *California* was bestowed by the Spanish conquistadors (possibly by Cortez) after an imaginary island — an earthly paradise — in *Las Serges de Esplandian*, a Spanish romance written by Montalvo in 1510. Indeed, Califor-

nia was portrayed as an island on early maps. Baja (lower) California in Mexico was first visited by the Spanish in 1533; the present U.S. state was called Alta (upper) California. (WA)

. . . .

California Current A cold-water ocean current in the North Pacific that flows southward from the Gulf of Alaska along the west coast of North America.

California Dream The pot of gold at the end of the rainbow, which many people move to California to find. Means many things to many people. To surfers, it means the California surfing experience.

"California Dreamin' " 1) A sixties song by the Mamas and the Papas written by John Phillips and Michelle Phillips and containing the line "I'd be safe and warm if I was in L.A." Cover versions were made by America (1978) and The

Beach Boys (1986). **2**) A Hollywood movie (1978).

California girl *n*. **1**) The pinnacle of female perfection; typically envisioned as a curvaceous bikini-clad female with blonde hair, blue eyes, and a deep golden-brown tan that is to die for. (AJM, P) **2**) A term popularized by The Beach Boys' 1963 hit tune "California Girls" with the lyrics, "I wish they all could be California girls."

Historical note: Early European explorers described the women they saw along the shores of California as Amazonian. (AJM, P)

California Myth The belief held by people living outside of California that everyone in California lives at the beach, has a palm tree in the yard, and surfs. These non-Californians also believe that the weather in all of California is like that in Southern California — sunny and warm.

"I think we had a lot to do with the population rush to California. People hearing The Beach Boys' songs envisioned California as sort of a golden paradise where all you did was surf and sun yourself while gorgeous blondes rubbed coconut oil on your body." —Al Jardine

California surf sound, California surfin' sound *n*. **1**) Instrumental surf music such as that played by Dick Dale, the Belairs, etc. **2**) Vocal surfing songs such as those by The Beach Boys, Jan & Dean, and others. See SURF MUSIC.

camber *n*. ROCKER.

can or no can Either you decide to go and take off on a big wave or you don't; similar to CHANCE 'EM. (Hawaii; SLS)

cane swell *n*. A big ocean swell generated from a hurricane. (Florida; TDW)

canoe leaping *n*. Leaping from a canoe with a surfboard in order to ride the wave. (Hawaii) Also called LELE WA'A.

canoe surfing *n*. **1**) Riding waves in outrigger canoes. (Hawaii) **2**) **Canoe Surf** A SURF BREAK at Waikiki.

canopy, wave canopy *n*. The curved overhead crest of a wave.

Cape Hatteras Located in North Carolina, the premier surf spot on the East Coast of the United States. Also called HATTERAS.

Cape Rollers *n*. Giant waves created off the southeastern coast of Africa. See FOLLOWING CURRENT and OPPOSING CURRENT.

Along a stretch of water known as South Africa's Wild Coast, "where the continental shelf abruptly drops away, the Agulhas Current sweeps in hard against this immovable barrier, concentrating the massive southwest flow of water into a relatively narrow stream [that] moves at four to six knots. . . . When storms to the southwest pump waves around the Cape of Good Hope and up into the channel, the wave length of the swell can be shortened dramatically and the wave steepness increased to precipitous angles. Under certain conditions the unusually swift current here actually doubles the height of the waves pushing upstream." —Drew Kampion, *The Book of Waves* (1989)

Captain Goodvibes A cartoon character created by Tony Edwards and featured in Australian surfing magazines.

card *n*. An old surfer. (East Side, Santa Cruz; R&F)

carve *v*. **1**) To maneuver by digging the rail of one's board into the water while turning, as in "to carve a turn." **2**) To surf excellently. Usage:

"He was carving." (NAT, 1985)
3) To perform constant, controlled maneuvering on a surfboard. (MVA) —**carving** *n.*

carving up the mob An Australian term for a reckless ride by one surfer through a group of surfers or swimmers. See MOB.

casper *n.* A tourist who comes out to the beach with a very pale complexion, looking white as a ghost. The term was derived from the TV cartoon character Casper, the Friendly Ghost. (PZ)

cast a spray *v.* The action of the board hitting the top of a wave and forcing water to fly up in the air. (MM) See FAN SPRAY. Usage: "You cast a huge spray on that cutback."

casual, cas' (kazsh) *adj.* Characteristic of a surfer's mellow attitude. Usage: "Stay casual, man." "It's cas'."

catalyst *n.* **1**) A hardening agent used to make resin set up in the fiberglassing process. **2**) Material added to resin, together with an accelerator, to make it cure rapidly by oxidation. This causes the heat that in turn cures the resin. The catalyst used in most polyester resins is methyl ethyl ketone peroxide, usually referred to as "M-E-K" peroxide — not to be confused with MEK solvent. (ORB)

catamaran, cat *n.* **1**) A twin-hulled sailboat. The modern-day catamaran was designed and built by Woody Brown and Alfred Kumalae at Waikiki in 1948. Fashioned after the giant double-hulled canoes of the ancient Polynesians, it rode the breakers like a surfboard. (GTM) **2**) A raft consisting of logs or pieces of wood lashed together and propelled by paddles or sails. (W9)

catch a rail, catching a rail *v.* Happens when the down-wave rail of the surfboard catches in the surf and dumps the surfer. See DIG A RAIL.

catch a tip *v.* To dig the nose of the surfboard under water, possibly followed by a wipeout; to PEARL.

catch a wave, catching a wave *v.* **1**) To ride a breaking wave, on a board or some other surf craft or with your body alone. (MF) Same as CRACK A WAVE. **2**) To view the world from a different perspective, as in the line "Catch a wave and you're sittin' on top of the world," from the 1963 song "Catch a Wave" by The Beach Boys.

catch air, catching air *v.* Happens when both surfer and surfboard fly off of a wave. (MM) Usage: "I totally caught air on that one." Same as GET AIR.

cathedral-like *adj.* A metaphor for what it's like being in the tube. —**whirling cathedral** *n.*

caught inside *v.* **1**) To be on the shoreward side of a breaking wave, with a mass of foam coming at you. **2**) In paddling out, to have a wave break outside — one of the worst situations to confront a surfer. (MW) **3**) To be unable to make it past breaking waves. (MM)

caveman campfire squat *n.* A bent-knee, squatting-down stance on a longboard with arms stretched out in front as if being warmed over a hot fire. (Malibu; KSO)

cavitation *n.* The rapid formation and collapse of vapor pockets in a flowing liquid in regions of very low pressure. When cavitation occurs on one side of a fin, the surfer loses control. (ORB)

chafe, chafing *v.* **1**) To receive an injury or irritation from rubbing against the board while paddling. **2**) To get a rash from a wetsuit rubbing against the skin. See RASH GUARD.

chair *n.* An Australian term for underwater cliffs that create a wave-breaking site.

caught inside
Photo: Bob Richardson

cheese feet
Art: Karen T. Delgadillo

channels
Photo: Tom Servais / Surfer Magazine

chalk people *n.* People who live far from the beach. (Southern California) See CASPER.

chalker *n.* A surfer with an all-white board and a black wetsuit; a common sight in the 1970s but a somewhat rare and endangered species today. (Oxnard grommet word, TJ)

chance 'em What you do when you have a 50/50 chance of making it when taking off on a wave — either you go or you don't. (Hawaii; SLS) See CAN OR NO CAN.

channel *n.* **1)** A deep spot where waves ordinarily don't break; usually used for paddling out to the surf. **2)** An entry to a destination over a relatively calm, deeper area of water; an exit over the same area. (MVA) **3)** A gap between sandbanks or reefs. **4) no channel** Describes a condition in which there's no easy way out through the surf. (BP) **5) channels** Grooves in the bottom of a surfboard that function to direct water flow and create lift.

channel concave *n.* A depressed bottom surface of a surfboard with grooves shaped into it.

channel hull *n.* A surfboard bottom contour with channels; a series of flat, concave planes.

chapped *adj.* **1)** The way you feel when you miss a perfect wave. (CVG) **2)** Bummed or depressed. Usage: "I'm chapped because my girlfriend left me." (SFG, 1989)

charge *v.* **1)** A term whose full meaning is obvious when it is said in a burned-out, shaky, laid-back voice ("Chaarrge . . ."); to hit the surf. **2)** To enthusiastically go surfing. Usage: "Let's charge it, bro, the waves are sweet."

chatter *n.* The sound of water slapping the underside of a surfboard. (MM)

cheater five, cheater five nose ride *n.* A surfing maneuver made famous by Paul Strauch, Jr., in the mid-sixties. (SFR, 6/88) The maneuver involves crouching down on the board while stretching out a leg and hanging five toes over the board's nose, as distinct from walking out to the end of the board in an upright position. Also known as STRAUCH CROUCH.

check out *v.* To look over and observe the surf at one or more spots in order to determine its quality, decide where to go out, etc. See SURF CHECK.

cheese feet *n.* The California equivalent of HAOLE FEET.

cherry *adj.* **1)** Boss, bitchin', neat. (A&M) **2)** Said of anything new or in good condition, as in "cherry condition."

chester *n.* Any mascot or companion to ward off evil forces and bring filthy waves. (South Australia; R&D)

chicken carl conditions *n.* Derived from an anonymous Marin County, California surfer who says the surf is eight feet high when it's really only one foot high.

chicken out *v.* To be overcome with fear; to hold back from catching a steep or high wave.

chill out *v.* **1)** Cool it. (MVA) Usage: "*Chill out,* dude!" **2)** To calm down, to relax. (MM) Usage: "We can chill out at your place."

chine rail *n.* **1)** A rail that is faceted or beveled rather than rounded. (ORB) **2)** A definite edge created by the shaper on the rails of a surfboard where the top and bottom surfaces meet. (MCR)

chinselbogger *n.* Someone who has a weak surfing style. (East Side, Santa Cruz; R&F)

chip, chip board *n.* The name given to the first all-balsa-wood boards constructed in the late 1940s. Much smaller than the giant planks, they were referred to as

POTATO CHIPS; later, they became known as MALIBU BOARDS.

choice *adj.* Great, as in "choice waves."

choiceamundo *adj.* **1**) Said of anything that's cool. **2**) The exhilarating feeling you get when you tube through a wave and flip over its back like an ocean pizza. (Hollywood, Florida)

choke *v.* **1**) To be leery of big surf. **2**) To fail under pressure. (P) **3**) To fail to accomplish one's goal. Usage: "I fell off my board. I choked, big time." (MVA)

chop, choppy *adj.* **1**) A light form of BLOWN OUT. (MVA) **2**) A term used to describe a certain condition of the water surface, usually when strong onshore winds are blowing. Many little waves are created, making a very bumpy and difficult surface to ride. —**wind chop, choppy conditions, choppy surf, choppy waves**

chopper gun *n.* A special spray gun used for spray-laminating a board by cutting, or "chopping," predetermined lengths of fiberglass roving or strands and depositing them together with catalyzed resin onto the surface of the mold. (ORB)

chubasco *n.* **1**) A storm off Baja California that produces large south swells (*chubasco* **lines**) that may reach Southern California. **2**) A big swell from the south, sometimes pumped in by a Mexican hurricane.

churly-churly *adj.* A churned-up surf carrying a heavy load of sand and gravel that smacks you in the face when you walk out into it. Usage: "It's churly-churly today." (San Francisco; RMYN, NTS)

churned, churning *v.* **1**) To be tossed around in a wave. **2**) To take a trip through the WASHING MACHINE.

churning action *n.* Mean-looking waves. (CC) Usage: "Look at that churning action."

churning cylinder *n.* A gnarly tube.

cigar *n.* **1**) You got it, as in "*Cigar,* dude!" A skate crossover term derived from "Close, but no cigar." (BHT) **2**) An old term for a wooden surfboard. (G)

clam-shelled *v.* To be engulfed; what happens when a wave closes over a surfer. (W&B) Usage: "I just got clam-shelled."

classic 1) *n.* A perfect surfing day. (MM) **2**) PERFECTION. **3**) Perfect surfing form. **4**) A fantastic day. **5**) The best. **6**) *adj.* Perfect, as in "classic conditions," "classic waves."

clean *adj.* Good glassy surf conditions (NAT, 1985), as in "clean waves," "clean peeler," "breaking clean."

cleanup or **clean-up** *n.* **1**) A wave or set that breaks outside of most of the surfers, causing them to lose their boards, thus "cleaning up" the area; a preleash term. **2**) **cleanup set** or **clean-up set** Large waves that catch surfers off guard, sweeping them into shore. (MM)

climb *v.* **1**) To steer the board up the face of the wave toward the top or crest; **climbing the wall**. **2**) To lean one's weight on the inside rail of the board to cause it to climb back to the ridge of the wave. Repeated, this act is referred to as **climbing and dropping**.

climb and drop *v.* **1**) To ride up the face of a wave and back down. (MM) **2**) To steer a rhythmic course up and down the face of a wave. — **climbing and dropping**

clocking in the green room A long ride inside the hollow part of a wave. (MM) Same as ROOM TIME. Usage: "I saw you clocking in the green room out there."

clocky *n., adj.* Jerky arm movements; used to describe the look of a surfer's arms twirling around to maintain balance. Usage: "That wave went from eight to four because the

clam-shelled
Art: Rick Stover

churly-churly
Art: Rick Stover

judges took off half a point for each of those clockies you did on take-off." (New Jersey and East Coast; SFR, 1989)

close haul *n.* A very fast slide when the board-to-wave angle is very small.

close out 1) *v.* To break all at once along the entire line or length of a wave; applied to waves that become too large to form suitably for surfing. Usage: "The waves are closing out." "It was totally closed out today." **2**) When waves break all the way across a bay or a normally safe channel, rendering a surf spot unridable. **3**) When the waves are so huge that surfers can't paddle out. **4**) **closeout** *n.* A wave that slams all at once. Usage: "Beware of closeouts." **5**) **close-out** *adj.* Usage: "It was a close-out set."

closeout
Pipeline
Photo: Robert Brown

. . . .

Breaking waves that close out are characterized by a lip that "throws out" all at once along the entire wall of the wave (as opposed to a lip that gradually peels off from one side to the other or from the middle toward either end), thus rendering the wave unsurfable. Close-out waves are usually caused by a formless bottom profile. When a spot is closed out, its surf is usually considered too big to ride.

. . . .

closed tail *n.* A design characteristic of a surfboard, featuring a squared-off tail as distinct from a rounded one. Square tail and squash tail are two examples of closed-tail boards.

cloth *n.* FIBERGLASS CLOTH, for example, "20-oz. cloth."

cloud breaks, cloud burst *n.* A large wave (or waves) breaking on an outer reef; same as BOMBORA.

cloud surf *n.* The biggest waves that one can remember.

clubbie *n.* A term often used in letters published in Australia's *Tracks* magazine, referring to members of

coffin
Photo: Rob Gilley

the Australia Surf Lifesaving Association, usually in a derogatory manner.

clueless *adj.* A troublemaker who does not quite understand life. (MVA) Usage: "He's *totally* clueless."

coastal access *n.* The ability to get to a beach or surf spot — an issue of vital importance to surfers. Access restrictions have limited surfers' ability to use some surf sites. (JRW) See MEAN HIGH TIDE LINE.

coastal development *n.* Any construction or project that alters the coastline in some way — a potential threat to surfers. Beach-widening projects, small-boat harbor development, and reef reclamation for land all contribute to overcrowding at prime surf sites. (JRW)

coastal terrace *n.* MARINE TERRACE.

coastal zone *n.* The area along the coast where development is regulated and controlled. In California, the boundary of the coastal zone varies depending on the "resources" in the area.

cobalt, cobalt napthanate *n.* **1**) An accelerator used in POLYESTER RESIN. **2**) An additive that will allow resin to be used at lower temperatures. (ORB)

cobble applause *n.* The tumbling sound made by retreating surf on a cobbled beach, for example at Cape Lookout, Oregon.

coffin, coffin ride, the coffin *n.* A hot-dog riding position on a longboard (under the curl or on the face) with the rider lying stiffly on the back with arms folded across the chest as if in a coffin or with hands pressed together as if praying. (KSO) This stunt was especially popular in the sixties.

cold-water wax *n.* WINTER WAX.

collapsing section *n.* **1**) A portion of a wave that breaks in front of a surfer and turns to white water, making it difficult to continue riding in

that direction. (RA) See SECTION.
2) A beer belly. (IBN)

comber *n*. A long, curling wave. (RHD) Usage: "Would'ja look at them there combers, Mabelle." (MVA)

combined seas *n*. A combination of local wind swell and ground swell. (WS)

Coming down! Comin' through! A warning cry to anyone who is down the line or taking off in front of you on a wave; usually accompanied by profanity. (A&M) Usage: "Coming down left!" Duke Kahanamoku use to yell "Coming down!" when he caught a wave on his 16-foot, 114-pound, solid koa board. (GTM)

coming off the bottom *v*. When a surfer cranks a bottom turn and shoots back up to the top of the wave.

committed *adj*. When a surfer decides to turn or take off on a wave; when there's no turning back.

common tit rash *n*. What you get from lying on your board; same as BOARD RASH.

competitive surfing *n*. One of the most subjective of all competitive sports because of the unlimited diversity of waves and conditions that make up the surfing arena. (L&L) Done on both amateur and professional levels. See SURFING CRITERIA.

competitive surfing rules *n*. The rules used to judge surfing contests. These vary throughout the sport depending on which group or association has jurisdiction over the competition. Generally, surfers are required to ride a certain number of waves in specified time periods, called heats. The surfer who executes the most radical maneuvers in the most critical sections of the biggest waves for the longest distance is deemed the winner. See BASIC DROP-

IN RULE, FIRST RIDER UP, RIDER ON THE INSIDE. (LL)

composite *n*. A type of construction using two or more different materials, such as resin and fiberglass. (ORB)

compression ding *n*. A depression in a surfboard, but not serious enough to cause the fiberglass skin to fracture. See DING.

conan *n*. A macho bodybuilder who can't surf but who tries to impress people on the beach. Taken from the Marvel comic book character Conan, who was played by Arnold Schwarzenegger in the movie of the same name. (South Australia; R&D)

concave 1) *adj*. Characteristic of a bottom contour or planing surface that curves in (is "concave"). (ORB) **2**) *n*. A design feature on the bottom of a board to give extra lift. (NAT, 1985)

conservative *n*. A rider who stays away from the curl or the hot part of the wave, taking no chances.

continental shelf *n*. The shallow, gradually sloping area of the sea floor adjacent to the shoreline, terminating seaward at the continental slope. (CCRG) On the East Coast of the United States, the continental shelf stretches far out to sea, diffusing ocean swells into small waves. By contrast, on the West Coast the shelf drops off close to the coast, so that big, powerful ocean swells can approach areas like California with full force and create larger waves.

contour *n*. **1**) The BOTTOM CONTOUR of a surfboard.   **2**) The configuration of the bottom of the ocean at a specific surf spot.

controlled *adj*. A requirement added to the ASP scoring criteria in 1985, intended to bring about a switch from extravagant free-form antics that frequently ended in wipeouts to specific and well-defined maneuvers that could be judged more eas-

conan
Art: Karen T. Delgadillo

coral
Brain coral

ily. The rules now read "radical *controlled* maneuvers" instead of "radical maneuvers."

cook, cooking *v.* **1)** To surf aggressively; to make fancy moves. Same as RIP, HOT DOG, LACERATE. **2)** (Of waves) To offer excellent surfing conditions. See PUMPING. (MVA)

cool *adj.* **1)** Hot. (SP) **2)** Really great, as in "way cool," "so cool," "fully cool," "too cool," "the coolest."

cool breezer *n.* A happy-go-lucky surfer type, usually a student. (MVA)

Coolite *n.* **1)** An Australian brand-name for a Styrofoam trainee surfboard. (MW) **2)** The first board of most Australian grommets, including MR, Rabbit, and Barton Lynch. (SFG, 1989)

coral atoll *n.* ATOLL.

coral cut *n.* A deep laceration resulting from a collision with the jagged surface of coral formations. The cut itself is usually not as dangerous as the microscopic bacteria that may get under the skin and cause serious infection. See KAKIOS.

coral reef *n.* An enormous living organism that can produce incredibly clean, tubing surf but is also dangerous because of the razor-sharp cuts that coral can inflict when a surfer is pounded into or dragged over the reef during a wipeout.

cord *n.* SURF CORD. Affixed to the board and strapped to the ankle, a cord allows poor swimmers and poor surfers alike to hop in the ocean; it prevents far more accidents than it causes. Same as LEASH, GOON CORD, SHOCK CORD.

corduroy to the horizon
Santa Cruz, California
Photo: Woody Woodworth

corduroy, corduroy to the horizon *n.* A strong, straight swell perfectly lined up, like the ribbed cotton fabric used for pants. (BP)

cork *n.* A surfboard that floats too high in the water. (BP)

corkscrew *n., adj.* Spinning action by a bodysurfer when catching a wave. (MF) Usage: "Nice corkscrew action."

corner, cornering *v.* An Australian term for ANGLE — to travel sideways across a wave.

corpuscle *n.* A HELGIE who hangs on the lip waiting for someone to fall. (East Side, Santa Cruz; SFR, 8/90)

cove *n.* The area beside the point (MVA); a small bay.

cover-shot surfing, cover-shot maneuvers *n.* A term used by competitive surfing judges to describe an exhibitionist style of surfing with little regard for technique.

Surfing magazines and surf photographers have created a tendency among young surfers to indulge in a style of surfing that places little value on making a wave or even completing a particular maneuver, because once they're on the cover they don't care if they fall off in the next frame. The photos that appear in the magazines are simply spectacular wipeouts about to happen in the next frame. (L&L)

cover-up *n.* GETTING TUBED; the term originated in the sixties and is still in use. A cover-up is similar to a tube ride, where the breaking white water covers the rider. (L&L)

covered *v.* To be inside the curl of a wave with water pitching out over one's head. (MM) Usage: "He's totally covered!" (SP)

Cowabunga! A surfer's hilarious and exultant shout. As Snoopy says, "That means surf's up!" and who is going to argue with that? (MVA) Surfers adopted the expression from *The Howdy Doody Show* in the 1950s. Sometimes spelled **Kowabunga.** See BANZAI and KOWABONGA.

Cowabunga stokaboka A sixties term for really super STOKED. (KSO)

crack *v.* An Australian term for ride. Usage: "Crack a good wave."

crack it *v.* Do it, go for it, go surfing. (A&M)

crank, cranking *v.* **1**) (Of really big waves) To break consistently. Usage: "Unreal, it's cranking out there." (MVA) **2**) **cranked** *adj.* Used to describe big surf. Usage: "The waves are really cranked." See COOK and PUMP.

crank a turn *v.* To lean into a turn at a radical angle.

crashing move *n.* Any hot maneuver that scores high in a surfing competition.

crazing *n.* Hairline cracks either within or on the surface of fiberglass laminates, caused by stresses generated by excessive heat during cure, removal from the mold, impact, or flexing. (ORB)

cream, creamed *v.* **1**) To be caught by the curl of a wave, thrown off the board, and spun around by the turbulence while being held underwater and tossed aside; a WIPEOUT. **2**) To be beat up; to be crushed to juice in the pilings of a pier. (A&M)

creek skimming *n.* Riding a skim board on a standing wave on a river. (TLH)

crest *n.* **1**) The highest point of a wave before it breaks. **2**) The tallest part of the wave, which usually breaks first. (ORB) Also called WAVE CREST.

crew, the crew *n.* A group of surfers, for example, "the Santa Cruz crew."

cripple *n.* A derogatory term for a KNEEBOARDER. Implied in the question, "What's the matter, can't you stand?"

critical *adj.* **1**) The condition when the wave is about to break. **2**) Applied to a board with hypersensitive response. **3**) Used to describe a very steep, fast-breaking, and difficult-to-ride wave — a "critical" wave.

critical point *n.* A situation on a wave in which there is no leeway, time, or room for alternatives. See COMMITTED.

critical section, most critical part *n.* **1**) The part of a wave that is very difficult to ride, usually deep within the curl or a very steep section. (L&L) **2**) The part right where the wave is breaking.

cross chop *n.* A water condition created by a cross wind or the convergence of waves. See CHOP.

cross curve *n.* The transverse profile or cross section of a surfboard.

cross step, cross-stepping *n.* The act of walking toward the nose of a longboard, one foot over the other — a stylish move. (A&M, MVA) Same as FOOT-OVER-FOOT WALKING.

cross wind *n.* A wind that blows directly across the path of a surfer.

crosscurrent or **cross-current** *n.* An ocean current that runs parallel to the beach. (GN) See LONGSHORE CURRENT.

crossover *n.* CROSS STEP.

crouch *n.* A leaning-forward, squatting position used to duck into the breaking part of the wave, reduce wind resistance, or obtain better balance on a big-wave drop. See STRAUCH CROUCH.

crowd, crowding *v.* Not giving another surfer enough space on a wave.

crowded, crowded conditions, overcrowded When there are too many surfers in the water. Usage: "This place gets too *crowded!*" (SP) See ZOO.

crown *n.* A convex curvature, such as under the nose of a surfboard.

crowned deck *n.* DOMED DECK.

crowned rail *n.* CHINE RAIL.

cruise, cruising *v.* To slide across the face of a wave with free and easy turns, nothing tight or radical.

cruisemobile *n.* A Holden station wagon. (South Australia; R&D) See SURF VEHICLE.

crowd
above:
Trestles lineup
Photo: Robert Brown

below:
Beach crowd
Photo: Don Balch

crumbling tube *n*. A tubing wave that collapses as the surfer rides through it. In competitive surfing, this kind of tube scores less than a DRY TUBE, where the surfer is completely enclosed. See TUBE RIDE.

cruncher *n*. **1**) A hard-breaking big wave that folds over and is almost impossible to ride (IDSM); same as BOOMER, DUMPER. Also called CRUSHER, CRASHER, BLASTER, WHOMPER, etc. **2**) A ding in a surfboard that can be repaired without a resin filler. To qualify as a "true" cruncher, three circumstances must be present: the fiberglass must be buried in the foam firmly; the glass must not be deeper than 3/16 of an inch; and the area surrounding the crunch must be solid and attached to the foam. (GCD) See SINKER.

cruzer *n*. Someone who surfs without exerting much energy; a semi-lazy surfer. (MVA) See CRUISE.

cup *n*. The upward curvature of the front end of a surfboard; the SPOON or SCOOP.

cure *v., n*. In building a surfboard, the changing of the liquid resin to a solid state. Once the resin begins to cure, the process can't be reversed. The technical term for this reaction is *polymerization*. (ORB)

cure time *n*. **1**) The time required for the liquid resin to become hard enough to undergo other processes, such as sanding or finishing, or to cease being tacky or sticky. **2**) Technically, the time required for the resin to reach a polymerized state after a catalyst has been added. (ORB)

curl *n*. **1**) The curved breaking portion of the wave, curling or pouring over in front of the rest of the wave and creating a space between the main body of the wave and the spilling crest. **2**) The hollow wave face under the lip of a breaking wave. (L&L)

curl line *n*. The path of the wave as it peels from one side to the other.

current *n*. **1**) A body of water that runs or flows, usually in, out, or along a beach or coastline. **2**) Local or large-scale water movements that result in the horizontal transport of water masses and surfers.

curtain floater *n*. Surfing across the top of the white water and down the front onto the flats. Usage: "Nice curtain floater, bro."

curve *n*. A surfboard design feature, as in a "curve in the bottom of a board." (NAT, 1985) The way a board is curved affects its hydrodynamics.

custom surfboard *n*. A surfboard built especially to the specifications of a rider. The weight of the surfer and the type of riding to be done are generally taken into consideration.

custom wetsuit *n*. A tailored garment with tapered arms and legs, incorporating various body measurements so that it fits the individual surfer like a glove.

cut *v*. To slide in or move at an angle to the direction of a wave's motion.

cut down *v*. To surf from the top of a wave to the bottom.

cut it up, cutting it up *v*. Same as RIP, but usually applies to more than one person. (MVA) Usage: "They were really cutting it up out there."

cut off 1) *v*. To terminate a ride. **2**) To be SNAKED or SHOULDER HOPPED. (RO) Usage: "That dude totally cut me off." **3**) **cutoff** *n*. An intrusion by someone who doesn't respect another surfer's right to ride a wave alone. (MVA) **4**) As the Surf Punks say in an album glossary, "Cutting off — valleys usually do."

cut out *v*. **1**) To exit a wave. (MM) **2**) To leave a wave by turning up the face and over the crest. (A&B) Same as PULL OUT or KICK OUT. **3**) To be forced out of a wave by another

surfer. Usage: "He cut me out."
—**cutout** *n.*

cutaway *n.* On the sides of the bow or stern of a surfboard, the section that is removed, or "cut away," in the design stage to permit a smaller board-to-wave angle.

cutback or **cut-back** *n.* **1**) An S-shaped maneuver in which a surfer turns sharply back toward the advancing curl, then turns sharply again to advance once more along the wave face. **2**) A turn toward the breaking section of the wave, or back into the wave. **3**) In competitive surfing, a horizontal change of direction of at least 130 degrees in which the board reverses its original path so that it returns toward the breaking part of the wave. This type of maneuver usually precedes the RICOCHET. The most difficult cutback is to extend far out into the shoulder of the wave and, with no loss of speed, return at 180 degrees in a figure-8 path into the breaking curl. (L&L) **4**) A complete change of direction. (MVA) —**cut back** *v.,* **butt-skimming cutback, cutback radical**

cyclops *n.* A grumpy old longboarder who burns everyone and never looks back. (East Side, Santa Cruz; R&F)

cylindrical *adj.* Describes the shape of a perfectly tubing wave.

caveman campfire squat
Art: Robbie Quine

da kine or **da' kine** (da KINE)
1) The keystone of Hawaiian Pidgin; you can use it anywhere, anytime, anyhow — very convenient. (DSN)
2) Another way of saying "what-chamacallit" or "what's-his-name." Usage: "Ey, Michael! Where da kine?" (ECN) **3**) A Hawaiian term for TOTALLY (SP); not to be confused with *the kind,* a California expression meaning "the best." **4**) The word used when you don't use the word, for instance to describe excellent waves, extremely good weather, or great looks, among other things. Usage: "Da kine waves, brah."

Dale, Dick Known as the "King of the Surf Guitar," he was the originator of the "surf sound" of surf music in 1958–1959. His hits include "Let's Go Trippin'" (1961), recorded live at the Rendezvous Ballroom in Newport Beach. Dick Dale and The Deltones was the name of his band.

dangle foot *n.* An old name for GOOFY FOOT.

darryl *n.* A Santa Barbara term for BARNEY. See DEREL.

Davidson Current A northward flowing, warm-water ocean current located inshore of the California Current along the California coast in late fall and winter. (CCRG)

dawn patrol *n.* **1**) An early-morning surfing session. (MM) Some people say of such a session, "Crisp and clean and no caffeine." **2**) Surfing or looking for surf at sunrise. (L&L)

day-after-storm surf *n.* A condition caused by local storms, when waves are typically close together

and very uneven in appearance but can be quite large, up to ten feet or more. In California, this happens from November to April. (S&C)

Day-Glo Radioactive neon colors, adopted by some surfers and much of the surf industry in the 1980s. Used for fluorescent, overstated clothes, wetsuits, surfboards, zinc oxide, etc.

dead dip *n.* A squatting position in which the surfer leans forward at an exaggerated angle. (IDSM)

dead section, **dead spot** *n.* A flat section of the wave that limits maneuverability or acceleration. (L&L). Also called DEEP GUTTER.

deal, dealing *v.* When the waves are good. (JP) Usage: "The waves are dealing today."

death *n.* The ultimate — you can't get better. A great wave or an attractive woman can be just like death; after that, you might as well die because it's over. Usage: "That wave was death." "She's death." (Southern California)

. . . .
This usage has been well documented in Shakespeare's sonnets, where to die was a euphemism for orgasm. To Jim Morrison of The Doors, sex was an enactment of death.
. . . .

debbie *n.* A derogatory term for a dumb beach bunny who never gets wet — for example, someone in a bikini contest. (Santa Monica; JB, 1985)

decal *n.* SURF STICKER.

Dick Dale
Photo: Surfer Magazine

decent *adj.* Used to describe good surfing conditions. Usage: "The waves are pretty decent today."

deck *n.* The top surface of a surfboard.

deck contour *n.* The shape of the top surface of a surfboard. See CROWNED DECK, DOMED DECK.

. . . .

The different contours also include a *flat deck,* where the rail turns down quickly, and a *deck very blended into rails,* where the transition from deck to rail is completely smooth.

. . . .

deck grip *n.* Adhesive tape strips or shaped pads that act as a WAX SUBSTITUTE.

deck line *n.* The length of the board, as measured along the stringer from the nose tip to the tail of the surfboard. Same as STRINGER LINE.

deck patch *n.* An extra layer of fiberglass cloth laminated into the area of the deck where the surfer lies, kneels, or stands. Its purpose is to avoid excessive dents or knee depressions in the deck. Also called STOMP PATCH, BUTTERFLY STOMP PATCH. (ORB) **—staggered deck patches**

deck profile *n.* The outline of a surfboard.

decoy *n.* A FLOUNDER BUOY, who on a crowded day is used by the other surfers as a marker on a slalom course; a spectator. (MCR)

deep, deep inside, **deep set** *adv.* To be closest to, or actually inside, the curling part of the wave, or the tube. **—deep inside the green room, deep in da tube, deep barrel**

deep gutter *n.* The area of deep water where a wave flattens out before it reaches the shorebreak. Also called DEAD SECTION. (L&L)

deep peak takeoff, deep takeoff *n.* Catching a wave at its most critical stage. (A&M) See LATE TAKEOFF.

deep setup or **deep set-up** *n.* A deliberate positioning far inside

either the tube or the power pocket before accelerating along the wave face.

deep turn *n.* A wide turn carved out near the curl of a wave.

deep-water wave *n.* A wave coming out of deep water. See BOMBORA.

delamination *n.* **1)** On surfboards, the separation of fiberglass layers from one another or from the foam, as in a "delaminated deck." This condition is most often the result of a failure of the foam-fiberglass bond. **2)** On wetsuits, the separation of materials from the neoprene layer. **3)** Peeling skin from a really bad sunburn.

derel *n.* A term used in a derogatory or joking sense to describe someone who is lacking in intelligence. Short for the word *derelict*. (AC) Usage: "What a derel." See DARRYL.

destructo *n.* The house-wrecker in the party scene of the movie *Big Wednesday* (1978). (A&M)

devil winds *n.* SANTA ANA WINDS.

dewey or **duey** *n.* A nerd. (MVA)

dial, dial in *v.* **1)** To plug in — like a telephone. Usage: "Let's go dial in on some waves." **2) dialed** To be connected or hooked up. Usage: "Ah, dude, your room is fully king, you're so dialed."

diamond tail *n.* A surfboard tail design that comes to a point, rather than being more rounded at the end.

Diego Short for San Diego.

dig a rail, digging a rail *v.* To have the edge or side of the surfboard cut or "dig" into the water. Often occurring when a turn is being attempted, digging a rail may result in a spill. The usual cause is poor positioning on a turn, for instance trying to turn from too far forward. Same as CATCH A RAIL.

ding 1) *n.* A damaged place in the surface of a surfboard, such as a hole, crack, dent, or deep scratch;

delamination
Art: I. B. Nelson

deck grip
Photo: Trevor Cralle

decoy
Art: Rick Stover

dolphin
Art: I. B. Nelson

dingage. See DUCT TAPE. **2**) A surf-related injury, such as a cut on the leg. **3**) **getting dinged up** v. When a surfer gets tossed around by a wave, or when a board has lots of dings. Usage: "I got all dinged up on that wipeout." "My board's all dung up."

ding-ding n. The way some Hawaiians refer to a ding. Usage: "You gotta ding-ding, brah."

ding kit n. A repair kit for dings, usually containing a small roll of duct tape, several different grades of sandpaper, and a variety of other things.

ding repair n. Patching or filling dings on a surfboard — one of those things in life that no surfer can elude. (GCD)

ding string n. A SURF LEASH; so named because using a leash may reduce your chances of dinging up your board.

dip n. **1**) GEEK. **2**) A not-with-it kind of chap; a goof. (MM)

disco move n. Any KOOK MANEUVER.

dismo n. A person who talks surf, lives surf, dreams surf, but never surfs. (P)

disorganized adj. Said of swell or waves that don't line up or break consistently. Usage: "It's pretty disorganized out there."

dissipate v. To flatten or disappear. Waves "dissipate" in size and shape depending on bottom contour and various other factors.

diurnal tides n. High and low tides that occur twice daily in many parts of the world, like California. See MIXED TIDES.

DMA Dimethylanaline — a promoter used in resins.

do a sauna, doing a sauna v. To piss in your wetsuit to stay warm while out in the water. (ELN)

doggers n. Multicolored swimming trunks, ordinarily made of canvas or some other tough fabric.

dol-fin n. A raked surfboard skeg (fin) originating with the hydroplane surfboard and resembling a porpoise's dorsal fin.

dolphin n. A playful marine mammal that occasionally joins in on surfing sessions.

domed deck, slightly domed deck n. A rounded, rather than flat, deck that provides a thicker stringer and increased foam volume (hence more flotation) down the center of the board. (ORB) Same as CROWNED DECK.

dommo v. To surf really well — to dominate. Usage: "I dommo Doheny." (SFG, 1989)

doom tube n. A tubing wave that's so long there's no way out. (BC, Spring 1990)

dope rope n. A derogatory term for SURF LEASH; same as KOOK CORD, GOON CORD.

dork n. Someone exhibiting unacceptable behavior, who doesn't know the unwritten surfer code; a twerp or turkey. For example, a surfer from San Jose or other inland cities — from "over the hill" — automatically has dork status. (CVG) Same as KOOK, GEEK. (A&M)

double, doubling v. What happens when a wave jacks up in size.

double bubble, double humper, double wave n. When a fast outside wave overtakes a slow inside wave, creating a larger and faster compound wave. Same as DOUBLE UP.

double-ender n. A surfboard that is almost symmetrical, with a slightly pointed tip at either end.

double-glassed adj. Used to describe longboards that have two layers of fiberglass instead of one.

double overhead n. A wave that is twice as high as the surfer riding it.

double ski n. A WAVE SKI designed to be used by two people. (MF)

double spinner *n*. Two consecutive 360-degree body spins on a surfboard. See SPINNER.

double up *v*. What two consecutive waves do when they meet or join. (L&L) See DOUBLE BUBBLE. Usage: "Did you see those two waves double up on each other?"

double-wing pin twin fin *n*. A pintail-shaped twin fin with two sets of bumps along the rails.

doughnuts *n*. Very round TUBES. (MVA)

dovetailed fin box *n*. A dovetailed slot on the underside of a surfboard for a removable skeg that can also be adjusted fore or aft along the stringer line.

down *adj*. Refers to surf that is FLAT. Usage: "Surf's down, bro."

down railed *adj*. A surfboard design by Gerry Lopez in which the rail has a lowered outer edge that produces less side spray and higher speeds. (SFR, 10/83) Also called DROPPED RAIL.
—**downrails**

down the face Surfing from the top to the bottom of a wave.

down the line 1) That portion of a breaking wave some distance away and toward which the rider is projecting his or her track. **2**) The spot to which a surfer maneuvers on a breaking wave. Usage: "The wave started to section on me down the line."

down the mine 1) An Australian term for PEARLING. **2**) WIPE OUT. (A&B) Usage: "I went down the mine on that last one."

Down Under Another name for Australia. Also called OZ, as in *The Land of Oz*.

drag *n*. **1**) BUMMER. **2**) A surfboard's resistance to forward motion caused by the shape of its bottom and its breakaway edges.

drag-foot turn *n*. An old-fashioned method of turning long, heavy surfboards by dragging one foot in the water. This maneuver was made famous by a surfer from Hawaii called Scoota Boy. (A&M)

dragging a hand *v*. Letting your trailing hand touch the wave while surfing across it.

draw out, drawing out *v*. To extend a turn. Usage: "He was drawing out a high-speed bottom turn." "I saw you carve a drawn-out turn."

draw the line, drawing the line *v*. **1**) To touch the wall of a wave with a finger or hand while surfing across it. Same as DRAGGING A HAND. **2**) To test your limits and push yourself, as seen in the movie *Big Wednesday* (1978): "It's time to draw the line."

dredge, dredging 1) *v*. The action of strong waves breaking in shallow water, which draw water from ahead of them and suck already shallow water up into their face. Usage: "It was really dredging out there." **2**) **dredging wave** *n*. The big brother of a SUCKEY WAVE. (Australia; MW)

dribble *n*. **1**) Small, powerless surf. **2**) A form of speech favored by surfers who have spent too much time in the sun without a hat on. (Australia; JARR) See TROPPO.

drift 1) *v*. To float in motion with a current, as in a surfer being carried away by a current. **2**) *n*. The SIDESLIP of a surfboard.

drill, drilled *v*. **1**) To be WORKED — the condition of a surfer who has unsuccessfully negotiated a killer wave. **2**) Used to describe a bad experience, usually with a rough or uncooperative wave. Usage: "Man, that wave really drilled me." (JP)

drip *n*. DIP.

drive, driving *v*. **1**) To accelerate on a wave. (NAT, 1985) **2**) To exert extra effort to trim the board and gain the most possible speed, as in "driving hard off the bottom."

dredging
Photo: Rob Gilley

dropping in
Photo: Woody Woodworth

dude
Art: Jimbo Phillips

drop-knee
Photo: Fred Swegles

drop 1) *v.* To move down on the face of the wave toward the trough. **2**) *n.* The initial downward slide after taking off on a wave. —**taking the drop**

drop in, dropping in 1) *v.* To slide down the face of a wave immediately after it is caught; to take off on a wave and ride from the top straight to the bottom. **2**) To take off on a breaking wave in front of a surfer already launched, thus cutting the other surfer off. **3**) To refuse to give priority to someone already on a wave. See DROP-IN RULE. **4**) **drop-in** *n.* Surfing's most offensive behavior, to paddle and then begin a ride on the inside on a wave that someone else is already riding. (MW) Usage: "Don't drop in on meeee!" See SNAKING, SHOULDER HOPPING.

. . . .

Stealing another surfer's wave is the ultimate taboo in surfing, often breached by surfers unfamiliar with the local PECKING ORDER. Some locals yell "Dropping in!" at intruding surfers to prevent getting snaked. (CVG, BHT)

. . . .

drop-in fade *n.* Stalling the surfboard after catching the wave to let the curl catch up.

drop-in rule, basic drop-in rule *n.* In competitive surfing, the rule that the surfer on the inside at the initial point of takeoff has unconditional right-of-way for the entire duration of the ride. "On the inside" means closest to the breaking curl of the wave. (L&L) See WAVE POSSESSION.

drop-knee *n.* **1**) A type of turn in which both knees are bent, with the trail leg crossed behind the lead leg and the trail-leg knee dropped closer to the board than the knee of the lead leg. **2**) A bodyboarding position. —**getting up drop-knee**

drop-knee cutback *n.* A dynamic longboarding maneuver involving bending one leg in order to turn in the opposite direction. (KSO)

drop-turn *n.* A turn, usually radical, just at the bottom of a drop down the face of the wave.

dropped rail *n.* DOWN RAILED.

dry suit *n.* **1**) A neoprene rubber full bodysuit (sometimes as much as five millimeters thick), which doesn't let water leak in, as distinct from a WETSUIT. Long winter underwear is worn under the suit. **2**) A necessary garment for surfing in places like Maine in the winter.

dry tube *n.* **1**) A tube ride in which the surfer is completely enclosed and emerges without the wave collapsing. **2**) In competitive surfing, a higher scoring maneuver than a CRUMBLING TUBE.

duck *n.* Someone who floats around in the lineup like a buoy. Also called MALLARD.

duck dive *n.* **1**) A maneuver in which the surfer pushes down on the front nose of the board to dive under a breaking or broken wave. (JP) **2**) A method of diving with the board under an oncoming wave on the way out through the break. (NAT, 1985)

duck feet *n.* Rubber fins used for bodysurfing, bodyboarding, and kneeboarding.

duct tape *n.* A shiny, silver-colored, heavy-duty adhesive tape used for on-the-spot ding repair and a bunch of other things; fixes everything.

dude *n.* **1**) A surfing enthusiast, usually of the male gender. Females are sometimes known as **dudettes**. The word was popularized in the 1982 movie *Fast Times at Ridgemont High* by the character Jeff Spicoli (played by Sean Penn). **2**) A lame, outdated Valley word; **the "d" word**. See VALLEY SHEEP. (SP, 3) **3**) Another surfer who is your friend. (H&R) **4**) How surfers refer to the other guy, usually because they can't remember his name. (MCR) Usage (various, depending on inflection or emphasis):

"Dude!" (Hello.) "Hey, dude." (What's happening?) "Hey. Dude." (Come over here.) "Killer, dude!" (Awesome.) "Later, dude." (Goodbye.) "Yo, dude," or simply, "Dude." (Said to get someone's attention.) If your friend has locked himself in the closet, you might say, *"Dude?"* —**surf dude**, **surfer dude**

dump *n*. WIPEOUT; often referred to in bodysurfing.

dumper *n*. **1**) A wave that curls over steeply as it is about to break, then suddenly washes down into shallow water. **2**) A wave that breaks and curls straight down from the top,

dumping the rider. **3**) A thick, powerful wave that curls from top to bottom with the texture of wet cement. (A&M) **4**) A wave that sucks out in shallow water and pounds when breaking. (NAT, 1985)

dweeb *n*. GEEK; a term allegedly coined by Corky Carroll. Usage: "Look at those two dweeby-looking types."

dwid *n*. GEEK.

dying cockroach *n*. A supine surfer who weakly waves arms and legs. (WLK)

E-glass *n*. A specific formula for fiberglass composition commonly used in building reinforcements for boats and surfboards. (ORB)

early surf *n*. An early-morning surf session. (Australia) —**an early** (Hawaii; GS, 4/90) Usage: "I woke up for an early today at 5 A.M."

earthquake *n*. A trembling movement of the earth's surface that sometimes generates SEISMIC SEA WAVES, or TSUNAMIS. See SEISMOGRAPH.

East Coast In surfing, refers to the East Coast of the United States.

east swell *n*. A swell that moves from east to west. (ORB)

east wind, easterly *n*. A wind that blows from east to west. (ORB)

eat it, eat shit *v*. **1**) To fall off one's surfboard; to WIPE OUT or GET WORKED. (P) Usage: "I ate it somethin' fierce." (GN) **2**) To eat the sand or a piece of your surfboard; to get MUNCHED. (MCR) See LUNCH.

eat the cookie *v*. To wipe out in the white water. (IBN)

eat the rocks *v*. To get crushed into a rocky shoreline, with or without a surfboard.

eat up *v*. Hawaiian Pidgin slang for what happens when a wave swallows a surfer.

ebb, ebb tide *n*. A tide that is going from high to low (ORB); an outgoing tide.

edge *n*. **1**) A design feature on the side or rail of a surfboard. **2**) The portion of a wave that remains unbroken; the SHOULDER. Usage: "I was forced out on the edge."

egg *n*. A 1960s term for KOOK.

egg board, egg round tail, egg-shaped rounded tail *n*. A surfboard shape featuring an oval tail.

eggroll *n*. A raw novice; same as EGG (1960s), KOOK (1970s), and RUBBERNECK (1980s). There's a heavy PECKING ORDER in surfing: an "eggroll" is anyone who isn't as good as you. (Australia; MW)

eight ball *n*. Another name for the PRIORITY BUOY used in competitive surfing. See GETTING BEHIND THE EIGHT BALL.

El Niño *n*. An anomalous warming of the ocean surface, associated with a vast fluctuation in atmospheric pressure, that triggers abnormal northward migration of southern species of seabirds and marine life and brings about global changes in weather patterns that have been linked to droughts, severe storms, flooding, and landslides. *El Niño,* Spanish for "the Christ child," got its name because of its periodic appearance around Christmas off the coast of Peru. (CCRG) Both the giant winter surf of 1983 and the occurrence during 1988 of possibly the flattest waves in recorded surfing history were attributed to *El Niño.* (SFG, 3/90)

el rollo *n*. **1)** Originally a hotdogging longboard maneuver, in which the surfer lies prone and rolls with the surfboard a complete 360 degrees — as seen performed by Corky Carroll and described by Bruce Brown in *The Endless Summer* (1964). Today, it is more commonly identified as a bodyboarding maneuver. **2)** A maneuver performed in small surf to exit a wave.

El Spontanio (el spawn-TANE-ee-o) *n*. A squatting position where the surfer looks back between the legs, ordinarily while riding at the nose of the surfboard. In a pure *El Spontanio,* the fingers must be interlocked behind the surfer's back. The term is a corruption of the Spanish *el espontáneo* (the spontaneous one).

El Telephono (el tel-e-FONE-o) *n*. A hot-dog riding stance invented by Mickey Muñoz in the late 1950s; looks roughly like a bullfighter's classic stance or like someone trying to

be thin in a telephone booth crush. The term is a corruption of the Spanish *el teléfono* (the telephone).

elephant gun *n*. A large surfboard designed especially for big surf, or the heavies; same as BIG GUN.

elevator effect, elevator-shaft drop, elevator-drop takeoff *n*. A sudden fall from the crest of the wave as the result of a sudden drop or elevation in wave height caused by a bottom shoal or depression or by a backwash or doubling.

elevator surfing *n*. The life- and limb-risking practice of riding up and down an elevator shaft on the *top* of an elevator. Generally practiced by East Coast frat boys suffering from alcohol poisoning.

elliptical rail *n*. A surfboard rail that is oval shaped in cross section and that produces a fairly low side spray and more speed than a round rail.

emmit, emmits *n*. **1)** A term used by Cornwall surfers to describe tourists or spectators; the old Cornish word for "ants." (England; TMN) **2)** A British DEWEY.

Endless Summer A double anthology album of early sixties surfing and hot-rod hit tunes by The Beach Boys, which was released in 1974 on Capitol Records and thrust the group into a second wave of popularity.

Endless Summer, The Bruce Brown's feature-length film, which followed two surfers around the world in their search for the perfect wave; premiered in Wichita, Kansas, in 1964. Brown was originally planning to fly round-trip to South Africa from Los Angeles, but it turned out to be $50 cheaper to fly around the world, so he went for it and produced what many consider to be the all-time classic surf movie.

The Endless Summer

On any day of the year it's summer somewhere in the world. Bruce Brown's latest color film highlights the adventures of two young American surfers, Robert August and Mike Hynson who follow this everlasting summer around the world. Their unique expedition takes them to Senegal, Ghana, Nigeria, South Africa, Australia, New Zealand, Tahiti, Hawaii and California. Share their experiences as they search the world for that perfect wave which may be forming just over the next horizon. BRUCE BROWN FILMS

TM & © Bruce Brown Films 1966
Art: John Van Hammersveld

The movie sound track was by the Sandals; the album featured the classic instrumental theme of the movie, a mellow surf tune that evoked the feeling of surfing under the sun. The movie poster, done in classic sixties fluorescent colors of purple, orange, and yellow, was created by poster designer John Van Hammersveld; the image has been reproduced on T-shirts.

The following may have been the very first use of the term *endless summer*:

". . . the slumbrous calm of an endless summer, the glorious tropical trees, the distant view of cool chasmlike valleys, with Honolulu sleeping in perpetual shade, and the still blue ocean, without a single sail to disturb its profound solitude." —Isabella Bird, "Impressions of Honolulu, 1873," from *The Spell of Hawaii,* edited by A. Grove Day and Carl Stroven (Mutual Publishing of Honolulu, 1968)

energy *n.* See OCEAN ENERGY.

enforcer *n.* A sixties term for a male surfer with a reputation for being very tough. He usually has a name like "Lunchmeat" or "Heavy Duty"; it's his job to keep law and order in the water, on the beach, or at a party. (MCR)

epic *adj.* CLASSIC; something of grand proportions, as in "epic conditions," "epic surf," "an epic day."

epoxy resin *n.* A thermosetting resin used in boat work and consisting of two parts that, when combined, cure and form into an extremely hard and tough product. *Epoxy resins* adhere better and shrink less than polyester resins and have generally greater strength; they are also much more expensive. (ORB)

equatorial tides *n.* Tides of minimum range that occur twice a month when the moon is over the equator. (CCRG) See TROPIC TIDES.

ESA Eastern Surfing Association.

Eskimo roll *n.* **1**) A technique for getting out through a wave by capsizing the surfboard and using the body as an anchor. (MF) **2**) A means of getting past a broken wave. **3**) A method of going under waves when riding Malibus and wave skis. (NAT, 1985)

evening glass-off *n.* **1**) A late-afternoon surf session that sometimes extends past sunset. Usage: "Let's hit the evening glass-off." **2**) **evening glass** The calm, glassy surface of the ocean in the evening after the wind has died down. (A&M) See GLASS-OFF.

excellent *adj.* Great, fantastic, exceptionally high-quality, as in "totally excellent," "excellent waves," "excellent conditions," "most excellent."

exit track *n.* The projected path of a surfer steering the surfboard up over the back of a wave in order to terminate a ride.

exostosis *n.* A bone thickening in the ear canal caused by exposure to cold water. Also called SURFER'S EAR.

exothermic heat *n.* The heat given off by the resin during the curing process, or polymerization; caused by the reaction of the accelerator and the catalyst when mixed in polyester resins, and by the hardener in epoxy resins. (ORB)

explosive *adj.* Used to describe a style of surfing characterized by high-speed cutbacks, blasting off the tops of waves, and throwing around lots of spray.

extraction operation *n.* Sending in a game fisherman to catch a rogue shark. (Victoria, Australia; RDTW)

extreme *adj.* RADICAL; pushing the limits while surfing, as in "going to extremes."

face plant
Pipeline, Hawaii
Photo: Bill Romerhaus

face *n.* **1**) The unbroken wall, surface, or nearly vertical front of a wave between the crest and the trough. **2**) The front portion of a wave — the part facing the shore — just before it breaks (JP); the unbroken inner curve of a wave. **3**) The desirable part of a wave to surf, as distinct from the white water. Also called WAVE FACE.

face plant *n.* WIPEOUT; a crossover term from skateboarding.

fade *n.* **1**) A move similar to a stall, in which a surfer slows down either to go deeper into the tube or to avoid colliding with another surfer on the same wave who is blocking his or her exit track. See STALL. **2**) Riding toward the curl or hot part of a wave before turning and riding across the face away from the curl; a maneuver used to stay in the hottest part of the wave. **3**) A motion after takeoff that directs the board toward the curl before the bottom turn. (L&L) —**fading to the inside**

fade turn *n.* A turning maneuver used to slow down so that one can wait for the advancing wave to catch up to the board.

fairing *n.* The way in which the contours of a surfboard blend together to produce a smooth appearance.

fall line *n.* The line of fastest descent from the crest to the base of a wave. (Australia; NAT, 1985)

fan spray *n.* The spray of water a surfer casts when carving a sharp turn on a wave.

fast *adj.* **1**) As applied to boards, usually means highly maneuverable.

faucet nose
Art: Rick Stover

May also be used to mean speedy. **2**) As applied to a wave, one that peels off along its length quickly or that travels shoreward at a fast rate. (RA) —**fast surf**, **fast zippers**

fast-closing *adj.* Applied to a wave on which the break begins at one end and moves rapidly across the wave line to the other end.

Fast Times at Ridgemont High
A 1982 Hollywood movie starring Sean Penn as Jeff Spicoli; responsible for bringing *gnarly* and *dude* into mainstream America's lexicon. (SFG, 11/89)

fat-out *v.* An Australian term for a wave that has become less hollow and fuller, due to a deepening ocean bottom. (MW) Usage: "The wave tends to fat out over by the channel."

fat wave *n.* A wave that walls up, looks like it's going to tube, but drops out (loses shape) because of backwash or more water rushing up from behind. (Australia, C&M)

faucet nose *n.* A phenomenon that occurs when you come in after surfing, bend over, and the whole ocean pours out of your sinuses. (MCR) The condition is caused by having water forced up your nose during a wipeout. Same as POST-SESSION NASAL DRIP, NASODRAIN.

fear *adj.* Used to describe scary waves or scary women. Usage: "The waves are fear, it's so good out there." "That girl was fear."

fear factor *n.* An element of surfing, a consequence of big waves, sharks, etc.; something you just have to live with.

feather 1) *v*. Used to describe the motion of a wave in the instant just before it breaks, when it seems to hang there suspended, or "feathering," just before its lip pitches out. **2) feathering wave** *n*. A wave that does not rise too steeply before breaking. The crest spills over, sliding down the wave face rather than rolling forcefully over. Also called SPILLING WAVE or FRINGING WAVE. (DSHJ)

feather edge *n*. The edge of a resin-saturated fiberglass material that has been tapered to blend with the adjoining surface, as opposed to ending abruptly. (ORB)

feebletosis *n*. Used to describe weak surfing conditions. (East Side, Santa Cruz; SFR, 8/90) Usage: "It was feebletosis."

femmie, fem grem *n*. A female GREMMIE. Also called FREMLIN.

fer sure Surfer and valley girl pronunciation of "for sure," meaning totally, definitely, full agreement.

fetch *n*. The distance, or area, over which the wind blows across the water to create waves and swell. The waves may travel out of the particular wind system and cover a long way before reaching the coast as a ground swell. (L&L)

fiberglass, fiberglass cloth *n*. **1)** A woven glass fabric used in surfboard construction; its application is often referred to as a **glass job**. **2)** Literally fibers of glass. (GCD) **3)** Glass fibers woven into a cloth and saturated with resin before being used to strengthen the exterior of a surfboard's foam core, or blank. (ORB) **4)** The material that provides the protective outer coating of a surfboard. (NAT, 1985)

Fiberglass was invented in a Paris, France, textile mill in 1836, though the term itself didn't come into use until 1936. It comes in weights of four-ounce, six-ounce, etc., per square yard of cloth.

fiberglass dust *n*. Microscopic bits of fiberglass produced during the shaping process that can be extremely itchy, especially when they work their way under your waistband and into your pants (GN); not good to inhale, either. See GLASS ITCH.

fifty-fifty *n*. A surfboard rail that is rounded or "soft." (MCR)

filthy *adj*. HOT, UNREAL, OFF ITS TITS — in other words, totally great. (Australia; MW) Usage: "The waves were filthy out there."

fin *n*. **1)** The vertical projection, or rudder, affixed to a surfboard's bottom near the tail for the purpose of enhancing directional stability and drive. Surfboards can have one (single-fin), two (twin-fin), three (tri-fin), four (quad), or more fins. Also called SKEG. **2)** The dorsal fin of a shark or dolphin.

fin area *n*. The shape or outline of a fin; the surface area of a fin.

fin base *n*. The width of the fin where it meets the board.

fin box *n*. **1)** The ⅜-inch-thick box that holds the base of removable fins, or skegs; generally made of molded plastic. **2)** The sliding, angled adjustment toward or away from the stringer that allows a board to be adapted to waves of various size. **3)** A plastic channel that the fin slides into. (ORB) See DOVETAILED FIN BOX.

fin canter *n*. The angle of the fin leaned away from the stringer, as distinct from FIN TOE IN.

fin height *n*. The distance from the bottom of the board at the fin base to the top of the fin.

fin placement *n*. The distance between the rear edge of the fin and

fiberglass dust
Shaper Bob Pearson, Arrow Surfboards
Photo: Bob Barbour

fin box with removable skeg
Note: leash damage due to lack of rail saver
Photo: Don Balch

fins
Maria Souza
Photo: Woody Woodworth

flappin'
Art: Bob Penuelas

finned
Art: Peter Spacek

the tip(s) of the tail, usually six or seven inches.

fin rake *n.* The degree the leading edge of a fin is swept back. A fin with more rake has a more drawn-out (longer) turning radius; one with less rake has a more pivotal (shorter) turning radius. See RAKE.

fin slot *n.* The track that an adjustable fin slides along in a fin box.

fin toe in *n.* The angle of the fin leaning toward the stringer, as distinct from FIN CANTER.

finned *v.* To be run over by someone's skeg. (A&M)

fins, swim fins *n.* Rubber flippers worn on the feet to help kick out and maneuver in bodysurfing, bodyboarding, and kneeboarding.

fio dental (FEE-o DEN-tal) *n.* Portuguese for "dental floss" — used to describe G-string bikinis. (Brazil) Same as FLOSS, BUTT THONG.

fire, firing *v.* GO OFF, GOING OFF.

first break *n.* **1)** The line of breakers farthest from shore on a given day. See ZERO BREAK. **2)** A specific location at a surf spot where the waves break only when they are sufficiently large.

first rider up Refers to a rule adopted by some competitive surfing organizations that gives priority (right-of-way) to the first surfer to stand up on a wave and ride it. All other surfers must yield to that person. See RIDER ON THE INSIDE.

five-finned board *n.* A surfboard with five fins.

five toes over *n.* HANG FIVE. (DM, 1962)

flagged areas *n.* Swimming areas at beaches where surfboards are prohibited. See FLAGS.

flags *n.* Used to demarcate surfing and swimming areas along a beach and also, at some places, to indicate the condition of the surf. For example, at La Jolla, a **checked flag**

denotes a surfing-only area; at Newport Beach, a **green flag** indicates light surf, a **yellow flag** means moderate, a **red flag** means heavy, and a **black ball flag** means no surfing.

flail *v.* To make eccentric, often funny, arm and body movements; to surf in a clumsy manner. Usage: "Tommy *flails*." (SFG, 1989)

flailer, flailing dork *n.* What beginning surfers are. (CVG) See FLOUNDER.

flap, flappin' *v.* To make spastic arm movements; to FLAIL. See BOOGIE FLAPPER.

flare *n.* A widened portion of the tail of a surfboard; characteristic of hot-dog boards. This design feature provides greater maneuverability and stability at lower speeds.

flat *adj.* **1)** Refers to surfless ocean or surfless conditions. Usage: "The surf's flat today." **2)** Said of the section of a wave that has no power. (NAT, 1985) **3)** A characteristic of some bottom contours or planing surfaces. Usage: "The rocker is very flat in the tail half."

flat spell *n.* A long period — maybe a few days, or even weeks — without surf.

flat spot *n.* **1)** The relatively horizontal water space between wave crests. Also known as FLATS. **2)** A large COMPRESSION DING.

flatlander *n.* INLANDER.

flats *n.* **1)** A surfboard shaper's term for the top and bottom of the board. **2)** The area out in front of a breaking wave.

flatten, flatten out *v.* What a wave does as it passes over a deep spot in the bottom contour. See BACKING OFF.

flex *n.* A measure of how rigid or flexible a surfboard is structurally; considered by many to be the most dynamic action a board exhibits.

Usage: "Your board really has a lot of flex in it."

flexible fin *n*. A fin that absorbs, stores, and then releases turning energy by snapping back into line, thus giving the surfboard added thrust through a delayed response.

flick-off *n*. A maneuver used to kick the board clear of the breaking wave. (NAT, 1985)

flick out *v*. An Australian term for PULL OUT or KICK OUT. —**flickout** *n*.

flip-flops *n*. Rubber sandals. Also called GO-AHEADS.

flipout *n*. A PULLOUT with a somersault.

flippers *n*. SWIM FINS.

floater *n*. **1**) A maneuver in which the board slides on top of a white-water section. **2**) Riding over the white water after a wave breaks, to get back onto the face. (JP) **3**) A move initiated by Cheyne Horan, where the surfer rides over the falling curtain of a breaking wave. (MW) See CURTAIN FLOATER. **4**) A large, buoyant surfboard.

. . . .

The floater maneuver requires the board to be projected up onto the breaking white water or lip and to traverse the section horizontally before descending into the unbroken face of the wave. A special example is a tail-slide floater, where the surfer allows the board to descend tail first down the breaking wave while still maintaining control. (L&L)

. . . .

floater reentry *n*. A maneuver in which the surfer heads up into, and comes over with, the breaking part of a wave; allows the surfer to travel over a closed-out white-water section and continue riding. Sometimes called ROLLER COASTER. See FOAM FLOATER.

floaties *n*. Pieces of shit in the water. (LH)

floating air biscuits What happens when a surfer farts in a wetsuit and the smell comes right out the neck. (Santa Cruz grommet)

floaty *adj*. Used to describe a surfboard that floats high in the water. Usage: "Your board's a bit floaty, mate." (Australia; ASL, 2/88) See CORK.

flood, flood tide *n*. A tide that is going from low to high. (ORB)

flop out *v*. To exit a wave.

floss, bun floss *n*. A thong-backed bikini. (Southern California) Same as BUTT FLOSS, BUTT THONG, FIO DENTAL.

flotation, floatation *n*. The ability of a board to float a surfer; its buoyancy.

flounder *v*. FLAIL. Usage: "You were floundering out there." **2**) To struggle after being pounded by the surf. Usage: "Did you get floundered out there?" **3**) **flounder buoy** *n*. Someone who is in the way of the other surfers. See BUOY.

flow **1**) *v*. To get free stuff from a surf shop. Usage: "Flow me some wax." "Flow me a leash with that board." (Santa Cruz; JMZ) **2**) To move or run freely; to hang loose, make a smooth motion. (RO) Usage: "Surfing is a sport that really *flows*." **3**) *n*. An incoming tide, as in "ebb and flow"; a FLOOD TIDE.

fluid *adj*. Smooth. Usage: "Greg really has a fluid style of surfing."

flyaway *n*. Stepping to the tail of the board and wrenching your body and board sharply to get out of a wave.

flying cutout *n*. A cutout in which board and rider fly back over the crest of the wave separately and through the air.

flying kickout *n*. **1**) An exit from a wave in which the surfer kicks the board out from underneath while up in the air. **2**) An attempted

floater
Vince De La Peña
Photo: Robert Brown

flying cutout
Brian McNulty, Haleiwa
Photo: Bill Romerhaus

aerial that ends in a wipeout. See COVER-SHOT SURFING.

flying swan *n*. **1**) A tandem surf-riding position, with the female sitting on the male partner's shoulders with her arms stretched out. **2**) A bodysurfing position with arms extended outward to the side.

foam *n*. **1**) A chemically produced hard plastic (polyurethane) cellular structure that is shaped into a surfboard; the core of the surfboard. **2**) The frothy aftermath of a broken wave.

The first person to try foam in a surfboard was Bob Simmons in 1950, using polystyrene foam. In 1955, Lorrin Harrison in Capistrano Beach became the first to try polyurethane foam, and in 1956 Dave Sweet in Santa Monica made the first sustained effort to develop polyurethane foam boards. Hobie Alter came out with the first successful polyurethane foam board design in June 1958. Then in 1961 Gordon "Grubby" Clark formed Clark Foam, which is still the largest foam-blank manufacturer in the world. Foam didn't change surfboard design all that much, but it did stabilize and streamline the boards. The same type of board could be made over and over again without worrying about different weights of wood, bad grain, etc. (GN)

foam blank, foam block *n*. The basic block of foam from which a board is shaped. Gordon "Grubby" Clark is the person most responsible for the development of the foam blank. (SFR, 6/87)

foam floater *n*. A distance-covering floater that originates and ends in the white water. It enhances white-water riding potential by offering an alternative to groveling, trimming, or hopping. (L&L) See FLOATER REENTRY.

foam pump turns *n*. Maneuvers in which the whole of the surfer's board is behind the section of white water on a horizontal plane. (L&L)

foam rot *n*. Decay of the core of a surfboard as a result of the board's becoming waterlogged and damaged by exposure to the sun.

foam trim *n*. Efforts, such as hopping or wiggling, aimed at maintaining momentum through white-water sections; carries no point value in surfing competitions. (L&L) Same as GROVELING.

foam turn *n*. Surfing the board up, around, and over a white-water section; an alternative to riding straight or groveling.

foamie, foamer *n*. An Australian term for a surfboard made of foam. Also known as POLY.

foff, foffing *v*. To GO OFF, but more so; said of waves or surfers. Usage: "Big Rock was foffing yesterday: 6 feet, glassy and offshore." (North San Diego County; Rob Gilley, 1989)

fog, fog bank *n*. Condensed water vapor in cloudlike masses, which can make good swells bad and bad surf even worse. Variations include **low fog**, **high fog**, or, if you've been on drugs, **foggy**. Light, onshore winds usually accompany fog and make the surf bumpy and sort of blown out. In very dense fog, though, the ocean is occasionally glassy. See MARINE LAYER. (W&B)

foil *n*. **1**) The distribution of foam on a surfboard, viewed lengthwise from the side; the **thickness flow**. **2**) The thickness cross section of a fin. (ORB) —**asymmetrical foil**

following current *n*. An ocean current that is flowing in the same direction that a swell is traveling, thus increasing wave lengths and decreasing wave heights, the opposite effect of an opposing current. (DKM)

foot-over-foot walking *n*. CROSS-STEPPING.

foot paddling *n*. While standing, dipping one foot over the side of a

In the beginning... Photo: Woody Woodworth

"Surf Swimming by Sandwich Islanders," 1878. Bishop Museum

Alaia board. First known photograph of a surfer, c. 1880's, Waikiki. Bishop Museum

Greg Noll at Pipeline, 1964. Photo *Surfer* Magazine, Courtesy of Greg Noll

HARRY MURRY — RICH THOMPSON — ALEX HOKAMP — BLAKE TURNER — BILL GRACE — BUSTER STEWARD — FRED HUNT — HARRY MAYO — PINKY PEDEMONTE

SANTA CRUZ SURFING CLUB

Photo: Ed Webber, Courtesy of Harry Mayo / Santa Cruz Surfing Museum

Pleasure Point Surf Shop

Santa Cruz, 1967. Photo: Bob Richardson

Jams, 1966. Photo: *Surfer* Magazine

Skateboarding, California, 1964. Photo: I. B. Nelson

Huaraches, 1965.
Photo: *Surfer* Magazine

Malibu. Photo: Woody Woodworth

Myth Beach. Photo: Bill Schwob

Antique surfboard. Photo: Philip Hellsten

Photo: Woody Woodworth

Balsa board, c. 1950.
Artwork: Mack Fowlie.
Photo: Tom Servais /
Surfer Magazine

Woody. Photo: Trevor Cralle

Photo: Woody Woodworth

Surfari. Photo: Woody Woodworth

Beach girl. Photo: Bill Romerhaus

Longboards new and old. Photo: Kirwan Fox

North Shore, Oahu. Photo: Woody Woodworth

longboard and paddling to increase forward motion.

football-type S fin *n*. An S-shaped fin with a narrow base.

forehand surfing *n*. Riding with the body facing the wave. (L&L) —**forehand floater**

forehand turn *n*. Making a turn with the body facing the wall of the wave; affords greater stability and control than a backhand turn.

formula ones *n*. Hammerhead sharks. (Australia; MW)

forward roll pullout *n*. A bodysurfing technique for getting off of a wave by somersaulting forward. (MF)

fossil *n*. Someone who is over the hill in the surfing world; one whose heyday is past and who now clings to some hope of regaining recognition. A fossil will sometimes "yarn" (spin yarns) about how great it used to be. (ALN)

four-fin *n*. A surfboard with four fins located near the rails, where they can dig in when the board is leaned on edge. Same as QUAD.

France The European country that provided surfing with two wonderful inventions: fiberglass and the bikini.

freak set *n*. A surprise set of big waves that catches surfers off guard or on the inside. See CAUGHT INSIDE.

Fred Flintstone The name of a Hanna-Barbera cartoon character, which is given to people who can't surf and get in the way. (KSO) Usually just called **fred**; same as BARNEY or WALLY.

free fall *n*. A mishap that can befall a surfer who is riding high or taking off on a very steep wave and whose surfboard slips out, so that both board and rider fall in midair down the face of the wave. May or may not result in a wipeout.

free-lapping *n*. The process of laying up a rail without trimming it.

free roundtrip ticket over the falls Getting pitched over the front of a wave. (Texas; H&R) See OVER THE FALLS.

freeboard *n*. The portion of the surfboard that extends above the water.

freeboarding *n*. Riding a surfboard while being pulled by a boat. (1960s)

Freeth, George (1883-1919) The Irish-Hawaiian who introduced surfing to Southern California. In 1907 Henry Huntington brought him to Redondo Beach and sponsored surfing exhibitions in an effort to boost ticket sales for the Pacific Electric Railroad and to promote a new saltwater plunge. (DM) Freeth's surfing demonstrations at Redondo are generally regarded as the first appearance of the sport on the California coast. However, see KAWONANAOKOA. A bronze bust of Freeth is located at the foot of the Redondo Beach Municipal Pier.

freeway surfer *n*. A would-be surfer who spends more time driving a car than surfing. (MM) See HIGHWAY SURFER.

freight trains *n*. **1)** Used to describe the appearance of a wave breaking fast in a perfect line down the beach. (MM) **2)** Big, powerful ocean swells. Usage: "Look at those freight trains starting to smoke in."

fremlin *n*. A female GREMLIN.

fringing wave *n*. FEATHERING WAVE.

Frisbee *n*. **1)** A polyethylene plastic flying saucer used by surfers on the beach. First began to be widely marketed in the late fifties and early sixties. *Frisbee* is a registered trademark of Wham-O Mfg. Co., San Gabriel, California. Also called FRIS or DISC. **2)** A popular device for entertaining surfers at surf movies. **3)** Something to eat off of during surf trips to Baja. **4) ultimate frisbee** A team sport played in an open area such as a beach or a field.

freeboarding
Photo: Don Balch

formula one
Art: The Pizz

frogskins
Art: Rick Stover

full-on stoked
Art: The Pizz

frogskins *n.* An outfit consisting of a wetsuit and other cold-water articles such as gloves and booties. (Texas; H&R)

frontside *adj., adv.* Riding with the body facing the wave. (ORB) Usage: "She took off frontside."

frontside layback *n.* An advanced bodyboarding maneuver. See LAYBACK.

frontside under-the-lip snap *n.* An advanced bodyboarding maneuver in which the rider gets under the wave lip and turns sharply.

full-on *adj., adv.* Complete, entire, total. Usage: "I had the full-on wipeout today." "We were full-on stoked." "That party was a full-on rager." —**full stoke**

full-power drift *n.* A sliding turn on a wave.

full rails *n.* Thick rails; a surfboard design feature for increasing flotation.

full stick *n.* A longboard that is full-size, as opposed to a routed shortboard.

full suit *n.* A one-piece wetsuit consisting of long sleeves and legs. Occasionally includes an attached hood (attached booties are rare in a surfing wetsuit). Also called STEAMER.

full template *n.* A surfboard that, viewed from above, is wider than normal. See PULLED TEMPLATE.

fully *adv.* Absolutely complete, as in "fully real," "fully stoked," and "The waves were fully throbbing." (SFR, 6/88)

fun surf, fun waves *n.* Small or medium surf not big enough to make a surfer think twice before taking off or to cause any worry about taking a wipeout. (CC) —**fun surfing**

functional distance *n.* One of the scoring criteria in competitive surfing; it involves being able to hold one's line (keep moving) through the smallest part of the wave while continuing to do maneuvers. (L&L) See SURFING CRITERIA.

functional maneuvers *n.* In a surf competition, any of certain well-defined maneuvers that can be scored, for example, a floater, cutback, or tube ride.

G-Land An abbreviation for Graja-gan (GRAHD-ja-kin), one of the world's hottest surf spots for lefts, on the island of Java in Indonesia.

gale *n.* A grade of storm. **Gale-force winds** range from 32 to 63 miles per hour.

gangreeneous (gain-green-e-us) *adj.* A surfer corruption of *gangrenous* that is used to describe a gnarly coral cut, as in "Gangreeneous, dude." (Southern California)

garbage *n.* No explanation needed. Usage: "The surf was garbage today." (EPZ)

gargantuan *adj.* Used to describe an immense wave; about the same as HUMONGOUS.

gas money *n.* What every surfer is always trying to dig up in order to get to the beach.

gassed *v.* Getting wiped out on a wave. See TAKING GAS.

geek, geekster, geek-a-mo *n.* **1)** A dorky surfer who behaves poorly at the beach; a jerk. **2)** Originally, a carnival sideshow freak who bit the heads off live chickens. **3) geeky, geeklified** *adj.* Usage: "That's completely geeklified." (RBQ)

gel *n.* **1)** A flake. Usage: "Did you see that guy trying to pick up my girlfriend on the beach today? What a gel." Or, occasionally, "Hey **gel brain,** take off on me one more time and I'll carve my initials in your back with my twin fin." **2)** A derelict or do-nothing. (SFG, 12/81) **3**) A stage resin goes through — the physical state in between a liquid

and a solid. (GCD) **4)** *v.* To MELLOW OUT. (SP) Usage: "Gel, dude!"

get air, getting air *v.* To maneuver the surfboard so that both rider and board leave the surface of the ocean. Usage: "Hey dude, check it out. Did you see me get air?" (MVA) Same as CATCH AIR.

get covered up *v.* To be TUBED. See COVERED.

get "L" *v.* To gain elevation (altitude) on an aerial. (TLH)

get launched *v.* To be catapulted from the board.

get piped *v.* To achieve a tube ride. (WW)

get pitched *v.* To become airborne.

get spun *v.* **1)** To experience the washing machine spin-cycle effect when you're held underwater in the surf after wiping out. **2)** To get CLOSED OUT for a very long time.

get tubed, getting tubed *v.* To ride or shoot a tube.

get worked *v.* To be put on "spin cycle"; to be punished by a bad wipeout. See WASHING MACHINE. (P)

getting a place wired *v.* To figure out how the waves break at a specific surf spot, as seen in the movie *The Endless Summer* (1964). See WIRED.

getting behind the eight ball *v.* To paddle around the priority buoy.

getting bombed *v.* What happens to a surfer who gets "avalanched" by a big wave.

geek
Art: Jim Phillips

getting caught in the white water *v.* When the avalanche-like mass of foaming white water overtakes a surfer from behind.

getting caught inside *v.* Describes the situation when continuously breaking waves prevent a surfer from paddling out through the white water or when one really big wave breaks on a surfer before he or she can paddle over the top.

getting stuffed in the pit *v.* To be left in the foam because a surfer down the line in front of you has stalled so much that you can't keep moving. (KSO) Usage: "That kook totally stuffed me in the pit."

getting up drop-knee standing up *v.* A bodyboarding maneuver in which the surfer quickly moves from the prone position to kneeling to standing up.

getting way back *v.* To surf deep inside the tube.

Gidget 1) The nickname of a real person named Kathy Kohner, whose father wrote a book about her called *Gidget,* which was a best-seller in 1957. **2**) The main character in the original *Gidget* film (1959), made after the book, and in several derivative films. See TUBESTEAK. **3**) A television series of the same name.

glassing
Gordon Arrendale
Photos: Woody Woodworth

Kathy Kohner got her nickname from the other surfers when she showed up at Malibu Beach, California, in the summer of 1955 to surf. She explained, "I'm so small [they] called me 'Midget.' I got mad. So now it's Gidget. A girl midget. A gidget. Get it?" After her father, Frederick Kohner, wrote a best-selling book about her adventures, her story was adapted into a popular movie called *Gidget,* which gave surfing its first national exposure. The film was shot at Secos, a Southern California surf spot; Sandra Dee played the starring role, with Mickey Muñoz doing her stunt work.

This was the first of several Gidget films (*Gidget Goes Hawaiian*, etc.) that set the stage for a wave of beach movies in the 1960s. Then the craze hit television, too, with Sally Field starring in a series about fun, fun, fun in the California sun along the shores of Santa Monica. Like the movie, the TV program chronicled the antics of Francine Lawrence (Gidget) and her surfer pals, Jeff Matthews (Moondoggie), Siddo, Larue, and Treasure. The half-hour sitcom aired thirty-two episodes on ABC from September 15, 1965 until September 1, 1966. "The New Gidget," a TV pilot in the 1980s, starred Don Stroud. According to many, surfing's image suffered irreversible damage as a result of all the Gidget-mania. (S&C; JJV)

gilligan *n.* Same as FRED, BARNEY, WALLY, etc.; derived from the character of the same name played by Bob Denver on the TV series "Gilligan's Island."

gitch *n.* Half girl and half bitch; derived from Gitch Anderson in the movie *Under the Boardwalk* (1989).

glass 1) *v.* To laminate resin-saturated fiberglass cloth to a shaped blank. **2**) *n.* Short for FIBERGLASS.

glass coat *n.* GLASS JOB.

glass itch *n.* A skin irritation caused by fiberglass dust. (A & M)

glass job *n.* The application of fiberglass to a surfboard.

glass-off *n.* **1**) A condition usually found in the early morning or evening when the wind dies and the waves become smooth and glassy-looking. **2**) A smooth water surface. (MM) —**afternoon glassy slick**

glass-on fin, glassed-on fin *n.* A fin that is permanently affixed to the surfboard, as distinct from a removable fin.

glasshouse *n.* A smooth ride inside a tubing wave. Usage: "Did you see me pull into that glasshouse?" Also called GREENHOUSE.

glassout *n.* A day when the surface of the ocean is unruffled and ideal for surfing. See GLASSY.

glassy *adj.* Used to describe an extremely calm ocean surface or wave, usually giving off a glasslike reflection; silky smooth. Glassy conditions usually occur early in the morning or evening when there is no wind.

gliding ability *n.* A surfboard performance characteristic. (L&L) A board's ability to glide through the water is affected by many things, including its shape, weight, and body contour. —**gliding demise**

gloss coat, gloss *n.* The thin, final finish coat of resin that is buffed out.

gloss resin *n.* **1**) A thinned resin that has leveling and surfacing agents added to it. **2**) The final coat applied to a surfboard, which is wet-sanded and polished to give the board its smooth, glossy finish.

glue foot *n.* A surfer who almost never falls off the surfboard. (MCR)

gluing up *v.* Joining pieces of foam together, for instance to form the block out of which a surfboard is shaped.

gnar-gnar *adj.* A Laguna Beach term for GNARLY (said in a high-pitched voice). (LWK)

gnarlatious *adj.* Anything that's really cool, huge, or awesome, like a wave. (RBQ) Usage: "Gnarlatious waves today, bro."

gnarly (NAR-le) *adj.* **1**) Treacherous; same as HAIRY. Big waves with glossy faces and clean barrels are considered gnarly. Usage: "In gnarly conditions, watch yourself." (A&M; JP) **2**) A dramatic term for a wave with a real mean streak — the kind of wave that can eat a surfer for breakfast and then use the board as a toothpick. (MW; CVG) **3**) A term for monster surf. (MM) **4**) According to a Surf Punks glossary, any wave over two feet, or any girl over 120 pounds; **nar** for short. (SP) **5**) Large and dangerous. Usage: "San Onofre was gnarly this morning." (SFG, 1989) "Those were the gnarliest waves out there." (BC, Spring 1990) **6**) **your gnarlyness** The proper way to address an important dignitary or good friend. **7**) **get gnarled** *v.* To get thrashed in the surf, as in "all gnarled up." —**gnarly ass**, **gnarler**, **total gnarl**

According to Webster's, the word *gnarly,* a variant form of *gnarled,* was used in 1829. Among surfers (with whom the word is most commonly identified), *gnarly* may have first been used at a California surf spot where Torrey pine or Monterey cyprus trees grew. Their gnarled roots and branches may have inspired comparisons with the waves.

go-abb *n.* A person like a geek, but not as bothersome. See ABB. (MVA)

go-aheads *n.* Rubber sandals. (GN) Same as FLIP-FLOPS.

go behind A hot-dogging maneuver where one surfer passes over another surfer, and then the surfer who was passed repeats the maneuver. (MCR)

go beyond vert *v.* To surf past the vertical plane.

go for it An expression meaning "Do it!" — take a chance, go ahead and try it. This phrase has been adopted by many, but it was probably popularized by California surfers in the early 1970s. Someone can be said to have a "go-for-it attitude."

go high on the wave *v.* To surf up close to the lip.

go off *v.* **1**) (Of resin) To change from a liquid to a solid. (GCD) See GEL. **2**) (Of a surfer) To surf radically. See GOING OFF.

go-out *n.* A surf session. Also called FULL GO-OUT. Usage: "We can go for the full go-out this afternoon."

gloss coat
Kurt Boeche
Photo: Woody Woodworth

go over the falls *v.* To be picked up by a large dumping wave and carried down in its curl. (DSHJ)

going off *v.* **1)** When waves are consistent and breaking smoothly. (JP) **2)** Same as RIPPING, UNREAL, HAPPENING. **3)** Said when someone is shooting along in perfect surf. Usage: "Keith was going off." (MW)

going to church *v.* Early sixties expression for GETTING TUBED. (Long Beach, DWK) Same as IN THE POPE'S LIVING ROOM.

Gold Coast A forty-kilometer stretch along Australia's east coast in the state of Queensland, beginning at Southport and ending at Tweed Heads and encompassing such surf spots as Surfers Paradise, Burleigh Heads, Kirra, and Point Danger. Has the finest collection of point breaks in such close proximity anywhere in the world. (NAT, 1986)

gone surf-o *v.* To be crazy over waves; STOKED.

goob *n.* GEEK.

"Good Vibrations" A 1967 song by The Beach Boys, composed by Brian Wilson; gave rise to such expressions as "getting good vibes." See VIBE.

goofy foot or **goofy-foot** *n.* **1)** Riding a surfboard with your right foot forward, left foot back; the opposite of a natural footer. **2)** A left-handed surfer who rides with the right foot forward, left foot back. —**goof, goofy footer, goofy-foot surfer**

goofy foot
Amy Zavala, Año Nuevo
Photo: Bud Clark

Goofy foot is one of the oldest terms still current in surfing jargon, and one never revised: someone who stands on the surfboard with the right foot forward. Most surfers are natural footers, meaning they use a left-foot-forward stance. Some well-known goofy footers are Gerry Lopez, David Nuuiwa, Rory Russell, Tom Carroll, Mark Occhilupo, and Derek Ho.

goon *n.* KOOK. The term was derived from a 1930s Popeye the Sailor animated cartoon in which Popeye gets shipwrecked on the Island of the Goonies. (IBN) See GYROGOON.

goon cord *n.* A derogatory term for a SURF LEASH. Also called KOOK CORD.

goon squad *n.* A derogatory term for a car full of surfers; about the same as MEAT WAVE.

goop *n.* Liquid resin used for surfacing surfboards.

Got it! What you say to someone down the line who's taking off or dropping in on a wave that you're already surfing on, meaning "This wave is mine." Same as MY WAVE.

gouge *v.* **1)** To hurt oneself while surfing. **2)** To ding a surfboard. **3)** To make aggressive maneuvers on a wave (MM); to carve a large divot out of a wave. (SFG, 1989) Usage: "Did you see me gouge that cutback?"

grab-rail aerial *n.* A move in which the surfer grabs the rail while flying through the air; has its functional roots in skateboard ramp riding.

grab the rail, grabbing the rail *v.* A maneuver used by a surfer who is about to be hit by a wave or white water, in which he or she holds onto the outside edge of the board, leans toward the wave, and pulls the board into the wave to keep from being knocked off; allows the surfer to continue on in the curl, through a section, or on the unbroken wave ahead.

grab your board, grab your stick *v.* To pick up your surfboard and go surfing.

grabbers *n.* Invading surfers who steal or grab waves from other surfers.

graveyard *n.* BONE YARD.

great white shark *n.* WHITE SHARK.

green, green wave *n.* An UNBROKEN WAVE. Sometimes referred to as the SHOULDER of a wave.

green monsters *n.* Very big waves.

green room *n.* **1**) The space inside of a tube. Usage: "I was deep inside the green room." Same as GLASS-HOUSE. It is every surfer's dream to spend even a second or two in that "green room." (GN) **2**) A room painted green. (SP)

". . . and these waves throw out over the top of you. Suddenly you're inside this enclosure, a green room, and the wave has broken completely over you. If you want, you can yodel or yell and the noise bounces off the side of the walls. You go on like this for a while, then you go flying out of the other end of this tube into daylight." —from a Bob Simmons story in Greg Noll's *Da Bull* (1989)

green waves *n.* Small unbroken waves that are steep enough for riding.

green womb *n.* Inside of a tube. Same as GREEN ROOM. See WOMB.

greenback *n.* **1**) An UNBROKEN WAVE. **2**) A swell that peaks higher and higher but has not yet begun to spill white water down its face. (Australia; AHK)

greenhouse *n.* GLASSHOUSE.

greenie in a bottle *n.* An Australian term for Heineken beer, which comes in a green bottle.

gremlin *n.* **1**) A beginning surfer. See GREMMIE. **2**) A selfish, undesirable pest who is constantly in trouble and constantly creating trouble for fellow surfers. (DSHJ) **3**) A trouble-maker; one whose misdeeds cause surfing beaches to be lost and give surfing a bad name. —**gremlin-devouring tubes**

"**Gremlins** Perverse, resourceful, and mischievous air pixies, or imps, charged with the blame for virtually anything that can go unexpectedly wrong with or in an airplane." —from "Glossary of Important New Words in the News," *Funk & Wagnalls New Standard Encyclopedia Year Book for 1942*

gremmer *n.* GROMMET; from the movie *Under the Boardwalk* (1989).

gremmie or **gremmy** *n.* **1**) A fifties and sixties term for a stoked pre-teen who inhabits surfing beaches and hangs out with, idolizes, and imitates his or her hero. **2**) Either an inexperienced and troublesome surfer or an objectionable nonsurfer who hangs around with surfers and tries to act like them in everything except aquatic skill. **3**) Any kid under fifteen who is stoked out of his or her gourd on surfing. (A&M) **4**) A young, poorly mannered surfer who is a beginner at riding the waves; sometimes a little kid, not necessarily troublesome. **5**) A young surfer, usually a trouble-maker, who usually has long blonde hair and baggy pants. **6**) A young and inexperienced surf enthusiast to whom nothing counts in life but a surfboard and waves. **7**) An uncomplimentary term for those who hang around the beach for reasons other than surfing, but less harsh than HODAD. Also called SURF PUNK. See GROMMET, WEED. —**gremmyville, beach grem**

gremmie coat *n.* Apparel worn by just about every surfer in the sixties on cold winter days. Trench coats, tanker jackets, Goodwill suit coats, Navy pea jackets, moth-eaten fur coats, and ankle-length Luftwaffe officers' coats were especially favored. (A&M) Same as BEACH COAT.

grim situation *n.* **1**) A close call. **2**) Big surf favorable for big-wave riders. —**grim** *adj.*

grind-down zone *n.* The low spot surrounding the actual ding in the surface of a surfboard; an extremely

important concept in ding repair. (GCD)

grinder *n.* A power tool used in combination with a #36-grit resin-backed disk to remove fiberglass and resin quickly and efficiently; it can also be turned on edge and used as a cutting tool to open up those dings that are caved in. Attachments such as a power pad or a buffing pad are used for fine sanding and polishing. (GCD)

grinders *n.* Big waves. See POINT GRINDER.

grinding 1) *adj.* Said of powerful waves that are breaking consistently. (MM) **2)** *v.* Used to describe an aggressive riding style. Usage: "You were fully grinding out there."

grit *n.* A cigarette. (Leucadia)

grit cloth *n.* A grit-coated screen used for blending rail contours during the foam-shaping process.

groin *n.* A wall or embankment, constructed at right angles to the shoreline, that projects out into the water. Its purpose is usually to prevent beach erosion, but in some cases it also creates waves for surfing. See JETTY, BREAKWATER.

grom *n.* GROMMET. (Australia; ASL, 2/88)

grommet *n.* **1)** A young surfer-type person, intent on maximizing beach and in-the-tube experiences. **2)** A sixties Australian term for GREMMIE that has been adopted worldwide and is in current usage. **3)** A trainee surf mongrel on the way to full "surf nazi" status. (MW) **4)** An adolescent or pre-adolescent surfer. (L&L) **5)** A cheeky young surfer. (NAT, 1985)

grommet
Photo: Rob Gilley

ground pounder *n.* SHORE POUND. See BEACH BREAK. (PZ)

ground swell *n.* **1)** Large waves generated by distant storms, usually seasonal, as distinguished from waves

formed by local winds. **2)** A swell that originated far away. (MM)

Surfers prefer a ground swell to a wind swell because it is even, well spaced, and lasts longer. The waves approach the coast in long, parallel lines. Ground swells break best at reefs and points.

grovel, groveling *v.* **1)** To maintain momentum on a broken wave in an attempt to find a re-formed wave face on which to make further maneuvers. (Australia; L&L) **2)** To extract the last bit of energy out of a wave. (SFG, 1989) Usage: "You were grovelin' on the inside there."

grunts *n.* Food; derivation unknown. (A&M)

guaraches (wah-RA-chees) *n.* A Spanish word for leather Mexican sandals with tire-tread soles. Sometimes spelled *huaraches.* Also called MAZATLANS, TREADS.

guava 1) *adj.* A grommet word for COOL. **2)** *n.* A yummy-tasting tropical fruit. (JHM)

guillotine *n.* The wave lip as it comes down and smacks a surfer on the head. Also known as HAMMER.

gun *n.* **1)** A long, thin, tapered surfboard for twelve-foot and larger waves, particularly in Hawaii. **2)** A big-wave board; a board designed for big-to-humongous surf, as in a "gun-style board." The old eleven-foot guns weighed forty-five to fifty pounds; they were double-glassed and had heavy, three-quarter-inch redwood sticks in them for reinforcement. By contrast, modern guns are longer, narrower, and lighter. See BIG GUN, ELEPHANT GUN, RHINO CHASER.

gunga *n.* Surf-wax residue that won't come off; the stuff that sticks to your board even after you scrape it. (WCH)

gunnish *adj.* Used to describe a surfboard that is too long for the rider or conditions. Usage: "Your board's a little gunnish."

gutter section *n*. The unridable, inshore white-water area close to shore. —**deep gutter**

gyrator *n*. A sixties term for a GYRO. (HJP) —**gyrating for the judges**

gyro, gyro wanker *n*. A derogatory term for an over-displayed surfer — someone who does a lot of wasted arm flapping while maneuvering on a wave.

gyrogoon *n*. A gyrating goon.

gyrospaz or **gyro-spaz** *n*. A derogatory term for someone who wrecks a wave by ripping, slashing, and tearing it up into tiny bits; someone who just really screws up a wave. (SP3) Usage: "Don't gyrospaz on the shoulder."

"You got a perfectly good wave — this guy's just like spazzing all over it, up & down and ripping and slashing and really screwing it up!" —Surf Punks, "Gyrospaz" (1988)

hair *n*. Nerve, the courage to take off on enormous waves. A surfer who is exceptionally brave or crazy is known as "having hair." (MVA)

hair ball 1) *n*. A big wave. Usage: "Look at that hair ball!" **2**) *adj*. Wild or radical. (NWT)

hair dry *adj*. Without getting your hair wet. (SFR, 1989) Usage: "I paddled out hair dry."

hair out or **hair-out** *v*. **1**) To chicken out. (JMZ, WCH) Usage: "Don't hair out, bro." **2**) Not committing to a wave or a venture because of fear. (MVA) Usage: "Everyone was completely hairing out." **3**) **haired-out** *adj*. Scared. (BP) Usage: "I was fully haired-out."

hairy *adj*. Scary, risky, or dangerous; something beyond normal limits, requiring nerve. See GNARLY.

hairy takeoff *n*. When the wave jacks up and starts pitching faster than you can paddle in and get to your feet — and all you can see is red lights flashing — that's a hairy takeoff. (MW)

haken (HAWK-in) *v*. **1**) To go surfing. This is the root of a surfing sublanguage spoken on the East Side in Santa Cruz. (R&F) **2**) **haken vees** Surfing waves. **3**) **hakenveesmo** (hawk-in-VEES-mo) To surf — with a meal afterwards. **4**) **haken visuals** Getting good barrels. **5**) **hakenmo sess** (like "session") To go eat.

half men *n*. A derogatory name for KNEEBOARDERS because they surf while kneeling instead of standing. (KSO) "Be a man, learn to stand." —Zuma Jay (1982).

hammer 1) *n*. What descends on a surfer when the wave lip comes over and there's nowhere to go. (C&M) **2**) **hammered** *v*. To be totally immersed in an uncomfortable situation. This baptismal spinning, tossing, and gasping for air while trying to find which way is up is the price a surfer pays for trying to ride juicy waves. (MVA) See WORKED.

hand gun *n*. A small hand-held device that improves bodysurfing planing speed.

hand plane *n.* **1)** A small bodysurfing device held with the hands out in front of the body to assist in planing. **2)** A small board. (MF, 1967)

handboard *n.* A sixties term for HAND PLANE.

hang five, hanging five *v.* **1)** To ride so far up on the nose of the board that the toes of one foot reach over the front end. **2)** To have five toes over the nose of the surfboard. (IDSM)

hang loose A Hawaiian term for "everything's cool," usually conveyed by a hand signal called the *shaka.* Usage: "Hang loose, brah."

hang ten 1) *v.* To ride so far up on the nose of the board that the toes of both feet are extended over the front end. This involves not only nose riding but also abandonment of the usual diagonal or one-shoulder-forward stance. **2) hanging ten** *n.* A hot-dog riding stance reserved for longboards. (A&M) Also called TEN OVER.

hang time *n.* Refers to time spent in the air during a maneuver. Part-time surf contest announcer Peter Townend borrowed the term from American football. Usage: "Look at that major hang time."

haole (HOWL-ee) *n.* (Hawaiian) **1)** A white visitor, resident, or surfer in Hawaii; anyone foreign to Hawaii. Not necessarily a bad thing to be called — depending on who says it. Usage: "Focking haole!" "He's a haole boy." **2)** A mainland surfer. (JP) **3)** A Hawaiian VALLEY. (SP3)

Ha means "breath" and *ole* means "without" or "no." So *haole* literally means "without breath." Before religious ceremonies, Hawaiians traditionally would cleanse themselves by doing deep-breathing rituals to ready their souls. After 1820, when missionaries arrived with their churches and religious beliefs, the Hawaiians noticed that the whites did none of these breathing exercises before entering a church; they therefore became *haoles.* (PHL)

haole feet *n.* Tender soles with no callus buildup; comes from not walking barefoot and can be spotted instantly. (Hawaii; MFM, 1982) Same as CHEESE FEET.

haole rot *n.* A fungus on the top part of the back and chest, acquired by surfers visiting Hawaii; curable by applying Phisoderm. (JMZ)

hapa-haole music *n.* Hawaiian music given a Western tilt to make it more appealing to tourists; it became a national craze when Albert ("Sonny") Cunha performed Henry Kailimai's "On the Beach at Waikiki" at the 1915 Panama Pacific International Exhibition in San Francisco. Johnny Noble, known as the "Hawaiian Jazz King," was a leading figure in hapa-haole music; he wrote such popular hits as "Hula Blues," "My Little Grass Shack," and "Hawaiian War Chant." (GTM)

happening *adj.* Cool, great. Usage: "It's a happening spot." "The waves are happening."

hard bottom turn *n.* While turning at the bottom of a wave, really leaning into it so that one's body is nearly parallel to the ocean surface.

hard-breaking *adj.* A wave that breaks with full force. Such a wave can cause problems if not negotiated properly.

hard-core or **hard core** or **hardcore** *adj.* Used to describe intense things, as in "hard-core surfers" or "hard-core locals." May be the most overused word in modern surfing. (SFR, 3/91) Usage: "That's so hard core."

hard planing edge *n.* The squared-off bottom of a surfboard rail.

hard rail *n.* A surfboard rail with a sharper corner and a more defined

hanging five
Cheyne Horan
Photo: Bill Romerhaus

hang ten
Wingnut, Santa Cruz
Photo: Bob Barbour

edge (ORB), as distinct from a round rail.

harsh 1) *adj.* Severe, unpleasant, irritating. Usage (after a bad wipeout): "That was harsh." —**harsh waves**, **harsh conditions 2)** *v.* To give someone a hard time. Usage: "She fully harshed on me."

hasake or **hasaki** *n.* From the Arabic *khasakay*, a diamond-shaped 12- to 13-foot-long wooden board 3½ to 4 feet wide at the center and weighing 130 to 155 pounds. Used in Israel for paddling out and riding small surf back in with a hand paddle. (AHK)

hassle, hassling *v.* To compete to gain the inside position at takeoff and thereby the right-of-way; same as HUSTLE. (CC, L&L) In competitive surfing contests, this practice has been virtually eliminated by the use of the priority buoy system.

hateful *adj.* Miserable. (LH) Usage: "It was such a hateful night."

Hatteras Short for CAPE HATTERAS.

Hawaii 1) The surfing mecca of the world, known collectively throughout the surfing community as "the Islands." **2)** A volcanic chain of islands including Kauai, Oahu (home of Honolulu, Waikiki, and the North Shore), Maui, and Hawaii ("the Big Island"). **3)** The fiftieth state of the United States.

. . . .

British explorer Captain Cook named this archipelago the Sandwich Islands in 1778; it was a U.S. territory from 1900 until it became a state in 1959. The name *Hawaii* is possibly derived from the native word for homeland, *Hawaiki* or *Owhyhee*. (WA)

. . . .

"Hawaii Five-O" A TV detective show filmed on location in Hawaii and starring Jack Lord. Theories as to where the famous wave at the beginning of each show was shot include Sunset Beach and the film was flopped or Ala Moana; however,

it was probably shot at Rockpile just west of Ehukai Beach Park. (BB 2/91). The show's opening theme song (recorded in March 1969) became the Ventures' second biggest hit, reaching #4 on the charts. (GSM)

Hawaiian A Polynesian language. See "A Brief Guide to Pronouncing Hawaiian" on page 167, and see Appendix A for a list of ancient Hawaiian surfing terms.

Hawaiian luau *n.* See LUAU.

Hawaiian music *n.* Vocals combined with ukelele, steel guitar, and drums; the music often takes its inspiration from the beach. The popularity of Hawaiian music reached a peak in the 1930s, owing largely to Harry Owens, whose 1935 song "Sweet Leilani" became the #1 hit nationwide. (GTM) See HAPA-HAOLE MUSIC.

Hawaiian Pidgin, Hawaiian Pidgin English An English-based dialect widely spoken in Hawaii; called "pidgin" for short. Examples are *brah, bra,* or *brudda* for "brother." See DA KINE.

Hawaiian print *n.* ALOHA PRINT.

Hawaiian pullout *n.* Going to the nose of the surfboard and sharply twisting one's body, right or left depending on the wave, in order to pull the board out of the wave. Also called ISLAND PULLOUT. See STANDING ISLAND PULLOUT, SQUATTING ISLAND PULLOUT, and SITTING ISLAND PULLOUT.

Hawaiian shirt *n.* A short-sleeved, loose-fitting, open-collar shirt originally worn in Hawaii and adopted by many surfers the world over; made of lightweight fabric. Same as ALOHA SHIRT. See ALOHA PRINT.

. . . .

Hawaiian shirts were originally made of silk or rayon, and later of cotton or polyester — the latter *never* worn by surfers except to be tacky at a party. The shirts feature colorful, often bold designs — a visual vocabulary including palm trees, romantic beaches, tropical jungles, airplanes, bamboo, volcanoes, exotic flowers, surfing scenes, pineapples, drums, outrigger canoes, and images from Polynesian legend. The functional use of creative colors and the amazing artistic renderings in these shirts capture the simplicity and spirit of Hawaii. As the saying goes: "Speak softly and wear a loud shirt" —Anonymous.

Hawaiian time *n.* Late. (SP) Same as ISLAND TIME.

Hawaiian Triple Crown In professional surfing, the Pipeline Masters, the Big Wave Classic at Waimea Bay, and the World Cup at Sunset Beach. All of these contests are held annually around December on the North Shore of Oahu, Hawaii.

hazelwood *n.* Anyone unable to maneuver a water craft, be it a surfboard, a motorboat, or an oil tanker, and who as a result causes great damage. This eponym may have been derived from Joseph Hazelwood, captain of the *Exxon Valdez,* the tanker that ran aground in the fall of 1989 off of Alaska, causing a massive oil spill. (AJM)

head dip *n.* While riding a wave, bending the head to touch the wave or white water. If your head gets wet from the wave, you've done a successful head dip.

headland *n.* A point of land, usually high and with a sheer drop, extending out into the ocean; a promontory. (CCRG)

headstand *n.* Standing on your head during a surf ride — a hot-dog maneuver performed on a longboard.

heat *n.* A specified time period in which to perform maneuvers on waves in a surf contest.

heavies, the heavies *n.* **1**) Very big waves, from twelve to twenty-five feet high and over; usually found in Hawaii. **—the local heavies, big**

head dip
Joel Woods, Secret Spot, Santa Cruz
Photo: Bob Richardson

locals **2**) Big-name surfers in the sixties. (A&M)

heavy *adj.* Intense, as in "heaviest surf spot" or "That was heavy."

hectic *adj.* Pretty NAR. (SP3)

hectic gnarler *n.* A really good-looking girl. (Santa Barbara, California)

heels over *n.* A hard-to-pull-off longboarding maneuver that involves walking out to the end of the board, turning around, and hanging the heels over the nose tip. (KSO)

heenalu or **he'enalu** or **he'e nalu** (hay-ay nah-LOO) *n.* Hawaiian for surfing.

heini *n.* Heineken beer. Also called GREENIE IN A BOTTLE (in Australia).

held down, held under *v.* **1**) Refers to wiping out and getting tossed around beneath the sea, when a few seconds can seem like an eternity. (CC) **2**) To be prevented by the force of a breaking wave from coming up quickly for air — an unpleasant situation. Happens when a surfer is caught in the white water or caught inside.

helgi *n.* A Santa Cruz word for a young, enthusiastic, "surf-stoked" wave rider (CVG); a GROMMET.

heli-surfing *n.* A kind of surfing that requires the help of a helicopter to lower the surfer into a remote or outside break.

helicopter, helicopter spin *n.* A THREE SIXTY turn (L&L); has nothing to do with being rescued from the surf by a helicopter on the North Shore of Hawaii.

hero *n.* A sixties term for anyone who thinks he's better on a surfboard than he is. (IDSM)

hideous, hiddie *adj.* **1**) Offensive to the senses, and especially to sight; exceedingly ugly. **2**) Morally offensive; shocking. Usage: "Scott's Reef, Oregon, is surfable up to 5', but at

8-12', the place is hideous." "The waves are pretty hiddie today." (SFG, 1989) See GNARLY, HAIR BALL.

high, high pressure system, high pressure *n.* A climatic condition characterized by warm weather, less turbulent air, and winds that blow clockwise around the weather system's center, in contrast to a low pressure system, in which winds blow counterclockwise around the center. (W&B)

high-energy winter waves *n.* Powerful seasonal waves generated by very large faraway storms.

high-flying backside reentry *n.* A surfing maneuver where the surfer, with back to the wave, leaves the water with the board and returns.

high tide *n.* When the sea level is at its highest mark. —**high tide line, high tide mark**

highway surfer *n.* 1) A HODAD who goes to the beach and spends all his time driving up and down the highway with a surfboard sticking out of the car. (ASKC, 1965) 2) Someone who spends all his time in the car and never gets to the surf. 3) A POSER whose surfboard stays on the roof rack. (A&B) Same as FREEWAY SURFER. —**highway surfie** (Australia)

hips *n.* The portion of a surfboard between its midpoint and tail; measured twelve inches from the tail.

hit a wave, hit the surf *v.* To ride a wave or go surfing. Usage: "Let's hit the surf."

hittin' 1) *adj.* Used to describe something of extreme goodness. For example, after a session Sambro is hungry, and when given a steaming hot bowl of home-cooked beans, he takes a bite and exclaims, "Dude! These beans are hittin'!" 2) **hitting** *v.* Usage: "There's a big swell that's supposed to be hitting tomorrow."

hodad or **ho-dad** or **hoedad, hodaddy** *n.* 1) A derogatory term for a nonsurfer. See GREMMIE. 2) A surfer who rarely goes in the water but still talks, acts, and dresses as if he were a minor god of the sport; a fake; a show-off. (DSHJ) Same as POSER. 3) A greaser, sort of a hot rodder with long hair and sideburns. 4) A street person as opposed to a beach person. Such a person usually spends a lot of time riding around in a lowered car. (A&M) 5) A hood from the back streets, generally driving a hopped-up car; may or may not be a surfer. 6) An antisurfer hoodlum, often just an ill-mannered beach bum who doesn't surf but loiters around the regular surfers; an undisciplined, antisocial character. 7) An all-out, nonsurfing surf bum — a person with questionable motives. 8) Anyone the surfers don't like. (IDSM) 9) An unknown surfer, a stranger to the lineup.

hold, holding *v.* Refers to the ability of a surfboard or fin to grab onto a wave. Usage: "My board was holding the wave face." —**holding power** *n.*

hold one's line *v.* To hold one's position on a wave. Usage: "Hold your line — I'm coming through!"

hold up *v.* 1) What waves do when, because of an offshore wind, they continue longer before breaking. Usage: "Look at that wave hold up." 2) To stall the board during a ride and then continue the ride. 3) **held up** To be lifted by an offshore wind while taking off on a wave. (RA) See HUNG UP.

hollow *adj.* 1) Used to describe an extremely concave wave, or a fast, deeply curling, plunging wave. 2) A descriptive term for a cylindrical wave. (NAT, 1985) See TUBE.

hollow out *v.* What happens when a wave begins to peel over into a tube.

hollow surfboard *n.* A surfboard with its core or insides removed. In 1926 surfer-swimmer Tom Blake, a Waikiki waterman originally from Wisconsin, accidentally invented the hollow surfboard when he was trying to replicate a sixteen-foot board and drilled the wood full of holes. After sealing the holes, he found that he had created a lighter, longer surfboard that was well suited for paddleboard racing. His discovery revolutionized surfboard design. (GTM)

hollowback *n.* An East Coast term for a DUMPER. (DSHJ, 1965)

hondo *n.* A derogatory term for non-local, or anyone living inland from the beach. Usage: "Did you see all those hondos at our break today?" Or, occasionally, "I think all you **inland hondos** should take the next bus back to Anaheim." (SFG, 12/81) Same as INLANDER, FLATLANDER, VALLEY.

honing *v.* When waves are huge and breaking at an accelerated rate. (MM) Usage: "The waves are honing up the coast."

honker, big honker *n.* A really big wave. (DPL)

hood *n.* A neoprene rubber head covering for surfing in cold water. (MM) See SQUID LID.

hook *n.* **1**) The curling part of the wave; BOWL. **2**) The innermost ridable part of a tubing wave. See CURL, POCKET. **3**) *v.* To ride the best part of the wave. Usage: "I hooked into the meaty part of the wave."

hook up *v.* **1**) To fix or set someone up. Usage: "I can hook you up with a wetsuit." **2**) To meet someone. Usage: "We can hook up over at Dave's apartment."

hoon *n.* Someone who tends to compensate for a lack of surfing ability with eye-catching performances in the car park. (Australia; MW)

hood
Photo: Bud Clark

hoota! The yell of a surfer who's stoked. (A&M)

hooter *n.* A really great party. Usage "That was a real hooter."

hooting *n.* Calling or shouting that compliments the quality of a ride or a wave. (Australia; L&L) See SURFER HOOTS, AAAAAHOOO!

hop, hopping it back and forth *v.* To bounce the front of the board up and down and from side to side in order to extend a ride on a wave that is petering out. See GROVELING.

horrendous *adj.* Used to describe a large or difficult wave. (DBF) Usage: "That was a horrendous wave."

hot *adj.* **1**) COOL. (SP) Usage: "Wow, hot ride." "Look at those hot chicks." **2**) A slang expression applied to a good-quality wave (NAT, 1985); **hot waves. 3**) Used to describe a batch of resin that goes off fast, or quickly changes from a liquid to a solid. Yes, resin will get *hot!* (GCD)

hot coat *n.* **1**) A fast-drying coat of resin applied between the fiberglass lay-up and the finish sanding. **2**) The resin layer that is sanded to blend and refine the contours of a board. (ORB) Also referred to as SAND COAT.

hot curl *n.* **1**) A 1930s term for a challenging, fast-breaking wave. **2**) HOT-CURL BOARD.

hot-curl board *n.* **1**) The name of Hawaiian surfboards designed from 1950 to 1955 for big-wave (hot-curl) riding. Such boards are fast and maneuverable. Also known as HOT-SLOPE or HOT-SHAPE BOARDS. (AHK) **2**) **hot-curl redwood board** A plank of solid redwood with no fins, used in the 1930s; the tail comes down in a V shape, the bottom is rounded, and there is no scoop in them. (GN)

hot dog *n.* **1**) Applied to a fancy and tricky style of surfing and also to the board design best suited to that style. **2**) A wide and heavy board. (IDSM) **3**) *v.* To show a great deal of ability in the surf, usually demonstrated by fancy turns, walking the nose, and taking chances. **4**) **hot-dogger** *n.* A surfer who is skilled in, and devoted to, fancy and tricky riding (DSHJ); one who exhibits tricky footwork and generally a snappy style of board riding. **5**) **hot-dogging** *n.* Fast maneuvering on small surf. (L&L) —**hot-dog maneuvers**

hot gooper *n.* A fast-drying resin made by adding an extra catalyst or cobalt.

hot little section *n.* A fast and fun section of a wave to ride. See INSIDE ZIPPER.

hot sand *n.* The sun-baked surface of a beach — yowch!

hot-shape board, hot-slope board *n.* HOT-CURL BOARD.

hotties *n.* **1**) Good waves. **2**) Great surfers.

houge (HO-ghee) *v.* To scarf down food after you surf. (San Clemente) Usage: "Let's go houge." See HAKEN-VEESMO and HAKENMO SESS, listed under *haken.*

howling *adj.* Strong, as in "howling winds."

Howzit brah? Hawaiian Pidgin expression meaning, "How's it going, brother?" See BRAH.

huaraches (hwah-RA-chees) *n.* GUARACHES.

huevos (HWAY-voes *or* WAVE-os) *n.* Spanish for eggs, but a cross-cultural surfer homonym for waves. See OLAS. (P)

Huey 1) The Australian KAHUNA. (NAT, 1985) **2**) The legendary god of the surf. (MM)

huge *adj.* **1**) Said of a wave that's bigger than large. **2**) **huge monolith** *n.* A gargantuan wave; Mount Everest, massive, mega-enormous —

Hawaiian style. (MM, CC) Same as BEHEMOTH WAVE.

human lure *n.* What a surfer feels like in sharky waters — not a nice feeling. (Australia; MW)

humongous *adj.* Used to describe waves. When the surf is bigger than big, it's huge; when it's bigger than huge, it's humongous. Same as GARGANTUAN. See BROWN BOARDSHORTS MATERIAL. (MW)

humpers *n.* Medium-to-large unbroken waves.

hung up *v.* **1**) To be tottering on the upper lip of a wave, usually held there by the updraft of a strong offshore wind. See HELD UP, listed under *hold up.* **2**) To have the skeg of one's board get caught in kelp.

Huntington Hop *n.* A typical bouncing maneuver used to make it through small waves; the term originated at the Huntington Beach Pier in California, where the annual Op Pro surf contest is held.

"When the swell is small there is an outside section followed by a deep gutter where the wave flattens out before it reaches the shorebreak. Often surfers will have to straighten off and bounce their board through this dead section to reach the inside. This has become so commonplace that the technique has become known as the 'Huntington Hop.'" —Michael Martin, "Surfing for the Judges" in *Competitive Surfing: A Dedicated Approach* (1988)

hurricane *n.* A powerful, destructive storm, stronger than a tropical storm, that starts over water and has winds rotating counterclockwise at speeds in excess of 72 miles per hour. Such winds develop in low pressure areas and are usually accompanied by very high tides. A storm's diameter may range from 150 to 300 miles. Hurricanes are assigned such names as "Gilbert," "Hugo," or "Ewa." A storm of this magnitude is

human lure
Art: Rick Stover

called a *hurricane* in the Caribbean Sea and the Atlantic, a *cyclone* in the Indian Ocean, and a *typhoon* in the China Sea and most of the Pacific. In the Philippines, it is called a *baguio*. (GVS, OA)

hustle *v.* HASSLE.

HV (high velocity) fin *n.* A fin designed to control and stabilize the natural drifting tendency of channel bottom boards; invented by Australian shaper Kym Thompson.

hydro *n.* HYDROPLANE SURFBOARD.

hydro hull *n., adj.* A bottom contour designed to channel water away to give maximum planing.

hydro-ironed *v.* To get flattened by a close-out set. (Pedro Point, Pacifica; BTV) Usage: "I just got hydro-ironed."

hydrocoffin *n.* A wave that encloses, and then breaks on, a surfer.

hydrofoil step, hydrofoil stepped *n., adj.* HYDROPLANE STEP.

hydroplane step *n.* An area on the front of a longboard designed especially for nose riding.

hydroplane surfboard *n.* A sixties surfboard incorporating a hydroplane step to produce both the highest possible speed and quick-turning maneuverability.

hydrothermal ceramic technician The job description of a dishwasher, a position commonly held by some surfers. When said with the proper delivery, the title earns instant respect from almost anyone (especially gullible surfers).

PRONUNCIATION OF HAWAIIAN

Hawaiian is a language of the Polynesian language family. It has just twelve letters: all of the vowels *a, e, i, o,* and *u,* and the consonants *k, h, l, m, n, p,* and *w.* Traditionally, each vowel is pronounced separately, and each is pronounced the same as in Latin or Spanish:

English	**Spanish**	**Hawaiian**
a is "ah" as in "father"	or "taco"	or "Makaha"
e is "a" as in "way"	or "peso"	or "he'e nalu"
i is "e" as in "beat"	or "hijo"	or "malihini"
o is "o" as in "flow"	or "dos"	or "moana"
u is "oo" as in "dude"	or "bruja"	or "nalu"

In modern-day Hawaiian, combinations of vowels, such as *ai, ei, ou,* and so on, are usually sounded together. Thus, *ai* becomes "i," as in "like"; *ei* becomes "ay," as in "way"; *ou* becomes "au," as in "owe." Consonants are pronounced the same as in English. When *w* is used as the first letter in a word, as in *Waikiki,* it is pronounced like the "w" in "warm." In the middle of a word, as in *Ewa, w* is usually pronounced as "v."

ice cream headache *n.* A piercing pain in the head resulting from ducking under freezing cold water while paddling out. (MM)

ice cube tube *n.* A curling cold-water wave. (P)

impact zone *n.* **1**) The area directly in front of a breaking wave, where the falling lip strikes the water or the beach; the place where the breaking wave lands and exerts maximum force. (NAT, 1985) **2**) The area where a wave first breaks. (ORB)

in-betweeners *n.* The smaller waves that come in between sets. (SFG, 3/90)

in position Said of a surfer who is in the right spot to catch a wave.

in thar Anything that's cool — the way it is "in there," or inside a tube. The expression can also be accompanied by a hand gesture, with fingers curled over like a breaking wave and thumb pointed in, as if getting tubed. (Santa Cruz; RPM) Usage: "That's in thar." "In thar!"

in the curl Refers to surfing inside of a barreling wave; getting TUBED.

in the Pope's living room Refers to a good ride in a good barrel. (JP) Jock Sutherland made this term infamous. Same as being in the GREEN ROOM or GOING TO CHURCH.

in the tube Inside a barreling wave; TUBED.

in-the-tube 360, in-the-tube forward 360 *n.* A bodyboarding maneuver in which the surfer spins fully around while riding in the tube. An **in-the-tube reverse 360** is currently under development.

in the tunnel 1) *n.* IN THE TUBE. **2) getting tunneled** *v.* Same as GETTING TUBED.

in the womb IN THE TUBE. Same as being in the GREEN ROOM or GREEN WOMB. See WOMB.

inboard *adj.* The side of a surfboard nearest the wall of a wave. Usage: "I was really leaning on the inboard rail."

inconsistent *adj.* Said of waves that do not break at regular intervals. Usage: "The waves were totally inconsistent today." See DISORGANIZED.

indicator *n.* **1**) A wave (or the place where it breaks), seaward of the usual takeoff point, that provides an indication of the size and shape of waves moving into the lineup zone. Rincon's Third Point is a good example. **2**) An outside wave that breaks over a shallow reef or sandbank and backs off, indicating that a wave or set is approaching. **3**) A surf spot outside of (seaward of) the spot you are riding that can be used to gauge approaching waves. **4**) A sign that a set of waves is approaching. (NAT, 1985)

Indo Australian slang for Indonesia.

Indonesia A republic in the Malay Archipelago, comprising hundreds of islands (including Bali and Java), each with its own culture, language and dialect; has many excellent surf spots. See "Speaking Indonesian" on page 58.

in the Pope's living room
Art: Rick Stover

in thar
Art: Karen T. Delgadillo

SPEAKING INDONESIAN

The country [of Indonesia] is so diverse, a Western Indonesian can be as unintelligible to an Eastern Indonesian as both would be to an English-speaking surfer. Fortunately for travelers, Bahasa Indonesia is the official language of the country. It is taught in schools, used on television, street signs and in newspapers, and makes it possible for a traveler to learn one tongue, and make himself understood whether he's in Timor or Sumbawa (Paul King, *Surfer* Magazine, 1/91). Bahasa Indonesian is a very easy language to learn. Here are some useful words and expressions for the traveling surfer to know:

surfer	*pesilancar*	wall	*tembok*
surfing	*bersilancar*	tube	*lengkung*
surfboard	*papan bersilancar*	ocean	*lautan*
surf wax	*lillin*	beach	*pantai*
sunscreen	*anti panas matahari*	point	*titik*
swell	*gelambang*	reef	*karang*
wave	*ombak*	channel	*saluran*
big	*besar*	offshore winds	*angin darat*
small	*kecil*	onshore winds	*angin laut*
fast	*cepat*	high tide	*air pasang*
peak	*puncak*	low tide	*air surut*
shoulder	*bahu*		

Thank you	*Terima kasih*
You're welcome	*Terima kasih kembali*
I'm sorry	*Maaf*
You're a good surfer	*Kamu pesilancar yang baik*
I'm stoked	*Saya bahagia*
I'm bummed	*Saya kecewa*
I come from . . .	*Saya datang dari . . .*
I am here to surf	*Saya disini untuk bersilancar*

(Adapted from PK in SFR, 1/91)

Art: The Pizz

injected molded fin *n*. A fin with a perfect foil. (SFG, 2/90)

inland invader *n*. Anyone who travels to the beach from deep inside the interior. Same as VALLEY, FLATLANDER.

inland squid *n*. A derogatory term for a surfer who doesn't live near the beach. (MM) See SQUID.

inland surfer *n*. **1)** Anyone who has to travel a great distance to get to the surf. **2) Inland Surfers** An organization based in Phoenix, Arizona, whose slogan is "Real surfers don't need water." (DS)

Inland Surfers Association (ISA) A Southern California organization.

inlander *n*. A derogatory term for anyone who isn't lucky enough to live within walking distance of the beach. See VALLEY.

insane *adj*. Really great, usually used to describe the surf. Usage: "It was totally insane." "It was an insanely hollow wave."

insepia (in-sa-PEE-a) *n*. Riding on the nose of a board with one foot forward and both hands stretched out in front. (Australia; ASKC, 1965)

inshore *adj., adv*. Refers to either the beach or the area of water just off the beach, or the area inside the break.

inside *n., adv., prep*. **1)** That portion of the white-water surf zone that is landward of breaking waves. **2)** The area between the breaking waves and the shore. (MM) **3)** Shoreward of the breaking waves. (NAT, 1985) See CAUGHT INSIDE. **4)** Toward the shore or near the shore. **5)** Toward or close to the curl. If two surfers catch the same wave, the one closest to the curl on takeoff is inside. (MF) **6)** Completely within the curling part of the wave, as in "inside the tunnel" or "inside the barrel"; IN THE TUBE. (A&M)

inside break *n*. Surf breaking shoreward of a larger outside (seaward) spot. See OUTSIDE BREAK.

inside of a tube Being completely covered by the curl of a wave — one of the supreme thrills in surfing. (A&M)

inside rail *n*. The edge of the board closest to the wave face. (L&L) See OUTSIDE RAIL.

inside reef *n*. A surf spot located shoreward of the outside break; usually smaller surf. (GN) See OUTSIDE REEF.

inside section, inside wave *n*. A wave that is shoreward of the main break. The waves inside the main break are often smaller and easier to ride.

inside zipper *n*. A really quick inside wave that is small but fast and fun. (KSO) See ZIPPER.

intense, totally intense *adj*. Extreme. Usage: "A repo man's always intense."

interference penalty *n*. In accordance with ASP rules, a surfer judged to have interfered with another surfer is scored on only three rides instead of four. (L&L)

interference rule(s) *n*. In competitive surfing, very strict prohibitions about hassling — crowding or impeding — an opponent. The ASP rule book has twelve pages, complete with illustrations, devoted to the interference rule. (L&L) See WAVE POSSESSION.

internal heating *n*. Warmth generated by pissing in a wetsuit. (PZ) See URINOPHORIA, PETER HEATER.

International Surfing Association (ISA) The worldwide amateur organization of competitive surfing.

inverted air *n*. A bodyboarding maneuver that involves turning upside down when catching air.

ISA 1) International Surfing Association. **2)** Inland Surfers Association.

Art: The Pizz

island *n.* **1)** A piece of land completely surrounded by water but not large enough to be called a continent or continental island; the result of volcanic action or coral formations. **2)** Unquestionably the best place to look for big surf, for some part always points straight into the swell. (W&B) One side of the island is always offshore!

island fever *n.* The feeling that you've spent too much time on an island and it's time to go. Usage: "After two months on that place I was starting to get island fever."

island pullout *n.* An exit from a wave identified with the first surf riders from Hawaii to popularize the sport in California and elsewhere; performed by grasping the nose of the board, swinging the stern shoreward, and pulling the board back through the wall of the wave. See HAWAIIAN PULLOUT, SITTING ISLAND PULLOUT, STANDING ISLAND PULLOUT.

island time *n.* The pace of the tropics: forget being in a hurry. Foreigners learn patience in the tropics. Same as HAWAIIAN TIME. See MAÑANA.

Islands, the *n.* The cool way to say HAWAII. (MVA) But what if you're from Fiji?

ISP International Surfing Professionals — a now defunct organization.

it Pronoun used to refer to the surf. Usage: "It [the surf] was so good out there."

jacking
Photo: Rob Gilley

J-Bay An abbreviation for Jeffrey's Bay, a famous right point break west of Port Elizabeth, South Africa.

jack, jack up *v.* **1)** (Of waves) To suddenly gather water and gain elevation in moving from deep into shallow water. (MW) Usage: "The wave really jacks up on the inside." "Look at that wave jacking." **2)** The motion of a wave when it suddenly lifts up just before breaking. Usage: "I saw you smack a jacking six-foot lip." —**jacking, jacking up**

jam *v.* **1)** To block the ride of another surfer. (MF) **2) jamming** To dance or groove to reggae music.

jams *n.* Very colorful swim trunks, almost knee-length and usually loose to the point of bagginess. Dave Rochlen started the jams trend in the early 1960s with the original Surf Line Jams, which were brightly colored Hawaiian-print trunks, cut just above the knee; every surfer wore them. (GN) See BAGGIES.

Jan & Dean Jan Berry and Dean Torrance, a sixties rock 'n' roll music group known for their songs about surfing and cars. Among their hits was "Ride the Wild Surf" (September 1964), the title song from the film of the same name starring Fabian and Tab Hunter. See SIDEWALK SURFIN'.

Japan The Asian country responsible for manufacturing some forty thousand surfboards per year in its surfboard factories. Also known for Nippon's surf-hungry populace and for fast-changing typhoon conditions.

Japan boards *n.* Small-wave boards that are super wide, super thick, and blocky. The name derived from a series of Japanese events held in tiny surf; the boards were made for one

jellyfish
Purple striped jellyfish
Art: Andrea McCann

thing — riding dribbly white water to shore. (SFG, 2/86)

Jaws 1) In case you were on Mars in the mid-seventies, there's this nasty shark off of Martha's Vineyard, see . . .   **2)** A best-selling novel by Peter Benchley about a New England beach community terrorized by a great white shark. **3)** Steven Spielberg's 1975 movie based on Benchley's novel.

Jaws was the biggest box-office powerhouse of all time, if you exclude movies with spaceships or ghosts; it featured the $2 million mechanical man-eating shark nicknamed "Bruce." This movie — more than any other single event — greatly fueled people's fear of sharks and drove many individuals away from the ocean, scaring them for life (hence, "The Jaws Syndrome"). John Williams provided the music, which won an Academy Award for Best Original Score. (SHS)

"Breathes there a soul brave enough to go near the beach after seeing this film?" —Arthur Cooper

jaws board *n.* A surfboard design.

jazz 1) *n.* Talk; business, miscellaneous thoughts, as in "all that jazz." **2)** *adj.* Having a good time. Usage: "I was jazzed."

jello arms *n.* Limp limbs from excessive paddling. (MM) Same as RUBBER ARMS.

jelly roll *n.* A 1950s hairdo, generally seen on ho-daddies or low riders. The hair is combed up on either side so that it spills over in the front and is glued to stay in place with Butch wax. (A&M)

jellyfish *n.* Any marine coelenterates of the class Scyphozoa, characteristically having clear purple or blue umbrella-like floats between two and twelve inches in diameter but with tentacles — containing stinging cells — that may extend down for fifteen or twenty feet. There are some four thousand varieties. They sometimes infest near-shore waters during the summer months. One treatment after an encounter: apply meat tenderizer to the sting. See SEA WASP.

jet *v.* To make a quick disappearance. (TMA) Usage: "Let's jet."

jet ski *n.* **1)** A useless ocean polluter. (DS) **2)** A loud and obnoxious motorized craft resembling a snowmobile and used to race around the water surface and spew totally offensive smelly gasoline fumes around surfers.

jetty *n.* **1)** A structure projecting into the sea, usually made of cement, steel, or large blocks of hard rock. **2)** A shoreline protective device intended to stabilize the beach and keep it from washing away, or to protect the entrance to a harbor. A jetty may destroy an existing surf spot (such as Dana Point) or create a new one, such as 56th Street in Newport Beach — one of the finest **jetty setups** known to mankind. (W&B)

jetty break *n.* A specific type of surf break created by the presence of a jetty. (KH)

jonesing *v.* Craving — how a frustrated surfer feels when begging for a great wave. (CVG)

juice *n.* **1)** The energy or power of a wave. **2)** Big, powerful surf. Usage: "Those were pure juice." **3)** In Hawaii, pure, unsweetened island juice. Usage: "Lotta juice, brah."
—pure juice, **blue juice**

junk, junky waves, **junk surf** *n.* **1)** Choppy waves created by local winds. When the surface is chopped up, the approaching swells are harder to ride. **2)** Surf that is barely ridable. (DSHJ)

junker *n.* A competitive surfing term for a ride that the judges score so low (a 1.5, for instance) that you toss it from your overall score. Also called THROW-OUT WAVE. See SURFING CRITERIA.

jet ski
above:
Herbie Fletcher
Photo: Tom Servais / Surfer Magazine
below:
Wave jumping
Photo: Woody Woodworth

jetty
Photo: Woody Woodworth

K35, K38, K39 Roadside kilometer signpost markings in Baja California, Mexico, where the surf is good.

K-cloth, K-glass *n.* A special fiberglass developed by John Kershaw of Kno-Naw Corporation.

K-den Hawaiian Pidgin for "OK, fine, everything's cool — I'll see ya later." (VAB)

Kaha Huna The mythical Hawaiian goddess of surfing. (IDSM)

Kahanamoku, Duke (1890–1968) The "father of surfing." Duke Paoa Kahinu Makoe Hulikohola Kahanamoku, known to most as Duke, was a Hawaiian Olympic swimmer (a gold medalist in the hundred-meter freestyle in Stockholm, Sweden, in 1912 and in Antwerp, Belgium, in 1920). He popularized surfing in California (on a visit in 1911) and introduced surfing to Australia at Freshwater Beach, Sydney (in 1915). A bust of "The Duke" is located at the foot of the Huntington Beach Pier in California. The first Duke Kahanamoku Invitational Surfing Championships were held at Sunset Beach, Oahu, in 1965.

. . . .

"I have never seen snow and do not know what winter means. I have never coasted down a hill of frozen rain, but every day of the year where the water is 76, day and night, and the waves roll high, I take my sled, without runners, and coast down the face of the big waves that roll in at Waikiki. How would you like to stand like a god before the crest of a monster billow, always rushing to the bottom of a hill and never reaching its base, and to come rushing in for half a mile at express speed, in a graceful attitude, of course, until you reach the beach and step easily from the wave to the strand?" —Duke Kahanamoku in *Waikiki Beachboy* by Grady Timmons (1989)

. . . .

Kahoona The self-described surf bum in the movie *Gidget* (1959).

Kahuna 1) A Hawaiian witch doctor adopted by modern surfers as an imaginary surfing god. **2)** The god of sun, sand, and surf. **3)** A Hawaiian priest of mysterious powers and rites. **4)** The only surf god, which true surfers make sacrifices to when the surf is flat. (H&R)

kahuna tuna *n.* KOOK.

kakios (ka-KEY-os) *n.* A Hawaiian word for very bad sores on the feet from stepping on coral; the coral sand gets in the sores and gets infected. (GN)

kaks *n.* **1)** A derogatory term for San Jose surfers; they don't surf, they just "kak." (Santa Cruz) **2) kak** A term for dick.

kamaaina (KAH-ma-EYE-na) *n.* **1)** The Hawaiian name for Island residents who either were born in Hawaii or have lived there twenty-five years or more. **2)** An old-timer to the waves of Hawaii; someone experienced in surfing the big waves. See MALIHINI.

kamikaze or **kami-kaze** *n.* **1)** A planned wipeout, done on purpose with no hope of saving the board or avoiding the swim. **2)** Riding the board at the nose with arms held straight out to each side. (IDSM)

opposite:
Duke Kahanamoku
Photo: Surfer Magazine

3) Any daredevil feat.   **4**) A Japanese word literally meaning "divine wind" but used to describe Japanese air pilots in World War II who were assigned a suicidal crash. (1945)

kamikaze run *n*. A suicidal takeoff on a big dumper; usually ends in a bone-crushing wipeout. (A&M)

Kawonanaokoa, Prince David The Hawaiian who was probably the first person ever to surf in California (in Santa Cruz in 1885). See FREETH.

kayak *n*. A canoe with a light frame covered with skins, canvas, marine ply, or fiberglass; sometimes used to ride waves. A kayak is paddled with a double-bladed paddle, the paddler sitting in a hole in the deck with only his or her trunk visible. **—sea kayak, ocean kayaking**

keckin' air *v*. CATCHING AIR. (Santa Cruz; WCH) Usage: "I saw you keckin' air out there."

keel fin *n*. WINGED KEEL.

kelp *n*. Seaweed; a large brown algae that grows off the Pacific Coast, usually giant kelp (*Macrocystis pyrifera*) or bull kelp (*Nereocystis luetkeana*).

. . . .

"Good kelp" grows in thick stands a quarter mile to a mile offshore, in water fifteen to fifty feet deep. It dissipates wave shock further from shore and cuts down wind chop while allowing strong swells to pass, so that protected surf stays glassy even when onshore winds are blowing.

"Bad kelp" grows in water so shallow that it can slow down the speed and shape of a wave. It often interferes with a surfer's ride by catching the skeg and inducing a surprise wipeout. (S&C; SFR, 3/91) Usage: "I kept getting hung up on kelp out there."

. . . .

kelp monster *n*. A California mythological sea beast that reaches up and grabs the passing fin of a surfboard, stalling the ride or causing the surfer to wipe out.

kelp
Giant kelp (Macrocystis perifera)
Art: Andrea McCann

kelp skeg *n*. A shallow, raked fin designed for riding over kelp. (MCR)

kelphead *n*. **1**) A beginning surfer who spends most of the time with his or her head in the kelp. (San Diego; LP, 1981)   **2**) A person lacking any knowledge of the ocean or the waves. (ATRL)

kelpie or **kelpy** *n*. **1**) A malevolent water spirit in Scottish legends, usually having the shape of a horse and causing or rejoicing in drownings. **2**) A sheepdog of a breed originating in Australia. (AHD2)

kevlar *n*. An aramid fiber cloth that is lighter and more durable than fiberglass. (ORB)

kick *n*. The rocker, or curvature, of the nose or tail area. **—nose kick, tail kick**

kick five *n*. A longboarding maneuver, in which the surfer goes out to the nose of the board, hangs five with one foot, kicks the other foot out in front of the tip of the board, and then shuffles back. (KSO)

kick out *v*. **1**) To pull out of a wave by jamming or kicking the back foot down on the tail section, a motion that lifts and pivots the nose of the board out of the water and back over the wave crest.   **2**) To flip the board over or through the back of a wave while falling off the tail of the board into the wave — a last ditch effort to keep from losing the board.   **3**) To leave a wave abruptly in order to avoid losing, or damaging, the board or to avoid wiping out. (IDSM)   **4**) To deliberately exit over the back of a wave while maintaining board control. (L&L) **5**) Loosely, to ride back over the crest of a wave. Also known as CUT OUT, FLICK OUT, PULL OUT. **—kickout** or **kick-out** *n*.

kick stall *n*. A hot-dogging maneuver in which a surfer shifts all of his or her weight to the tail of the surfboard, causing it to stall, and then quickly shifts forward again, retrimming the board. (MCR)

kicked *adj.* Turned up or scoop-shaped — used to describe the nose or tail of a surfboard.

kickoff or **kick-off** *n.* The act of kicking the board out in front in a bailout.

killer *n., adj.* **1)** A complimentary word, meaning awesome or great. Usage (said of an excellent wave): "That was a killer wave." (JP) Or (said of a great ride) "Killer, dude." **2)** Can also mean something bad. Usage (after a wipeout): "That last wave was a killer." **3) killer wave** *n.* Either a good or a bad wave. **4) Killer Dana** A famous surf spot that no longer exists.

killer board *n.* A board on a wave with no rider; same as LOOSE BOARD.

killing it *v.* Surfing good. Usage: "You were killing it out there today."

kind, the kind *n.* A Southern California expression for the best. See DA KINE.

knee dragging or **knee draggin'** *v.* Catching a knee on the wave while surfing. (JWN)

knee pad *n.* Extra padding on the knee section of a wetsuit.

knee paddle, knee paddling *n., v.* Stroking through the water with the arms while balanced in a kneeling position on a longboard.

knee slapper *n.* A very small whitewater wave. See ANKLE SLAPPER.

knee wells *n.* Pressure marks on the deck of the longboard caused by excessive knee paddling (MCR); same as KNEELING DENTS.

kneebangers *n.* Real long shorts. (PZ)

kneeboard *n.* A surfboard, usually short (five to six feet in length), ridden on the knees. (NAT, 1985)

kneeboarder *n.* A surfer who rides a kneeboard.

kneeboarding *n.* Surfing on the knees on a specialized board. The rider can maintain a compact and stable position, good for quick, radical maneuvers and tube riding.

kneeling dents *n.* KNEE WELLS.

kneeling patch *n.* An extra sheet of fiberglass cloth applied to the center deck of a board to prevent kneeling dents; same as DECK PATCH.

kneeling position *n.* A paddling position on a longboard.

kneelo *n.* An Australian term for a kneeboard rider. (NAT, 1985)

kneerider *n.* KNEEBOARDER. (SFR, 1989)

knobs *n.* KNOTS.

knock with both elbows An Australian saying meaning to bring enough beer to a party — that is, both arms full. Usage: "Yeah, come on over at eight — and remember to knock with both elbows." (BMS)

knot *n.* An international measurement of speed equal to one nautical mile, or 6,076.115 feet (1,852 meters), per hour; of interest to surfers because it is used to measure wind speed. For example, in a calm sea or glassy conditions, wind speed is less than one knot, whereas a gale ranges from thirty-four to fifty-five knots. (WB, AJM)

knots *n.* **1)** A buildup of excess tissue caused by friction between the body and the surfboard. Also called SURF KNOBS or SURF BUMPS. **2)** Calcium deposits over the knees and on the feet where the knees and feet come into contact with the board in a kneeling position. See VOLCANO.

The medical term for knots is Osgood-Schlatter disease (also known as housemaid's knee). A nonmalignant condition, it can be very painful for beginning surfers or for those just returning from a long absence. It's particularly common among young surfers.

kneeboarder
Head dip, Bill Siler
Photo: Woody Woodworth

knock with both elbows
Art: Rick Stover

kona (KO-nah) *n*. Hawaiian for the leeward side of an island, for example, the Kona Coast of the Big Island.

kona wind *n*. A south wind in the Hawaiian Islands, generally onshore at most of the beaches with a southern exposure, where it causes mushy surfing conditions. Occasionally, however, it blows offshore and makes it glassy on the North Shore.

kook or **kuk** *n*. **1**) A rank beginner; a know-nothing; someone who is generally blundering, out of control, and in the way or who gets into trouble because of ignorance or inexperience. **2**) A lame surfer, rule breaker, idiot; same as GOOB, GEEK, UNLOCAL, VALLEY. Sometimes called HODAD or GREMMIE. (JP) **3**) Someone who imitates others badly. (MF) **4**) Anyone who doesn't know how to surf. (H&R) **5**) One who practices **kookism** — a pseudo surfer, fake, goon, pretender, wannabe, beginner, novice, etc. (BP) —**longboard kook** (W&B)

. . . .

Kook is an especially derogatory term, applied specifically to someone who lives inland. Kooks are always getting in the way of "real" surfers, letting their boards get away and sometimes crashing into other surfers. *Kook* spelled backwards is still *kook*.

. . . .

kook box *n*. A 1940s term for a PADDLEBOARD or HOLLOW SURFBOARD used by lifeguards; so named because you felt like a kook on them. (GN)

kook cord *n*. A derogatory term for a SURF LEASH; same as VALLEY LIFELINE.

kook maneuver *n*. A stupid move, such as taking off in front of another surfer. (IBN)

kook repellent *n*. A novelty spraycan product by Runman; the successor of Silly String. Works best on yourself.

Kookmeyer, **Wilbur** A cartoon character introduced in 1986 in Bob Penuelas' cartoon strip "Maynard and the Rat" in *Surfer* magazine. Wilbur is a young beach kid, the quintessential wannabe and the epitome of what it's like to be a kook — whether it's surfing, hanging out with the cool group, or trying to impress the most beautiful girl on the beach.

kookster *n*. A spazzy kook.

kooky 1) *adj*. Having the characteristics of a kook. Usage: "This really kooky guy just cut me off." **2**) **Kooky** A character on the 1960s TV series "Route 66."

Kowabonga! The cry of the legendary Chief Thunderthud (played by Bill Lecornec) on "The Howdy Doody Show" (1947–1960). This all-purpose expletive and greeting was coined in 1949 by Eddie Kean at a

MAYNARD & THE RAT PRESENTS... BY BOB PENUELAS
WILBUR **KOOKMEYER**

*KOOK (kо̄о̄k) ONE WHO PRACTICES KOOKISM. PSEUDO SURFER; FAKE, GOON, PRETENDER, WANNABEE, BEGINNER, NOVICE, ETC.

HI, MY NAME IS WILBUR KOOKMEYER. IM WHATCHA CALL A KOOK. NOW MOST PEOPLE WOULD BE ASHAMED TO BE KNOWN AS A KOOK, BUT NOT ME, IM PROUD TO BE A KOOK. THERES NOTHING WRONG WITH BEING A KOOK, ALOT OF KOOKS MAKE FINE HONEST CITIZENS IN FACT THEY SAY THAT SOON KOOKS WILL OUT NUMBER REGULAR SURFERS BY AS MUCH AS TEN TO ONE. ITS ALREADY HAPPENING JUST LOOK AROUND... WE'RE EVERYWHERE...

Art: Bob Penuelas

script meeting. Surfers eventually turned the term into "Cowabunga!"

. . . .

"'*Kowabonga* was a nonsense word that originally meant an expression of anger, like "dammit!" But the way Bill first said the line, it sounded more like an exclamation of surprise, and that's mostly the way we used it.' Years later, Baby Boom surfers weaned on Howdy Doody would scream "Kowabonga!" on an ecstatic wave, which evolved into Cowabunga! Young officers in Vietnam,

incredibly, used it as a battle cry."
—Stephen Davis, *Say Kids! What Time Is It?* (Boston: Little, Brown, 1987)

. . . .

Kowabunga! or **Kawabunga!** COWABUNGA.

kracka-pow!! The sound a surfboard makes when it goes flying off a roof rack as you drive away. (GCD) See RACK FLYER.

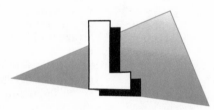

lacerate *v*. To tear up a wave (BP); to make aggressive maneuvers on a surfboard. Same as COOK, RIP.

lagoon *n*. A shallow body of water separated from a larger bay or from the ocean by a landform such as a sand spit or a reef (CCRG); used to gain access to surf spots.

laid-back *adj*. Relaxed. Used to describe someone's style in the surf or an attitude on land. Usage: "He's really laid-back."

Lake Atlantic The surfers' name for the flat summer conditions in Florida. (TDW)

laminate *v*. To apply resin over fiberglass during surfboard construction.

laminating resin *n*. The base resin used in applying fiberglass cloth to a shaped blank.

land breeze *n*. A light wind blowing offshore.

"Land Shark" The "Saturday Night Live" TV skit involving a Jaws-like great white shark posing as a delivery person.

land yacht *n*. A really big station wagon used to transport surfers and boards to and from the beach. (LWK)

landlocked *adj*. **1**) The state of being too far inland to reach a beach in a reasonable amount of time, for instance, from Kansas or Bolivia. **2**) Also used to describe nonsurfers. (JP)

. . . .

"There is no life east of I-5."
—California bumper sticker sold at surf shops in the early 1980s

. . . .

lands end *n*. The extreme seaward tip of an island or promontory.

lap line *n*. The edge of laminated fiberglass cloth, usually trimmed. (ORB)

late drop-in, late takeoff *n*. Catching a wave as it starts to break, a move that usually ends in disaster because the wave has already started to crash.

later, lates, late "See ya later."

later for that "Forget it." (MLI)

lateral drift *n*. The motion of a surfer carried in a cross current. See LONGSHORE CURRENT.

layback
Rockies—"He made it!"
Photo: Bill Romerhaus

Art: I. B. Nelson

leash cups aplenty
Photo: Bob Barbour

latronic (lay-TRON-ic) "Later on." This expression was possibly derived from Mike Latronic; it has been further simplified to **lonic**. (North San Diego County; LH) Usage: "Latronic, dude."

launched *v.* To be thrown or catapulted off a board up over the back of a wave; same as PITCHED.

lava tube *n.* A hollow cave carved out of lava rock; generally refers to submarine caves beneath surfing spots.

lay up *v.* To place a sheet of fiberglass over a foam blank and trim it to fit.

layback *n.* **1)** A stalling cutback maneuver in which the surfer, instead of carving an S-turn, jams into a skidding slide while leaning back toward the curl, then allows the body's forward momentum to return him or her to an upright posture before continuing along the wave face. **2)** A 1980s maneuver in which the surfer is surfing backhand and leans way back on the wave face. (NAT, 1985) See BACKSIDE LAYBACK.

Lazor Zap *n.* A wide-tailed surfboard popularized by Cheyne Horan; it had a brief tenure. (SFG, 2/86)

leanback *n.* A backward-leaning stance on a surfboard.

leap-off-and-catch When a surfer terminates a ride, swings back over the top of a wave, and lands prone on the surfboard in position to paddle back out. (AHK, 1967)

leash *n.* SURF LEASH.

leash cup *n.* A small, round cup laminated into the tail section of a surfboard and finished with a cross-pin, to which the surf leash is attached. Same as PLUG.

leash loop *n.* A small piece of a fiberglass product called rope that is laminated to the rear deck of a surfboard and used to attach a surf leash.

ledge *n.* An underwater formation, usually a reef, that causes incoming swells to jack up quickly and pitch foward in a powerful, thick lip. (MW)

leeward *n., adj.* Refers to the protected side of an island, where the wind is calm and the surf is small or nonexistent; the opposite of windward.

left *n.* **1)** Any wave breaking in such a manner that a surfer taking off must turn to his or her left to stay ahead of the curl. **2)** A wave that breaks from left to right, as viewed from the shore, or from right to left, as viewed from the water looking toward the beach. (ORB, MW) Surfers always define left and right from their vantage point out in the water, facing the shore. **—left hander** or **left-hander**

left point *n.* A point break that produces waves that break to the right.

left slide *n.* A ride where the surfer slides to the left on a wave that is breaking from right to left.

leg rope or **leg-rope, leggie** *n.* **1)** An Australian term for a SURF LEASH.

legalese grommetspeak *n.* See SURF CRIMES.

legend *n.* An Australian term for someone who rides a Mal, or longboard. (R&D) Usage: "The place was full of legends."

length *n.* The dimension of the surfboard from the tip of the nose to the tip, or tips, of the tail.

let down *v.* (Of a wave) To break. Usage: "The lip let down on his head."

"Let's Go Trippin'" The instrumental surfing tune by Dick Dale that was the first acknowledged surf music hit. (PJN) In the late fifties and early sixties, *trippin'* was another word for surfing.

lifeguard *n.* A person trained in life-saving who watches over the beach and ocean area, rescues people from drowning in the surf, patrols up and down the beach in a jeep, and sits in a tower and scopes out the scene with a pair of binoculars. This individual is a keen observer of the beach scene and a good source for local surf conditions.

lift *n.* **1)** The force created when the water flow is faster across one side of a fin than the other. (ORB) **2)** ROCKER.

lifted rail *n.* A surfboard rail whose outer edge is above the center line of the side rail.

line *n.* **1)** A long wave or set of waves. **2)** A wave that forms a steep, long wall of water, ordinarily making for an extremely fast ride. **3)** A strong, well-developed swell that is pumping in toward shore like a freight train. **4)** The contour of a surfboard.

. . . .

"A wave is a blank canvas, and you're able to draw on it whatever wild lines you want." —Body Boarding (December/January 1990)

. . . .

line up *v.* **1)** (Of surfers) To sit in the lineup. **2)** (Of waves) To start to break evenly. Usage: "The waves are lining up nice." **3)** To keep track of one's position in the water in relation to two fixed land objects, called **lineups**. (GN) Usage: "I was lining up with the palm tree and your car."

lined up *adj.* Used to describe long, even swells. (NAT, 1985) **—lined-up waves**

lineup or **line-up** *n.* **1)** The place in the water where the surfers gather to pick up waves; the takeoff area. **2)** The area where surfers straddle their boards waiting for waves to begin curling. (B&F) **3)** The point where the waves are consistently starting to break. (A&B) **4)** The term used to describe the wave and swell formation at a surfing location. (NAT, 1985)

lining surf *n.* A wave that stretches a long distance from end to end and often provides a lengthy ride. (MF, 1967)

lip *n.* **1)** The top edge of the wall of a breaking wave. **2)** The fringing crest of a wave that is starting to break. **3)** The part of a wave that comes over first when the wave breaks. (ORB) **4)** The leading edge of a clean-breaking wave. (MW) **5)** The pitching crest of a hollow or semihollow wave. (L&L) **—wave lip, thick lip**

lip attempt *n.* Any attempt to perform an off-the-lip maneuver.

lip bash or **lip-bash** *n.* Snapping a turn off of the wave lip. (SFR, 10/83) Usage: "Nice lip bash."

lip floater *n.* A surfing and bodyboarding maneuver in which the surfer glides over the wave lip.

lip-slasher, lip-slamming *n.* Surfing off-the-lip.

lip slide *n.* Floating the board across the wave lip. (SFG, 3/90)

lipper *n.* Any off-the-lip maneuver. (Santa Cruz)

liquid smoke *n.* The effect when an offshore wind rips the tops off of waves, giving the spray a smoky, jet-blown appearance.

littoral drift *n.* The relocation of sediment as a result of two factors: its transport by a longshore current and its wave-induced deposit on the beach. (CCRG)

lit-up *adj.* What it feels like to be stung by a Portuguese man-o'-war — your skin's on fire. (Florida; TDW)

live *adj.* Great, awesome. Usage: "That was live."

loady *n.* Someone who's more interested in smoking weed than surfing. (San Clemente)

local, locals *n.* **1)** Anyone who lives in a particular area and surfs it the

lifeguard
Art: Rick Stover

liquid smoke
Photo: Rob Gilley

most. (ORB) **2)** Inhabitants of a private beach area; must live within two miles of the ocean. (SP) **3)** Anyone who's been there a day longer than you. (MW) —**local heavies**

local knowledge *n.* **1)** Knowledge about a particular surf break — which way the wave breaks best, where the easiest access is, what tide works best, etc. (SFR, 7/90) A lack of local knowledge can sometimes be partially made up for in enthusiasm. **2)** Having all the information about a surf spot. See WAVE KNOWLEDGE, WIRED.

log
Art: I. B. Nelson

local wind *n.* Wind caused by factors in the immediate area, rather than by well-developed storms coming from afar. **Local wind conditions** kick up surf that is generally weak and very short-lived, with wave periods very close together. See SEA BREEZE, WIND SWELL.

localism *n.* **1)** Territorial defiance in defense of a surf spot. The activity was born in 1779 when angry Hawaiians killed Captain James Cook at Kealakekua Bay. (SFG, 11/89) **2)** When surfers who frequently ride the same surf break are jerks to those who don't. (MM) **3)** An attitude that can easily be identified by the warnings that are painted on signs and fences: "If You Don't Live Here, Don't Surf Here." "No Unlocals." "Warning!! Windansea May Be Hazardous To Tourists!" "Valley Go Home!"

localism
Heather Cralle with Windansea graffiti, La Jolla, California, 1979.
Photo: Trevor Cralle

local/valley switch *n.* The name surfers give to the "local/distant" button on a car radio that improves reception. (DBF, 1981)

locies (LO-keys) *n.* LOCALS. (North County San Diego)

locked in *v.* **1)** To be in a position on a fast-closing wave, trimming just ahead of the curl, so that there is no choice but to drive straight across the wave's face as fast as possible to avoid being wiped out. **2)** To

be in a position where it is impossible to pull out even if you wanted to. **3)** The situation when a surfer is caught on such a fast-moving wave that he or she is forced to hang on to the board for dear life. (IDSM) **4)** To be positioned in the perfect spot on the wave — that is, inside the curl. (MM)

log *n.* **1)** A very heavy surfboard. **2)** A long surfboard. (JP) **3)** A longboard. (MM) **4)** Any board over seven feet and weighing over fifteen pounds. (H&R) **5) logger** An old MALIBU. (NAT, 1985)

logjam *n.* **1)** The situation when there are too many longboards on the same wave. **2)** Constipation; the opposite of TOURISTA.

logman *n.* LONGBOARDER.

lone-star session *n.* Surfing all by yourself. (RMN)

long crested swell *n.* A swell that produces large waves.

long hair *n.* A heavy-metal surfer. Usage: "He's a long hair." (San Clemente)

long john *n.* A sleeveless wetsuit with full-length legs. See SHORT JOHN.

long-line drive *n.* A long, fast ride on a hot wave.

longboard *n.* A surfboard eight to ten feet long, used during the forties, fifties, and sixties and revived in the eighties.

A longboard provides more flotation than a shortboard because it contains more foam. It also paddles and catches waves more easily, and is more stable in big, fast, bumpy surf. In addition, the longer rail line gives control. Longboards are known for gliding, carrying speed, and keeping their momentum through slow or mushy sections of a wave.

longboard club *n.* A group of surfers who have organized to promote longboarding.

longboarder *n*. A surfer who rides a longboard.

longest functional distance, functional length of ride *n*. **1**) In professional surfing, the longest possible distance that a surfer can ride along the horizontal plane in the judges' field of vision while performing maneuvers. The length of the ride is both the least important and the most controversial aspect of the scoring criteria. See SURFING CRITERIA. (L&L) **2**) The length of the ride. **3**) Continuing to perform functional maneuvers for the maximum distance that the wave allows. Riding for the maximum distance does *not* mean riding straight in with the white water (groveling).

longshore current *n*. A stream of water flowing parallel to and near the shore; caused by waves hitting the beach at an oblique angle. (CCRG) This current often carries a surfer down the coast during a session, making it difficult to paddle out or line up.

loomer *n*. A big wave suddenly appearing outside.

loop *n*. A surfing and windsurfing maneuver in which the surf craft is ridden through a complete circle in the air or in a wave.

looper *n*. A wave that curls or throws out in front of itself, often breaking over a surfer to create a ride in the tunnel.

loose 1) *adj*. Used to describe a board-handling characteristic, as in "loose and responsive." **2**) **looseness** *n*. The maneuverability of a surfboard. (L&L)

loose board *n*. An incoming surfboard with no rider! Also called KILLER BOARD.

louie *n*. Someone with a ripped tank top who rides a motorcycle or drives around in a jacked-up pickup truck with fluorescent shocks and a Local Motion decal. (Newport Beach)

lovelys *n*. Good-looking girls, as in "scopin' on some lovelys." (North San Diego County)

low, low pressure system, low pressure *n*. Unstable moving air and winds that blow counterclockwise around the center of the system, in contrast to a high pressure system, in which the winds blow clockwise around the center. Low pressure systems make surf, highs don't. (W&B)

low-energy summer waves *n*. Fun surf that never gets very big.

low tide *n*. A lowering of sea level. Some spots break best at low tide; some break only at low tide.

lowk *n*. LOCAL; a term used in the movie *Under the Boardwalk* (1989).

luau *n*. A feast and party with music and hula dancers.

lull *n*. **1**) A period in which there is no constant roll of waves breaking on the bank. **2**) The period between sets when the waves are smaller or nonexistent. (ORB) **3**) A long wait between waves. (MM) **4**) **major lull** A longer than normal wait between sets, which often means that a bigger set is coming next. (L&L)

lunch *v*. HAMMERED or WORKED. (MVA) Usage: "I got completely lunched out there." —**lunch time** (SFG, 10/87)

lurker *n*. **1**) Someone from the Midwest who lives at the beach, doesn't work or go to school, drinks a lot of beer, has a tattoo, scams to get by, mooches off girlfriends or lives off a trust fund, may or may not surf. **2**) A Sunset Boulevard type (Hollywood, Los Angeles), who rides a skateboard or a beach cruiser. These characters lurk around, going from place to place to look for drugs, a free meal, a sack of herb, or parties. (Mission Beach, Newport Beach, and Huntington Beach)

longboarder
Art: Jim Phillips

lurker
Art: Keith Hunter

Maalaea, Maalaea Pipeline (ma-LAY-ah) *n.* A spectacular surf site located on the south shore of Maui, Hawaii, and known as the "fastest wave in the world"; breaks fast only a few times a year. Recently has been threatened by a harbor expansion project, and the Protect Maalaea Coalition is fighting to save this endangered surf spot (1990).

mack, mack out *v.* To eat enthusiastically and without inhibitions, usually after a surf session. (P) Same as SHOVEL, MOW. Usage: "Let's mack."

macked *v.* To be smacked by a big wave. (SWH) Usage: "I got completely macked."

macker *n.* A very large wave. (Ocean Beach, San Francisco; BTV) Usage: "Here comes a macker!"

macking *v.* When huge waves roll in, big and powerful as a Mack truck. (RQN) Usage: "The waves are fully *macking*."

major *adj.* BIG TIME, as in "a *major* lull."

major hang time *n.* A long FLOATER. Usage: "Look at that major hang time." See HANG TIME.

major hazard *n.* Any hidden obstacle that can suddenly derail a surfer, such as a storm drain, underwater cables, or submerged rocks.

major maneuvers *n.* In competitive surfing, the outstanding or eye-catching moves that most influence a judge's score. They are (in descending order of degree of difficulty): TUBE RIDE, COVER-UP, REENTRY, CUTBACK, RICOCHET, FLOATER, and BOTTOM TURN.

macking
Art: Rick Stover

(L&L) Also see METHODS OF FINISH, MINOR MANEUVERS, TRANSITIONAL MANEUVERS.

makable wave *n.* Any wave that's fairly easy to catch. —**makable takeoff**

Makaha A Hawaiian beach and surf spot on Oahu that is famous for its backwash and awesome bowl (the **Makaha bowl**).

Makaha board *n.* A board designed in the 1950s, especially for riding through the Makaha bowl. The design featured a pointed tail and a flat bottom, which were supposed to help the board glide across the flat part of the wave and thus enable the surfer to make it through the bowl. Another distinctive design element was the sharp breakaway edge on the bottom of the tail block.

make a section 1) *v.* To surf through a particular section of a wave to another section. 2) **making a section** *n.* A scoring move in a surf contest.

make waves, making waves *v.* To catch a wave and ride it. "Surfers don't make waves they ride 'em" —California bumper sticker. (1989)

makeitaudible (make-it-audible) To ride in and out of a big barrel; the term was coined by Nathan Fletcher. May have to do with yelling as you ride in and out of a tube, or with the sound that you hear inside the wave. Usage: "Makeitaudible, dude."

Mal, Mal-rider *n.* Australian slang for a MALIBU BOARD, or LONGBOARD.

Windsurfing. Photo: Woody Woodworth

Ward Coffey tubed, Carmel. Photo: Woody Woodworth

Skimboarding, Laguna Beach. Photo: Dennis Junor

Session. Photo: Woody Woodworth

Bobby Owens in trim, Backdoor, Hawaii.
Photo: Bill Romerhaus

Underwater view of a tube. Photo: Rob Gilley

Offshore wind. Photo: Woody Woodworth

Windsurfer wave jumping. Photo: Woody Woodworth

Mike Johnson in the green room. Photo: Rob Gilley

Derek Ho getting tubed, Pipeline. Photo: Woody Woodworth

Glassy conditions, Laguna Beach. Photo: Woody Woodwort

Malibu 1) A Southern California coastal community known for its beaches and surf spots. **2**) The place where antivalley sentiments originated. **3**) The birthplace of the Malibu board.

Malibu Barbie *n*. A label given to a girl with the IQ of a Barbie doll. See BARBIE. Usage: "She's such a Malibu Barbie."

Malibu board, Malibu or **malibu** *n*. A lightweight balsa board designed by Malibu surfers Matt Kivlin and Joe Quigg.

The Malibu board was developed in the late forties and early fifties, when it was ridden mainly at Malibu Beach, California, and referred to as a "chip board." It was based on the Simmons theory of reducing weight, but it went one step further by improving the shape and thus the maneuverability of the board. Originally made of balsa wood (plywood in Australia), the **modern Malibu** is constructed of foam and fiberglass and is from 8½ to 10½ feet long. Also called MAL (in Australia), ZIP BOARD, and LONGBOARD.

* * * * * * * * * * * * * * *

malihini (MAH-le-HEE-nee) *n*. A newcomer to the Hawaiian Islands. Newcomers to the sport of surfing are also referred to as *malihinis*. See KAMAAINA.

mallard *n*. A KOOK; someone who floats around out in the lineup like a duck. (San Clemente)

man-made waves *n*. Artificially produced waves, like those at Big Surf in Arizona. See WAVE POOL.

man-on-man *n*. A system introduced to professional surfing by Australian Peter Drouyn at the inaugural Stubbies Contest at Burleigh Heads, Australia, in 1977. Although having two surfers in the water was a breakthrough then, it is now standard practice in competitions, except in the big waves of Hawaii. The catch in the system is that inside positioning is the key to

dominating the man-on-man heats, making them more of a paddle race than a surfing contest. (L&L) See PRIORITY BUOY.

mañana *n., adv*. Spanish for morning, tomorrow, or in the near future. An important concept and state of mind that it's necessary to grasp and accept when traveling in Baja and other Spanish-speaking areas south of the Mexican border. Same as HAWAIIAN TIME or ISLAND TIME.
—*mañana* method, *mañana* time

In his book *Demon Box* (New York: Viking Penguin, 1986), Ken Kesey says the Arabic version of *mañana* is *bukra fi'l mish-mish* ("Tomorrow, when it's the season of the apricot").

* * * * * * * * * * * * * * *

mane *n*. Spray thrown aloft from a breaking wave, caused by an offshore wind. See LIQUID SMOKE.

maneuverability *n*. How well a surfboard turns on a wave. For example, a shortboard is more maneuverable than a longboard.

manson *n*. **1**) A psycho surfer. Usage: "Some manson snaked Johnny-Boy this morning at Beach Park, and did a cutback right into him." (Sunset Beach Surf Shop, Hawaii; SFR, 1989) **2**) A term used by shortboarders to describe out-of-control longboarders. (RJS)

marauder *n*. A sixties term for a reckless surfer. (IDSM)

marine layer *n*. **1**) Fog and low clouds that frequently form along coastlines in the late spring and early summer; caused by the mixing of cold, upwelling water with warm air. Although the cold, opaque marine layer blocks the sun at the beach, a short distance inland the fog ends and it is hot and sunny. (California; W&B) **2**) An inverted climatic condition that pervades certain coastlines.

Malibu
Photo: John S. Callahan

mallard
Art: Rick Stover

marine terrace *n*. **1**) Uplifted sea floor that was cut and eroded by wave action, forming a flat plain edging the ocean. **2**) A good spot for a surf check. (CCRG) Also called COASTAL TERRACE, WAVE-CUT BENCH.

massive *adj*. Used to describe waves that are really superbig.

mat *n*. SURF MAT.

max out *v*. **1**) To be over the limit, over the top. Usage: "The huge swell maxed out." **2**) Used to define the upper limit of a particular wave. Usage: "This wave maxes out at two meters." (MW)

maxi-pad cowboy *n*. A derogatory term for a bodyboarder so called because the bodyboard resembles an absorbent feminine pad in shape. (Hawaii)

Mazatlans *n*. Mexican sandals with tire-tread soles; same as GUARACHES.

mean *adj*. Nasty but good. Usage: "Those waves look pretty mean."

mean high tide line (**MHTL**) *n*. The highest point that the tide reaches on the shore. In California and certain other areas of the globe, the beach is public property up to the mean high tide line, even on a so-called private beach posted with "no trespassing" and "keep out" signs. This means that a surfer may walk along the beach (up to the MHTL) in order to reach a surf spot; it's always smart, though, to respect the property owner's land.

mean wave height *n*. See WAVE HEIGHT.

mean wave period *n*. See PERIOD.

meat wave *n*. A carload of valleys. (SFR, 8/90)

meaty *adj*. Used to describe the part of a wave with the most energy. Usage: "I saw you trim through that meaty section."

medium tide *n*. **1**) Somewhere in between high and low tides. Some spots break best during a medium tide. **2**) A tide that doesn't get superhigh.

mega *adj*. An intensifier, as in "mega-enormous waves" or "mega-tubular."

mellow *adj*. **1**) Relaxed, laid-back, enjoying a kicked-back pace. See GEL. **2**) Used by jazz musicians in the 1930s to describe their scene; it was *mellow*. **3**) Used by East Coast types, quite fairly, to ridicule California's "laid-back" pretensions. "If I start to get too mellow, I ripen and rot" —Woody Allen, *Annie Hall* (1977). Or, "When Californians use leaf blowers, life is less mellow" —*The Wall Street Journal* (December 4, 1990). **4**) "**Mellow Yellow**" A 1966 pop song by Donovan Leitch.

Mellow had an established slang usage among surfers and other beach kids well before the word became associated with the hot-tub-and-long-hair crowd. The surfing connection may have been initiated by Mark M. Wagner when he was a junior at La Jolla High School; his poem "Day Chant" (published in *Surfer* magazine, March 1970) featured the line, "Let's hug the mellow day and come back again tomorrow!"

"In Orange County, California, in 1981, wanting to be mellow is like wanting to be dead." —Kief Hillsbery, "Clockwork Orange County," *Outside* magazine (August/Sepember 1981)

mellow out *v*. **1**) To relax, veg. **2**) "Cool it!" Usage: "Mellow out, dude!"

meltdown, the meltdown *n*. A phenomenon you experience when it's low tide, really hollow, and you take acid drops off of waves. (Ocean Beach, San Francisco; BTV)

melting lines *n*. Well-harmonized contours of a surfboard.

methods of finish *n*. Any of several maneuvers used to end a ride. In competitive surfing, they are (in descending order of degree of difficulty): KICKOUT, PULLOUT, STEPOFF, and

UNCONTROLLED. (L&L) Also see MAJOR MANEUVERS, MINOR MANEUVERS, TRANSITIONAL MANEUVERS.

Mexi-gringo surf drawl *n.* The lingo of Spicoli-type surfers who venture into Mexico and speak Spanish with a very poor accent. (P)

"Who's got the beaucoup dollares?" ..."I got uno nicklea." —Jeff Spicoli (Sean Penn) in *Fast Times at Ridgemont High* (1982)

Mexican hurricanes *n.* Storms off Baja that bring short-term south to southwest swells to the California coast. Also called CHUBASCOS.

Mexico, Mex A major surf destination, especially among California surfers. See "Spanish for the Mexico-bound Surfer" below. Also see BAJA.

micro *n.* A perfectly shaped wave but unridable because of its small size. (Newport Beach)

mid-face turn *n.* Any minor directional change, for example between 60 and 130 degrees, that has little influence on speed. (L&L)

mid-latitude cyclones *n.* Strong low pressure systems that track across the North Pacific in winter. Depending on how far north or south these storms are steered by the jet stream, California experiences a west, northwest, or north swell. (BB, 10/90)

milk, milking *v.* To get the most out of a wave, as in "milking speed and energy from small surf."

milky *adj.* Used to describe the white-water section of a broken wave.

micro
Six inches high, Baja
Photo: Woody Woodworth

SPANISH FOR THE MEXICO-BOUND SURFER*

For many American surfers, a burning desire to escape the crowded conditions of the home break spells MEXICO. Travel is one of the most exciting aspects of surfing — and possibly the most educational part of life — but it requires some minimum language skills to maximize the possibility of positive contact with the natives of the country visited. Anybody who has ever traveled in Baja or mainland Mexico knows the advantages of being able to communicate with the people. Most Mexicans have become used to the "stupid gringo" who travels south to take a cut-rate vacation, drink cheap beer, and buy souvenirs; so don't be surprised if you get treated less than warmly when you make requests to a Mexican in English.

The following simple guidelines will help you increase your chances of having good, even memorable, experiences. Even if your Spanish is horrible, it's worth it to make an effort because it is the recognition of this effort that creates a bridge of understanding and shows that you are different from the *gringo típico* to whom the Mexicans have numbed themselves. As you will learn, Mexicans are very generous and hospitable to travelers who are hip to their culture and language. So don't be shy, put yourself on the line and try to speak what you know, even if you think it's really bad. (P)

*May be useful in Spain as well.

Art: The Pizz

(continued on next page)

SPANISH PRONUNCIATION MADE EASY

Pronunciation of vowels:

a	ah	as in *taco*
e	eh	as in *cerveza* (a key word)
i	ee	as in *hijo* (pronounced EE-ho)
o	oh	as in *hola* and *ola* ("hello" and "wave," respectively — very important words)
u	oo	as in *rubio* ("blonde," something Mexicans are fond of calling anyone who has light-colored hair)

Pronunciation of tricky consonants:

g	pronounced like *h* in English when followed by *e* or *i*, for example, *gente* ("people"); when followed by *a, o, u,* or a consonant, pronounced like *g* in English *grommet*
h	always silent, for example, *hombre* ("man")
j	pronounced like *h* in Hawaii, for example, *jardín* ("garden")
ll	pronounced like *y* in *your,* for example, *Me llamo . . .*
ñ	pronounced somewhat like *ni* in *onion,* for example, *año, enseñar* ("year" and "to teach," respectively)
q	pronounced like *c* in English *come*; always followed by *ue* or *ui,* in which the *u* is silent, for example, *querer* and *quitar* ("to want" and "to remove" or "to take away," respectively); the sound of English *qu* is represented in Spanish by *cu,* for example, *cuenta* ("bill" or "check")
z	pronounced like *s* in English *surf* in Latin America and like *th* in English *thruster* in Spain (Castilian Spanish), for example, *zapato* ("shoe")

Key Words and Phrases

por favor	please	*arrecife*	reef
gracias	thank you	*patinaje sobre las*	
de nada	you're welcome	*olas, surfear*	surfing
lo siento	I'm sorry	*tabla de surf*	surfboard
ola	wave	*cera de surf*	surf wax
la playa	beach	*grande*	big
el tiburón	shark	*pequeño*	small
el pilluelo	sea urchin	*océano*	ocean
el viento	wind	*canal*	channel
terral	offshore wind	*marea*	tide
tubo	tube	*alto*	high
punta	point	*bajo*	low

¿Dónde está . . . ?	Where is . . . ?
¿Cuanto cuesta?	How much does it cost, how much is . . . ?
La cuenta, por favor.	May I have the check, please?
¿Cómo se llama, usted?	What is your name?
Me llamo . . .	My name is . . .
¿De dónde es, usted?	Where are you from?
Yo soy de . . .	I am from . . .
Soy Norteamericano.	I am American. (It's important to say "norte" because in Latin America the people also consider themselves American.)

mindless *adj*. Used to describe insane waves that are beyond the wildest imaginings of the mind. (MM)

miniboards *n*. The new shortboards, which are usually teardrop or bullet shaped.

minigun *n*. A surfboard that is somewhere between a shortboard and a big gun in length.

minilog *n*. A shortened version of a longboard. (GTV)

minor maneuvers *n*. In competitive surfing, moves that are not in the category of major maneuvers but that have some influence on scoring potential. They are (in descending order of degree of difficulty): TOP TURN, FOAM FLOATER, FOAM TURN, and FADE. (L&L) Also see MAJOR MANEUVERS, METHODS OF FINISH, and TRANSITIONAL MANEUVERS.

minus tide *n*. An extremely low tide that occurs during a spring-tide period.

miragey *adj*. The effect when a wave looks huge from far away but is actually quite small by the time it reaches you. (MPZ) Usage: "It was really miragey out there today."

mixed tides *n*. A widespread phenomenon in the Pacific and Indian oceans, in which pairs of high and low tides are unequal in height, so that there is a **higher high tide**, followed by a **lower low tide**, a **lower high tide**, and a **higher low tide** each day; caused by changes in the moon's and sun's positions with respect to the earth's equator. (CCRG, WB) See TIDES.

moana (mo-AH-na) *n*. Hawaiian for ocean.

mob *n*. An Australian term for a group of surfers — usually many. See CARVING UP THE MOB.

mo'bettah Hawaiian Pidgin English for "more better."

modern surfboard eras *n*. Specific periods in the history of surfing in Australia, identified with the kinds of board in use, including: **1**) the solid board, from 1912 to 1938; **2**) the hollow board, from 1938 to 1956; **3**) the balsa-wood Malibu board from America, fiberglass covered and fitted with a fin, from 1956 until 1965; **4**) the American-invented polyurethane/glass-covered board, from 1965 to the present. (ASKC)

modern surfing *n*. A surfing era that was born in the 1940s and 1950s and that was characterized by the transition to lighter surfboards.

moke, big moke *n*. A local heavy surfer dude who may or may not be aggressive or in a good mood. (Hawaii; PDX, PZ)

MOLTO man (Man Of Late Take-Offs) *n*. Someone who consistently catches a wave late, thus making the drop-in very hairy. (ATRL)

mondo *adj*. Used to describe huge surf conditions, of epic proportions. (ATRL) Usage: "It was mondo."

monkey hop *n*. Surfing straight out to the flats.

monster *n*. **1**) A gigantic wave. (MM) **2**) **monster surf** Huge waves. — **monsta** (Hawaiian Pidgin), **monster air**

". . . waves that bulged and grew monstrous, like mountains . . ." —*The Odyssey Of Homer*, translated by Richmond Lattimore (New York: Harper and Row, 1975), page 58

moon *n*. The earth's natural satellite, whose gravitational pull is the primary force controlling the tides. It takes the earth twenty-four hours and fifty minutes to revolve, which is why the moon "rises" fifty minutes later each day. (CCRG) Tides are highest and lowest during a new

Art: I. B. Nelson

multifin
Is eight enough?
Photo: Don Balch

Murphy
Cover of Surfer Magazine,
Aug-Sept 1962
Art: Rick Griffin

and a full moon. See SPRING TIDES, SURFER MOON.

Moondoggie A character in the book/movie *Gidget*, who lived in a grass shack on the beach and was based on a real guy named Billy Bangston. (CC) Sometimes misspelled "Moondawg" or "Moon Dog."

Morey Boogie *n.* The original Boogie Board invented by Tom Morey in the 1970s; developed from aircraft foam. See BODYBOARD, BOOGIE BOARD.

most excellent *adj.* Supremely wonderful; used to describe waves and other favorable situations. (From the 1989 movie *Bill and Ted's Excellent Adventure*)

Mother Bu MALIBU.

mountains *n.* Used as a metaphor for waves. "Surfing is like mountain climbing, only in surfing the mountain chases you!" —Phil Edwards (1967)

mow *v.* To eat; to MACK OUT.

multifin *n.* Any surfboard with more than one fin placement.
—**multifin designs**

munch *v.* **1)** To get eaten up by a wave. (P) Usage: "I got totally munched on that last one."
2) To scarf down some food.

munchies *n.* Sharks. (Victoria, Australia; RDTW)

Murph the Surf 1) The nickname of surfer-turned-jewel-thief Jack Murphy, who together with Allan Kuhn stole the Star of India sapphire from New York's American Museum of Natural History in 1964. **2)** A 1975 movie starring Don Stroud and Robert Conrad, based loosely on Murphy and Kuhn's adventures.

Murphy Rick Griffin's fictitious cartoon characterization of a typical gremmie, who made his debut in

1961 in the second issue of *Surfer* magazine.

mushburger *n.* A shapeless wave, sometimes caused by unfavorable winds. In other cases, though, a spot just doesn't have a good bottom contour and the waves are always mushburgers. (MW) See MUSHY.

mushing wave *n.* A wave that breaks in the top and dies quickly, resulting in a very short ride. (MF, 1967)

mushroom cloud *n.* The white, inverted-mushroom-shape cloud produced underwater by the impact of the falling crest of a large wave on its forward slope. Seen only from beneath the surface.

mushy *adj.* **1)** Applied to waves that are blown over by onshore winds. The walls collapse, creating much white water and making conditions poor for surfing. **2)** Said of a slow, sloppy or rolling wave that has little power or speed. **3)** In general, used to describe poor-quality, small surf. (L&L) **4) mush dog, mush doggie** A wave that never breaks. **5) mush** Surf under one foot high that is barely ridable. (H&R)
—**mush out** *v.,* **mushier** *adj.*

My wave! A surfer's claim to own the wave he or she is riding; a presumption documented in the Surf Punks' song "My Wave." Also used to signal someone to stay out of the way. See GOT IT.

mysterioso *n.* An "adornment" or surf trick created by Mickey Muñoz in the late 1950s, in which he bent over and hid his head in his hands. Spelled "mysteriouso" in the first issue of *Surfer* magazine (1960).

mysto-spot *n.* A surf spot that breaks big when other places are flat.

nailed *v.* To be wiped out badly, to get dumped on — happens after a surfer "closes the lid" on a coffin ride. (MCR) Usage: "I got nailed by the lip."

nalu (na-LOO) *n.* Hawaiian for a wave; the surf. See "Ancient Hawaiian Surfing Terms" in Appendix A.

nami nori (NAH-mee NOR-ree) *n.* Japanese for surfing.

napper *n.* Anyone sleeping on the beach. (California, San Onofre Surf Club, 1940s)

nar *adj.* Short for GNARLY. (SP) Usage: "Those waves look pretty nar out there."

narly *adj.* GNARLY.

narrow nose *n.* A design used on a big-wave board so that offshore winds won't hold up surfers at the crest of a wave as they attempt to paddle into it.

nasodrain *n.* When the large quantity of seawater that is lodged in one's nasal passages as a result of the previous surf session empties out through one's nostrils in the space of a nanosecond. (SFG, 1990)

natural, natural foot, natural-footer *n.* A surfer (usually a right-handed one) who rides with the left foot forward; the opposite of a goofy foot. **—natural rider, natural surfer**

natural high *n.* The feeling you get from surfing.

nautical mile, international nautical mile *n.* A unit of distance designed to equal about 1 minute of arc of latitude; its length is 6,076.115 feet (1,852 meters), approximately 1.15 times as long as the statute mile of 5,280 feet. (GVS) See KNOT.

neap tides *n.* Tides of less-than-average magnitude that occur at the first and third quarters of the moon, when the sun and moon are at right angles to each other with respect to the earth, so that the sun's effect on the tides partially cancels the effect of the moon. (CCRG, WB) See SPRING TIDES.

nectar *n.* **1**) The juice, or energy, of a wave. **2**) Any fruit juice, such as papaya, passion fruit, or mango, especially after a surf; the **nectar of the goddess. 3**) *adj.* Sweet, like nectar; used to describe an attractive female. Usage: "She's really nectar." **—nectar betty**

needle nose *n.* The sharp pointed tip of a surfboard. See SHARKY.

neoprene *n.* **1**) The rubber used in the construction and repair of wetsuits. **2) neoprene rubber cement** The substance used to glue together and repair wetsuit seams, booties, etc.

Neptune's Revenge What you get when you drink too much salt water; derived from an instrumental surf tune by The Mermen (1990). Named after Neptune, the king of the ocean in Roman mythology.

New Zealand swells *n.* Southern-hemisphere swells caused by low pressure systems off Antarctica that develop to full strength just south of New Zealand. Whether California receives a southwest or a straight south swell depends on how far east

natural foot
Art: Robbie Quine

these storms continue to intensify. (BB 10/90)

nibbler *n.* Anyone eating at or near the beach. (California, San Onofre Surf Club, 1940s)

night surfing *n.* A unique nighttime experience, especially under a full moon. Tiny plankton (bioluminescent phosphorescence) that light up at night when disturbed can make a whole wave glow a bright lime green, adding a new dimension to tube riding. (W&B) This phenomenon occurs all over the world.

ninth-wave theory *n.* The notion that each ninth wave is the highest; generally not the case.

nip factor *n.* Much in evidence when the water gets a bit nippy. (Santa Cruz) Usage: "The nip factor today was way high."

nipple *adj.* Used to describe freezing cold water. (Santa Barbara) Usage: "It was nipple out there." —**nipson** (Newport Beach)

"No Fat Chicks" A slogan perpetuating anorexia, bulimia, speed walking, the dieting craze, and possibly other serious disorders yet to be seen; originated around 1980 in Santa Monica and Malibu and is used by brainless, superficial types who want to live in a society of Barbie dolls.

no-hesitation situation *n.* The split second that you have in which to make that drop down the wave face; otherwise you enter the TOADS zone. (RO)

no ka 'oi (no kah OY) Hawaiian for the best. Usage: *"Maui no ka 'oi."* ("Maui is the best.")

no one out 1) A joyous sight — perfect surf and nobody around to crowd it up. **2)** Possibly also a sign of bad surfing conditions, like maybe there's a reason nobody's out surfing.

no-paddle takeoff *n.* Rocking into a wave and catching it without having to paddle the board (A&M) — an extremely difficult maneuver.

no see 'ums *n.* Invisible biting insects encountered on shore in Baja and other parts of the globe. Vanilla is said to keep them away.

No Surfing The sign that every surfer hates to see. Some beaches have posted times or restricted areas for surfing.

noah *n.* Rhyming slang for *shark,* as in Noah's ark. (Australia, MW) Usage: "Did you see that noah out there?"

non *n.* A nonsurfer.

nonlocal *n.* Anyone who's not from the area. Same as UNLOCAL. See LOCAL.

nor'easters *n.* The prevailing summer winds along Australia's east coast. (MW)

North Shore The surf center of the planet Earth, located on Oahu, Hawaii; the proving grounds — site of a number of world-famous surf spots, including Haleiwa, Waimea, Pupukea, Pipeline, and Sunset. (GN)

north swell *n.* A swell that moves from north to south. (ORB)

north wind *n.* A wind that blows from north to south. (ORB)

nose *n.* **1)** The bow or front end of a surfboard. **2)** The tip of a board. **3)** The front third of a surfboard. (ORB)

nose guard *n.* A small, triangular silicone plastic cover that is glued onto the nose tip of contemporary surfboards and acts as a shock-absorbing bumper. It was developed by Island Classic Surfboards shaper Eric Arakawa and partner David Skedeleski in response to the increasing number of injuries from pointed nose tips. Because of its softness, the nose guard can also improve the safety of blunted noses. (ORB)

nose kick *n.* The upward curve, or rocker, in the front third of a surfboard.

nose ride or **nose-ride** *n.* **1**) Riding a longboard by putting one or both feet on the board's nose. **2**) Shooting across a hollow wave while standing on the nose of a board. (A&M) —**nose riding**, **noseriding**

nose rider *n.* **1**) A longboard with a rounded nose tip that makes it suitable for nose riding; originally created by Phil Edwards. **2**) A surfer who rides at the front end of a surfboard. (MM)

nose tip *n.* The pointed front end of a surfboard.

nose under, nosing *v.* To slip the front of a surfboard under water while riding a wave. Usage: "I was nosing under on that last section." See PEARL, PEARLING.

nose width *n.* A dimension used by shapers; measured twelve inches from the tip of the nose of the surfboard.

. . . not "I really like it . . . not" — a surfer's favorite way of turning a positive into a negative. Used on the "Saturday Night Live" TV skit "Wayne's World."

NSSA National Scholastic Surfing Association; the governing body of amateur surf competitions. Consists of seven conferences nationwide.

nuclear wave *n.* A wave generated by the explosion of a nuclear bomb. "Nuclear wave — if you can surf it, you can survive it" —John Leffingwell (Maybeck High School, Berkeley, California, 1978).

nugs *n.* Rippable waves — waves you can really tear into. (East Side, Santa Cruz; SFR, 8/90) See BUCKET O' NUGS.

nose ride
Herbie Fletcher
Photo: Rob Gilley

YAAAAAAAAAAAAAAAAAA AAAAAAA

nose ride
Art: I. B. Nelson

off-the-lip
Terry Simms
Photo: Bud Clark

o-double *v*. TO GO OFF, or surf radically; an abbreviation of "g double-o double-f," an expression that has fallen into disfavor. Usage: "Peter o-doubled his quarterfinal, but went down in the semis." (Santa Cruz; SFR, 1989)

oatmeals *n*. Little mushy waves. (Florida; TDW)

ocean *n*. **1**) The entire body of salt water that covers about 72 percent of the earth's surface. **2**) Any of the principal divisions of this body of water, including the Atlantic, Pacific, and Indian oceans, their southern extensions in Antarctica, and the Arctic Ocean. **3**) The source of a surfer's pleasure. See SEA.

The word *ocean* comes from the Latin *oceanus,* which came from the Greek *Okeanos,* in Greek mythology the god of the great outer sea thought of as a river encircling the earth. (AHD2, W9)

ocean briefs *n*. Monologuist Spaulding Gray's term for surf trunks in his performance piece, book, and film entitled *Swimming to Cambodia* (1985).

ocean consciousness *n*. Being in tune with the ocean, regardless of the activity — surfing, sailing, scuba diving, body surfing, living in close proximity to the beach, or whatever.

ocean energy *n*. Wave power in action; the juice of a breaking wave.

ocean pulse *n*. What Cheyne Horan says governs the rhythm of the sets and allows one to anticipate the bigger waves. (L&L)

"My soul is full of longing
For the secret of the sea,
And the heart of the great ocean
Sends a thrilling pulse through me."
—Henry Wadsworth Longfellow,
"The Secret of the Sea"

ocean roar *n*. **1**) The sound of the surf. See ROAR OF THE OCEAN.
2) **Ocean Roar** A California coastal community on Tomales Bay.

off its tits An Australian expression for outrageous; said of great surfing conditions. Usage: "The reef was off its tits yesterday."

off-the-bottom *n*. A maneuver in which the surfer springs from the bottom of a wave face up to the top.

off-the-face *n*. Any maneuver performed on the front of an advancing wave face.

off-the-lip *n*. **1**) A maneuver performed by cutting sharply up the wave face to a near vertical stall on the lip, then quickly turning down again. **2**) Snapping the board off the top of a wave. (MM)

off the Richter *adj*. A term used by surfers to describe something very good, or off the scale, as in "totally off the Richter." (Australia and USA; MW) Same as OFF ITS TITS, AWESOME, OUTRAGEOUS, TO THE MAX. See RICHTER.

off-the-top *n*. **1**) Smashing off the top of a wave lip. **2**) Turning on the top portion of the wave. (L&L)

off-the-wall *n*. **1**) A banking maneuver off of the wave face.
2) **Off-The-Wall** A Hawaiian surf spot. See OTW. **3**) **off the wall** The

ocean energy
Brian Bulkley
Photo: Don Balch

slogan on the back of Van's tennis shoes. **4)** *adj.* An early seventies expression meaning "outrageous."

offset or **off-set** *n.* A surfboard with an asymmetrical shape. (MF, 1967)

offshore *adv.* **1)** Refers to the direction of the wind, as in "offshore breeze" or "offshore wind." **2)** Used to indicate the location of a surf spot, such as an offshore island. **3)** Indicates a favorable wind condition. (JRW)

offshore breeze *n.* A lighter form of OFFSHORE WIND.

offshore wind *n.* Wind blowing away from shore, off the land, or from land to sea. In California, hot winds blowing offshore are called Santanas or devil winds. (A&M) See SANTA ANA WINDS.

An offshore wind creates the best conditions for good-quality waves. It smooths out the ocean's surface and causes the waves to hold up longer than usual and to hollow out before breaking. It also blows spray from the crest of the waves.

Oi! An exclamation like "Hey!" "Cowabunga!" or "Yo!"

oil spill, oil slick *n.* An environmental disaster that happens all too frequently today; usually caused by giant oil tankers running aground and disgorging their contents into the water. One of the consequences is damage to surf spots. See BLACK TIDE.

Two infamous oil spills that affected surfers were the huge Santa Barbara spill that coated beaches from Point Conception south in 1969 and the nearly 400,000-gallon spill of crude that stained the Orange County coastline in 1990.

olas *n.* Spanish for waves.
 —*olas grandes* (big waves)

old-man baggies *n.* Oversized surfing trunks. (A&M) See BAGGIES.

olo board *n.* A long surfboard used exclusively by ancient Hawaiian kings. (A&M) *Olo* means "thick" — and the boards were up to twenty feet long and weighed as much as 180 pounds. (DM) They were made from wili wili, ula, or koa wood.

omega fin *n.* A skeg designed so it won't grab kelp.

on the die 1) Used to describe a subsiding wave. Usage: "The wave was on the die." **2)** Said of a surfer who's about to eat it. Usage: "I was on the die."

on the nose *n.* Surfing in polluted waters. (Australia; MW) Same as YUK, WOOFY, SURFING UNDER TURD. Usage: "It was on the nose out there."

one eighty *n.* A 180-degree turn.

180-degree forehand turn *n.* After fading in a backhand direction, a turn back to the original tracking direction (RA); this shift is usually necessary to continue riding the wave.

one man–one wave One of the interference rules put into force for the ASP circuit at the beginning of the 1985/86 pro surfing season. (L&L) It dictates only one person on a wave at a time.

one-way board *n.* A board designed mainly for traveling in one direction. (MF, 1967)

onshore *adv.* Refers to the direction the wind is blowing. Usage: "It was completely onshore."

onshore breeze *n.* A light form of ONSHORE WIND.

onshore wind *n.* **1)** A wind that blows from sea to land. (ORB) **2)** A wind that blows from behind the waves. (MW)

ookei nami (OH-key NAH-me) *n.* Japanese for big wave.

open door *n.* A wave that has no close-out sections. (Australia; L&L)

offshore wind
Puerto Escondido, Mexico
Photo: Woody Woodworth

oil slick
Art: Rick Stover

opposing current *n*. An ocean current that is flowing against the direction that a swell is traveling. An opposing current decreases wave lengths and increases wave heights, thus steepening the wave face — the opposite effect of a following current. (DKM)

. . . or what? A slang expression of enthusiasm. "Or what?" is the last phrase of a rhetorical question, and implies an affirmative answer. Usage: "Is that a great sunset, or what?" "Are we playing cards, or what?" (LMY)

OTA Optimum tanning angle — positioning one's body in direct line with the sun in order to absorb the maximum amount of sun rays.

OTW The abbreviation for OFF-THE-WALL, the Hawaiian surf spot where Shaun Tomson's tube riding was made famous in the 1978 movie *Free Ride*.

"Our Mother Ocean" (**OMO**) *n*. A monthly column in *Surfer* magazine on the environment; has the slogan "To Save Our Mother Ocean."

out *adv*. Used to mean "to go out surfing." Usage: "I went out today at Black's." —a **go-out**

out of control 1) Said of a surfer who is unable to control the board as he or she is coming down a wave. **2**) Heading for a wipeout. Usage: "He's out of control." **3**) Said of a gnarly wave. Usage: "That wave's out of control."

out of sight *adj*. The greatest, terrific.

out the back *adv*. **1**) To be outside, or seaward, of the breaking waves. (Australia) **2**) To be behind where the waves are breaking.

outboard *n*. The direction or side of a surfboard away from the wall of a wave. Usage: "I caught my outboard rail on the wave."

outer reef *n*. OUTSIDE REEF.

outrageous, outrageous to the max *adj*. Incredible; said of unbelievable waves, food, or women.

outside *n*. **1**) Seaward of the breaking waves. An **outside wave** is one that unexpectedly breaks outside the surf zone. **2**) An area beyond which most set waves are breaking. (ORB) **3**) A position beyond the line of breaking waves or outside the lineup. (NAT, 1985) Same as OUT THE BACK. **4**) A warning cry. When you're out in the water and someone yells "Outside!" it usually means there's a big set approaching the break. (MW)

outside break *n*. The area farthest from shore where the waves are breaking. See INSIDE BREAK.

outside rail *n*. The edge of the board closest to the shore. (L&L)

outside reef *n*. **1**) A reef farther out to sea, beyond the inner reef. **2**) A surf spot that breaks beyond the first reef. (GN) Also called OUTER REEF.

over the falls 1) To be trapped in the plunging lip of a wave, hurled to the bottom, and sometimes sucked up the wave face and launched again — an unpleasant experience. Being poured over with the descending water, from the top of the breaking wave to the bottom, is like going over a waterfall. **2**) To topple off the very top of a wave instead of riding it out. (IDSM) **3**) To free-fall with the breaking lip of a hollow wave. (A&B) Usage: "I got sucked over the falls on that last one."

over the hill, over the hillers *n*. A derogatory expression for surfers who drive to Santa Cruz from San Jose or elsewhere in the San Francisco Bay Area via Highway 17 through the Santa Cruz Mountains.

overgunned *adj*. Riding a board that's too big for the surf, for instance a seven-foot-plus surfboard in three-foot waves (SFR, 10/83); the opposite of being underboarded.

THERE'S NOT MUCH OF A SHOULDER BUT IT'S A HECK OF A DROP !!

YOSEMITE FALLS 2,870 FT

over the falls
Art: I. B. Nelson

overhead *adv*. Used to describe waves higher than a surfer is tall — nice. **Double overhead** is even nicer. Usage: "It was double overhead for about two hours."

overlap *n*. The place along the rails of a surfboard where top and bottom layers of fiberglass converge; **double overlap** is stronger.

Oz *n*. Another name for Australia, as in *The Land of Oz*.

Pacific High *n*. A very large high pressure system off the West Coast of California that influences weather.

Pacific Ocean *n*. The largest ocean in the world with a surface area of 63.8 million square miles; bounded on the east by the continents of the Americas, on the north by the Bering Strait, on the west by a line from the Malay Peninsula through Cape Londonderry in Australia and Tasmania, then along meridian 147E to Antarctica. The Pacific includes all adjacent semienclosed seas that connect with it. (GVS)

paddle 1) *v*. To lie in the center of a board and take deep rhythmic strokes through the water. (WWK) **2**) **paddling** *n*. A means of propelling a surfboard through water; arm stroking. (MF)

paddle gloves, paddling gloves *n*. Gloves specially designed to create a wider paddling surface to help surfers catch waves; same as WEBBED PADDLING GLOVES.

paddle out *v*. **1**) To stroke out through the incoming surf to the lineup. See OUTSIDE. **2**) **Paddle out!** An exclamation used to signal fellow surfers that an outside set of waves is approaching. (Byron Bay, Australia) Same as OUTSIDE!

paddle out reentry *n*. A difficult-to-pull-off longboard maneuver requiring the surfer to stroke up the face of a wave that is just about to break and turn the board around with the advancing wave. (BBD)

paddle takeoff *n*. Stroking with one's arms to catch a wave on a skim board. (TLH) See NO-PADDLE TAKEOFF.

paddleboard *n*. A square-sided, hollow surf craft invented by Tom Blake

paddleboard
13-foot hollow plywood
Photo: Tom Servais / Surfer Magazine

in 1926 at Waikiki. It is usually constructed of plywood and is used in long-distance racing competitions.

paddler *n.* Someone who rides a paddleboard. (GN)

paipo, paipo board (PAY-po) *n.* A small polyurethane-foam bellyboard used in the Hawaiian Islands.

papa nui (pa-pa NU-ee) *n.* A Hawaiian term that literally means "big surfboard" but is loosely applied to big surf or a big surf site.

paradise *n.* In the eyes of a surfer, the ultimate tropical island reef break.

paraffin *n.* A waxy-like substance that is commonly applied on the deck of a surfboard to reduce slickness. Unlike modern surf wax, paraffin doesn't rip hair from the legs and chest. (DWK)

pass *v.* To sleep. Usage: "Are you gonna get **passious**?" (North San Diego County; LH)

passmodious *adj.* Really tired. (North San Diego County; LH)

patience *n.* The most important word in ding repair. (GCD)

PCH The abbreviation for Pacific Coast Highway, a section of California's Highway 1, which passes by Malibu.

peak *n.* **1)** The highest point of an advancing wave, marking the spot where the wave will begin to spill, break, or plunge. **2)** A narrow, humping wave that has little wall and that generally tapers fast from the middle or high point of the wave to almost flat on the shoulders; produced by a triangular reef or sandbank. **3)** A wedge-shaped wall of water that throws out as the wave breaks. **4)** The best spot for the takeoff; for example, Sunset Beach, Hawaii, is famous for its peak. **5)** The part of the wave over the shallowest section of an undulating bottom. (MW)

peak
Larry Blair at Pipeline, Hawaii
Photo: Bob Barbour

peak break *n.* One of several kinds of surf breaks; distinguished by waves that form peaks at the point at which they begin to break. Usually associated with a reef or sandbar. See SURF BREAKS.

peak surf, peaking surf *n.* **1)** Waves whose tops form peaks. (MF) **2)** Waves that peak up due to the shape of the sea bottom. (WWK)

peak takeoff *n.* A takeoff on the highest and steepest part of a wave.

peak up *v.* (Said of a swell) To begin to build up to break. Usage: "The waves peak up at low tide."

peaking tide *n.* The phase when the tide is approaching its highest or its lowest point.

peaky *adj.* Said of irregular wave crests caused by a cross swell (WB); hard to line up in.

pearl, pearling *v.* **1)** To catch or bury the nose of the board in the water; usually occurs on a takeoff and is caused by the steepness of the wave or because the surfer has put too much weight toward the front of the board. (MM, A&M) Usage: "I pearled on that last one." Called in Australia going DOWN THE MINE. (DSHJ) **2)** To nose the surfboard under a wave. (IDSM) —**pearl dive, pearl diving**

pecking order *n.* **1)** Seniority at a given surf spot. **2)** How you figure out whose turn it is to ride; determined by many factors, including paddling strength and just waiting your turn.

The tradition of pecking order goes back to the earliest days of surfing. In the early 1960s, when there were more people capable of riding than there were waves, no one wanted to share waves. The pecking order at point breaks and reefs is easy to figure out because takeoff areas are small and well-defined. At beach breaks or peaks that shift, pecking order begins with the person in the best position to get the best ride. If there's more than one surfer in position, whoever has waited longest for a ride (on an equal-quality wave) should get it. A hyperjerk who out-positions someone who's been waiting longer has no respect for pecking order. (HJP)

• •

peel 1) *v.* (Of a wave) To break fast from end to end. (MM) **2) peeler** *n.* A fast, curling wave that curls perfectly without sectioning ahead. **3) peeling** *adj.* Typical of the way good surfing waves break. (A&B) Usage: "Look at those peeling waves."

peel-off *n.* CUTOUT; turning back off the shoulder of a wave to terminate a ride.

Pendleton, Pendleton shirt *n.* A brightly colored plaid wool shirt worn by some surfers; originally popular in the fifties and sixties but still considered a stylish article of clothing.

peninsula *n.* A projection of land into a body of water, for example, the Palos Verdes or Monterey peninsulas in California.

perfect *adj.* Said of nice waves. Usage: "It was a perfect six foot with no one out." —**perfect conditions**

perfect wave *n.* A wave that files off, or peels, with mechanical perfection. (A&M) The movie *The Endless Summer* (1964) involved a search for "the perfect wave," discovered at Cape St. Francis.

• •

"Remember, there are no perfect people, perfect relationships, etc., just perfect waves."
—Filenea Bahris (1990)

• •

perfection *n.* Perfect waves, a perfect surfing day, flawlessness.

period *n.* **1)** The time interval between the passing of two wave crests; same as WAVE PERIOD, SWELL PERIOD. **2)** The time between sets — a relatively calm period.

peroxide, hydrogen peroxide *n.* A bleach; commonly used in the 1960s to achieve instant surfer blonde.

pet the cat, petting the cat *v.* The motion of a surfer who crouches down and strokes the air or water to get through a section; doesn't create speed and has no functional purpose, but everyone does it. Usage: "Bro, you never saw Derek Ho pet the cat at Pipe, right?" (New Jersey and East Coast; SFR, 1989)

peter heater *n.* Urinating in a wetsuit.

Petroleum Transfer Engineer *n.* An impressive-sounding job description for any surfer who works at a gas station; a euphemism for gas station attendant. (San Juan Capistrano; JRN)

pick up, picking up *v.* (Said of the waves) To get bigger. Usage: "The surf is picking up."

pidgin *n.* A simplified mixture of two or more languages, used for communication between groups speaking different languages. In Hawaiian Pidgin English, for example, *da* means "the," and so on.

pier *n.* An elevated structure projecting out into the ocean, most commonly used for fishing and boat access; sometimes blocks the wind.

pier break *n.* Waves breaking near or underneath a pier. See SHOOTING THE PIER.

pier hook *n.* A wave that is hooking or curling as it goes through a pier. Such a wave is very fast and permits little error when riding it.

pier out *v.* To hide behind the pier pilings while waiting for calm periods in which to make it out to the surf. (Manhattan Beach; anonymous bodyboarder dudette, 1990)

pig, pig board *n.* A surfboard with an extremely pointed nose and the

Pendleton
Photo: Tom Servais / Surfer Magazine

...There's only one thing wrong with surfing that pier...

Art: Jim Phillips

greatest width toward the rear (wide hips and a broad tail).

pigment *n.* An opaque coloring agent for resin. (ORB)

piling *n.* A large cement or wooden pillar used in the construction of a pier. See SHOOTING THE PIER.

piña colada *n.* **1)** A flavor for every-thing — surf wax, lip balm, suntan oil, etc. **2)** An alcoholic beverage, containing pineapple and coconut juices mixed with rum.

pineapple juice *n.* **1)** A rain squall in Hawaii. **2)** A tasty beverage made from the fruit of the pineapple.

pintail or **pin-tail** *n.* A surfboard configuration characterized by a reduced-area tail section that comes rather sharply to a point.

pipe *n.* **1)** The inside curve of a wave that creates a tunnel. (MM) Same as TUBE, BARREL. **2) Pipe** Short for PIPE-LINE.

pipe cleaner or **pipecleaner** *n.* A surfboard that has been tube ridden. (SFG, 2/90) See TUBE RIDER.

Pipe shots *n.* A surf photographer's term for Pipeline pictures.

pipeline *n.* **1)** A very long and large TUBE. **2)** The curl of a breaking wave that spreads onto each shoulder of the wave so rapidly that the rolling water resembles a pipe. (DSHJ)

Pipeline *n.* **1)** Probably the most famous wave in the world, located on the North Shore of Oahu, Hawaii, between Waimea Bay and Sunset Beach, off Ehukai Beach Park. **2)** Site of the annual Pipeline Masters surfing competition held in December. **3)** A classic instrumental surf tune by the Chantays from Santa Ana, California, in December 1962; it got to #4 on the charts in the spring of 1963. Other notable versions include those of the Ventures in 1963 and of Agent Orange in 1982.

pintail
Photo: Tom Servais / Surfer Magazine

Originally named by Bruce Brown, Pipeline was renamed Banzai Beach by John Severson. Then it became Banzai Pipeline, and now it's back to Pipeline again — Pipe for short. Pipeline is famous for its tube ride; deep-water swells hit the extremely shallow reef very quickly, making the waves hollow. The first person to surf it was Phil Edwards in December 1961; Outside Pipeline was first ridden by Greg Noll on January 3, 1964. (GN)

pipeliner *n.* Any surfboard that has been ridden at Banzai Pipeline, Hawaii. (SFG, 2/90)

pit *n.* **1)** The crashing foam of a breaking wave adjacent to the smooth shoulder of the wave. See GETTING STUFFED IN THE PIT. **2) The Pit** An area just north of the Malibu Pier, along a chain-link fence near a wall on the beach where the heavies used to hang out in the 1960s (KSO); known for its graffiti.

pitch *v.* A term used to describe the way the top part of a wave jacks up (gains height) and throws forward, caused by the wave suddenly mov-ing from deep into shallow water. (MW) Usage: "Look at that pitching barrel."

pitched, getting pitched *v.* Get-ting thrown or tossed off of one's board. (MDF)

pivot point *n.* The general area near the center of the surfboard that the surfer turns on.

pivot roll *n.* A surfing maneuver involving rolling with the wave.

pivot turn *n.* A very sharp turn.

planer, power planer *n.* A hand-held power tool used by shapers to remove foam from blanks quickly, easily, and accurately. (ORB)

planing *n.* A long, steady ride on a steep wave in which the board-to-wave angle is small. A portion of the forward end of the board may be partially supported by the flow of air rising up the face of the wave.

planing surface *n.* The bottom of the surfboard — the part that skims on the top of the water.

plank *n.* The name given to heavy, unmaneuverable boards, usually referring to the redwood giants ridden prior to the 1950s. **—redwood plank**

planshape *n.* The outline of a surfboard when viewed from above. (MF) Same as TEMPLATE.

plow *v.* A surfer term for sexual intercourse. (Marin County, California)

plug *n.* **1)** A small cup cut into the surfboard so that a shock cord can be attached. See LEASH CUP. **2)** A piece of foam cut into a wedge to repair a surfboard.

plugged *adj.* Used to describe a crowded surf spot. Usage: "The place was really plugged." (GN)

plunging breaker *n.* A kind of wave where the crest falls in front of the lower part of wave, rather than spilling down the face — the most dynamic, exciting manifestation of wave action on the ocean. (DKM)

pocket *n.* **1)** The portion of the wave inside the curl. **2)** The portion high on the wave wall as the lip begins to curl over. (RA) **3)** The part of a wave under the breaking lip. (NAT, 1985) **4)** The point on the wall of a breaking wave where the maximum power for surfing is found. **—deep pocket**

pocket beach *n.* A small, crescent-shaped beach inside a cove or between rocky headlands, often inundated at high tide. (CCRG)

pocket surfing, surfing in the pocket *n.* Riding in or near the curl — fundamental to the modern shortboard era because the shortboards of today are incapable of maintaining their momentum out on the shoulder of a wave. (L&L)

pod 1) *v.* To pass out. Usage: "He's poddin'." "He's fully podded." **2) POD** *n.* Passed-out dude. (LH)

point *n.* Refers to a jutting piece of land or the surf breaking directly off of it.

point break *n.* A type of surf break where waves wrap around a promontory and peel as they break; sometimes occurs in combination with a reef break. Rincon Point, just south of the Santa Barbara/Ventura county line in California, is a classic example of a point break. See BEACH BREAK, SURF BREAKS.

point break
Rincon Point, California
Photo: Don Balch

point grinder *n.* **1)** A tubular wave that spits and breaks off of a point with a grinding, churning motion. **2)** In the movie *Big Wednesday* (1978), a girl from The Point who is widely acclaimed for her amorous activities. (A&M)

point surf *n.* Surf breaking off a point. (MF) Same as POINT BREAK.

pole set *n.* Waves breaking adjacent to or immediately inside of a large pole jutting out of the water at Ala Moana on Oahu, Hawaii.

political waves *n.* What surfers make when their salty playground is threatened by pollution and overdevelopment. (FLD)

pollution in the ocean *n.* In some areas, an inescapable part of modern surfing. Surfers variously describe the experience of surfing in polluted waters as YUK, WOOFY, FLOATIES, SHIT PIPE, SURFING UNDER TURD, ON YOUR NOSE, and SURFING WITH POO.

poly or **pollie** *n.* FOAMIE.

polyester resin *n.* A liquid plastic widely used in surfboard construction; mixed with a catalyst and accelerator to form the hard outer shell, or skin, of the board.

Polynesian Paralysis (**PP**) *n.* A tropical malaise to which surfers are particularly susceptible. An attack of the PPs can mean almost total inca-

pollution in the ocean
Art: Peter Spacek

pacitation for up to a week. Apart from surfing four to six hours a day, the victim lies motionless on the hotel-room floor watching television and drinking six-packs of beer. Speech, thought, or personal hygiene are out of the question until the fever passes. (JARR)

polyurethane board, polyurethane foam board *n.* THE modern surfboard. See FOAM.

polyurethane foam, polyfoam *n.* A type of plastic foam (a petroleum by-product) that is commonly used in the construction of surfboards. (ASKC, 1965)

pop up, popping up *v.* (Of waves) To jack up suddenly over a shallow spot.

popeye *n.* Someone who exhibits above-average paddling strength, no doubt due to the regular ingestion of pounds of spinach. (Santa Monica; LJE)

popout or **pop-out** *n.* A relatively inexpensive mass-produced surfboard made in the early sixties by molding foam and fiberglass mat together. Popouts were cheap (because they involved little handwork), heavy, and weak; the process was abandoned, and the term is obsolete.

popping air off the lip *v.* To do an aerial; same as SLASHING OFF THE LIP. (RO) Usage: "Bro, I was fully popping air off the lip."

Portuguese man-of-war, man-o'-war (*Hydrozoa physalia physalis*) *n.* A stinging jellyfish indigenous to warm seas and having a bluish, bladderlike float from which are suspended numerous long stinging tentacles capable of inflicting severe injury (AHD2); found off Florida, in the Caribbean, etc. Also called BLUE BOTTLE (in New Zealand and Australia). See LIT-UP.

poser, surf poser *n.* **1**) A would-be surfer; someone who only dresses

post session nasal drip
Art: Karen T. Delgadillo

the part. (MM) **2**) An imitation surfer. (JP) —**pousuer**

post-session nasal drip (PSND) *n.* A gushing of sea water out of the nasal passages; this almost always occurs after a grueling skim session while talking to an extremely fine girl. (Santa Monica; RC) Same as FAUCET NOSE, NASODRAIN.

potato chip *n.* CHIP or CHIP BOARD.

pounder *n.* **1**) A hard-breaking wave; a wave that breaks with **pounding ferocity**. **2**) A big perfect wave. —**poundah** (Hawaiian Pidgin)

pour it on *v.* To trim a board on a wave and assume a stance that achieves maximum speed and control.

pour over 1) *v.* What a wave does when it breaks. **2**) **pour-over** *n.* An over-the-falls wipeout, in which the surfer gets caught and goes over with the breaking wave into the white water.

powah surf *n.* A Hawaiian term for spots that get heavy surf.

power move *n.* **1**) Any impressive maneuver on a wave, such as a "power cutback." (CC) **2**) **power surfing** Making big moves. **3**) **power it** *v.* A seventies term for doing just about anything, as in "to power a sandwich."

power pocket, power section *n.* That part of the wave closest to the curl.

power set *n.* Big waves.

"Pray for Surf" A caption that appeared on many surfing publications in the 1960s.

premium waves *n.* Waves with good size and shape and the potential for high scoring in competitive surfing contests. See WAVE SELECTION.

press, pressing *v.* **1**) When a rider on the outside (away from the curl) is crowded by a rider on the inside (near the curl). **2**) Any crowding while riding.

pressure ding *n.* COMPRESSION DING.

primo *adj.* Top rate. Usage: "The waves are gonna be really primo-bitchin' today."

Primo beer *n.* A Hawaiian brew that is no longer produced.

priority *n.* The right to the first or next wave in a surfing contest because you 1) have won the toss of a coin; 2) have paddled around the priority buoy; or 3) have the position closest to the curl.

priority buoy *n.* A brightly colored float anchored in the water outside the break and used in competitive surfing to determine who has the right-of-way on the next waves. Also called EIGHT BALL. See GETTING BEHIND THE EIGHT BALL.

. . . .

The old rule for right-of-way was that whoever was on the inside had it. Then in 1982, Peter Townend and Ian Cairns unveiled the priority buoy system at the first Op Pro surf contest in California. Originally, after each surfer had completed one ride, the first to paddle back outside and around the buoy had the choice of the following waves. This changed with the 1984/85 ASP World Tour season, when the first priority for every heat began to be decided by the toss of a coin. Thereafter in the heat, the first surfer who paddles out and around the priority buoy has the right-of-way on the upcoming wave.

. . . .

private beach *n.* An exclusive property right that in California and certain other areas of the world extends only to the mean high tide line.

pro circuit board (PCB) *n.* A surfboard made from a foam-sandwich mold, developed by veteran super-shaper Bob McTavish in the late 1980s based on a technique first developed for use with sailboards. A double foam-layer shell is glued up using a vacuum mold and then injected with expanding polystyrene foam; then a polyester gel coat is sprayed on to give the board a color design. Because a mold is used, a perfect copy can be made of any surfboard or shaped blank and reproduced as a PCB. A high-density foam reduces the weight of the boards to about five or six pounds. (SFG, 2/90)

professional surfing *n.* Born in the late 1970s. See ASP.

projection *n.* Thrusting out of a turn. Usage: "Did you see the projection he got on that wave?"

prone out or **prone-out** *v.* **1**) To ride one's board to the beach by lying down and holding on to the rails, often done to get ashore safely through heavy surf. **2**) To drop back to a prone position to keep from being knocked off the board when paddling out. **3**) To straighten out in front of a wave and lie down on the board, rather than risk being separated from the board in the turmoil of white water. Usage: "I had to prone out through the white water."

prone position *n.* Lying outstretched and stomach down on a surfboard.

prone turn *n.* Angling one's board while lying down by dropping one foot in the water. The right foot will turn the board right, the left foot will turn it left.

Proplugs *n.* Dr. Scott's ear plugs (with leash) from Santa Cruz; worn for the prevention of surfer's ear.

prosecuted *v.* To get wiped out to the fullest extent. Usage: "Guy got *prosecuted* on that wave." (LH) See SURF CRIMES.

protected *adj.* Describes any surf spot that is sheltered from wind by kelp, a cove, etc.

PSAA Professional Surfing Association of America; founded by Joey Buran in 1985.

pseud *n.* Australian slang for PSEUDO. (JARR)

pseudo, pseudo surfer *n.* Someone who only pretends to be a surfer.

psyched out *v.* To be mentally incapacitated; to be overcome with fear. Generally refers to a surfer's reaction to big surf.

pterygium *n.* An eye ailment caused by exposure to sun and surf; the medical term for SURFER'S EYE.

Puertas Abiertas A surf spot on Isla Natividad off Baja; means "open doors" in Spanish. See OPEN DOOR.

puff *n.* WIND SQUALL.

puka *n.* Hawaiian for hole; used as a substitute for DING.

puka shells, puka-shell necklace *n.* An adornment worn by many surfers in the 1970s. Mike Purpus began wearing these tiny white shells in 1973. (SFG, 11/89)

pull back *v.* To abort a takeoff to prevent the nose of the board from going underwater.

pull into a wave *v.* To drop down the face of a wave and turn back up for a ride. Usage: "Dane is pulling into a monster wave."

pull off *v.* To succeed in making a maneuver. Usage: "Did you see me pull off that last move?"

pull out *v.* **1)** To steer a board over or through the back of a wave in order to end a ride. **2)** To exit a wave. (MM) **3)** To exit through the bottom of the wall of a wave, with board and body moving in the same direction. (L&L) **4) pullout** *n.* A maneuver to guide the board out of a wave. (WWK) Same as CUT OUT.

pull root *v.* To masturbate; what surfers do when there are no waves. The term came up in a conversation with an Italian surfer that was carried on mostly in sign language. When asked what he did when there were no waves (which is almost always in Italy), he promptly responded with an up-and-down movement around his groin area. (P)

pulled template *n.* A surfboard that, viewed from above, is narrower than normal. See FULL TEMPLATE.

Pump House Gang, The Tom Wolfe's second collection of essays (1968), named after a "California surfing elite" at Windansea, La Jolla. The book was critically attacked by surfers, who over the years have inspired such graffiti as "Tom Wolfe is a dork!"

pump out *v.* To break vigorously, as in a point that "pumps out" some pretty unreal waves.

pump the board *v.* To extend a ride through small surf by swinging the board back and forth to keep up momentum. See HOP.

pump turn *n.* A hopping motion that generates forward momentum in a slow section of the wave. In surf contests, a pump turn lacks the scoring potential of other turns because it maintains horizontal direction and doesn't make a significant climbing or dropping direction change — that is, less than 60 degrees. (L&L)

pumping *v.* When huge powerful waves break in consistent intervals, or come one after another; going strong. —**pumpeen, pom-ping to da max** (Hawaiian Pidgin)

pumping down the line *v.* To work one's board along the wave to extract the most energy out of a fast ride.

punch through *v.* To negotiate an oncoming wave. See PUSH THROUGH.

punchy *adj.* Used to describe a wave that delivers a full blow; some waves are punchier than others. Usage: "The waves are a bit punchy." (Newcastle Surf Shop, Australia)

push through *v.* **1)** Originally meant to get your surfboard through a wave by climbing off the board and, holding on to the rear of the board, pushing it ahead of you through the wave; now means to get through the surf or white water by any means whatsoever.   **2**) To paddle the board seaward through broken waves.   **3**) To paddle out through the surf by ducking under incoming waves. (MM) Same as PUNCH THROUGH.

pushing the limits *v.* Going beyond one's personal limitations while surfing. —**pushing it to da max** (Hawaiian Pidgin)

pushing it to da max
Art: The Pizz

quad
**Willy Morris and Al Merrick,
Ventura, California, 1983**
Photo: Bob Barbour

Quasimoto
Mickey Muñoz

Q-cel *n*. A resin additive designed to take up maximum volume with minimum resin; makes an excellent filler to keep weight down. (GCD)

quad *n*. A 1980s term for a four-fin surfboard.

quakers *n*. Big waves. (Florida, TDW)

quaper (QWAY-per) *n*. A wave that is a quantum leap beyond a gaper. Usage: "Dude, that wave was the full quaper. You were six feet back and you're still hair-dry!" (North San Diego County; SFR, 1989)

quash *v*. To make void; a legal term applied to the sport of surfing. (ECN) Usage: "That wave totally quashed me." See SURF CRIMES.

Quasimoto, The Quasimoto *n*. A hot-dog riding stance invented by Mickey Muñoz; performed riding on the nose of a surfboard in a crouched, hunchback position with one arm stretched forward and the other arm stretched to the rear.

The term derives from the name Quasimodo, the hunchback of the title in Victor Hugo's novel *The Hunchback of Notre Dame*. However, in *John Severson's First Annual Surf Photo Book* in 1960 (the first issue of *Surfer* magazine), it was spelled "Quasimoto," and that spelling stuck. In surfing, the term is Quasi*moto*, not Quasi*modo*.

queber *n*. GEEK. (MM)

Queen Mary *n*. A board too big for the rider, one that is usually very large and buoyant.

quimby *n*. Pencilneck geek, dork, idiot (boogie boarder); mom drops you off at the beach in a station wagon, you get nosebleeds and have allergies. (Oxnard; TJ)

quiver *n*. An assortment or collection of different surfboards to accommodate varying wave conditions, like a quiver of arrows.

Quonset hut *n*. A prefabricated World War II shelter with a semicircular arching roof of corrugated metal that served as basic lodging for early big-wave riders at Makaha; also used for surf stomps in Southern California.

quiver
**Martin Potter, North Shore,
Hawaii**
Photo: John S. Callahan

R&D *n*. Research and development — what surfers do when looking for new surf spots, especially on expeditions to places like Baja.

RCMs *n*. RADICAL CONTROLLED MANEUVERS.

rabbit-ear skeg *n*. A twin skeg, joined at the base and designed to increase holding power on sharp turns as well as minimize spinouts.

rack flyer *n*. A surfboard that you forget to tie down on the roof rack of your car and that becomes airborne when you drive away. (RBS)

rad *adj*. Super cool; short for RADICAL. Usage: "Those waves were rad!" —**way rad**

radical *adj*. **1**) Heavy-duty, extreme, outrageous. (WWK) **2**) PUSHING THE LIMITS; going for broke. (A&M) **3**) Used to describe a difficult surfing maneuver or an outrageous surfing style. (MM; NAT, 1985) — **totally radical, super radical, radical turn, radical bottom turn**

radical controlled maneuvers *n*. The highest scoring component of the ASP criteria for judging a surf contest; RCMs for short.

. . . .

Walking around and posing may have been popular surfing moves in the sixties, but competitive surfing judges want to see more defined moves now. Originally two factors distinguished a radical maneuver commitment and positioning. "Controlled" was added in 1985. (L&L)

. . . .

radical maneuvers *n*. In competitive surfing, dynamic moves with a high degree of difficulty. (L&L)

radio weather channel *n*. The most accurate and up-to-date information available to most surfers, including the positioning of lows and highs, the size and direction of swells and seas, and wind velocities. (W&B) See WEATHER RADIO.

rage *v*. GO OFF; refers to a surfer. Usage: "I fully raged on that wave."

rager *n*. A good surfer party. (CVG) Usage: "That was a real rager last night." —**raging**

raging surf *n*. Really big waves.

rail *n*. The rounded side or outside edge of a surfboard. Usage: "Feel the rails on this board."

rail apex *n*. The point where the rail meets the tip of the surfboard nose.

rail design *n*. The shape of a surfboard rail; a crucial element in overall surfboard design in that the rails direct water flow and aid in turning. There are many different rail designs, but broadly they can be divided into hard rail (those with a sharply defined edge on the board's underside) and soft rail (those that are rounded above and below).

rail grab *n*. Holding onto the outside rail of the surfboard with your hand while crouching and tracking in critical situations; adds to stability. (RA) See GRAB THE RAIL.

rail line *n*. The outside edge of a surfboard. (ORB)

rail radius *n*. The curve joining the top and bottom of a surfboard.

rack flyer
"Did I check the racks before we left?"
Art: I. B. Nelson

rager
Simon Anderson after he won the Pipe in 1981, celebrating with Rabbit
Photo: Don Balch

rail sandwich
Photo: Fred Swegles

rail saver
Photo: Don Balch

rail-to-rail transition
Art: I. B. Nelson

rail sandwich *n.* A surfboard between the legs. (A&M)

rail saver *n.* A flat nylon strap, one to two inches wide and eight to ten inches in length, used to prevent the leash from tearing into the rail. (ORB) A rail saver is attached between the board and the leash.

rail shift *n.* The shifting of one's weight from one rail to the other, something done during every cutback but rarely accomplished in the tube. Same as RAIL-TO-RAIL TRANSITION.

rail slash *n.* Carving a sharp turn so that the rail digs into the wave and casts a spray.

"I hope the current phase of surf/body English is soon massacred by the surf media so we can all get on with doing some hard core rail slashes for the public instead of breakdancing performances for them and fooling ourselves." —Mitch Thorson (TRKS, 6/89)

rail-to-rail transition, rail-to-rail turn *n.* RAIL SHIFT.

rain squall *n.* A brief period of rain, usually lasting a few minutes or less; sometimes heavy, and sometimes accompanied by strong winds; a common occurrence in the tropics. Same as SQUALL. See WIND SQUALL.
—blinding rain squall

"Just relax folks, it's pure pineapple juice." —Surf contest announcer Lord Tally Ho Sanders describing a rain squall at Sunset Beach, Hawaii, in December 1982

raize *v.* To bother someone or give them verbal abuse. Usage: "If that guy raizes on me one more time I'm gonna rub Vaseline over his wax." (SFG, 12/81)

rake *n.* The way the fin area is arranged in relation to the fin base. (ORB) See FIN RAKE.

rakeback skeg *n.* A fin with its lower extremity or axis angled toward the rear.

Ranch, the *n.* A well-known collection of surf spots offshore of the Hollister and Bixby ranches between Santa Barbara and the Vandenburg Air Force Base.

rapper *n.* A wave that you ride into on a skimboard and get barreled in as it breaks over the top of you. (TLH)

rappin' *adj.* **1**) Used to describe a wave as it pours over. (KTD) Usage: "The lip was fully rappin'." **2**) Said of a swell that bends or wraps around a point. See WAVE REFRACTION.

rash guard *n.* A thin, short-sleeve stretch-lycra jersey worn to protect against skin irritation caused by the body rubbing against a wetsuit and a surfboard; can be worn as an undergarment beneath a wetsuit or by itself in warm waters for sun protection. Some of the newer wetsuits have a rash-guard lining. See BOARD RASH.

rat pack *n.* Surfing competitors vying for top place or recognition. (L&L)

rave *n.* After a good session, five to ten minutes of indulgence during which surfers go on about the unbelievability of their performance and about what a great pity it is that no one saw the barrel roll three sixty they pulled off up the beach a bit. (JARR)

raw *adj.* Happening, hot, cool; similar to LIVE. Usage: "That's *raw.*"

rays *n.* **1**) Sun rays. Usage: "Let's catch some rays." **2**) STINGRAYS. **3**) **ray** A stingray bicycle used as a beach bomber or beach cruiser.

reach-for-the-sky reentries *n.* Coming high off the wave with arms reaching straight up in the air — as if signaling a touchdown — and then dropping back down. See REENTRY.

real surfer *n*. Somone who meets a well-defined set of criteria concerning ocean, surf, and other life experiences. See "Real Surfers" on page 98.

really *adv*. Truly, as in "really primo-bitchin' surf."

rebound *n*. A turn off of the lip or white water of a wave. See RICOCHET.

rebound wave *n*. An outgoing wave, one going away from the beach. (TLH)

reckless abandon *n*. **1**) Surfing with wild style. **2**) A go-for-it attitude.

recovery *n*. Standing up again after having lost footing. (L&L)

red hot *adj*. Fantastic, awesome, the best, hard-core. Usage: "The surf here gets red hot in the summer."

red-hot surfing *n*. Hard-core surfing; performing at a high degree of excellence.

red tide *n*. **1**) A misnomer for a phenomenon that is neither a tide nor necessarily red; the sea may take on colors ranging from dirty brown to reds and violets, or it may show no discoloration at all. A "red tide" is caused by a high concentration of minute organisms called dinoflagellates, whose population explosion, or "bloom," produces a toxin that can kill off huge amounts of fish. It is also responsible for paraletic shellfish poisoning (PSP), which may be harmful to humans who eat shellfish during quarantine months. (OA, P) **2**) That time of the month. (SP)

Red Triangle *n*. In Northern California, the offshore area between Monterey (including Santa Cruz), the Farallon Islands off San Francisco, and Tomales Bay in Marin County that has the highest number of reported great white shark attacks in the world.

redirection *n*. Changing directions while surfing. Usage: "Look at that scorching redirection."

redwood plank *n*. A premodern surfboard; generally used in the early 1900s and in the 1940s in Santa Cruz.

reeds *n*. **1**) A kind of pants worn by surfers that extend just below the knee. (IDSM) **2**) BAGGIES from the 1950s; made by the wife of a Huntington Beach lifeguard named Mr. Reed. (MCR) See SURF FASHION.

reef *n*. **1**) A line, ridge, or assemblage of rock, coral, or sand lying at, below, or near the surface of the water. **2**) A natural underwater formation that creates good waves. See CORAL REEF, INSIDE REEF, OUTSIDE REEF.

reef break *n*. A surf spot where waves break over a reef.

reef configuration *n*. The underwater formation, or shape, of a reef. If you are familiar with a surf spot's reef configuration, you may be able to get in a better position to catch waves.

reef rash *n*. What you get surfing in the tropics when you scrape yourself on a coral reef. (KSO) See CORAL CUT.

reef surf *n*. Surf breaking on a reef. (MF) Same as REEF BREAK.

reef walkers *n*. Footware specially designed to protect feet from getting cut on sharp coral.

reentry *n*. **1**) A maneuver in which the surfer shoots to the very top of a wave, briefly skates along the top of the lip just ahead of the curl, and then drops back down along the face. The most difficult reentry is to go past vertical in ascent or to recross the path of the original vertical ascent when descending. **2**) An extreme version of a roller coaster, in which the surfer has all but kicked out and then radically cuts back into the breaking wave. See FLOATER REENTRY.

rebound wave
Skimboarder
Photo: Woody Woodworth

REAL SURFERS

Here are some views of what it takes to be a "real surfer":

Real surfers dress cool; have fixed dings; know how to ride bikes while holding surfboards; have been to Hawaii; have trouble choosing between girlfriends and waves; know how to surf with their hands (describe a ride); have made their own surfboards; have taken long, gnarly swims to shore; have cut school; can smell saltwater from more than a mile away; have stepped on sea urchins; have had at least one great tube ride; have surfed at sunup and sundown; have ridden skateboards; have had sunburned noses and lips; have done three-sixty maneuvers; love any food that comes from the ocean; have lived by the beach at least once in their lifetime; have had saltwater run out of their noses while kissing; hoot at surfing movies; have been the only ones in the water some-where; know how to look at surfboards; have entered contests; have written surfing graffiti; go on surfaris; have surfing pictures in their rooms. (SGE, P)

"Real surfers don't wear pink wetsuits: never wash their cars: surf standing up: don't have green hair: are nice to young girls (trust me): don't gyro-spaz on the shoulder: never clean their wax and never ever buy it: puke on trail mix: don't have pink bodies: don't own a tie: don't straighten out: meditate in the tube (not on the beach): stay in the tube (not in the car): don't wear earrings (unless they're chicks): don't read GQ: can stay down longer: don't wear bun huggers: gag on sprouts: like it big and hairy: like it steep and deep: don't wear shoes: don't wear leather: don't wear gold chains: don't wear polyester: don't listen to Wayne Newton tapes: don't watch the news: hate the Dallas Cowboys (red neck team from Baja Oklahoma): aren't Seymoors: aren't into vinyl: don't make their beds: don't drive cars that use unleaded: don't smoke Camels: don't jog or diet: don't get caught: don't drink un-cola: don't use baby oil: don't wear designer anything: don't chicken out: don't sleep until noon and miss it: still surf when it's blown out: surf in the rain: can't read "no trespassing" signs: don't listen to the "mellow sound": think Fila is what you do to Italian girls: don't want any mercy (or give any): have fat chicks for lunch (but never din-ner): don't do dishes: get down on the first date: never do laundry: don't read: don't write: can't spell: don't care: just surf." —Corky Carroll, "Real Surfers," (in *Surfer* Magazine, 5/84).

Corky Carroll
Photo: Tom Servais / Surfer Magazine

re-form *v.* **1)** (of a wave) To jack up and break again after crossing deep water and moving once more into the shallows. Waves often break on an outer sandbank or reef before moving across deep water and then re-forming, usually as shore breaks. (MW) **2)** When a wave becomes green again after having broken. (L&L) See BACK OFF, HUNTINGTON HOP.

refraction *n.* See WAVE REFRACTION.

reggae, reggae music *n.* **1)** Popular music that originated in Jamaica and has been adopted by many surfers worldwide. **2)** In Caribbean dialect, the feel-good irie vibes and heavy bass line roots dub riddim to accompany the natural soul lifestyle and help combat the dread forces of babylon (concrete jungles). **3)** Live and direct inna strictly massive ragamuffin surf posse stylee. **4)** Peace warrior sounds including those of Bob Marley, Steele Pulse, and Pato Banton. —**Jahwaiian** (Hawaiian reggae music)

regular foot *n.* A surfboard stance with the left foot forward, right foot back. (ORB) Same as NATURAL FOOT.

release *n.* The separation of water flow from the bottom or rails of a surfboard; akin to breaking suction.

releasing and reengaging rails *n.* **1)** Bending and flexing the legs to exert pressure on the surfboard, allowing for ultimate maneuvering in critical situations. **2)** Also a bodyboarding maneuver, where it is done with the arms.

rental *n.* A surfboard or wetsuit for hire, clearly marked "RENTAL" — a sure sign of a geek or hodad.

reo *n.* Short for REENTRY. (Australia; L&L)

reshape *v.* To reconstruct a surfboard by modifying its original shape.

resin *n.* In surfboard construction, the liquid plastic that is poured on fiberglass to bind it to the surfboard; used to laminate the fiberglass cloth to the foam.

resin fumes *n.* Extremely toxic vapors encountered during surfboard construction.

respirator *n.* A mask used to filter toxic fumes and dust from the air during the building and repairing of surfboards.

responsive *adj.* A surfboard performance characteristic. Usage: "Your board is really loose and responsive." —**responsiveness** *n.*

restaurant board *n.* A surfboard made specifically to hang as art.

rev-head *n.* A fool who thinks that cars are more important than surfboards. (Australia; JARR)

reverse kickout *n.* The same as a KICKOUT, except that the surfer executes a half spinner in kicking the board out of the wave.

reverse pullout *n.* **1)** Kicking out of a wave by quickly twisting the body to the rear, thus propelling the board over the top of the wave. **2)** Swinging the board around and off the wave in the direction opposite to that of the slide.

reverse takeoff *n.* A skeg-first takeoff in which the surfer lies on the board and once in the wave, spins the board around and stands up, riding in the correct manner. (MM)

reverse 360 air *n.* A bodyboarding maneuver. See THREE SIXTY.

reverse twist *n.* A hot-dog peel-off with the board turning off the wave to one side and the rider's body twisting around the other way. Also called REVERSE PULLOUT.

revetment *n.* A structure built along the coast to prevent erosion and other damage by wave action; similar to a SEA WALL. (CCRG)

rhino *n.* **1)** A bodacious wave; the ultimate surfing experience. (CVG) **2)** A board over seven feet long and weighing over fifteen pounds.

rental
Art: I. B. Nelson

(H&R) **3) rhino chaser, rhino-chaser gun,** BIG GUN.

richter (RICK-ter) **1)** *v.* To do a hard turn; to GO OFF. Usage: "Potter richtered his bottom turn, made it around the section and pulled into the barrel." (Australia and U.S.; SFR, 1989) **2) Richter scale** *n.* A scale, ranging from 1 to 10, used for expressing the intensity of an earthquake; developed by U.S. seismologist Charles Richter (1900–1985). See OFF THE RICHTER.

ricochet *n.* The end result of the most difficult type of cutback, where the surfer bounces the board off the breaking wave and again reverses horizontal direction. In competition, the difficulty of this move is determined by how far the board projects back into the breaking white water and how steep a vertical plane the board achieves. (L&L)

rider on the inside *n.* The surfer riding closest to the breaking portion of the wave; this person has the right-of-way.

riggin *n.* A surfer who won't stop talking. (MPZ) See YARNER.

right *n.* **1)** Any wave breaking in such a way that a surfer taking off must turn to the right to stay ahead of the curl. **2)** A wave that breaks from right to left, as viewed from shore, and from left to right, as viewed from out in the water. (MF) See LEFT. —**rights** *pl.,* **right-hander** (Australia)

right-of-way *n.* The first rule of surfing etiquette — that a surfer already on a wave and riding has the right-of-way, especially if he or she is on the inside closest to the curl. Anyone else coming into the wave should respect this right. See INSIDE.

right point *n.* A point break that produces waves that break to the right.

Art: The Pizz

right slide *n.* A ride where the surfer slides to the right on a wave that is breaking from left to right.

righteous Something that's right on, killer. Usage: "Righteous, dude."

ring around the collar Said of the collar of a wetsuit that is a different color than the rest of the suit. (SP)

rinse cycle *n.* See WASHING MACHINE.

rip *v.* **1)** To perform aggressive maneuvers on a wave; a complimentary term. Usage: "That dude really rips." **2)** To surf radically. **3) rippin'** or **ripping** Surfing hard. Same as RIP IT UP, RIP 'N' TEAR.

rip current, rip *n.* **1)** A powerful seaward movement of water created by waves breaking in rapid succession onto a beach, then rushing back through the lowest portion of the beach, thereby eroding an underwater exit channel in the sand. **2)** A narrow river of water moving seaward, the result of breaking waves and the subsequent accumulation of water in the near-shore zone. Generally accompanies big surf because the masses of water moving shoreward must have a way to get back out to sea. **3)** A current of water moving away from the beach. See LONGSHORE CURRENT.

A rip current is easily recognized by waves crossing diagonally over each other rather than rolling toward shore in parallel. The outward flow is sometimes called an **offset, runout, sea puss,** or **sea pussy.** It is sometimes mistakenly thought of as "undertow" — even though it doesn't drag you under the water but rather pulls you out to sea. It is also wrong to call it a **riptide,** since it has nothing to do with the tides.

rip it up, ripping it up *v.* To attack a wave; same as TEAR IT UP.

rip 'n' tear *v.* To surf radically; same as RIP. Usage: "I saw you rip 'n' tear out there."

ripe *adj*. Used to describe a perfect wave waiting to be surfed.

riprap *n*. Boulders or rock rubble used to construct a jetty or revetment. (CCRG)

ripper *n*. **1**) Someone who tears it up when surfing. **2**) Used to congratulate someone on a great ride, as in "Ripper, dude!" —**rippah** (Hawaiian Pidgin)

riptide *n*. A misnomer for RIP CURRENT.

river bodyboarding, river boogie *n*. Using a special board to surf river eddies, or the reversing foam of river "holes"; works best on deep and narrow "drop-and-pool"-type rivers. Also called WHITE-WATER SURFING.

The bodyboard adapted for river running is cut big for high flotation (4½ feet long, 2 feet wide, and 4 inches thick), equipped with two sets of handles, a slick bottom coat of high-density polyethylene, and a scalloped hip recess. In addition, a river bodyboarder needs a drysuit to ward off the river's chill; soccer shin guards, skateboard kneepads, and a kayaker's helmet to prevent bangs from river rocks; and swim fins and webbed gloves to enhance propulsion. (MHG)

"Kayakers are separated from the water by their gear — they touch a paddle here, poke the bow over there. Very artistic. Bodyboarding is full immersion; it's more like wrestling. You go down on the mat with the river." —Bob Carlson of Carlson Designs (1990)

river mouth *n*. **1**) Sometimes a good surf site due to the presence of sandbars. See RIVERBAR BREAK. **2**) Sometimes a feeding ground for sharks.

river surfing *n*. **1**) Riding a surfboard on river rapids while holding onto a line attached to an upstream bridge. In addition, as fast-running rivers flow over submerged obstacles, they sometimes form stationary waves that can also be surfed. See STANDING WAVE. **2**) Surfing upstream on a tidal bore.

riverbar break *n*. Waves breaking over a sandbar at the mouth of a river; can be dangerous because of the currents, including rips, that are common at river mouths. (WWK)

road trip *n*. A surfing adventure. See SURFARI, SURFIN' SAFARI.

roar of the ocean *n*. The sound of the surf. —**ocean roar**

"The three great sounds in nature are the sound of the rain, the sound of the wind . . . and the sound of outer ocean on a beach.

I have heard them all and that of the ocean is the most awesome, beautiful, and varied. . . ." —Henry Beston

rock dance, rock dancing *n*. A slippery walk over sharp, moss-covered rocks to retrieve a lost surfboard; often occurs at low tide. Your feet are at the mercy of sea urchins, pinching crabs, sea slugs, sea anemones, and barnacles — a miserable experience. (A&M, KSO)

rock reef *n*. A reef formed of rocks, as distinct from a CORAL REEF. This kind of reef is common in California.

rocker *n*. **1**) The gradual curve along a surfboard's fore-to-aft axis; the curvature of a surfboard in profile. A board with a lot of nose rocker has a pronounced upward curve toward the nose. **2**) The lengthwise bottom curvature of a surfboard. (L&L) **3**) **flat rocker** A rocker with little or no curve. **4**) **full rocker** A surfboard with an exaggerated upward curve in the nose and tail. **5**) An Australian HODAD. **6**) A member of a motorbike cult opposed to surfies. (Australia; MF)

When viewed from the side, a surfboard is higher at both ends than in the center. This fact has given rise to a number of colorful names; in addition to *rocker,* there is **banana**, **scoop**, and **spoon**. The curve is also called **camber** and **lift**.

. . . .

rocker block *n.* A hard foam block that attaches to the back of a thruster-style board and against which the back foot can be braced. (NAT, 1985)

rocks *n.* A part of the surfing landscape that one encounters, in one circumstance or another, in just about every surf session. Lost boards, for instance, are carried into hungry rocks that produce efficient board-digesting enzymes. See ROCK DANCE, EAT THE ROCKS.

rocky *adj.* One kind of shoreline or ocean bottom. Surf breaking over a rocky bottom or beach performs differently from surf breaking over a sandy beach or a mud flat.

rocky point *n.* A headland with a rocky shoreline that may feature a point break.

rodney wave *n.* A wave where everyone drops in on you and you get no respect; named for comedian Rodney Dangerfield. (MCR)

rogue wave *n.* **1**) A wave that appears unexpectedly and does not follow the pattern of previous waves. **2**) An unpredictably large wave in the open ocean, often in very deep waters, which sometimes exceeds 100 feet in height. (SFR, 6/88) **3**) A mid-ocean freak wave that is formed when a series of waves, commonly called trains, get "in step" for a short time, often less than a minute, and jack up into a single wave; not to be confused with a tsunami. (SFG, 10/82)

rogue shark *n.* A shark that roams alone. *Rogue,* as applied to animals, also means "vicious and destructive" — which in some circumstances aptly describes shark behavior.

rogue shark
Art: Deano

roll, rollover *n.* A maneuver used to get out through the white water. In the face of an oncoming broken wave, the surfer rolls over with the board, so that the bottom of the board is facing up, and hangs onto the rails — sometimes wrapping his or her legs around the board — until the wave passes over, then turns the board right side up and continues paddling outside. **—rolling over** *v.*

roller *n.* **1**) A wave that does not curl or tube; instead, the white water slides down its face. **2**) A wave that breaks gently and evenly toward a beach or shoreline. Same as SPILLING WAVE.

roller coaster *n.* **1**) A surfing maneuver in which the surfer comes out of a fast bottom turn, slides up the face of the wave, and rebounds off the lip at the crest of the wave. **2**) A surfer's up-and-down movement on the face of a wave. (MM) See CLIMB AND DROP.

roll in *v.* Said of large, unbroken waves or swell moving toward shore. Usage: "Look at that swell roll in."

rolling thunder *n.* Big ocean waves; taken from the name of a Great Plains Indian. (PZ)

roof of the wave *n.* The underside of the wave lip; the CANOPY.

roof rack *n.* SURF RACK.

room time *n.* Time spent in the tube. (DS) Same as CLOCKING IN THE GREEN ROOM.

roost *v.* To BAIL, fast. Usage: "Let's roost." "We're roosting." (Santa Monica; TMA, 1985)

rooster, rooster tail *n.* **1**) An upward-curving spray of water directly astern of a fast-moving surfboard. **2**) The arching trail of spray that shoots up off the back of the board as the surfer carves into a good turn. (A&M)

rope *n.* **1**) An Australian term for a SURF LEASH. Also called LEG ROPE. **2**) A fiberglass product used in fin laminations and leash loops. (GCD)

roto-moto *n.* The performance of continuous spinners while surfing; a surfing maneuver.

round rail *n.* A surfboard rail, the cross section of which is round and thickened, and which generally produces a slow and stable, or stiff, response.

round tail or **roundtail** *n.* A surfboard design featuring a rounded tail section, as distinct from one that is squared off or pointed. (NAT, 1985) See ROUNDED PIN.

'round the island, 'round the world *n.* A tandem maneuver where the female partner is rotated 360 degrees around the male partner's shoulders or waist.

rounded diamond tail *n.* A surfboard design feature.

rounded pin *n.* A surfboard design featuring a narrow, rounded tail; the standard by which all other boards are judged.

rounded square tail *n.* A surfboard design feature.

roundhouse, roundhouse cutback *n.* **1**) A maneuver in which the surfer cuts back into the wave and forces it to break, making an otherwise dull wave surfable. (JP) **2**) A cutback during which the surfer maintains speed and momentum through a turn of large radius (180 degrees). (L&L) —**sweeping roundhouse cutback**

roundhouser *n.* Any roundhouse maneuver. (PT)

routed skeg *n.* A strong method of attaching a skeg in a routed slot.

routed stick *n.* **1**) A surfboard with inlayed, decorative stringers. (MCR) **2**) A cheap method of inlaying a nonfull stick.

router *n.* A high-speed precision power tool used to install leash cups and fin boxes.

rubbah slippahs *n.* Hawaiian Pidgin for rubber sandals; same as THONGS, FLIP-FLOPS, GO-AHEADS.

rubber arms *n.* **1**) The term for a surfer who doesn't paddle hard enough to get a wave because it's too large or too critical. **2**) The feeling you occasionally get in your arms when you're paddling for an unusually large wave and you're not quite sure you want it.

rubber suit *n.* A cold-water insulating suit made of sponge rubber; the old term for WETSUIT. (JKMJ, 1965)

rubberneck *n.* An Australian term for KOOK. (1980s)

rule *v.* To go dominate the waves. Usage: "Let's rule, dude." (San Diego)

rumbled *v.* To get tossed in a wave. (TMA) Usage: "I was fully rumbled out there."

runback *n.* Fast back-stepping on a surfboard.

runup *n.* Fast forward-stepping on a surfboard.

roundhouse cutback
Kaipo Guerrero
Photo: Rob Gilley

rumbled
Art: The Pizz

S turn *n.* **1)** A move intended to keep the surfer nearer the pocket, like an abbreviated cutback and fade, followed immediately by a turn in the original tracking direction. **2)** CLIMBING AND DROPPING.

sacred *adj.* Used to describe something really cool; **sacy** (SAKE-ee) — if you're from Pt. Loma, California. (TJ)

sailboard *n.* **1)** A specialized board that is similar to a surfboard but outfitted with a mast, boom, and sail; first tested in the waters off Waikiki by Tom Blake in 1935. (GTM) See WINDSURFER. **2)** A small light sailboat with a flat hull designed to carry one or two persons. **3)** **Sailboard** A name trademarked in 1962.

sailboarding, sailsurfing *n.* WINDSURFING.

sampan roll *n.* **1)** An area seaward of Waikiki Bay frequented by fishing sampans on their way to sea, where only the largest swells break in blue water. **2)** A 1960s term for any site where large swells break.

San Jose *n.* **1)** Northern California's VALLEY. **2)** A densely populated urban area east of Santa Cruz and south of San Francisco. See OVER THE HILL, VALLEY SURPRISE.

. . . .

"You can take a valley out of San Jose, but you can't take San Jose out of the valley." (MCR)

. . . .

sand *n.* **1)** The more or less fine debris of rocks found at the beach, consisting of small, loose grains, often of quartz and feldspar. Other kinds of beaches are covered with volcanic black sand or coral white sand. See BEACH. **2)** Unpleasant yellow particles that form a buffer zone between ocean and earth. Sand burns your feet on hot days, it gets into your board wax, and it can ruin an amorous adventure under the stars if it gets where it's not wanted. (JARR)

SAND Surfers Against Nuclear Destruction — an Australian group of concerned surfers.

sand coat, sanding coat *n.* In surfboard construction, the resin layer that is sanded to blend and refine the contours of the board. (ORB) Also known as HOT COAT.

sand dune *n.* A mound, ridge, or hill of wind-blown sand, either bare or covered with vegetation; an aeolian landscape. Also called *dune.*

sand flea, sand fly *n.* Someone who avoids the water and just stays on the beach. (IDSM)

sand spit *n.* **1)** A narrow, finger-like embankment of sand deposited by littoral drift into the open water of a bay. **2)** The seasonal or permanent sand or sediment deposit at the mouth of a river. (CCRG)

sandals *n.* Open-air shoes favored by surfers, for example, thongs, rubbah slippahs (Hawaiian Pidgin), zorries, getogs, flip-flops, and go-aheads.

sandbank *n.* A submerged area of sand that causes waves to break. (NAT, 1985)

sandbar *n.* **1)** A submerged offshore deposit of sand or sediment created

sailboard
Art: The Pizz

by littoral drift or wave action; also occurs at a river mouth. (CCRG) **2)** A mound or plateau of sand caused by wave action or sea currents and occasionally acting as an underwater reef, creating good surfing waves and causing them to break further offshore.

Sandbars form parallel to the beach, but are not permanent — they shift around seasonally. Winter storm waves erode the summer beach profile and deposit sands offshore.

sandbar break *n*. A kind of surf break caused by swell moving over sand deposits just offshore; can be unstable, given that sandbars shift seasonally with changes in weather. See SURF BREAKS.

sandboarding *n*. Riding a specialized board down a sand dune. Unfortunately, this activity is destructive to a dynamic yet fragile landform. Sandboarding is an offshoot of surfing that now incorporates snowboarding technology as well. It first appeared in the movie *The Endless Summer* (1964), which showed surfers in South Africa using longboards to slide down large dunes on the way to a remote break.

sander *n*. In surfboard construction, a power tool used by the shaper to smooth out ridges left by the planer and to sand out the board.

sanding agent *n*. A resin additive used to transform laminating resin into hot-coat resin. (GCD)

sanding block *n*. A small piece of wood with sandpaper wrapped around it, making it easier to sand certain areas of a surfboard.

sanding resin, surfacing resin *n*. A special resin used to fill in the texture and lap seams in the fiberglass cloth of a surfboard. This resin contains a surfacing agent, which floats to the surface once the resin is applied and blocks air, causing the

resin to set up hard and tack-free. The resin is then sanded to make the board smooth. Same as HOT-COAT RESIN.

sandpaper *n*. The magic wand of ding repair; comes in a wide range of grits. For instance, #60 grit paper takes down the excess resin and glass and leaves a good surface for a gloss coat to bond to. Among the **finishing sandpapers,** #220 is used to take the gloss lines off, and #400 and #600 grit are used to prepare the gloss for buffing. (GCD)

sandsliding *n*. SKIMBOARDING. (Hawaii; ELK)

sandwhichable syndrome *n*. Getting crunched by a wave. (SFR, 10/83)

sano *adj*. Used to describe very, very clean waves. (MVA) Usage: "It's sano out there."

Santa Ana winds, Santa Anas, Santanas, Santa Ana condition *n*. **1)** Named for the Santa Ana Canyon in Southern California but occurring throughout the Los Angeles Basin, winds that form in fall and winter when air in the interior deserts piles up against the transverse ranges and begins streaming down the mountain passes toward the coast. The air heats as it moves downhill, sometimes raising coastal temperatures to over 100 degrees. **2)** Hot, dry winds that blow offshore all day and create excellent surfing conditions; may also reach gale strength — up to sixty miles per hour — and create dangerous waves offshore. (CCRG) Also called DEVIL WINDS.

"In the morning, standing at the busstop, you know the waves are classic and you can smell the wind." (SFR)

Santa Cruz A Northern California surfing community, first surfed by Hawaiian Prince David Kawonanaokoa in 1885 and home of the

Santa Ana winds
Huntington Beach, California
Photo: Rob Gilley

sandboarding
Monterey Bay, California
Photo: Don Balch

sanding coat
Gary Lill
Photo: Woody Woodworth

Santa Cruz Surfing Museum. Surf spots include Steamer Lane and Pleasure Point.

Santa Monica Bay 1) The site of numerous surfing communities, including the Palos Verdes Peninsula, Manhattan Beach, Redondo Beach, Hermosa Beach, Santa Monica, and Malibu. **2**) One of the most polluted bays in the world, especially during heavy rains, when millions of gallons of raw, untreated sewage run off into the bay.

sardine *n.* An old term for SHARK. (JKMJ, 1965)

Sargasso sea *n.* A large tract of the North Atlantic that is covered by vast blankets of sargassum seaweed, for which the sea is named; fed by the Gulf Stream, which deposits seaweed transplanted by hurricanes from the reefs of Florida and the West Indies. (OA) See SURF SOUP.

satu lagi (SAW-two LAH-ghee) An Indonesia word meaning literally "one more," and in surfing meaning "Outside!" Usage: "That Indo guy's screaming *satu lagi* at us! I'll get the anchor, you start the motor!" (SFR, 1990)

sausage board *n.* A special shape of surfboard rounded at both ends. (MF)

scam *v.* To hit on someone — to look for and hopefully get together with someone you are attracted to. Usage: "Look, he's totally scamming."

scareamundo *adj.* Scary.

scend *n.* The back part of a wave. **—wave scend**

schooling tuna *v.* To dial in on some butter. (Florida; TDW) Usage: "Let's go school some tuna."

scoop *n.* **1**) The turned-up shape in the nose of a surfboard. **2**) The camber, or uplifted shape, of the forward or rear portion of a surfboard. Also called SPOON, CUP. See ROCKER. (DSHJ)

scope, scope out *v.* To check something out, as in "to scope out the surf" or "to scope out a person you're attracted to." **—scopin'**

score *v.* To achieve or accomplish a goal, usually said in regards to waves, food, or babes. Usage: "I scored the full-on drumstick."

scoring criteria *n.* SURFING CRITERIA.

scorpion tail *n.* The tail scoop aft of the step on a hydroplane surfboard.

scratch *v.* **1**) To paddle hard. Usage: "I had to scratch really hard to make that wave." **2**) **scratching over the top** To paddle rapidly and still barely make it over a huge incoming wave. (MM)

scratch-up zone *n.* In surfboard construction, an area just outside of the grind-down zone that gets scratched up during sanding and later covered with gloss resin. (GCD)

screw foot *n.* Someone who rides a surfboard with the right foot forward, left foot back. (ORB) Same as GOOFY FOOT.

scrozzling (SCRAW-zuhl-ling) *v.* A move beyond GROVELING. Usage: "Yeah, I saw you scrozzling through that section, but I didn't think you'd make it, so I went." (Santa Cruz; SFR, 1989)

scungies *n.* Trunks worn for surfboard riding. (Australia; MNL)

sea *n.* **1**) The ocean. **2**) A tract of water within an ocean. **3**) A relatively large body of saltwater partially or completely landlocked. **4**) The condition of the ocean's surface, as in "a high sea." **5**) Something that suggests the sea in its overwhelming sweep or vastness, as in "a sea of wildflowers." (AHD2) **6**) **the seven seas** All the major waters of the world.

sea anemone *n.* Any sedentary marine animal of the phylum Coelenterata, having a flexible cylindrical body and numerous tentacles surrounding the mouth and superficially resembling a flower. Anemones come in bright and varied colors; some species in tropical waters are highly toxic to touch.

sea breeze *n.* **1**) A thermally produced wind blowing from a cool ocean surface onto adjoining warm land. (RHD) **2**) A light cooling breeze blowing onshore. **3**) A local wind rising as land heats up during the day.

. . . .

Sea breezes bring wind chop to the majority of surf spots. They sometimes die down an hour or two before sundown, allowing surfers to enjoy an evening glass-off. (S&C)

. . . .

sea chariot *n.* SURFBOARD.

sea hag *n.* An ugly woman.

sea lice *n.* Tiny insects that make you itch all over. (Florida, TDW)

sea puss, sea pussy *n.* A rip current found at open beaches; happens when waves breaking over a sandbar create an excess of water that has to flow out through a hole in the sandbar. (DSHJ) See RIP CURRENT.

sea rats *n.* Another name for sea gulls, because they crap everywhere and eat anything. (PZ)

sea snake, sea serpent *n.* Any of numerous venomous aquatic viviparous snakes (of the family Hydrophidae) found in warm seas. (W9) Although potentially deadly and a bit startling when encountered swimming around surfers in certain South Pacific surf spots, these snakes are not aggressive, and they have such tiny mouths that the only place they can bite is the webbed skin between the fingers of a surfer's hand.

sea state *n.* A condition in which waves are formed locally by winds blowing close to the coast; the crests are generally rounded and the waves are close together and travel slowly.

(L&L) Usage: "I think we're getting a bit of a sea state developing."

sea ulcer *n.* A sore usually on the feet or ankles that is a common problem among surfers; typically starts as a cut, often a deep one, then instead of healing shut, as most wounds do, it deepens and becomes encircled by a thick, rubbery kind of callous. A sea ulcer may last for weeks, months, or even years, all the while not looking particularly infected, but just never healing. The best treatment is to keep it clean and dry. (SFR, 4/19)

sea urchin *n.* Any of a class (Echinoidea) of echinoderms usually encased in a thin brittle shell that is covered with movable spines.

. . . .

Urchins can be quite abundant in rocky areas with shallow water, and if you lose your board and are forced to stand up and walk ashore, you may find your foot punctured by needle-like spines that can break off under the skin, emitting a poison and causing a wound that can hurt for months. The treatment is to dissolve the spines — which are composed of calcium carbonate — in any weak acid such as vinegar, lemon juice, or uric acid. This last suggests a possible emergency procedure: urinate on the injured foot and the reaction may force the spines out.

. . . .

sea wall *n.* A strong wall or embankment erected to prevent the encroachment of the sea and to protect the shore from erosion; serves as a breakwater.

sea wasp *n.* Any of various highly poisonous stinging jellyfish of the order Cubomedusae, found in tropical seas. (RHD) Surfers along Australia's northeastern coast wear pantyhose in the warm water to guard against their potentially lethal stings. Also called *box jelly* or *marine stinger.*

seawater *n.* Salty water in or from the ocean, large amounts of which

are involuntarily swallowed by surfers during heavy wipeouts.

seaweed *n.* An algae generally
divided into four groups: blue-green,
green, brown, and red. Kelp is the
familiar brown variety; mermaid's
hair is a common blue-green species
that lives on rocks and pilings. (OA)

Sebastian Inlet The most famous
surf spot in Florida.

second break *n.* **1)** The area where
waves break a second time, closer to
shore than the first break. **2) Second Break** A specific surf site at
Waikiki, Oahu, Hawaii.

secret goo *n.* A very useful mixture
of resin and fiberglass clippings used
in ding repair. (GCD)

secret spot *n.* A relatively undiscov-
ered surf site.

section *n.* **1)** A part of a breaking
wave. **2)** The difficult part of a
wave. (L&L) **3)** The fast part of a
wave, where ten or fifteen yards of
the wall fold over at once instead of
peeling off. (A&M)

sectioning *v.* **1)** What happens
when a wave breaks in front of a
surfer, making it difficult to make
the wave **2)** When a wave breaks in
two or more places at once, instead
of peeling from one side to the
other. **3)** When a portion of a wave
breaks all at once, rather than peeling. (A&B) Usage: "The wave started
sectioning on me just as I took off."

sectiony *adj.* Said of a wave that is
not breaking evenly, or is breaking
ahead of itself. Usage: "The waves
are a little sectiony."

seismic sea wave *n.* A long-period
wave generated by an underwater
earthquake, landslide, or volcanic
eruption; a TSUNAMI. Erroneously
called a tidal wave. (CCRG)

seismograph *n.* An instrument that
detects, measures, and records
ground motion (for instance, the
vibrations of earthquakes and distur-
bances from wave shock). This
device is an excellent indicator of
surf conditions. If the recorded lines

SURFING VERSUS SEX

Although many surfers take up sex as a second sport, aesthetically speaking it is
not in the same league. True, many of the maneuvers are similar, but the feeling
of satisfaction and exhilaration that floods over the surfer when he penetrates the
deepest recesses of a bitchin' barrel knows no rival. (JARR) Is surfing better than
sex? The first international surfing and sex survey by Wilson-Horsechester Market
Research included the following (GS, 4/90):

You wake up for an early because you know the surf is going off, but your
partner wants to have sex. Do you:

a) Go surfing regardless **17%**
b) Have a quickie and go surfing **77%**
c) Forget surfing and spend all morning in bed **6%**

In addition:
72% said their sexual appetite was increased during flat spells
51% said they thought about surfing during sex

are parallel to each other, little or no seismic activity is indicated and the surf is probably small or flat; if the lines are squiggly and crooked, probably the surf is up. Some colleges display seismographs in their earth sciences department.

semigun *n.* A big-wave surfboard modified to move at a slower speed and with somewhat increased maneuverability.

semipig *n.* A pig board modified to be less pointed in the nose and not quite as wide, or fat, in the rear.

seppo *n.* Short for Septic Tank Yank — an Australian derogatory term for an American. Some say the term originated way back, when some Americans visited Australia and noticed that when Australians had to relieve themselves, they just let it run all over the place. So the Americans explained what a septic tank was, but the Australians turned it around on them and said, "Wha'd ya mean, mate, you have this big tank full of shit — and you keep it?"

Serfin *n.* The name of a Mexican bank, preferred by many a visiting surfer to Mexico.

session *n.* **1)** Any time spent surfing; **sesh** or **sess** for short. Also called SURF SESSION. **2)** An Australian term for a SET.

set, wave set *n.* **1)** A series of waves — two, three, or four in a row — generally arriving at regularly spaced intervals. **2)** The largest waves to come through on a particular day or during a particular session, usually three or four or seven or eight at a time, the groupings separated by intervals of relative calm ranging from less than a minute to half an hour or more. **3)** A series of waves following rapidly one after the other. (Waves usually come in sets.)

Set waves come in many varieties: **kitchen sets** are waves you can really cook on; **dining room sets** are close-out waves that you eat; **living room sets** provide easy-chair types of rides — waves anyone can ride; in **bathroom sets** everyone gets flushed on. (MCR)

set *v.* To be carried down the coast in an ocean current. Usage: "I was set down the coast."

set an edge *n.* DIG A RAIL. (L&L)

set up 1) *v.* To incorporate a surfer's desired specifications into a surfboard design. Shapers can "set up" shortboards and longboards for various conditions by adjusting length, width, rocker, bottom contours, wide point placement, rail design, number of fins, and so on. **2)** A resin term; same as GO OFF. (GCD) **3) deep setup** *n.* The position of a surfer way back in the tube.

set waves *n.* Big surf that is breaking consistently.

setting the scale *n.* In competitive surfing, the practice of using the first ride that is scored in a heat as the standard against which all subsequent rides in that heat are judged. On the ASP tour the scale is set using a scoring range of 1 to 10, with increments of one-tenth of a point to reduce the likelihood of a tie. (L&L)

sex *n.* An activity that competes with surfing as the number-one priority in a surfer's life. Or does it? See "Surfing versus sex" on page 108.

Sex Wax *n.* A brand of surf wax, Mr. Zog's Sex Wax in full, which features the slogan "The Best For Your Stick."

shacking the lip *n.* A combination maneuver, something between a cutback and an off-the-lip. (Newport Beach)

shaka, shaka brah *n.* **1)** Hawaiian Pidgin for "Right on!" **2)** A hand signal meaning howzit, hello, so long, great ride, I agree, take it easy, hang loose, and various other things; a greeting. The shaka is

shaka
Art: Rick Stover

made by wiggling a raised hand with only the thumb and little finger extended. **3)** An internationally understood sign known by true surfers around the globe as "What's up?" (H&R)

. . . .

There are several explanations for the origin of *shaka*. The gesture is believed to have been invented by Hamana Kalili, a Hawaiian folk hero, fisherman, tug-of-war champion, *hukilau* (party) organizer, and resident of Laie (a tiny town on Oahu), who used the sign — not the word — as a sort of blessing and community calling. His right hand was missing three fingers; the thumb and the little finger were all that was left. Kalili is said to have lost his fingers from (a) using dynamite to kill fish; (b) being smashed in the rollers at Kahuku Sugar Mill; or (c) being bitten by a ferocious shark.

The word *shaka* was used in the 1960s by Lippy Espinda, a Honolulu used-car salesman and TV movie host. But it may have derived from much earlier times, for instance from a Buddha named "Shaykanuma," who prayed with his fingers folded except for his little finger and thumb. And some old-time Japanese residents of Hawaii say that *shaka* dates back to the 1880s; they claim it means "Praise the Lord" and was used when someone did something good. (SFG, 5/86)

. . . .

shaper
Art: Jim Phillips

shape *n*. **1)** Refers to the configuration, or form, of waves — well-shaped, poor, fair, etc. Usage: "It was a perfect six foot with really good shape." **2)** The foam blank as completed by the shaper (ORB); **board shape**. **3)** *v*. To form or sculpt a foam blank into a specified surfboard shape.

shaper, surfboard shaper *n*. The craftsperson who shapes foam blanks into surfboards.

shark *n*. **1)** The animal all surfers dread — even though Duke Kahanamoku believed that the shark was his *aumakua*, his guard-

ian. **2)** A type of elasmobranch fish that has existed for over 415 million years, that comes in a variety of shapes and sizes, that resides in various habitats, and that sometimes travels far afield. Also known as, among many other names, *the landlords, hermann,* and (in Australia) *"the man in the gray suit"* (from the movie *The Endless Summer*). See "A Few Facts about Sharks" on next page. Also see HUMAN LURE, RED TRIANGLE, WHITE SHARK.

shark attack *n*. **1)** The reason that surfers dread sharks. See "Myths and Facts about Shark Attacks" on page 112. **2)** Mr. Zog's Shark Jerky with the slogan "Bite Back." **3)** **"Shark Attack"** A song by the Surf Punks.

. . . .

"More people are killed in the United States by pigs (especially in the Midwest) than by sharks." —Camm Swift (Natural History Museum of Los Angeles County, 1990)

. . . .

shark nose *n*. A surfboard shape with a pointed nose. (ASKC, 1965) See SHARKY.

Sharkbusters *n*. An airborne coastal beach and bay patrol based in Victoria, Australia, and founded by Ric D. T. Wilson in January 1988. From a single-engine airplane equipped with shark-alert sirens, the patrol looks out for sharks near water users, as well as for major pollution and coastal abnormalities.

sharkin' *n*. To go surfing. (Texas; H&R) Usage: "Let's go sharkin'."

sharky *adj*. **1)** Used to describe a surfboard with a sharp pointed nose, or a shark nose. Usage: "The nose is a bit sharky." (New Castle, Australia) **2)** Said of a shark-infested area. Usage: "The waters there are supposed to be a little sharky."

shave ice *n*. A Hawaiian snow cone — a popular surf snack.

A FEW FACTS
ABOUT SHARKS

Sharks range in size from the tiny, six-inch bioluminescent spined pygmy shark up to the forty-five-foot-long, quite docile whale shark. The fastest known shark, the mako, has been clocked at up to twenty-two miles (thirty-five kilometers) per hour. Sharks have good vision and are sensitive to light, movement, and contrast—all important to their success as hunters. Prey is detected by sight, sound, and smell; sharks can detect odors from a hundred yards or farther away, and electrical reception and vibration from about six feet away.

Sharks that live near the sunlit surface or in shallow water are usually nocturnal, that is, active at night; others are crepuscular, active at dawn, dusk, or both (this is a busy time, when fish are waking up or settling down for the evening). A shark's eyes glow in the dark like a cat's.

A surfer may encounter a variety of sharks, including the fearsome great white (see WHITE SHARK), tiger sharks, hammerheads, and bull sharks. The large and ferocious tiger shark, a tropical species, has been known to eat anything in sight; it prowls reefs, bays, and river mouths in shallow, warm waters worldwide. Scientists think the broad, odd-shaped head of the hammerhead shark helps it steer and enhances its ability to see, smell, or detect the electrical fields given off by hidden prey. Dangerous bull sharks have been found 1,800 miles up the Amazon River and up the Mississippi River as far as Illinois.

Surfer terms for different shark species include **bronzies** (for bronze whalers), **formula ones** (for hammerheads), **terries** (for tiger sharks), and the surfer's favorite, **white pointers** (for great whites). (NHMLA)

Art: The Pizz

MYTHS AND FACTS ABOUT SHARK ATTACKS

Public hysteria over sharks was fueled by Steven Spielberg's movie *Jaws* (1975), which drove many beachgoers away from the ocean. Contrary to popular belief, however, sharks are not vicious man-eaters. Only about 27 of the more than 250 known species have attacked humans; these include the bull shark, gray shark, white-tip shark, blue shark, tiger shark, mako shark, white shark, and hammerhead shark. About one hundred people are attacked each year worldwide (twelve in the United States); in California, attacks average one per year.

Most shark attacks do not end in death, which results mainly from loss of blood and shock rather than from being eaten. In fact, sharks usually take one bite and swim away, leaving some 70 percent of their victims to survive. Most reported shark attacks occur in warm, tropical waters near large cities (where there are more people in the water), and most occur in shallow water (because there are more people near shore) or at the surface offshore. To a shark swimming below, the silhouette of a surfer floating on a shortboard may resemble the shape of a seal or a sea lion (its favorite foods). The increase in shark attacks in recent years is thought to be due in part to the growth in the marine mammal population brought about by the Marine Mammal Protection Act of 1973.

Some advice for the prevention of shark attacks:

- Don't surf alone.
- Don't surf in murky water.
- Don't surf while wearing brightly colored clothing. (See YUMMY YELLOW.)
- Don't surf at night; some sharks see well in dim light and hunt by moonlight.
- Don't surf if you are cut or bleeding; sharks have a keen sense of smell and are able to detect one part of blood in one million parts of water (equivalent to one drop in twenty-five gallons of water).

(GVS, NHMLA)

Art: The Pizz

border:
Masi (tapa cloth from Fiji)

shelf *n.* A reef or rock formation underwater that drops off sharply. Shore-bound waves hitting this shelf often jack up, creating a larger and faster-breaking wave than if the wave ran its normal course. Waimea Bay is a good example of a shelf-type break.

shifting peak *n.* A wave breaking over a seabed dotted with many small bars or reefs, whose irregularity causes the breaking depth to change from wave to wave, so that the peak — and hence the takeoff point — is constantly shifting.

shifty *adj.* Said of waves that don't break in a consistent spot. Usage: "The waves are extremely shifty." See DISORGANIZED.

shine, **shine it**, **shine on that** *v.* Forget it now. (TMA) Usage: "Let's shine this place." "We fully shined it." "Shine on that. Come to the party."

shinner *n.* What you get when a skimboard hits your shin. (TLH)

Shit Pipe *n.* A Redondo Beach surf spot next to a sewage outflow pipe.

shishi *n.* A local (Hawaiian) word of Japanese origin for urine; also an old Hawaiian remedy for removing embedded sea urchin spines and other marine-organism stings (to be used locally, not orally). (S&S)

shoal *n.* A sandbar or reef formation that creates shallow water.

shoaling waves *n.* Waves that, because of the way they jack up and shift around in shallow water, are said to feel the bottom as they approach shore.

shock cord *n.* An early term for SURF LEASH.

shock wave *n.* A side-wake caused by the motion of a fast board across the face of a large wave.

shoot *v.* To ride a wave, as in "shoot the curl." (DSHJ)

shoot the curl *v.* **1)** Riding through the curling or tubing part of a wave; making a hot section. **2)** Catching a wave at exactly the right moment and riding it all the way in to the beach. Usage: " Did you see me shoot the curl?" —**shooting the curl** *n.*

shoot the pier *v.* To ride a wave in between and through the pilings of a wharf or pier, or to attempt such a ride. —**shooting the pier** *n.*

shoot the tube *v.* To ride through a tight curl, so that the breaking wave is actually arching over the board, the rider, or both. —**shooting the tube** *n.*

shoot the tunnel *v.* To slide very rapidly through a tunneling wave; same as SHOOT THE TUBE, SHOOT THE CURL. —**shooting the tunnel** *n.*

shore break or **shore-break** *n.* **1)** Waves (usually small) breaking close to shore or directly on beaches. **2)** A breaker line caused by an abruptly shoaling bottom close to shore. The waves of such a break usually steepen and topple over quickly in shallow depths, and are therefore difficult and dangerous to ride. (DSHJ) Same as BEACH BREAK. —**whomping shorebreak**

shore pound *n.* A very hard-breaking wave, usually thick in the lip and hitting right on the shore.

short john *n.* A sleeveless wetsuit with the legs cut off above the knees, as distinct from a LONG JOHN. Usage: "I've got a short john in my trunk."

shortboard or **short board** *n.* **1)** A lightweight surfboard designed for high-performance surfing; usually five to seven feet long. **2)** The Australian term for a general-purpose or hot-dog board. (JKMJ, 1965)

shooting the pier
Art: Robbie Quine

shore break
Waimea Shorebreak
Photo: Robert Brown

A shortboard can be turned more easily and is quicker and more maneuverable than a longboard. It is also sensitive to

Shortboard Revolution
George Greenough
Photo: Don Balch

front/rear weight transfer, which helps in negotiating a steep drop in small surf without pearling. A surfer can generate speed by quickly maneuvering through critical sections of a wave.

Shortboard Revolution *n.* A trend toward using shorter boards that began in Australia in the late 1960s. George Greenough is the California innovator who most influenced the movement in Australia. (SFR, 6/88) Other names associated with shortboards are Bob McTavish and Nat Young.

shortboarder *n.* Someone who rides a shortboard.

shoulder *n.* **1**) The smooth hump of a breaking wave that moves ahead of the curl but has not yet become an actual wall. **2**) The unbroken section next to the white water, or next to the curling hook. **3**) The part of a wave that hasn't broken yet (ORB); the flat, slow part of the wave. **4**) The smoothly rounded end or edge of a wave away from the soup. **5**) The section to either side of the peak of a wave. Usually, the peak breaks first, with the curl spreading progressively along the shoulders. (DSHJ)

shoulder city *n.* Waves that are shoulder-high. (JP)

shoulder hopper *n.* **1**) Someone who insists on sharing a wave, thereby breaking the taboo of one wave, one surfer. (CVG) **2**) A surfer who cuts in on another surfer's right-of-way. (MM) See DROPPING IN, SNAKING WAVES.

"Shoulder hopper, don't drop in on me." —Surf Punks, "Shoulder Hopper" (1980)

shoulder turn *n.* Turning with the shoulders rotating in the direction of the turn.

shoulder hopper
Art: Jimbo Phillips

shoulder zip *n.* A horizontal zipper that runs along the upper back of a wetsuit. (IBN)

shralp or **schralp** *v.* Kind of a lame word used to describe someone who is SHREDDING or TEARING IT UP. (SP) Usage: "Dude, you were fully shralping out there."

shred *v.* To tear up the waves while surfing; to ride the waves well. (H&R, JP) Usage: "Those guys were really shredding it up." See RIP.

shuffle, shuffling *v.* **1**) To move toward the nose of the board without crossing foot over foot, usually a sliding maneuver. **2**) To change position on a surfboard without a walking step. **3**) To slide up or down the board without letting one's feet leave the deck. (A&M)

side current *n.* CROSSCURRENT.

side drift *n.* See RIP CURRENT.

side ride *n.* Riding a bodyboard lying on one's side, possible only on a very steep wave.

sider *n.* A skimboarder's term for any beach where you can ride a rebound wave out and catch an incoming wave back in to shore. The Wedge is a good example. (TLH)

sideshore wind *n.* A wind that blows parallel to the waves, making them a bit choppy and causing them to break early.

sideslip *n.* The act of releasing the rail that is in the wave so that the surfboard slides sideways; somewhat like a skiing sideslip.

sideslipping or **side-slipping**. *n.* The drift of the forward end of a surfboard diagonally down the face of a wave, a natural component of the motion of wave riding. —**sideslipping on the nose, sideslipping in the curl**

sidewalk surfin' *n.* **1**) A sixties term for SKATEBOARDING. (MM) **2**) **"Sidewalk Surfin'"** A song by Jan & Dean (October 1964) about the skateboard craze. Brian Wilson originally penned the tune for The Beach Boys as "Catch a Wave"; Roger Christian rewrote the lyric.

Silver Surfer A Marvel comic book character.

SIMA Surf Industry Manufacturers Association, formed in 1989.

Simmons, Bob A Southern California surfer with an engineering background who made major contributions to surfboard construction and who provided the link between the redwood board and the modern surfboard in the 1940s and early 1950s. He died in 1954, when his own board slapped him on the head at Windansea. (GN)

Simmons played a central role in the following innovations: **1**) the transition to lighter-weight boards (he experimented with different materials, such as sandwiching balsa, plywood, and Styrofoam together); **2**) the use of fiberglass (he was the first to combine lightweight materials and fiberglass); **3**) the use of foam in a surfboard (he was the first person ever to try foam in a surfboard — polystyrene foam in 1950).

single fin *n.* A surfboard with one fin.

sinker *n.* Any ding in which there is a hole to be filled; the most common type of ding on earth. (GCD) See CRUNCHER.

sitting island pullout *n.* An ISLAND PULLOUT in the sitting position.

sizzler *n.* Someone who is boisterous and at the same time conspicuously out of place; inappropriately vain. (Newport Beach; ALN)

skag *n.* **1**) An occasional spelling of SKEG, the fin at the end of a surfboard. (IDSM) See SKEG. **2**) An ugly woman.

skankamangus *n.* A rather large woman walking down the beach. (Southern California)

skateboard *n.* Originally a skate mounted on a short piece of wood shaped like a miniature surfboard. Made of fiberglass in the 1970s and again of wood in the 1980s.

skateboarding *n.* A pastime and sport that originated in Southern California in 1963 when an unknown creator put together a simple vehicle consisting of a small, short board with round ends and two pairs of roller skate wheels mounted to the underside. Like a surfboard, a skateboard is ridden standing up or squatting down. Also called ASPHALT SURFING, SIDEWALK SURFIN'. See SURF-SKATE SYNTHESIS.

The initial fad for skateboards lasted only about two years in the early sixties, though it was nationwide. Interest revived around 1975, again in Southern California, with the introduction of fiberglass boards whose polyurethane wheels allowed riders to move at great speeds and to perform athletic movements resembling those achieved on surfboards. Professional teams and championship tournaments soon came into being, as did a popular literature of magazines on the subject, such as *Thrasher*. Moves like "the McTwist," "hydro ollie-hop," and "fakie" and expressions like "boneless" and "boomin'" have grown out of the culture, which has also given birth to a punk skate band called McRad. (JDH) Skateboarders do their thing in (or on) all sorts of places, including empty swimming pools, skate parks (in the 1970s), large drain pipes and half pipes, homemade backyard ramps, ditches, curbs — and, of course, streets and sidewalks.

skating *n.* **1**) PUMP TURN — a surfing maneuver that helps the rider traverse the slow part of a wave. (L&L) Usage: "I was skating through that last section." **2**) A bodysurfing technique using the hands as a planing surface. (MF)

skeg *n.* The fixed, rudder-like fin on the bottom rear of a surfboard that

sidewalk surfing
Art: I. B. Nelson

Art: The Pizz

skateboarding
Jon Newman—speed with style.
Photo: Don Balch

skeg
Longboard fins: solid wood (left); laminated wood (right)
Photo: Bob Barbour

skimboarding
Photo: Dennis Junor

skimboarding
Wipeout, Maui
Photo: Don Balch

allows the surfer to steer; also provides directional stability and holds the stern of the board in the wave. The skeg was invented by Tom Blake in 1935. Also called FIN.

skeg first, skeg reverse *n.* Intentionally dropping into a wave tail first, just for the fun of spinning around with the board. (MVA, WWK)

skeg hum, skeg whine *n.* See WHISTLING SKEG.

skeggin' *adj.* Having great fun, as in a "skeggin' party" or a "skeggin' time."

Skegness *n.* A town in England. As far as is known, has nothing to do with surfboard fins.

skimboard or **skim board** *n.* A rounded plywood or fiberglass board two or three feet across, used to slide over the shallow water at the water's edge.

skimboarding, skimming *n.* Standing up on a flat board and riding it along the shoreline on top of a thin layer of water. Also called SANDSLIDING.

skin *n.* **1)** The outside layer of a foam blank. **2)** What you lose when dragged over the coral reef at Banzai Pipeline in Hawaii. (ATRL)

skin it *v.* Surfing without a wetsuit, as in "Let's skin it." (CSD) Same as TRUNK IT, BARE BACK.

skitter board *n.* **1)** A fast, finless, flat-bottomed bellyboard or paipo board about forty-two inches long and thirty inches wide and around three-eighths of an inch thick — one of the fastest wave-riding devices. **2)** An old term for SKIMBOARD.

skurfing *n.* A combination of water skiing and surfing, where the rider is towed behind a speedboat on a **skurfer,** a specialized board with foot straps; a poor substitute for the real thing.

skysurfing *n.* Hang gliding. (From Dan Poynter's book *Hang Gliding: The Basic Handbook of Skysurfing*)

slab *n.* An extremely hollow, cold, thick, dark, spooky wave. (Marin County, California)

slack, slack tide, slack water *n.* **1)** The period between the ebb and flow of the tide, when the water is relatively motionless. **2)** The quiet period between sets of waves.

slaps it off the top A phrase commonly used by surf contest announcers to describe a sharp turn at the top of a wave; same as WHACKS IT OFF THE TOP. Usage: ". . . and she slaps it off the top!"

slash 1) *n.* A radical, carving cutback, performed on the steep face of a wave. (MW) **2) slashing** *v., adj.* Usage: "I saw you slashing on the inside." "He ripped a slashing backside bottom turn." **2) slashing off the lip** Doing an AERIAL.

s'later "See you later."

sleeper, sleeper wave *n.* A wave that sneaks up on you and is larger than usual.

sleeper set *n.* SNEAKER SET.

slibity *n.* The police. (Half Moon Bay; PPJ)

slice, slicing *v.* **1)** To carve a turn or cut through a wave. **2)** To run over another surfboard. Usage: "I sliced his board."

slide *n.* **1)** A long track down a large wave from which a safe deviation is usually not possible without wiping out. **2)** A diagonal descent on a wave. (MM) **3) sliding** Movement across the face of a wave, as opposed to going straight in with the wave. **4)** *v.* To ride either left or right, on a track somewhat parallel to shore. See STRAIGHT OFF.

slimeball *n.* An undesirable person or obnoxious surfer. (JP)

sling off *n.* To maneuver out of a wave; to PULL OUT. (JKMJ, 1967)

slop *n*. **1**) Small, mushy, sometimes blown-out surf that is chopped up by cross winds and tides but is otherwise surfable.   **2**) Very poor surf.   **3**) Wind-forced wavelets a maximum of two feet high. (L&L)   **4**) Unridable waves. (H&R)

slope *n*. The curvature of the face of an unbroken wave.

slopey *adj*. Used to describe steep waves. Usage: "The waves are real slopey." (T & C Surf Shop, Ala Moana, Honolulu)

sloppy *adj*. Characteristic of surf in an onshore wind, when waves collapse and are formless or irregular. Usage: "Sloppy surf today, bro." (MW, MF)

slot *n*. **1**) A hole in which a skeg can be affixed; same as FIN SLOT.   **2**) The most desirable riding area of a wave, where the rider is in position to plane; a little less than halfway up from the forefront to the crest — that is, in the curl. To be **slotted in** is much preferable to being far out on the shoulder of a wave.

slot wave *n*. A wave in between the peaks of other waves, such as at Steamer Lane, Santa Cruz. (IBN)

slow surf *n*. Slow waves, as distinct from ZIPPERS. In slow surf, you have to work really hard to catch a wave, and the ride usually doesn't last very long.

sluggo *n*. An Australian term for a G-string bikini.

smack *v*. To hit or rebound, as in "to smack the lip of a wave."

smash, smashing *v*. SLASHING.

smog monster *n*. A derogatory term for an inland surfer. (Southern California; KH)

smokin' a pipe *v., n*. Speeding down the face of a wave in the tube. (MM) Usage: "I was smokin' a pipe out there."

smurf *n*. **1**) Small surf. (Texas; H&R)   **2**) **smurfage** Many small waves.

snake, snaking waves *v*. To drop down in front of another surfer who is already riding a wave. See SHOULDER HOPPER.

snake pit *n*. A wave full of shoulder hoppers. (San Francisco; JWN)

snap *n., v*. Riding directly into a wave and flipping around 180 degrees to begin riding the face. (JP) Usage: "Did you see that lip snap I pulled off?" "You really snapped it out there on the shoulder."

snap off the face *n*. A surfing maneuver. See SNAP.

snap turn *n*. A radical change in direction. (L&L)

snapback or **snap-back** or **snap back** *n*. A move invented by Ian Cairns in the early 1970s; rather than easing into a long, sweeping cutback, you race out onto the shoulder and then jam the full force of your body weight back onto the inside rail so violently that the board virtually comes to a stop. (L&L)

snapped board *n*. A surfboard that has broken into two pieces. Usage: "I snapped my board." See BROKEN BOARD.

snappy *adj*. Said of bitchin' waves or babes.

sneaker set *n*. A surprise group of larger-than-normal waves that come out of nowhere. (KSO) Same as SLEEPER SET.

sneaker wave *n*. SLEEPER WAVE.

snibbler *n*. Someone who tries to get everything for nothing — free lunch, free wax, free boards, etc. (Southern California; TMA)

snog, snog up *v*. A term with a flirtatious, sex-driven connotation — to encroach on someone's personal space, for example when some slimeball is sleezing up to a girl at the beach. Not necessarily a bad thing to have happen if the person being **snogged** is interested in the person

Carrying a spare—the answer to a snapped board, 1964
Photo: Bob Richardson

doing the **snogging**. (Newport Beach)

snowboarding *n*. Riding a specialized board on snow-covered mountain ski slopes. This surfing spin-off sport was featured in the opening sequence of the James Bond movie *A View to a Kill* (1985), where 007 surfs down the mountain.

. . . .

A miniglossary of snowboarding terms follows: **1**) **boardhead** Someone who snowboards all the time. **2**) **boardin'** Snowboarding, as in "Let's go boardin'." (RO) **3**) **lame air** Not very high. **4**) **lawn-chair air** Going really high in the air, then falling on the snow and collapsing like a lawn chair. **5**) **hairspray air** Jumping so high that you puncture the ozone. (JGD)

. . . .

snowsurfing *n*. An old term for SNOWBOARDING. (SFG, 10/85)

snuff, snuff out *v*. To WIPE OUT really fast; to be covered by the curl or tube and either disappear or be blasted off the board. Usage: "That wave totally snuffed me."

So Cal SOUTHERN CALIFORNIA.

soaker *n*. **1**) A surfer who never takes a wave; a DUCK or a BUOY. **2**) Someone who just sits out in the lineup and **soaks up** the sun and the saltwater.

soft *adj*. Used to describe slow, gentle surf that hasn't much energy. Usage: "The waves are pretty soft today."

soft board *n*. **1**) A surfboard made of soft sponge foam. **2**) A compliant surfboard that is easily maneuvered.

soft rack *n*. A surf rack made from foam pads strapped across the roof of a car.

soft rail *n*. A rounded rail with a softer, less defined edge.

soft wing *n*. A wing with a less defined edge. **—soft-wing swallowtail**

sognar, sognared *v*. When a dog that's been playing in the ocean

solid
A solid 10-foot wave—
if not bigger
Photo: Don Balch

sognar
Art: Rick Stover

comes up and shakes off on you; to get sprayed. Usage: "I got sognared by my dog." (Santa Barbara; TJ and his dog, Mort)

solid *adj*. **1**) Used to describe the feel of a surfboard or a wave. Usage: "Your board feels really solid." "That last wave felt really solid." **2**) Looking like a good-size wave; solid waves are five to six feet. (WWK) Usage: "It was a solid six feet out there today."

soul arch *n*. A back bend while surfing; a wave rider's posture. Also called ARCH.

soul surfer *n*. **1**) A surfer who surfs for the joy of it. **2**) A noncompetitive surfer. (MM) **—soul surfing**

sound *v*. **1**) To deliver harsh words to an unwelcome surfer. Usage: "That dude totally sounded me." **2**) To dive to the bottom of the ocean. (JKMJ, 1965)

soup *n*. **1**) The turbulent foam created by a wave's breaking; not very suitable for surfing, and often dangerous in big surf. Also called FROTH, SWASH, WHITE WATER. **2**) A mixture of air bubbles and moving water. **—soupy** *adj*.

soup bowl *n*. The white-water area known as the bone yard.

south swell *n*. A swell that moves from the south to the north. (ORB)

south wind *n*. A wind that blows from south to north. (ORB) Usage: "The wind has a little south in it."

Southern California *n*. **1**) The mythological capital of the sport of surfing and its attendant lifestyles — a creation helped along by music and movies about surfing. George Freeth was the first person to surf Southern California, at Redondo Beach in 1907. (BHP) See CALIFORNIA MYTH. **2**) In a strict geographic sense, the area in California beginning at Point Conception and continuing to the Mexican border. As a social and stylistic boundary within the surfing world, however, the dividing line between the northern and southern part of the state is debatable; the transition begins somewhere around Santa Barbara and Oxnard. (SFR) Also called SO CAL.

southers *n.* A derogatory term for Southern California surfers.

south-facing beach *n.* Where the coastline is oriented in an east-west direction, such as at Malibu and Santa Cruz.

spaghetti arms *n.* A condition caused by surfing for hours on end. In Australia when the classic point breaks are happening, you can't stop even after riding incredibly long waves because the good waves are so numerous you can't stand to see them go to waste. So you continue surfing for hours, and all that paddling makes your arms and legs tired and heavy. (MW)

Spanish for surfers See "Spanish for the Mexico-bound Surfer" on page 75.

sparkle factor *n.* **1)** The diamond-like glistening of the sun's rays reflecting off of the ocean, especially in the afternoon as the sun goes down. **2)** The glitter of moonglow on the ocean. **3)** Whether created by sun or moon, one of the most pleasing visual sensations of being at the beach or floating in the lineup.

"Innumerable twinkling of the waves of the sea." —Aeschylus (525–456 B.C.) in *Prometheus Bound*

sparkle room *n.* Inside the tube; same as GREEN ROOM.

speed bead *n.* A resin ridge near the rail on the bottom of a surfboard, the purpose of which is to direct water flow and increase speed. (ORB)

speed bump *n.* SPONGE. (SWH)

speed finish *n.* A thin layer of fiberglass applied to a surfboard to enhance high-performance surfing; makes the board lighter but doesn't last as long as a regular glass job.

speed run *n.* A skimboarding maneuver in which the skimboarder rides out into an incoming wave and surfs it back onto the beach.

speed shape *n.* A surfboard shape featuring an elongated nose and tail; developed around 1972.

speed tails *n.* A surfboard with a sleek shape designed for speed. (A&M) See SPEED SHAPE.

specialty fins *n.* Fins designed for specific surfing conditions, such as the omega fin, which is designed so it won't grab kelp.

SPF Sun protection factor — the rating number on sun screen tubes and bottles (2, 4, 6, 8, 10, etc., up to total blockout) that refers to the amount of time you can expect to be protected from the sun's harmful ultraviolet rays. For example, an SPF #8 rating means that you can stay in the sun eight times longer and be protected. Nonetheless, the time varies for each individual.

Spicoli, Jeff 1) A character played by Sean Penn in the movie *Fast Times at Ridgemont High* (1982). Pot smoking, long haired, and a poor student, personified one version of the modern surfer. Because of Spicoli, terms like *dude* and *gnarly* entered the mainstream ("Hey, dude — let's party!"). **2) spicoli** Someone who acts or looks like the character in the movie. Usage: "He's a total spicoli."

spider ding *n.* A small, cobweb-like fracture of the fiberglass skin on the rail of a surfboard. (BP)

spilling wave, spilling breaker, spiller *n.* **1)** A cresting wave that breaks forward gradually, crumbling at the top and spilling down the front. Such a wave breaks slowly and without the violent release of energy needed to fling the crest for-

sparkle factor
Tex Wilson
Photo: Bob Richardson

ward into the trough ahead. A good example is the surf at Waikiki in Hawaii. (WB) **2)** A wave that spills over instead of breaking clean. See FEATHERING WAVE.

spin out *v.* What happens when the skeg and tail lose contact with the wave face, usually because of the sharpness of a turn or the tightness of the trimming, and the rider takes a spill. Usage: "Did you see me spin out on that wave?" —**spinout** *n.*

spinner *n.* **1)** A maneuver in which the surfer turns around 360 degrees on the board while riding a wave. This move is distinct from a three sixty, where the board itself is rotated in a full-circle turn. **2)** A 360-degree body spin or twist on a Malibu. (NAT, 1985)

spinning board *n.* The fate of a board thrown into the air by the force of a wave, aided by its buoyancy. Usage: "Look at that spinning board."

spiral V *n.* A vee in the tail section of the bottom of a surfboard that comes to a point under the backfoot area. (L&L) This design helps channel water away from the board.

spitter *n.* A tubing wave that emits air and spray as it collapses. Air caught in a curl must go somewhere when a wave collapses; if there is an open end, the air and spray hiss out and the wave is called a "spitter." See TUBE SPIT.

splampted *n.* To get wiped out. (LH)

spleet *n.* GEEK or GOON. (Florida; TDW)

spock out, spock *v.* To check, peruse, or look over. Usage: "Hey man, spock this out." "Did you spock out that last cutback I did?" (SFG, 12/81)

sponge
Art: Peter Spacek

sponge *n.* **1)** A degrading term for boogie boarders, who surf on soft, flexible foam boards. Also called *sponge heads, sponge people, sponge riders, spongers.* Usage: "Kind of a sponge problem out here, dude." (California) See BOOGIE FLAPPER. **2)** A leach.

spoon *n.* The upturned nose of a surfboard, whose purpose is to keep the board from pearling; made popular by Reynolds Yater. (MCR) Also called SCOOP, CAMBER, ROCKER.

spot *n.* The place where waves are generated; a SURF SPOT. Usage: "That spot is totally happening." —**hot spot**

spring suit *n.* A wetsuit with either long or short arms and short legs cut above the knees.

spring tides *n.* Tides that occur twice a month, at the new and full moons, when the sun and the moon are in line with the earth and their combined gravitational force produces tides that are of greater magnitude than average. The highest high tide and the lowest low tide occur during spring tides.

squall *n.* A gust of violent wind, often accompanied by heavy rain, and lasting only a short while; a common occurrence in the tropics. See WIND SQUALL, RAIN SQUALL.

squall line *n.* An advancing wall of rain. Usage: "Look at that squall line out over the water."

square *n.* **1)** An extremely hollow wave whose bottom drops quickly as the top pitches, stretching the wave face vertically and creating "corners" on the wave profile; can be dangerous to surfers. The term originated in Australia but is also used in the U.S. (MW) **2)** One of the tail shapes of a surfboard; also the name of a surfboard with a square tail.

square tail or **squaretail** *n.* A surfboard with the tail squared off, rather than rounded or pointed.

squared-off fin *n.* STRAIGHT-EDGE FIN.

squash tail or **squashtail** *n.* A surfboard design. A squared-off tail looks like either a square tail with

Slab. Photo: Woody Woodworth

Bodyboarder kneeling bottom turn.
Photo: Bill Romerhaus

Aerial. Josh Loya. Photo: Bud Clark

Gerry Lopez. Pipeline. Photo: Bob Barbour

Ben Severson bodyboarding. Photo: Woody Woodworth

Bodyboarder Maria Souza. Photo: Woody Woodworth

Cover-up. Photo: Bob Richardson

Longboard virtuosos. Photo: Don Balch

J. P. Patterson and son Travis. Photo: Woody Woodworth

Snowboarding. Photo: Tom Servais / *Surfer* Magazine

Tube ride sequence, Dane Kealoha, Backdoor, Hawaii. Photos: Rob Gilley

Tom Carrol quiver. Photo: Robert Brown

Shaper Bill Barnfield. Photo: John Callahan

Grommet. Photo: Fred Swegles

Surf art by Peter Schroff

blunted corners or a pintail that's been dropped on the ground. (SFG, 4/87)

squatting island pullout *n*. An ISLAND PULLOUT made in a squatting position. See SITTING ISLAND PULLOUT, STANDING ISLAND PULLOUT.

squatting through *v*. To crouch down to avoid being caught by the curl of a wave as it pours over. Usage: "Did you see me squatting through that cover-up?"

squealy *adj*. Used to describe a surfboard that performs very loosely, in contrast to one that is stiff and has stable handling characteristics.

squeegee *n*. In surfboard construction, a rubber tool used to force resin into fiberglass cloth so that the cloth becomes saturated.

squid, squid head *n*. KOOK; sometimes spelled skwid. **—inland squid**

squid lid *n*. A derogatory term for the neoprene hood that some surfers wear in cold water.

squid lips *n*. **1**) GEEK. **2**) A term for an overweight surfer. (H&R) Usage: "Hey — outta my way, squid lips."

stable *adj*. A surfboard handling characteristic; said of a board that maintains stability on a wave, for example by holding on the wave face through a turn. The opposite of SQUEALY.

stacked, stacked up *v., adj.*
1) Describes the situation of several surfers grouped closely — one above another — in or on a wave. Usage: "Check out that wave — those guys are completely stacked." **2**) Said of a group of many parallel waves, or lines, coming toward shore. **3**) Crashed; wiped out. Usage: "I fully stacked it on the rocks."

stall, stalling *v*. **1**) To slow one's forward speed in order to reposition oneself on the face of a breaking wave; similar to FADE. **2**) To slow the board when it has outdistanced a wave, usually by climbing up the wave's face, so that the curl can catch up with the surfer. **3**) To slow a board down and pull it out of a wave. (IDSM) **4**) To slow the board while waiting for the wave to steepen ahead. **—stall** *n*.

. . . .

To stall a board, the surfer steps back, shifting his or her weight to the rear of the board, and angles the board up toward the top of the wave. A bodysurfer can stall by raising head and shoulders.

. . . .

stall out 1) *v*. To lose the wave by letting the nose of the surfboard ride too high (DSHJ); **stalled out.**
2) **stallout** *n*. A stall held long enough to let the wave pass by.

stacked
Photo: Robert Brown

skwid

Foam

squid
Art: The Pizz

stand-up tube
Joey Buran
Photo: Robert Brown

stingray
Southern stingray
Art: Andrea McCann

stand up 1) *v*. The motion of a swell as it comes out of deep water and rises to break. (MW) Usage: "That swell really stands up on the outside reef." See JACK.   **2**) **stand-up** *n*. A beginning bodyboarding move.

stand-up tube *n*. A tube large enough for a surfer to stand up inside of it.

standard *n*. **1**) A type of surfboard. Same as STOCK.   **2**) A surfer who rides with the left foot forward; a left-foot-forward stance. Same as NATURAL. See GOOFY FOOT.

standard foil *n*. See FOIL.

standing island, standing island pullout *n*. **1**) An ISLAND PULLOUT made in a standing position. See SITTING ISLAND PULLOUT, SQUATTING ISLAND PULLOUT.   **2**) A pullout in which the rider slashes through the back of a wave while standing toward the front or on the nose of the board.

standing up The normal surfboard position — standing on two feet as you ride a wave in to shore, as opposed to kneeling or lying on your stomach.

standing wave *n*. A spot on a river where water coursing over a rock consistently forms a wave that a surfer can ride while remaining in one place. This happens, for example, on the Snake River in Wyoming and on the Eisbach River in Munich, Germany. Same as STATIONARY WAVE. See RIVER SURFING.

star tail *n*. A surfboard tail that ends in two points, rather than in a single point, as in a pintail.

stationary wave *n*. STANDING WAVE.

Statue of Liberty *n*. A cutback or snapback right in the hook, in which the surfer's leading arm raises high like the Statue of Liberty's. (SFG, 12/81)

stay dry An expression meaning "Don't take that wave." (LH) Usage: "Dude, stay dry."

stay-wag *n*. A station wagon. (LWK) See LAND YACHT.

staying high in the section *v., n.* **1**) Riding in the upper portion of the wave crest as a means of gaining speed.   **2**) Taking a track across the wave's lip in order to get the most out of the available energy. (A&M)

steamer *n*. An Australian term for FULL SUIT, a wetsuit with long arms and legs. (NAT, 1985)

steamer lane *n*. **1**) The general area where ships pass by offshore.   **2**) Loosely, any place far out from the shore.   **3**) A deep-water surfing site.   **4**) **Steamer Lane** The Santa Cruz surf spot known locally as **Steamers** or "**the Lane**"; the site of the annual Cold Water Classic, a stop on the ASP World Tour.

steep *adj*. Said of waves or wave faces that incline sharply. Usage: "Man, that wave was steep." —**wave steepness, steep takeoff**

step *n*. On a hydroplane surfboard, the line or shoulder differentiating the planing surface from the scorpion tail. See HYDOPLANE STEP.

stepoff *n*. **1**) A move to terminate a ride by walking back, one foot at a time.   **2**) A stall or exit necessitated by coming to the end of a wave or reaching the shore line. (L&L)

stern *n*. The rear end of a surfboard.

stick *n*. **1**) A SURFBOARD.   **2**) A STRINGER — a piece of wood, such as redwood, that is glued between the two sides of a surfboard for strength; when preshaped, it helps the shaper to shape the board. Additional off-center or curved sticks are sometimes added for greater strength, weight, and design.

sticker placement *n*. The orientation and display of surf stickers and decals on your surfboard. Whether you have the "right" stickers or even the right number of stickers is viewed by some as a measure of how cool you are. See SURF STICKERS.

stiff *adj.* A surfboard handling characteristic that has to do with how easily a board maneuvers; the opposite of LOOSE.

stiffener *n.* STRINGER or STICK. Usage: "We can add an additional stiffener to the board."

sting, stinger, stinger board *n.* A surfboard design that features pronounced wings and, consequently, a more forward pivot point. (SFR, 6/88) **2)** A shift in the template that alters the rail line. (ORB)

stingray *n.* An elasmobranch fish of the family Dasyatidae that has a flattened body, greatly enlarged pectoral fins, and a long, flexible tail armed near the base with a strong, serrated bony spine that can inflict a very painful puncture wound in the foot if the ray is stepped on. (S&C)

Stingrays inhabit sandy bays with flat bottoms, so be extra careful when wading through shallow murky water. One preventive technique is the "Jake Shuffle" (named after a Long Beach fireman who invented it in Baja): simply move your feet in small, sweeping circles as you walk out into the water, and the disturbance will cause any rays in the vicinity to swim away.

stink eye *n.* A hostile, threatening, contemptible, or utterly curious way of looking at someone. (Hawaii; S&S) Usage: "Wow, you saw da stink eye she wen geev me?" (DSN)

stinkbug stance *n.* An awkward squatting position in which the surfer's rear end protrudes like a stinkbug's. (A&M)

stitches *n.* The means of sewing together the gash in your head after you get smacked or speared by a surfboard, or mauled by a coral reef.

stock *n., adj.* The basic board type, which today is the rounded pintail — the standard by which all others are judged; a very versatile design that can deal with a wide variety of situations. Usage: "He's riding a stock." "I bought a stock board." Same as STANDARD.

stokaboka or **stoka boka** *adj.* Superstoked. (1960s)
—cowabunga stokaboka

stoked *adv., adj.* **1)** Excited, thrilled, jazzed — usually about the surf; chock-full of enthusiasm or satisfaction. **2)** Feeling the ultimate in exhilaration; feeling high on life — can't wait to go surfing. **3)** An impressed reaction to something "boss." (IDSM) **4)** A reaction to the ultimate ride on the ultimate wave. (MM) Usage: "I'm stoked!" "I was stoked to the max." **5) stoke** *n.* A term sometimes used to mention an encounter with marine animals. Usage: "Did you see the pelican stoke I had out there?" "No, but I got seal stoked." **6) stoke** *v.* To feed a fire on the beach, or to feed hungry individuals. For instance, Pacific Northwest lumberjacks often stoke themselves with a huge breakfast. **7) stoker** *n.* Something that makes you feel stoked. Usage: "What a stoker." "That was a real stoker." **—surf stoked, stoke-a-rama, stoking**

"To catch a wave was (and is) to stoke the fires of the heart and soul. Hence the terms: to be stoked, the stoked life, degrees of stoke, and pure stoke." — John Grissim, *Pure Stoke* (1982)

stomp patch *n.* DECK PATCH.

storm *n.* A disturbance of the atmosphere marked by wind, rain, thunder, lightning, etc., and responsible for whipping up the surf. In weather language, storms are low pressure systems, which have unstable moving air and winds blowing counter-

stoked
Art: Bob Penuelas

Photo: Tom Dodd

clockwise around their center. (W&B)

storm-drain runoff *n.* A major contributor to ocean pollution, especially during heavy rains when raw, untreated sewage filled with bacteria and heavy metal residue spills into the ocean, putting surfers at risk of contracting hepatitis. See SANTA MONICA BAY.

storm front *n.* The leading edge of a storm; may bring good surf.

storm surf *n.* Waves generated by a local storm, which are usually big but not clean.

storm-surge waves, storm surges, sea surges *n.* Wind-driven waves caused by cyclones, superimposed on storm-swollen tides. Usually produce a systematic, pounding surf, but can also form single crests up to forty feet high and do incredible damage. (OA) Not to be confused with tsunamis.

storm track *n.* The path a storm takes.

straight-edge fin *n.* An old concept (the **squared-off fin** — 1968–1972) with a new application and a simple design premise — that straighter lines beget cleaner, more efficient release. The extra area at the tip increases holding power, so that the fin can be shorter and still hold in. (B, 6/83) Same as ANGULAR 757 FIN.

straight in, straight off or **straight-off** *adv.* **1)** Refers to riding straight toward shore, without turning or angling, directly in line with the movement of the wave, rather than sliding across the wave. **2)** A term applied to the riding style of novices.

straight out "I mean it." "That's it." (TMA)

straight ride *n.* The last ride of a session — straight in to the beach. (SWH)

storm surf
Santa Cruz, Westside, winter '83
Photo: Woody Woodworth

straighten off, straighten out *v.* **1)** To turn from riding at a definite angle across a wave to heading directly toward shore or in the same direction as the wave is moving. **2)** To ride directly toward shore in front of the white water to escape the wave. (ORB)

Strauch crouch *n.* A riding position developed by Paul Strauch in the Hawaiian Islands in the 1960s. Traveling parallel to the wave, in trim, the surfer moves forward on the board, crouches, not right on the nose but a few feet from it, then extends the forward foot and hangs it over the nose. (MF) Also called CHEATER FIVE, CHEATER FIVE NOSE RIDE.

stretch five *n.* A longboard maneuver; same as CHEATER FIVE. (KSO)

stretched *adj.* Describes what happens to a swell that, because it is coming in at an angle, must bend around to fit the contour of a point; consequently it loses much of its size. See WAVE REFRACTION. Usage: "That swell is really stretched."

stringer *n.* **1)** The wooden runner or runners (1/16 to 1/4 inch thick) that most well-made surfboards have inside of them, aligned from front to back along the longitudinal centerline, for the purpose of strengthening the foam and fiberglass. The stringer sets the rocker, that is, it determines how much curvature (nose scoop) the surfboard will have. **2)** Narrow strips of wood, usually redwood, laminated into a surfboard, generally for strength or decoration. **3)** Thin pieces of wood glued down the middle of the foam core, or blank, to give lateral strength. (NAT, 1985) Also called STICK, STRIP.

Although stringers are commonly made of redwood, balsa, butternut, and spruce can also be used. Canadian cedar gives a rich dark effect or, if a blonde appearance is required for the finished job, Pacific maple (which is slightly stronger) can be used. (ASKC) Greg Noll was the first to use light-weight sticks (aircraft-grade spruce) for stringers, which he did to reduce the weight.

. . . . , , ,

stringer line *n.* A line measured from the tip of the nose to the tail of a surfboard; a measure of the length of a board.

strip *n.* A narrow piece of wood used to reinforce a surfboard; sometimes used for decoration only. Same as STRINGER.

stripes *n.* Decorations applied on the outside of a surfboard.

stroking into a wave The act of paddling and taking off on a wave.

strong swell *n.* A swell that is well developed and bringing good waves.

style *n.* The distinctive quality in the way individual surfers ride the waves.

styling, stylin', stylish *adj.* **1)** Fully cool. Usage: "That's so styling." **2)** Used to compliment a fancy maneuver. Usage: "That was a way stylish cutback." "Dude, you were fully stylin' out there."

styrene *n.* A resin thinner.

submarine *n.* A board that is too small, short, or thin for the rider, so that he or she is floated partially under the surface.

submarine canyon *n.* A steep, underwater, V-shaped valley cut into the continental shelf and slope. The part of a wave that comes in over the canyon moves at full speed when nearing the beach, while the part that is over the shallower fringes of the canyon slows down; this creates a bend in the swell — a bowl or pocket — where generally a large peak forms that is larger than the original swell, and the wave peels off in both directions from the center of the peak. (CCRG, W&B)

submerger *n.* A wave that forces the front end of a surfboard to pearl.

suck milk *v.* To WIPE OUT, EAT SHIT, drink white water. Usage: "Sucking plenty milk, brah." (Hawaii; BNJ, P, 1983)

suck out, suck up *v.* What happens when an advancing wave draws water into, and up, its face as it breaks. Usage: "That wave really sucks up at low tide near the jetty." **—hollow suckular tubes, heavy suckouts** *n.*

sucked out *v.* To get carried away in a current. Usage: "I was sucked out to the point."

sucked over *v.* To be pulled back by the force of a breaking wave and creamed in the white water. (A&M) **—sucked over the falls**

suckey wave or **sucky wave** *n.* **1)** A wave that breaks extremely fast, throwing its lip out in front of itself and creating a space or tube; caused by the wave passing suddenly over a shallow spot and throwing forward. A suckey wave is like a DREDGING WAVE, only slightly less awesome. **2)** An extremely hollow wave. (Australia; NAT, 1985; MW)

sudden-death takeoff *n.* KAMIKAZE RUN. (A&M)

summer *n.* The time of year when the beach gets crowded and things start to heat up, as in "Summer Means Fun" (1964), a song originally by the Fantastic Baggys and later by Jan & Dean.

summer break *n.* A break that occurs only in summer; a seasonal surf spot, usually the result of a shifting sandbar or of swell coming from a particular direction. See WINTER BREAK.

summer swell *n.* A south swell generated by storms in the South Pacific, most commonly between April and October, or by chubascos (hurricanes) off of the coast of Baja California from June to November.

style
J. Riddle
Photo: Don Balch

"You'll like this place, it's all fresh baked daily."
Art: I. B. Nelson

Sunset Beach
North Shore, Hawaii
Photo: Bob Barbour

surf art
"Birth of Venus" by Tim
Smith; mixed media on
surfboard

surf bomb
Will Natilla
Photo: Don Balch

The waves come in strong, clear lines, usually two to five feet high but occasionally over fifteen feet. (S&C)

sun *n*. **1)** A source of gravitational pull on waves. Compared with that of the moon, however, it has little influence. **2)** The source of **sun rays,** celebrated in such music as "The Warmth of the Sun" by The Beach Boys and "We All Live for the Sun" by the Surf Punks. On the negative side, too much time spent in the sun can cause skin cancer. See TROPPO.

sunglasses *n*. Fashion articles that make you look cool and that filter out harmful ultraviolet (UV) rays. Also called *darkglasses, shades,* etc.

sunscreen *n*. A protective lotion applied to the skin to minimize sunburn. See ZINC.

Sunset Beach A famous surf spot on the North Shore of Oahu, Hawaii, known especially for its peak. Originally called Pau Malu, it was later named after the Sunset Market just down the road. It was first surfed by Greg Noll and others in 1957 and is now the site of major surfing contests, including a leg of the Hawaiian Triple Crown.

suntan *n*. The deep golden-brown color that a surfer acquires from hanging out under the sun all the time; an indispensable part of the surfer image.

suntan lotion *n*. See SPF.

suntan oil *n*. A means of greasing up before exposure to the sun that provides little or no protection against the sun's harmful rays.

Supertubes or **Super Tubes** *n*. A name given to various surf spots, for instance the ones in Ventura County, California, and in Peniche, Portugal.

surf *n*. **1)** The area of any body of water adjoining the shoreline in which the wave action is accelerated by reason of the decreasing depth of water approaching the shoreline. **2)** The line or mass of foamy water caused by the sea breaking against the shore or rocks. Variously called *sea, waves, breakers, rollers, whitecaps, white horses, billows, surge, spume, sea foam, froth, spindrift, spray.* **3)** The foam, splash, and sound of breaking waves. **4)** *v*. To ride the surf (as on a surfboard). *Oxford English Dictionary's* etymology of surf on next page.

surf *n*. A SURF SESSION. Usage: "I had some nice surfs last week." "I went out for a surf today."

Surf 1) A small coastal town (elevation 10) in Santa Barbara County, California. **2)** A brand name of laundry detergent, popular among surfers.

surf art, surfing art *n*. Art created by people who surf. Examples are giant wall murals painted on the outside of surf shops, surf graffiti, and furniture made from surfboards. In recent years, collecting surf paintings has become increasingly popular.

surf band *n*. A group that plays surf music, such as Dick Dale and The Deltones.

surf beat *n*. **1)** The action and impact of sets of waves crashing against the shore. **2)** The sound of surf music.

surf bomb *n*. A clunker car. (BP)

surf breaks *n*. Places where waves are breaking. There are several kinds of surf break, depending on the ocean bottom contour or the obstructions causing the waves to break: **1) beach break, shore break** Where the surf breaks close in to shore and sometimes directly onto the beach. **2) peak break** Waves that form peaks as they begin to break; usually formed in conjunction with a reef. **3) pier break** Surf generated by pier pilings in the water. **4) point break** Surf that breaks in along a line that wraps

surf (sɜːf), *sb.* Also 8 **surff**. [Continues SUFF *sb.* in chronology and meaning, but the relation between the forms is not clear. (Not in general Dicts. before Todd, 1818.)

Both *suff* and *surf* are used particularly in reference to the coast of India, a circumstance which would make a native origin for the words probable.]

1. a. The swell of the sea which breaks upon a shore, esp. a shallow shore. (In recent use usually with implication of sense 2.)

1685 W. HEDGES *Diary* (Hakl. Soc.) I. 182 [At Fort St. George, Madras] This unhappy accident, together with yᵉ greatness of yᵉ Sea and Surf ashore, caused us to come aboard again. **1719** DE FOE *Crusoe* I. (Globe) 50 My Raft was now strong enough to bear any reasonable Weight; my next Care was..how to preserve what I laid upon it from the Surf of the Sea. **1745** P. THOMAS *Jrnl. Anson's Voy.* 35 The Landing is bad by reason of pretty much Surf, and great Stones like Rocks. **1774** GOLDSM. *Nat. Hist.* (1862) I. xvii. 97 This rising of the waves against the shore, is called by mariners the surf of the sea. **1783** W. MARSDEN *Hist. Sumatra* (1811) 34 The surf..is used in India, and by navigators in general, to express a peculiar swell and breaking of the sea upon the shore. **1836** W. IRVING *Astoria* II. 100 Low bellowings..like the hoarse murmurs of the surf on a distant shore. **1840** E. E. NAPIER *Scenes & Sports For. Lands* I. p. xii, The progress of the neophyte..in that far land, from the moment when having crossed the 'surf' [*Note.* An expression equivalent to entering or leaving India, as a person is never supposed to venture across this tremendous barrier of the Coromandel coast, unless on such momentous occasions.] **1886** RUSKIN *Præterita* I. 379 Half-a-mile of dangerous surf between the ship and the shore. **1906** MAX PEMBERTON *My Sword for Lafayette* xxiv, The distant thunder of the sea surf upon an angry shore.

b. with *a.* Also *transf.* (in first quot.).

1698 FRYER *Acc. E. India & P.* 14 A notable Fish..It might be in length forty Feet..bolting out of the Water with a great Surf. **1748** *Anson's Voy.* II. ii. 134 The wind..occasioned such a surf, that it was impossible for the boat to land. **1763** THOMPSON *Temple of Venus* i. 14 A dull promiscuous sound a-far..like..southern surffs upon an iron shore. **1803** WITTMAN *Trav. Turkey* 3 A military artificer was unfortunately washed off the vessel by a surf. **1840** MACAULAY *Ess.*, *Clive* ⁸8 Fort St. George had arisen on a barren spot beaten by a raging surf. **1879** A. R. WALLACE's *Australasia* xvi. 303 The southern coast..is exposed to a heavy and dangerous surf, which rolls in upon the shore at all seasons.

2. a. The mass or line of white foamy water caused by the sea breaking upon a shore or a rock.

1757 tr. *Keysler's Trav.* IV. 141 *note*, Salt..was not produced here as in other countries by a desiccation of the surf of the sea [tr. Tacitus *Ann.* XIII. lvii. *non ut alias apud gentis eluvie maris arescente unda*]. **1784** COWPER *Task* V. 155 Light as the foamy surf That the wind severs from the broken wave. **1833** TENNYSON *Dream Fair Wom.* viii, White surf wind-scatter'd over sails and masts. **1882** 'OUIDA' *Maremma* I. 78 She played with the surf, with the sand, and with the crystals of the salt.

b. *transf.* and *fig.*

1847 LONGF. *Ev.* II. iii. 24 Just where the woodlands met the flowery surf of the prairie. **1873** LOWELL *Above & Below* II. i, To behold The first long surf of climbing light Flood all the thirsty east with gold.

3. *attrib.* and *Comb.*: Simple *attrib.*, 'of or pertaining to surf', as *surf barrier*, *-beach*, *-beat*, *-billow*, *line*, *-rock*, *-sound*, *-thunder*; locative, as *surf-bathe* vb., *-bather*, *-bathing*, *-fish* vb., *-fisherman*, *-fishing*, *lifesaver*, *lifesaving*, *-rider*, *-riding*, *-swimmer*, *-swimming*; *surf-sunk* adj.; instrumental, as *surf-battered*, *-beaten*, *-bound*, *-showered*, *-tormented*, *-vexed*, *-washed*, *-wasted*, *-worn* adjs.; similative, as *surf-white* adj.; also **surf-bird**, a small, plover-like bird, *Aphriza virgata*, found on the Pacific coast of America; **surfboard**, a long narrow board on which one rides over a heavy surf to shore; hence as *v. intr.*, to ride on a surfboard (also *fig.*); **surfboarder**, **surfboarding** *vbl. sb.*; **surf-boat**, a boat specially constructed for passing through surf; hence **surf-boatman** = *surfman*; **surf-bum** *slang*, a surfing enthusiast who frequents beaches suitable for surf-riding; cf. *ski bum* s.v. SKI *sb.* 2 b; **surf-casting** *vbl. sb.*, fishing by casting a line into the sea from the shore; so (as a back-formation) **surf-cast** *v. intr.*, **surf-caster**; **surf-clam**, a large clam, esp. *Mactra* (or *Spisula*) *solidissima*, found on the Atlantic coast of the United States (*Funk's Standard Dict.* 1895); **surf-coot** = *surf-duck*; **surf day**, a day marked by rough surf along the shore (see quot. 1854); **surf-duck**, a North American species of sea-duck of the genus *Œdemia*, esp. *O. perspicillata*, found sometimes in Great Britain; **surf-fish**, any one of the numerous species of the family *Embiotocidæ*, abundant on the coast of California; **surf-grass**, any of several species of marine grass of the genus *Phyllospadix* (family *Zosteraceæ*), having thickened rootstocks and slender stems and growing underwater on rocky shores in temperate regions; **surf-man** *U.S.*, a member of the crew of a surf-boat; hence **surfmanship**; **surf music**, a variety of rock music which celebrates the sport of surf-riding; **surf-perch** = *surf-fish*; **surf-ride** *v. intr.* [back-formation from *surf-riding* above] = *surfboard* vb. above; also *fig.* and as *v. trans.* and *sb.*; **surf safari** = SURFARI; **surf-scoter** = *surf-duck*; **surf-shiner**, a small California fish, *Cymatogaster aggregatus* (Webster 1911); **surf-smelt**, a species of smelt, *Hypomesus olidus*, found on the Pacific coast of the United States; **surf-whiting**, the silver whiting, *Menticirrus littoralis*.

1940 V. BRITTAIN *Testament of Friendship* xii. 192 You'll look at the Rhodes Memorial and the Union Buildings..; you'll.. *surf-bathe* at Durban..and then you'll begin to think you know everything. **1893** KATE SANBORN *S. California* 163 *Surf* bathers go in every month of the year. **1884** *Encycl. Brit.* XVII. 461/1 Conveniences for *surf-bathing*. **1902** *Temple Bar* May 579 Like *surf-battered* swimmers. **1932** N. PALMER *Talking it Over* 137 *Surf-beaches* of any size are rare in the world. **1966** *Weekly News* (N.Z.) 19 Jan. 11/1 Mt. Maunganui is probably one of New Zealand's best-known surf beaches. **1977** *Herald* (Melbourne) 17 Jan. 14/4 Within 16 km of Wollongong are 17 superb surf beaches. **1873** 'MARK TWAIN' *Gilded Age* I. 543 A receding of tides, a quieting of the storm-wash to a murmurous *surf-beat*. **1974** *Encycl. Brit. Micropædia* IX. 689/2 Surf beat, ocean waves of uncertain origin, with the relatively long periods of 1 to 5 minutes. These low-frequency waves appear to be related to the interaction of normal wind waves and swell. Surf beat is believed responsible for the generation of seiches in bays. **1801** CAMPBELL *Lochiel's Warning* 82 Like ocean-weeds heaped on the *surf-beaten* shore. **1890** 'R. BOLDREWOOD' *Col. Reformer* (1891) 154 The deep-toned ceaseless roll of the *surf-billows*. **1872** COUES *N. Amer. Birds* 245 *Aphriza*, *Surf Bird*. *c*1826 RICHARDS in Gosse *Ocean* vi. (1849) 285 Those who were standing on the beach saw the *surf-bird*..floating on the water. **1931** T. E. LAWRENCE *Let.* 14 July (1938) 729 Here is a final report..on the little surf-board target. **1934** WEBSTER, *Surfboard*, *v.i.*, to ride the surf on a surfboard.—*surfboarding*, *n.* **1938** E. HEMINGWAY *Fifth Column* (1939) III. iv. 103 Or what about Malindi where you can surfboard on the beach. **1962** *Coast to Coast 1961–62* 63 He wished he could stand up and walk away from Pammie and go out with the surf-board riders. **1962** M. McLUHAN *Gutenberg Galaxy* 248 (*heading*) Heidegger surf-boards along on the electronic wave as triumphantly as Descartes rode the mechanical wave. **1953** *Pop. Mechanics* July 157 Hitching a ride on a beach-bound ocean wave with a featherlight surf-board is rated tops in water sports by practiced *surf-boarders*. **1969** *Britannica Bk. of Year* 1968 801/1 *Surfari*, a group of surfboarders who travel together in search of good surfing areas. **1964** *Sunday Mail Mag.* (Brisbane) 17 May 1 *Surfboarding* was virtually forgotten until the late 1930's. **1898** DICKENS *Wreck Golden Mary* (1898) 22, I gave..the word to lower the Long-boat and the *Surf-boat*. **1883** J. D. CAMPBELL *Fisheries China* 5 (Fish. Exhib. Publ.) The catamarans are surf-boats of South Formosa. **1886** *Encycl. Brit.* XXI. 804/2 The Madras surf boats. **1880** *Scribner's Mag.* Jan. 323 It is an erroneous notion that the experience of the sailor qualifies him for a *surf-boatman*. **1884** *19th Cent.* Feb. 239 The noisy tumult of a *surf-bound* shore. **1958** *Surf-bum* [see PETITE *a.* 2]. **1971** Surf-bum [see PIPE-LINE *sb.* c]. **1975** *Country Life* 16 Jan. 131/2 *Surf-cast* for corvina..on a California beach and you will probably have to show your California fishing licence. **1958** 'S. JAY' *Sleepers can Kill* xxiv. 248 When you've walked through to the beach, you'll see a *surfcaster*, fishing by himself. **1928** *N.Y. Times* 8 Oct. 21/4 Charles Vollum of Philadelphia became *surf casting* champion of the United States today at the annual tournament of the Dover Fishing Club of Philadelphia. **1963** *Weekly News* (Auckland, N.Z.) 8 May 56/6 Pukehina surfcasting beach. Near Te Puke, Bay of Plenty, one of the best surfcasting beaches in New Zealand. **1979** *Angling* July 45/3 As a contemporary guide to the basics of all shorefishing it gives excellent surfcasting instruction. **1884** *Bull. U.S. Nat. Museum* No. 27. 260 Hen Clam, *Surf Clam*, or Sea Clam. Florida and Gulf of Mexico to Labrador. **1949** [see SKIMMER *sb.* 1 c]. **1978** *Times* 29 July 3/6 More than two weeks after the wreck..we saw millions of dead molluscs, urchins, razor and surf clams. **1885** SEEBOHM *Brit. Birds* III. 610 To the hunters on Long Island it [the Surf-scoter] is known as the 'Spectacled Coot' and *Surf-Coot*. **1854** G. W. PECK *Melbourne & Chincha Islands* 187 Often when the mornings are still, and the surface of the sea undisturbed by a ripple, the surf will be rolling tremendously on the narrow beaches.. These are called '*surf-days*', and special allowance is made for them in the charter parties of vessels loading at the islands. **1950** J. S. LEARMONT *Master in Sail* 60 Surf days did not count as working days. These surf days are peculiar to the northern part of the coast of Chile. **1808–13** A. WILSON & BONAPARTE *Amer. Ornith.* (1832) III. 70 Black, or *Surf Duck*, *Anas perspicillata*... This duck is peculiar to America, and..confined to the shores and bays of the sea. **1882** JORDAN & GILBERT *Fishes N. Amer.* 585 Embiotocidæ. The *Surf-fishes*... Fishes of the Pacific coast of North America, inhabiting bays and the surf on sandy beaches. **1940** O. H. P. RODMAN *Handbk. Salt-Water Fishing* iii. 99 We will make a definite statement in regard to wetting down your cutty hunk line before you really start surf fishing. **1979** 'A. BLAISDELL' *No Villain need Be* vii. 120 They like to surf-fish, and they claim rain..drives 'em in toward the beach. **1920** HEILNER & STICK *Call of Surf* i. 5 Those great and goodly fish which so frequently take into their capacious jaws the bait of the *surf-fisherman*. **1967** O. E. MIDDLETON in *Coast to Coast 1965–66* 123 The surf-fishermen leaned out over the shallows. **1920** HEILNER & STICK *Call of Surf* i. 4 *Surf fishing* is by no means a new development of the angler's art..but only of late years has it begun to achieve real popularity. **1949** S. K. FARRINGTON *Fishing the Atlantic* iv. 82 Surf fishing at Narragansett should be a revelation. **1923** L. ABRAMS *Illustr. Flora Pacific States* I. 94 *Phyllospadix torreyi* S. Wats. Torrey's *Surf-grass*. **1981** *Sci. Amer.* Mar. 92/1 The sea grasses number 12 genera and ..about 50 species... Eelgrass and surfgrass are familiar examples in temperate regions. **1977** *N.Z. Herald* 8 Jan. 1–6/4, I have been talking to the wife of a *surf lifesaver*, and she spoke of the apparent indifference people show on being saved from drowning. **1968** W. WARWICK *Surfriding in N.Z.* 1 It is difficult to imagine how closely it was once associated with the *surf lifesaving* movement. **1887** O. J. HUMPHREY *Wreck of Rainier* 33 When the *surf line* was hauled tight the boat would run on the line and be kept head to the sea. **1923** H. BELLOC *Sonnets & Verse* 1. 28 Above the surf-line, into the night-breeze; Eastward above the ever-whispering trees. **1965** P. L. DIXON *Compl. Bk. Surfing* 142 If the dory broaches in the surf line and turns over, bail out and get clear of oars and falling boat. **1880** *Scribner's Mag.* Jan. 322/2 The keeper [of the surf-boat] commands the crew of six *surfmen*. *Ibid.* 334 Until 1871..*surfmanship* was not a standard of qualification. **1965** *N.Z. Listener* 17 Dec. 4/1 The million-dollar industry of *surf music*, surf movies and surf-wear. **1977** *Sounds* 9 July 28/2 The Turtles started out playing surf music at High School hops in LA. **1889** *Amer. Naturalist* Oct. 923 *Micrometrus aggregatus*, one of the viviparous *surf-perches*. **1953** 'S. RATTRAY' *Bishop in Check* 101 One-half per cent of them play tennis—or swim, or *surf-ride*. **1958** *Listener* 2 Oct. 494/1 This motorization wave is not something on which the rich alone can surf-ride. **1973** *Times* 1 June (Australia Suppl.) p. i./3 The Whitlam Government has been in office just six months tomorrow. For the Prime Minister it has been a *surf ride* so far'. **1976** *National Observer* (U.S.) 19 June 1/3 Now, surf-riding his victory in the California Presidential primary last week, he's racing to a showdown with Gerald Ford. **1882** *Hawaiian Almanac* 52 At one time they sent their champion *surf-rider* to compete with chiefs in the sport at Hawaii. **1981** L. LEAMER *Assignment* iii. 43 They take this drug. They have learned this from these hippie surf-riders. **1882** *Hawaiian Almanac* 52 Among the various sports and pastimes of the ancient Hawaiians..the principal one..is that of surf-bathing, or more properly speaking, surf-riding. **1898** JEAN A. OWEN *Hawaii* iii. 81 Surf-riding on boards is still much practised. **1800** COLERIDGE *Piccolom.* I. xii, The *surf rocks* of the Baltic. **1962** *Austral. Women's Weekly* 24 Oct. (Suppl.) 3/4 *Surf safari*, a trip around different beaches to find a good surf. **1835** JENYNS *Man. Brit. Vertebr. Anim.* 240 *O[idemia] perspicillata*, Steph. (*Surf Scoter*.) **1882** JORDAN & GILBERT *Fishes N. Amer.* 294 Hypomesus, Gill. *Surf Smelts*... H[ypomesus] pretiosus... Surf Smelt.— Pacific coast, from California northward; abundant, spawning in the surf. **1828** CAMPBELL *Death-boat Heligoland* 22 Now *surf-sunk* for minutes, again they uptossed. **1845** GOSSE *Ocean* vi. (1849) 283 The cry of 'A Shark!' among the *surf* swimmers will instantly set them in the utmost terror. **1858** R. M. BALLANTYNE *Coral Island* xxv. 305 'What sort of amusement is this *surf swimming*?'.. 'Each man..has got a short board or plank, with which he swims a mile or more to Sea, and then, gettin' on the top o' yon thunderin' breaker, they come to shore on the top of it.' **1890** 'R. BOLDREWOOD' *Col. Reformer* (1891) 150 The wind is..from the south, we shall have the *surf-thunder* in perfection. **1829** POE *Dream within a Dream* ii, I stand amid the roar Of a *surf-tormented* shore. **1852** MUNDY *Antipodes* (1857) 24 Green turfy knolls sloping abruptly to the *surf-vexed* beach. **1861** L. L. NOBLE *Icebergs* 180 The bleak, *surf-washed* rocks. **1854** H. MILLER *Sch. & Schm.* xxiv. (1858) 532 The picturesque *surf-wasted* stacks of the granitic wall of rock. **1897** MARY KINGSLEY *W. Africa* 391 The young women..with their soft dusky skins,..pretty brown eyes, and *surf-white* teeth. **1882** JORDAN & GILBERT *Fishes N. Amer.* 933 M[enticirrus] littoralis... *Surf Whiting*.— South Atlantic and Gulf coast. **1878** GEIKIE *Geol. Sketches* ii. (1882) 34 Weather-beaten or *surf-worn* sheets of rock.

surf (sɜːf), *v.* [f. the *sb.*] **1.** *intr.* To form surf. *rare*.

1831 J. WILSON in *Blackw. Mag.* XXIX. 141 The breakers surfing on a lee-shore. **1832** *Ibid.* XXXII. 131.

2. To go surf-riding; to surf-ride. Also *transf.* and *fig.*

1917 *Chambers's Jrnl.* Apr. 280/2 The depth of the lagoon is trifling.., and this it is which makes surfing there so safe and enjoyable. **1932** *Ibid.* Aug. 462/2, I had snaps, too, of the children, riding or surfing, and of the whole family in their ocean-going yacht. *a*1957 R. CAMPBELL *Coll. Poems* (1960) III. 83 Over its surge in red tornadoes rolling My heart goes surfing on the waves of fire. **1965** *N.Z. Listener* 17 Dec. 4/5 Once a person is bitten by this surfing bug he seems to become insatiable. He surfs every day he can, the whole year round. **1970** *Motor Boat & Yachting* 16 Oct. 29/1 *La Russhe* surfed handsomely down the backs of the heavy swell and buried herself into the short steep seas on the way. **1976** M. BIRMINGHAM *Heat of Sun* iv. 51 Biriwa has..a comparatively safe beach..where you can surf when the tide is right.

3. *trans.* **a.** To ride (a boat) on the surf. **b.** To surf-ride at (a specified place).

1965 P. L. DIXON *Compl. Bk. Surfing* 18 Dories, canoes, sailing catamarans, and a few special motorboats can be surfed by experts. Where waves break far from shore and spill gradually forward. **1967** W. MURRAY *Sweet Ride* vi. 85 Ten years ago..no one surfed this place but him. **1968** *Surfer Mag.* Jan. 56/1 Paulo surfed a beach break off the famous Rio Copacabana called Posto Six Pier.

Hence **ˈsurfing** *vbl. sb.*, surf-riding, surfboarding.

1955 A. ROSS *Australia* 55 xv. 214 The essential art of surfing is timing. **1959** H. HOBSON *Mission House Murder* xviii. 119 When they'd had enough surfing, they brought the boards back up the beach. **1963** *Wall St. Jrnl.* 22 July 1 Surfin' music is characterized by a heavy echo guitar sound, supposed to simulate the roar of surf on the beach. **1971** 'D. HALLIDAY' *Dolly & Doctor Bird* i. 2 Skin diving, rum punches, calypso night-clubs, surfing, dancing, gambling.

Art: **Surf Toons Magazine, 1967**

around a rocky point.   **5) reef break** Surf that breaks over a rock or coral reef.   **6) sandbar break** Surf that breaks in sections over sand deposits just offshore of the beach or at a river mouth.

surf bum *n.* Someone who lives only for surfing. "Ride the waves, eat, sleep, not a care in the world" — Kahoona in the movie *Gidget* (1959).

surf bumps *n.* Gnarly looking calcium deposits that develop on various parts of the body as a result of constant contact with a surfboard. A common location is below the kneecap, where they are caused by resting on the knees while paddling a surfboard, but they also form on bottom ribs and the tops of feet and toe joints just from lying down on the board. Surf bumps were frequently cited as the reason for classifying surfers 4-F during the Korean War.

(A&M, DWK) Same as SURF KNOBS, SURF KNOTS. See VOLCANO.

surf bunny *n.* **1)** A sixties term for a surfer's girlfriend.   **2)** A female surfer, usually deeply tanned, with sun-bleached, wind-blown hair. Sometimes called *beaver.* (IDSM) **3)** A girl who hangs around with surfers; usually not a surfer herself, but attracted to boys who surf. Also called BEACH BUNNY.

surf camp *n.* An organized camp for surfers; became popular in the 1980s.

surf cartoons *n.* Cartoons with stereotypical characters and situations centering on the surfing scene. John Severson, the first acknowledged surf illustrator, published drawings in *Surfer* magazine in 1961. He established a panoramic genre — capturing a day's worth of action in a single frame — that was copied by a whole generation of surf artists. Rick Griffin set the standard in the early

surf cartoons
Surf Crazed Comics by Roy Gonzales and Salvador Paskowitz 1991

surf bomb
Art: Bob Penuelas

1960s. Among the broad stereotypes drawn by many surf cartoonists are the clueless kook, the pampered surf star, the superhuman wave warrior, the rabid local, the cosmic soul surfer, and the average Joe. (SFR) See CAPTAIN GOODVIBES, MURPHY, WILBUR KOOKMEYER.

surf cats *n*. Surfers.

surf change *n*. The act of changing into, or out of, your clothes, surf trunks/bathing suit, or wetsuit, with or without a towel, sometimes in full view of the public.

surf chaser *n*. An Australian term for a surfer's jalopy. (JKMJ, 1965)

surf check *n*. An appraisal of the surf at one or more spots to determine its quality, where to go out, etc.

surf chicks or **surf chix** *n*. Female surfers. See BETTY.

surf chowder *n*. Any warm, nourishing seafood soup, usually clam chowder.

"Surf City" *n*. A hit surfing tune about a mythical place in California, written by Brian Wilson and sung by Jan & Dean (June 1963). It was Jan & Dean's first #1 hit.

Surf City 1) Another name for Huntington Beach, California. **2)** A real place in New Jersey. **3) Surf City, U.S.A.** The prototypical surf town.

surf club *n*. Any organization of surfers, such as a longboarding club.

surf conditions *n*. The state of the surf — how the waves are breaking at any particular time. Usage: "Let's check the surf conditions."

surf contest *n*. An amateur or professional competition, usually held over a period of several days or a week; may be delayed or postponed if the swell is poor. Popular professional contests include the Op Pro, Stubbies, and Pipeline Masters. See ASP, SURFING CRITERIA.

surf cord *n*. SURF LEASH.

surf check
Art: Bob Penuelas

surf dog
Art: Rick Stover

surf craze *n*. A general reference to the period during the first half of the 1960s, when the sport grew tremendously.

surf crimes *n*. Legalese applied to surfing; originated in Southern California in the late 1980s; popular among grommets. Usage (to describe a really heavy wipeout): "That bailiff took him straight to the slammer." Also called LEGALESE GROMMETSPEAK. See PROSECUTED, QUASH, WITNESS.

surf culture *n*. A pervasive subculture, one that thrives over much of the globe. (BC, Spring 1990)

surf day *n*. Any day in Peru when the surf is too large for freighters to dock at piers to load or unload their cargoes.

surf dreads *n*. Bleached-blonde dreadlocks — a surfer hairstyle that became popular in the 1980s.

surf dog *n*. **1)** BEACH DOG. **2)** A veteran surfer.

surf dude, surfer dude *n*. A male surfer.

surf fashion *n*. Fashion trends inspired by surfer clothing, which has been an influence in the fashion world for many years. The first surfwear trend started with the cutoff sailor pants worn by Dale Velzy and his cohorts at the Manhattan Beach Surf Club in the 1950s. (GN) Other surfer fashions include jams, reeds, Hawaiian shirts, and Day-Glo neon clothing. And don't forget J.C.'s/Percells — 1960s surfer footware.

surf fever *n*. **1)** A condition prevalent along all coastlines of the world. *Symptom*: a burning desire to go surfing. *Cause*: a lack of waves. *Treatment*: to go surfing — the only known cure. **2)** *Surf Fever* A 1960 John Severson surf flick.

surf flick *n*. Surf movie.

surf god *n.* The legendary god of the waves, KAHUNA in Hawaii, HUEY in Australia.

surf grass (*Phyllospadix scouleri*) *n.* A sea grass found in and around Pacific Coast tidepools; encountered by surfers on their way to the surf.

surf groupie *n.* Someone, usually a female, who hangs out around surfers. As Corky Carroll said in 1989, "A real surf groupie has sand in her butt."

surf guitar *n.* An instrumental reverb guitar imitating the hypnotic crashing sound of waves, pioneered by Dick Dale; consists of tremolos and reverbs (echoes). See SURF MUSIC.

surf hearse *n.* **1)** An old hearse rehabilitated for carrying surfboards. **2)** Any jalopy used to transport surfers and boards to and from the beach. **3)** **"Surfin' Hearse"** A song by Jan & Dean. (1960s)

surf hog heaven *n.* Where you are when you are really superstoked. Corky Carroll coined this term.

surf knobs, surf knots *n.* SURF BUMPS.

surf leash *n.* A three- to four-foot elastic cord connecting a surfboard to a rider's ankle (via a velcro cuff). The cord is affixed to the top side of the surfboard's tail and to the surfer's trailing foot. Originally, leashes were attached to the nose of the board and the wrist of the surfer. (SFR, 6/87) Also known as LEASH, LEG ROPE, DING STRING, SHOCK CORD.

surf legends *n.* Surfers who have made a name for themselves in the history of surfing, for example, Lance Carson ("No Pants Lance"), Mickey Dora ("Da Cat"), Greg Noll ("Da Bull"), and Jack Murphy ("Murph the Surf"). See SURFERS' NICKNAMES.

surf lore *n.* See SURF STORIES.

surf mag *n.* Any magazine on surfing.

surf mama *n.* **1)** A female surfer. **2)** The ocean; same as THE BIG MAMA.

surf mat *n.* A rubber mattress inflated and used to ride the waves. (Australia) Also called MAT, SURF-O-PLANE.

surfmobile *n.* SURF VEHICLE.

surf mongrel *n.* A hyper young surfer. (Australia)

surf movies *n.* **1)** A genre of independently made films pioneered by Bud Browne in the 1940s and 1950s. It was further developed by Greg Noll, John Severson, and Bruce Brown in the late 1950s and early 1960s, and included such feature-length documentaries as Brown's *The Endless Summer* (1964). Also including some zonko surf-flick titles over the years, such as *Barefoot Adventure, Cat on a Hot Foam Board, Five Summer Stories, Free Ride*. In the early days, surf movies were screened with live narration. They were then, and still are, always accompanied by hooting and howling from the audience. **2)** Hollywood's version of the surf culture, including films like *Gidget* (1959), *Beach Party* (1963), *Beach Blanket Bingo* (the "Beach" movies starred Annette Funicello and Frankie Avalon), and *Ride the Wild Surf*. **3)** And in a class by itself, *Big Wednesday* (1978) by John Milius. In this film, Hollywood rendered the California surf culture from the perspective of a real surfer.

surf music *n.* **1)** A sound representational of the ocean landscape, associated with the late fifties and early sixties and created by two main "families" of musicians: the *Orange County* bands descended from Dick Dale, who generally used more reverb (**full reverb surf music**), and the *south bay* bands descended from the Belairs, who tended to use less reverb. Examples of surf music range from "Walk Don't Run" by

surf movie
Barefoot Adventure (1960)
TM & © Bruce Brown Films
Dave Kinstle Collection

surf knobs
Art: I. B. Nelson

surf legend
Mickey Dora
Photo: Ron Stoner / Surfer Magazine

surf photographer
In-water shot
Photo: Bob Barbour

Cameraboard shot of Adam Replogle, Baja
Photo: Bob Barbour

surf photographer
Brian Bielmann
Photo: Bill Romerhaus

the Ventures to the spy-surf theme sound of "Outer Limits" by the Marketts to "Mr. Moto" by the Belairs. Also known as *intro*
2) Rock-'n'-roll music from California in the early 1960s, characterized by close treble harmonies and with lyrics that celebrated the exhilaration of surfing and beach life. The Beach Boys are a prime example.
3) Any music you can surf to — Jimi Hendrix, Led Zepplin, Ramones, Santana, punk, reggae, etc. See HAWAIIAN MUSIC, SURF GUITAR.

With the introduction of the "reverb" unit by guitar maker Leo Fender in 1962, lots of lead guitars took on the big, hollow, tubular tone of the reverb. The Fender reverb gave the guitar a slippery, "wet" sort of tone, which naturally served to solidify the music's identification as "the sound of surfing." Some of the most memorable surf sounds (such as the Chantays' "Pipeline," the Surfaris' "Wipe Out," the Pyramids' "Penetration," and Dick Dale's "Miserlou") were literally *drenched* in reverb.

The surf sound peaked in 1963; the advent of the Beatles in early 1964 and the "British Invasion" marked what is generally regarded as the end of the surf music era. Yet original surf music still has the energy, simplicity, and rawness of the setting that inspired it. (PJN)

"... **and you'll never hear surf music again**" was Jimi Hendrix' phrase from the song "Third Stone from the Sun" on the album *Are You Experienced?* Hendrix tunes in which the influence of surf music is obvious include "Drifting" and "Pali Gap."

surf music revival *n.* A resurgence of instrumental surf music in the late 1970s and early 1980s, led by groups like Jon and the Nightriders, the Surf Raiders, the Halibuts, and Agent Orange.

surf-n-turf *n.* A generic term for any dish with meat and seafood.

Surf naked! An exclamation on T-shirts and bumper stickers, meaning something like "Go for it!" (North Carolina; 1981)

surf nazis *n.* **1**) Originally, young gremlins of the 1960s, who took to wearing German Luftwaffe officers' coats for warmth on the beach on cold winter days; they also adopted the iron cross and the swastika as their emblems. (MCR) **2**) Loosely applied, refers to hyper young surfers.

"The swastika became a symbol of some surfers just because it pissed off people. It was a rebellious act. That's why Mickey Dora painted swastikas all over his boards. Most surfers didn't even know what it meant. It was just another way of shaking the pillars of society, something we excelled in doing." —Greg Noll, *Da Bull* (1989)

surf-o-plane or **surfoplane** *n.* An inflatable rubber mat used in Australia in the 1950s. (MF) Same as SURF MAT.

surf party *n.* A full-on raging good time, as seen in the "Crashers!" scene in the movie *Big Wednesday* (1978).

surf photography *n.* An area of photography that often requires the photographer to be positioned in the breaking wave in order to shoot the surfer coming down or through. Doc Ball was the first acknowledged surf photographer; other pioneers include John Severson, Bud Browne, and Bruce Brown. Today there are many surf photographers, among them Robert Brown, Jeff Divine, Aaron Chang, Rob Giley, Don King, and Woody Woodworth.

surf punk *n.* **1**) A young surfer. **2**) A surfer who is part of the punk rock scene — reads *Maximum Rock 'N' Roll* and *Thrasher* magazines, has spiked hair, listens to punk music, and so on.

Surf Punks *n.* A satirical music group from Malibu, formed in 1977 and led by Drew Steele and Dennis Dragon, which mirrored events experienced in the water and on the sand. Their observations of the Southern California beach and surf scene are mixed over a richly layered soundtrack; their songs include "My Beach," "My Wave," and "Locals Only."

"By over-simplifying our statements, I thought the surfing public would interpret the message as an obvious parody targeted at the beach communities. But I was wrong. Many of the younger surfers took on "My Beach — Go Home" as their anthem. However a few *did* understand and appreciated the comedic aspects of the show." —Dennis Dragon (SFR, 5/83)

surf rack, surfboard rack *n.* A metal, foam pad, or wooden apparatus attached to the top of a car and used to carry surfboards. Also called ROOF RACK. See SOFT RACK.

surf rasta *n.* A term loosely applied to any surfer who sprouts dreadlocks, listens to reggae music, enjoys living naturally, but doesn't necessarily subscribe to the Rastafarian religion. Usage: "He's a total surf rasta."

surf rat *n.* A young and enthusiastic surfer.

surf rebel *n.* A surfer who lives for surfing, and nothing else. Same as WAVE REBEL.

surf report *n.* **1)** An accounting of up-to-date regional surfing conditions given on local radio stations each morning. **2)** A telephone report offered by many lifeguard services. **3)** *The Surf Report* An informative publication put out by *Surfer* magazine and offering monthly summaries and forecasts of worldwide surfing conditions. For various other sources of information about the surf, see "Where to Get Surf Reports" on page 134.

surf rider, surfrider *n.* SURFER.

surf riding or **surf-riding** or **surf-riding** *n.* The sport of riding the surf on a surfboard (W9); SURFING.

surf rocking *n.* Dancing, grooving to the music.

"Surf Route 101" *n.* A song by Jan & Dean about driving a woody up and down the coast. (1960s)

surf run *n.* A long trip in the car with the destination of catching some waves, for example, a "Mexico surf run."

surf sacrifice *n.* The ceremonial burning of a surfboard on the beach, usually an old or discarded board; not recommended for today's environmentally conscious surfer.

surf scooter *n.* One means of transport to the beach — a vespa or other type of motorcycle, but almost never a moped.

surf scoter (*Melanitta perspicillata*) *n.* An abundant sea-going duck that floats in flocks and rides waves; a sea duck.

surf scruff *n.* Facial stubble from not shaving; an element of the surfed-out look.

surf session *n.* See SESSION.

surf shop *n.* **1)** A store that sells surfing equipment and beach apparel; known for the intoxicating smell of surf wax, neoprene rubber wetsuits, and fiberglass surfboards. **2)** The original "Surf Shop," a name registered to Jack O'Neill in 1962, which later became a generic term. (SCSM) In the early 1960s, the common surf shop was also a surfboard factory. (GN)

surf shorts *n.* A surfer's swimsuit. Also called BOARDSHORTS, SURF TRUNKS.

surf site or **surfsite** *n.* **1)** A location where waves break in a form suitable for surfing — the result of swell interactions with the bottom and wind interactions with the water surface. **2)** A spot composed of a take-

surf rat
Art: The Pizz

BULLETIN AT MALIBU

WHERE TO GET SURF REPORTS

One of the most accurate sources of information about the surf is the marine weather channel on a weather radio, which sometimes provides information about the swell that you can't see just by looking at it. Information found on the newspaper weather page is reasonably accurate but always seems to be a day or so behind. A toll call to various 976 telephone numbers can provide you with surf predictions using state-of-the-art meteorological technology. Turn to TV weather on the news only as a last resort. (W&B; SFG, 3/90)

In addition, surf shops and lifeguard stations usually post some or all of the following information daily:

A sample surf report

- skies: "clear," "hazy," "foggy," "partly cloudy," "overcast"
- swell: "2–4," "4–6," and so on (height given in feet)
- swell direction: "SW" (southwest), "West," "NW" (northwest)
- wave shape: "clean," "good," "fair," "poor"
- air temperature: "72°"
- water temperature: "68°"
- wind speed: "15–25" (knots or miles per hour)
- high tide: "12:00," "12:01"
- low tide: "6:00," "5:58"

Art: Jim Lucas / Big Stick Surfing Association

off area, a riding area, an end-of-ride area, a board-recovery area, a return path, and an access route. (JRW) Also called SURF SPOT.

surf-skate synthesis, surf-skate crossover *n.* The transference of terminology and maneuvers between surfing and skateboarding. Examples are aerial and face plant. (SFR, 11/83)

surf ski *n.* An Australian paddleboard invented in 1933 by Dr. G. A. Crackenthorp of Manly Surf Club in Sydney. Surf skis have a lot of scoop in the nose, are very long (about nineteen feet), and narrow (about seventeen inches), and have a rudder. The rider sits on the board with feet in holders and propels the craft with a double-bladed paddle — occasionally standing while surfing. Surf skis were very popular in Australia before Malibu boards arrived. (DM) Sometimes called *racing ski. Not* a wave ski.

surf sound *n.* **1**) The music of American surf bands in the early 1960s; **California surf sound.** (IDSM) See SURF MUSIC. **2**) The sound of powerful ocean waves, crashing against the beach or onto the water surface. Same as OCEAN ROAR, ROAR OF THE OCEAN.

surf soup *n.* **1**) An unappealing condition of the water surface when southeast winds off of Florida blow a Sargasso sea-like mat of algae into the surf zone — it's like paddling through pea soup. (TDW) **2**) SURF CHOWDER.

surf spot *n.* SURF SITE.

surf spot names Names used by surfers to identify specific surf spots; may be confined to surfer use initially but usually spread into general use after a while. Surfers name spots for a variety of reasons; for example, Garbage Pit, Hawaii, is named for the pollution in the area, and K38 in Baja California, Mexico, is so named because of the location of the break

near roadside signpost K38. See Appendix H, "Major Surf Spots around the World."

surf stickers *n.* Sticky-backed decals displaying the logos of surf-industry equipment. Stuck on surfboards, cars, gas pumps, and road signs; also good for temporary ding repair.

surf stoke 1) *n.* Adrenaline stoking the body's fire. (JGM) **2**) **surf stoked** *adj.* Usage: "I was completely surf stoked." See STOKED.

surf stomps *n.* Dances in the early 1960s named after the popular dance style, the stomp, which became known as the **surfer stomp**. Another indigenous "surf" dance was trippin', a creation of Dick Dale's crowd. Together the two dances became a sort of surfer "tribal ritual"; these dances were exclusive to the folk culture of surfing. (PJN) See SURFER'S STOMP. —**surf stomping**

surf-skate synthesis
Art: Jim Phillips

· · · · · · · · · · · · · · · · · · ·

"It was an intense experience to be among hundreds of surfers all doing nothing but stomping their sandals on the dance floor to the pulsating beat of the band!" —Paul Johnson (1987)

· · · · · · · · · · · · · · · · · · ·

surf stories *n.* Stories exchanged among friends, usually about a hot ride or a surf trip adventure; an important element of surfing. Same as TALK STORIES.

surf strap *n.* A stretch band used to secure surfboards to the roof rack or a soft rack to the car roof.

surf town *n.* Any small coastal community that has a beachy feeling about it.

surf trip *n.* A road trip in search of waves. See SURFARI, SURFIN' SAFARI.

surf trunks or **surftrunks** *n.* A swimsuit designed especially for surfing; made of heavy-duty fabric, double stitched, with a pocket for a bar of wax in the rear.

surf tunes *n.* SURF MUSIC.

surf vehicle
Photo: Dennis Junor

**Surfers Medical
Association**
Photo: Peter Spacek

surf types *n*. See SURF BREAKS.

surf vehicle *n*. **1)** A mode of transport to and from the beach, such as a VW Bug or a microbus (combi). **2)** A rusted-out heap if you surf in the tropics. See BAJA BUG, CRUISEMOBILE, SURF BOMB, SURFWAGON, WOODY.

surf video *n*. A means of seeing surf movies in your very living room; available in almost every surf shop these days. Unfortunately, watching videos can't duplicate the feeling of watching a surf movie on a big screen together with a screaming surfer audience.

surf wax or **surfwax** *n*. Wax spread on the surface of a board to give better traction, so the feet won't slip. (IDSM)

surf widow *n*. A surfer's wife or girlfriend. (San Francisco) "When a woman meets a surfer, she thinks she's lucky. He's tall, blond and handsome. Eventually she gets jealous of the surf. It can be hard sharing your husband with the ocean." —Kathleen Bergerson (CVG, 1988)

surf zombie *n*. Someone who is totally obsessed by a strange power so that all they wanna do is surf (there's no fighting it); a state caused by a new swell. You can spot surf zombies by their fried eyeballs and leaky sinuses. The term derived from a Wilbur Kookmeyer cartoon, "Surf Zombies."

surf zone *n*. The area affected by wave action, extending from the shoreline high-water mark seaward to where the waves start to break. (CCRG)

surfable *adj*. Used to say whether or not waves are ridable. Usage: "Are they surfable?"

Surfabout *n*. A famous Australian surfing competition.

surface chop *n*. A ruffled ocean surface; caused by local winds.

surfari *n*. **1)** A caravan of surf-hungry surfers. **2)** A surfing trip. (MM) See SURFIN' SAFARI. **3) the Surfaris** A 1960s surfin' band with hits such as "Wipe Out!"

surfatorium *n*. WAVE POOL.

surfboard *n*. **1)** A narrow, somewhat rounded board used by surfers for riding waves into shore; sometimes spelled *surf-board*. (DM, 1962) **2)** A kind of wave vehicle; a form with which to communicate with a wave. **3)** A long narrow buoyant board used in the sport of surfing. (W9)

surfboard polo *n*. A sport probably invented by the Kahanamoku brothers (Louis, Sam, and Sargent) in 1929 at Waikiki, where it became the rage during the 1930s. The game was similar to water polo, except that it was played on surfboards. (GTM)

surfboard rack *n*. SURF RACK.

surfboard riding *n*. Surfing. —**surf board riding** (WPA Guide to Los Angeles, 1941)

surfboard stand *n*. A structure used for ding repair, usually padded with a chunk of old rug or a discarded wetsuit. (GCD)

surfboard width See WIDTH.

surfboarder *n*. A SURFER. (W9)

surfboarding *n*. SURFING.

surfboat *n*. A boat made especially for use in the surf. (MF)

Surfdom *n*. The kingdom of surfing. (MM)

surfcut *n*. Any hip or stylish-looking haircut on a surfer. See BOWL CUT, SURF DREADS.

surfear *v*. Spanish for to surf. (Puerto Rico)

surfed out 1) *adj*. How someone looks — tan, bleached hair, salt caked on the skin, etc.; the **surfed-out look**. **2)** *adv*. How someone feels after a long surf session — tired. Usage: "I'm surfed out."

surfer *n.* **1**) Someone who surfs. **2**) In Chinese, "he who dances upon the water." (MGE) **3**) An endangered marine mammal. (SJN) **4**) In the Southern California surfer mystique, someone with sand between the toes, eyelids caked with salt, bleached-blonde hair, and a lifestyle that includes being surrounded by girls in string bikinis. (SMH)

surfer girl *n.* **1**) Any female who surfs. **2**) **"Surfer Girl"** A romantic ballad by The Beach Boys (1963), showcasing the harmonic influence the Four Freshmen had on Brian Wilson.

surfer hoots *n.* Screams of encouragement or appreciation while surfing, such as "eeeyuuuu!" "aaaahooo!" "ahoooo!" "aawh wooo!" "AWOOO!" or "OWOOOOO!"; also yelled at the surf flick.

surfer image *n.* As perpetrated by the media, the negative image of a surf bum. However, any true surfer knows that there are many different types of surfers. (BP)

Surfer Joe The character in a 1963 Surfaris song of the same title, about a guy who surfs Doheny, gets drafted into the marines, and has his long blonde locks cut off; written and sung by Ron Wilson, drummer for the Surfaris; the flip side of "Wipe Out."

surfer moon *n.* **1**) A full moon. **2**) **"The Surfer Moon"** A song by The Beach Boys. (1963)

surfer stomp *n.* A dance step popular in the early 1960s. See SURF STOMPS.

surfero, surfera *n.* Spanish for male and female surfer, respectively.

Surfers Against Apartheid *n.* A group of professional wave riders who have boycotted surfing competitions in South Africa since 1985. (FLD)

surfer's ear *n.* A condition in which the channels to the inner ear constrict in cold water, and over a period of time a bony growth closes the ear canal, sometimes causing intermittent deafness. Surfer's ear can be prevented by keeping the ear canal warm and dry with ear plugs.

surfer's eye *n.* A condition caused by excessive exposure to the sun's glare and the irritation of salt water, in which soft tissue forms on the white of the eye and begins to grow over the cornea. The medical term is *pterygium*.

surfer's knee, surfer's knobs, surfer's knots *n.* Tumorlike growths of connective tissue just below the knees, on the tops of feet, and often on the toes; caused by pressure on the skin and tissue exerted by the surfboard. Same as SURF BUMPS, SURF KNOBS, SURF KNOTS. See VOLCANO.

Surfer's Medical Association (SMA) *n.* A San Francisco-based organization of surfing doctors interested in the prevention and treatment of surfing-related injuries; founded by Dr. Mark Renneker ("Doc Hazzard") in 1985.

surfer's nicknames *n.* Names given to famous surfers, sometimes in recognition of their surfing style. Examples are "Buffalo" (Richard Keaulana) because of his shaggy, reddish-brown hair; "Da Bull" (Greg Noll) for his tenacity and aggressiveness in big waves; "Da Cat" (Mickey Dora); "Burrhead" Drever; "MR" (Mark Richards); "PT" (Peter Townend); "Bugs" or "Rabbit" (Wayne Bartholemew); and "The Animal" (Nat Young).

Surfers Paradise A built-up beach strip in Queensland, Australia.

surfers rule 1) Common graffiti in the 1960s claiming a beach as surfer territory. (DWK) **2**) **"Surfer's Rule"** A song by The Beach Boys. (1963)

surfer's squat *n.* **1**) A dance. **2**) A stance on a surfboard.

surfer
above:
Larry Blair, Hawaii
Photo: Don Balch

below:
surfer girl
Photo: Rob Gilley

Margo Oberg, Hawaii
Photo: Bob Barbour

"Surfer's Stomp" *n.* A 1962 song by the Marketts from Balboa, California. Also recorded by the Belairs as "The Surfer's Stomp." See SURF STOMPS.

Surfeteria, Lucy's *n.* A restaurant/bar in Manhattan, New York.

surfhead *n.* BOARDHEAD.

surfin' *n.* **1)** A near mythic concept that embodies all the elements of a certain kind of "California Dreamin'" — sun, sand, surf, blondes in bikinis, and so on. See SURFING. **2)** "Surfin'" The Beach Boys' first hit tune, recorded in December 1961.

"Surfin' Bird" *n.* A song by the Trashmen of Minneapolis, Minnesota (December 1963); one of the most repetitive songs ever recorded. The Ramones did an excellent version of the song in 1977.

surfin' safari *n.* **1)** A trip in search of surf, generally considered to be more than just a short drive — an expedition. See SURFARI. **2)** "Surfin' Safari" The Beach Boys' second album and hit tune (September 1962); a Brian Wilson–Mike Love composition.

surfing *n.* **1)** A combination of water torture and simulated womb regression practiced by masochists and misfits. (JAR) **2)** A water sport in which the participant stands on a floating slab of wood resembling an ironing board in size and shape, and attempts to remain perpendicular while being hurtled toward the shore at a rather frightening speed on the crest of a huge wave. (Especially recommended for teenagers and all others lacking the slightest regard for life or limb.) (TBB, 1963) **3)** In general, a sport in which one attempts to ride a surfboard toward the shore. **4)** Riding across the face of a wave standing on a board especially made for the purpose.

surfari
Art: The Pizz

"Surfing is the art of harnessing that ocean energy, and in doing that the surfer momentarily becomes a sea creature, moving in rapport with the waves." —Richard Wolkomir, *Oceans* magazine (June, 1988)

surfing criteria *n.* In competitive surfing, the factors by which a ride is judged. A good ride has four components: **1)** radical controlled maneuvers (RCMs); **2)** the most critical section; **3)** the biggest or the best waves; **4)** the longest functional distance. (L&L) Also called SCORING CRITERIA.

"The surfer who executes the most radical controlled maneuvers in the most critical section of the biggest and/or best waves for the longest functional distance shall be deemed the winner." —ASP Rule Book

surfing museums *n.* Places that store surfing paraphernalia and memorabilia to give a sense of the history of surfing and the surfing culture. Two of the more permanent ones in California are the Santa Cruz Surfing Museum and the Huntington Beach International Surfing Museum. In addition, many museums come and go, but there are also many private collections, especially in California, that can be tracked down by word of mouth through local surf shops. See Appendix G.

surfing spin-off sports *n.* Activities inspired by and sometimes imitating surfing maneuvers but done in other settings, for example sandboarding, snowboarding, and windsurfing.

surfing under turd Surfing in polluted waters; same as ON THE NOSE, YUK, WOOFY. (Australia; MW)

surfing with poo Surfing in an area full of excrement. See FLOATIES. (Australia; SAB)

surfish *n.* A blend of surf slang and English; a term coined by Dr. John Cohen in *Surfer* Magazine (9/84). See "Surfish as a Second Language" on page xxx.

surfistas (surf-EES-tahs) *n.* Portuguese for surfers. (Brasil)

surflets *n.* Special words for emotions, actions, or moments that only surfers experience. The term was coined by Eric Fairbanks at *Surfing* Magazine (1990); possibly it was inspired by the HBO TV "sniglets." See NASODRAIN, URINOPHORIA.

surfman *n.* BOARDMAN.

surfmanship *n.* An unwritten code of "fraternal and noncompetitive coexistence" that guides surfers in sharing waves. (NWT)

surfology *n.* The study of good surf — identifying where the surf will be good and understanding why it will be good at some breaks in certain conditions and not in others. Elements that allow surfers to predict and find good surf include swell direction, wind, tides, land and underwater topography, and wave size. Satellite photos are also useful. (W&B)

surform *n.* A hand plane with removable blades used in shaping foam, fiberglass, and resin.

Surfrider Beach *n.* A surf site located within Malibu Lagoon State Beach and popularized by surfing movies in the early 1960s; one of the finest surfing spots in California, especially during summer when strong southwest swells refract around a rock reef at Malibu Point and break over a gently sloping sandy bottom, offering long rides.

Surfrider Foundation *n.* A California-based nonprofit organization, founded in 1984, dedicated to the preservation and enjoyment of ocean waves and beaches worldwide. Its projects include protecting and improving beach access, promoting a long-range surf enhancement program, stopping encroachment of coastal structures, and supporting clean surfing conditions by advocating full sewage treatment and strict enforcement of toxic dumping regulations. See Appendix G for the address.

surf's down An expression meaning flat surf — which is possibly even unridable.

surf's up A statement indicating that the waves are breaking at a high level, ideal for surfing. (IDSM)

surfsailing *n.* WINDSURFING.

Surfside *n.* A residential beach community located on the south spit of Anaheim Bay within the city of Seal Beach, California. Surfside Beach, adjacent to the Pacific Coast Highway, was an excellent surf spot until the early 1960s, when the beach was rebuilt after heavy storms.

surfsuit *n.* WETSUIT.

Surftones *n.* A surf band from Newport Beach. (1980s)

Surfurbia *n.* Historical architecture professor Reyner Banham's term for the seaside communities of Redondo Beach, Hermosa Beach, and Manhattan Beach in Southern California. Also called *Surfurbs*.

surfwagon *n.* A woody or other station wagon used for transporting surfboards. Also known as STAY-WAG.

surfwear *n.* Surfer apparel such as neon boardshorts, long-sleeve T-shirts, and wetsuits.

surfy 1) *n.* An Australian term for a surfer or surfer type; also spelled *surfie*, as in "a barefoot, surfie-looking dude." (CC) **2)** *adj.* Abounding with surf; forming surf or like surf. **—surfier, surfiest**

surfy head *n.* A surfer. (Australia: MON)

surge, surge channel *n.* A narrow gap in rocky intertidal areas along the coastline through which waves

swallowtail winger
Photo: Tom Servais / Surfer Magazine

surge; if timed right, can be used to carry a surfer on a board to or from a surf spot. (But beware of sharp creatures such as barnacles along the way.)

swallowtail, swallow tail *n.* A surfboard tail design featuring two pintails side by side. (NAT, 1985)

Swami's *n.* A surf spot in Encinitas, California.

swan *n.* FLYING SWAN.

swash *n.* Incoming water, water moving up the beach; the opposite of backwash. (TLH) Usage: "I rode the swash up to the berm."

sweeping cutback *n.* A long, drawn-out turn.

sweet *adj.* Cool; said of anything you like. (PZ) Usage: "That's sweet."

sweet ride *n.* **1**) A nice ride. **2**) *The Sweet Ride* A Hollywood surf movie.

sweet spot *n.* **1**) The area on a surfboard that feels comfortable when you stand over it and that allows for ultimate maneuvering. **2**) A really good surf spot.

sweets *n.* A group of good-looking girls.

swell *n.* **1**) Unbroken waves; either one unbroken wave or all of the waves coming from one particular storm. **2**) A large, unbroken wave, usually of distant origin. **3**) Any wave before it breaks. **4**) Waves generated by wind in a particular storm. Two or more different swells may be present simultaneously. (S&C) **5**) **good swell** Regular, well-shaped waves created by distant storms and breaking consistently for several days.

Swells move in the open ocean at about thirty-five miles per hour; they move more slowly in shallow water. Once they hit shore, they may continue coming for a day, a week, or even a month, depending on the intensity of the distant storm and various other factors.

For example, a storm in the North Pacific may send waves to the North Shore of Hawaii that are ten feet the first day, twenty feet the second day, and twelve feet the third day, all with good shape.

swell classification *n.* Identifying the type of swell, "west swell," "south swell," etc. Detecting this from the beach is a fine art; there aren't any hard and fast rules.

swell characteristics *n.* The multitude of qualities that any given swell may exhibit, such as pumping in consistently or not being well defined.

swell direction *n.* **1**) The direction from which a swell is coming. **2**) Usually the first thing to check when deciding where to surf, since it can cause one spot to have better surf than another on any particular day. Surf spots break differently with different swells; for example, Cardiff reef will break on any swell, but it peels and has more bowls when the swell comes in from a northerly direction. (W&B) —**north swell**, **east swell**, **south swell**, **west swell**, **southwest swell**, etc.

swell period *n.* The time it takes for two swells to pass a given point; the longer the period, the stronger the swell. (BB, 10/90) Same as PERIOD, WAVE PERIOD.

swell window *n.* **1**) A gap between offshore islands that allows swells to pass unobstructed to shore and break with full force. Also called WINDOW. **2**) The direction from which surf can come and reach the shore; islands, points, and peninsulas may block swells from reaching certain areas. (W&B) An **open window** means that nothing is blocking the swell.

swim *v., n.* What you do to retrieve a surfboard that got away. Usually necessary with boards, such as longboards, that don't have leashes.

Usage: "I had about fifteen swims today." (GN)

switch-stance *n.* The ability to ride frontside on both rights and lefts. (ORB)

switchfoot *n.* A surfer who rides with either the right foot or the left foot forward, depending on which direction the waves are breaking, in an effort to face the wave at all times.

Swami's
Art: I. B. Nelson

T-band *n.* A surfboard whose wood stringer and wood tail block form a T.

tabis (TAH-beez) *n.* Hawaiian split-toe booties — the neoprene equivalent of toe socks; used for bodysurfing. (ECN)

tablista Hawaiiano *n.* Literally a Hawaiian surfer, but loosely applied to any visiting California surfer in El Salvador in the 1960s. (PDX)

tablistas (tab-LEES-tahs) *n.* A Spanish word for surfers. (Peru)

tag *v.* To leave one's signature as graffiti under a bridge at a local surf spot. (PZ) Usage: "Yeah, we tagged our names over by the river mouth."

tail *n.* **1**) The stern or back end of a surfboard. **2**) The rear third of a surfboard. (ORB) Also called *rear* or *butt*.

tail block or **tailblock** *n.* The back or tail section of a surfboard.

tail corner *n.* A sharp edge in the tail of a surfboard that allows water flow to break away.

tail curve *n.* A rounded place in the tail of a surfboard that holds water flow.

tail design The shape of the rear end of a surfboard. Tail designs include single-winged swallow, double-bump rounded square, round, double-winged rounded swallow, single-bump rounded pin, rounded diamond, square, winger, flyer, stinger, and screwdriver. (ORB) Same as TAIL PLANSHAPE.

tail fin *n.* SKEG.

tail flutter *n.* Instability in the tail of a surfboard, which sometimes happens on bigger waves when the tail goes out of control and the board slaps up and down; caused by too wide a tail or a board bottom that is too flat, or by riding too far to the rear of the board.

tail hook *n.* A metal hook attached to the tail of an old-style paddleboard.

tail kick *n.* The part of a board from the rear edge of the fin(s) to the tip of the tail. See ROCKER.

tail patch *n.* A sticky-backed foam pad affixed to a surfboard deck and used as a wax substitute to give added traction. Same as DECK PATCH.

tail planshape *n.* TAIL DESIGN.

tail-slide floater *n.* FLOATER.

tail width *n.* The distance across the tail of a board, measured twelve inches from the tip(s) of the tail.

take gas *v.* **1**) To have trouble, especially the kind that leads to a wipeout. **2**) To get trapped in the curl of a wave and lose one's board; to WIPE OUT. Usage: "I saw you taking gas out there."

takeoff or **take-off** *n.* **1**) The act of catching a wave. **2**) In general, the start of a ride. (A&M) **3**) In competitive surfing, the beginning of a ride, defined as the space of time between the hands leaving the rails and the commencement of the first maneuver or turn. (L&L) **4**) The moment of truth for surfers and astronauts alike. Surfers probably have a marginally better chance of coming back alive, but you wouldn't know it to see their eyeballs as they

takeoff
Photo: Woody Woodworth

peer down the face of a concave monster. (JARR) See LATE TAKEOFF (LATE DROP-IN), TOADS. —**screaming takeoff 5**) **take off** *v*. To paddle into a breaking wave in order to ride it, to catch a wave or begin a ride, to launch.

takeoff point *n*. The exact spot where the waves are consistently breaking in such a way as to provide a good ride.

taking the drop *n., v*. **1**) Coming over the top of a wave in order to take advantage of its velocity to stay ahead of the curl and avoid being wiped out. (IDSM) **2**) Dropping down the face of a wave. See FREE FALL. Usage: "Taking the drop at the Wedge is insanely gnarly."

taking the whip *v*. Going OVER THE FALLS. (CSD) Usage: "You were taking the whip in that shore break."

talk stories *n*. Accounts of surfing adventures. Every surfer has stories to tell; some surfers talk more than others. Same as SURF STORIES. See RIGGIN, YARNER.

talking to the seals *v*. Vomiting; same as AQUA BOOT. Usage: "I got seasick this morning and started talking to the seals."

tandem, tandem surfboard *n*. A large surfboard used for tandem riding. Tandem boards are usually extra wide and at least nine feet long, to give increased stability and compensate for the weight of two riders.

tandem surfing *n*. **1**) Two people — usually a man and a women — riding a wave together on the same surfboard. **2**) Two bodysurfers riding a wave together, one on the back of the other.

tank, tanker *n*. A very old and heavy longboard.

tanning center *n*. Skin-cancer ward. (SP)

tapered *adj*. Used to describe rails that gradually blend smoothly into the contour of the surfboard.

tar *n*. Sticky, black gobs of oil that adhere to your feet when you step in it on the beach. The beaches of Santa Barbara are notorious for this stuff.

taste or **tasty** *adj*. Said of fine-looking waves or babes. (MVA) Usage: "Oh, dude, that's taste."

tear, tear it up *v*. To shred waves, to surf very hard; same as RIP IT UP, RIP 'N' TEAR.

teardrop *n*. A surfboard shape, one with a wide tail. (1967)

ted *adj*. **1**) Bloated from eating too much. Usage: "Dude, I'm ted." **2**) **get tedly** To eat a lot. (North San Diego County; LH) Usage: "Let's get tedly."

Teenage Mutant Ninja Turtles *n*. Sewer-dwelling amphibians who co-opted valley and surf lingo ("Cowabunga!" "Go for it," "radical," "pizza dude," "awesome," "gnarly"). Originally comic-book characters, then stars of a Saturday morning TV cartoon show, they were later brought to life through animatronics for a 1990 Hollywood blockbuster movie. The immense popularity of these "heros on the half shell" has been capitalized on by more than three hundred products in the marketplace, including sugary children's cereal, stuffed animals, and bubble gum trading cards.

template *n*. The silhouette or outline curve of a surfboard, viewed from the top or bottom; same as PLANSHAPE.

ten over *n*. A riding stance where the surfer is so far forward that both feet extend over the nose of the board. Also called HANGING TEN. (IDSM)

"Tequila" *n*. **1**) An instrumental surfy tune (except for the word "Taaah-KEEEY-laaah") originally per-

tandem surfing
Steve Farwell and Chrissy Morrison
Photo: Bob Barbour

formed by The Champs; later popularized by the Ventures in 1960. Pee Wee Herman did the best dance to it in *Pee Wee's Big Adventure*. **2**) Mexican liquor.

terlines *n.* Form-fitting, nylon trunks designed for swimming; used by many Australian surfers.

textured deck *n.* A nonslip surface on the top of a surfboard.

thaw-out *n.* A quiet period after a winter surf session during which the only sound heard is the chattering of teeth and the cursing of the elements. You can tell a thaw-out is ending when the surfer is able to manipulate his tongue in such a manner as to form the words, "Unzip me, please." (JARR)

thick *adj.* Characteristic of some waves; can apply to the whole wave but usually relates to how big the lip is. A thick wave will pound you heavily or smack you in the face with full force. Usage: "That lip was really thick." See THIN.

thickness flow, thickness foil *n.* Refers to the distribution of foam along the length of a surfboard — from the nose to the tail — as seen from the side. **—nose thickness, middle thickness, tail thickness**

thin *adj.* Characteristic of some waves; applies mainly to the wave lip, which may be said to "peel thinly." Distinguished from THICK or SQUARE waves.

thongs *n.* Approved footwear for surfers, worn for all occasions all year round, often teamed with socks in winter. The beauty of the thong is its versatility. It can be used as a musical instrument, weapon, fly swatter, and sex aid. Any establishment that won't let you in wearing thongs is run by nerds. (JARR)

thrash, thrashing *v.* **1**) To rip or shred on a wave. Usage: "Did you see me thrashing on that wave?" **2**) **thrashed** To get wiped out.

Usage: "I got completely thrashed on that last wave." **—thrashed-out**

thrasher *n.* A surfing show-off.

three sixty *n.* **1**) A maneuver in which the surfer turns the board 360 degrees. **2**) A modern maneuver in which the surfer continues the bottom turn up through the lip; the fins then break loose, and board and surfer continue around in a 360-degree loop on the same wave. (NAT, 1985) Not the same as a spinner or three-sixty spinner.

360 air *n.* A three-sixty board spin in the air.

360 curtain floater *n.* A three-sixty board spin on top of the white water.

three-sixty spinner *n.* A move in which the surfer, not the board, does a quick 360-degree pirouette while standing on the moving board. Same as SPINNER.

throat *n.* An anatomical nickname for a hollow wave; a TUBE.

through the back *n.* A move to get through a wave before getting sucked over the falls. Usage: "I saw you made it out through the back."

through-the-lip el rollo *n.* A bodyboarding maneuver. Sometimes spelled *thru-the-lip*. See EL ROLLO.

through-the-lip rebound *n.* A maneuver normally attempted at the conclusion of a fade toward the main curl, at which point the surfer rides through the curl, instead of turning back to the original direction, and then takes the drop with the soup. Between hitting the curl and regaining a track in the original direction, the surfer has to turn the board through more than 180 degrees. (RA)

throwing the brains *n.* When male surfers expose themselves in front of their friends. (North San Diego County)

throwing the fin *n.* Hitting the top of a wave and exposing a fin. (MM)

thruster *n*. Australian Simon Anderson's revolutionary three-fin surfboard design (revealed in 1981), which incorporates a very wide winged, rounded square tail. The wide point is located at or within a few inches of center; the nose is extremely narrow. The two side fins are toed in and canted out, the third fin is set only a few inches from the tip of the tail. Board characteristics are loose and fast; boards are from 5½ to 6½ feet long. They are called thrusters because they tend to come out of a turn with a little more thrust. (CC) Also called TRI or TRI-FIN. —**thrusties** (STM)

thunder crusher *n*. A gnarly wave. (A&M) See DUMPER.

tiburón *n*. Spanish for shark; this is a significant term for anyone surfing in Mexican waters. (BBD)

tidal bore *n*. **1**) A phenomenon that occurs where rivers enter the ocean via long funnel-shaped bays; in such estuaries, especially during high spring tides, the broad front of the incoming tide is restricted by the narrow channel and the shoaling water so that it abruptly increases in height, and a visible wave front, or bore, develops. When conditions are right, this bore can be ridden upstream. See RIVER SURFING. **2**) A person who talks about nothing but the height of the tide in relation to the surf and can tell you at any given time of day when the best tide is. (IBN)

The bore of the Amazon is said to attain a height of twenty-five feet, giving it the appearance of a waterfall traveling upstream. It moves at a speed of twelve knots per hour and extends for three hundred miles. Other famous tidal bores are those of the Chientang River in northern China and the River Severn in England. (WB)

tidal pull and **tidal flow** *n*. EBB and FLOW — the tide coming in and going out.

tidal wave *n*. In the ocean, a train of waves generated by an earthquake, volcanic eruption, underwater landslide, or nuclear explosion, containing a huge amount of energy and moving at high speed. Can be tremendously destructive when they reach shore, inundating low-lying areas, because they steepen and increase in height on approaching shallow water. (WB)

This popular term is entirely misleading in that the phenomenon it identifies has no connection with the tides. Consequently, American oceanographers adopted the Japanese word *tsunami*, which is still in general use, even though it merely means "tidal wave" in Japanese. A more descriptive term that applies to waves caused by earthquakes is *seismic sea wave*.

tide book *n*. A reference book available at most surf shops that, in addition to a tide table with times and feet for high and low tides, contains such other useful information as the phases of the moon, times for sunrise and sunset, a wind chill factor table, and clam chowder recipes.

tide graph *n*. The daily tidal range plotted on a graph.

tide range, tidal range *n*. The difference in feet or meters between high and low tides. For example, at Fistral Beach in Cornwall, England, the notorious tides can cause the break to shift in or out fifty yards during a single heat in a surf contest; during the annual Fosters Contest, numerous competitors fail to score their minimum waves simply because they "get lost" and out of position for the sets. (L&L) The Bay of Fundy, Nova Scotia, has a tidal range of sixty-five feet.

tide wave *n*. TIDAL BORE.

Simon Anderson with thruster
Photo: Peter Crawford / Surfer Magazine

thrusters with coconuts
Photo: Don Balch

tourists
Art: Rick Stover

tides *n.* **1)** The periodic rising and falling of sea level as a consequence of the earth's rotation and the gravitational forces (or pull) of the moon and, to a lesser extent, the sun. Because these astronomical motions are very regular, tides are highly predictable. Tides are also influenced by the ocean's bottom topography. (CCRG) See TIDE BOOK. **2)** An important indicator as to when a surf spot is breaking best. See EQUATORIAL TIDES, MIXED TIDES, NEAP TIDES, SPRING TIDES, TROPIC TIDES.

tint *n.* A transparent coloring agent for resin. (ORB)

tip *n.* **1)** The pointed front end of a surfboard. Also called NOSE TIP. **2)** Cabo San Lucas at the southern tip of Mexico's Baja California peninsula. Usage: "We're going to the tip." (BMS)

TK *adj.* Totally killer. Usage: "TK, dude."

to da max Hawaiian Pidgin for all the way, 100 percent. Usage: "Da surf is pompeen to da max."

TOAD Take Off And Dissolve — said of San Francisco's surf spot "The Dump," which is located offshore of the municipal dump and is off-limits to surfers. The lineup is inundated by toxic pollution (after a rainstorm the water turns purple from the dump runoff), and tons of broken rebar (rusty World War II antisubmarine spikes) and concrete litter the paddle-out zone. (SFR, 3/91)

TOADS Take Off And Die Syndrome — a late takeoff that results in a heavy wipeout. Like a toad crossing the road, the surfer just goes for it and gets squashed. (DWK)

toast, toasted *adj.* A term for California surfers who are "burnt-out," usually from too much sun. (New Jersey; KAH) Usage: "Look at him, man, that dude is toast." See TROPPO.

toes-on-the-nose, toes over *n.* Riding the forward tip of a surfboard with toes hanging over the nose. See HANG FIVE, HANG TEN.

tombolo *n.* A bar of gravel or sand connecting an island or rock with the mainland or with another island. (CCRG)

too many guys out Said of way crowded surfing conditions.

tool, wave tool *n.* A surfboard. (MM)

toothpick *n.* An Australian surfboard from the 1940s and 1950s, usually sixteen feet long by fifteen inches wide, that was used primarily as a racing board and relatively little for wave riding. Toothpicks were constructed of plywood with a light timber frame. (NAT, 1985)

top-to-bottom *adj.* **1)** Used to describe a wave that pours out in front when it breaks, with the initial point of contact matching the height of the wave. **2)** The term for a very thick, hollow wave, for instance a "top-to-bottom barrel." (MW)

top of the wave *n.* WAVE CREST — what Jack London described as the "giddy summit." (1907)

top rack *n.* A surfboard rack for carrying boards on a car. Also called ROOF RACK, SURF RACK.

top turn *n.* **1)** A simple turn at the top of a wave. (NAT, 1985) **2)** In competitive surfing, a turn performed in the top one-third of a wave that does not extend into the lip of the wave, as in a reentry, and does not reverse the surfer's horizontal direction by more than 130 degrees. (L&L)

totally *adv.* Completely, entirely, utterly, absolutely — as in "totally bitchin'," "totally radical," "totally awesome," "totally intense," "totally insane," and, all by itself, "*Totally.*"

totally covered *adj.* TUBED.

TOADS
Art: Robbie Quine

tourist *n.* A visitor to the beach, a valley or nonlocal; **tour** for short. (MCR, MM) —**touristy**-type cars

"*Hootervillus Touristimostus* is a species of tourist found in Hawaii, who probably just bought a matching set of aloha wear from a Waikiki tourist trap for self and spouse. The male of this species is easily recognized by his brightly colored Hawaiian-print short pants with black socks and dress shoes. The female's favorite color seems to be red since she spends many hours sunning herself to get the desired color change — perhaps it is related to a mating ritual. One of this species' favorite migratory areas is Hanauma Bay, where the first day is spent sunning, swimming, and snorkeling. The second day is often spent in the hotel room or emergency room recovering from reef cuts and second-degree sunburns." —Ken Suiso and Rell Sunn, *A Guide to Beach Survival* (1986)

tourista *n.* What you get when you go on a surf trip to Mexico — the runs (diarrhea), an intestinal disorder characterized by abnormal frequency and fluidity of fecal evacuations. Also called *Montezuma's revenge* or *mud slide*. A LOG JAM (constipation) is the opposite of tourista. (PZ)

track *n.* The line in which the surfboard is traveling, and which the surfboard usually wants to continue traveling even though you may be trying hard to turn it.

tracker *n.* A surfboard shape, circa 1968.

tracking *v., n.* **1)** Surfing along the length of the wave wall. (RA) **2)** Making long trails with the surfboard's wake. (MVA) Usage: "I was really tracking on that wave."

trade winds *n.* **1)** A system of winds that blow regularly in one direction or another, occupying most of the tropics. (AHD) **2)** The prevailing winds in the Caribbean, the Hawaiian Islands, and the South Pacific.

At most of the good Hawaiian surfing beaches, the trade winds blow offshore. (See KONA WINDS.) In the northern hemisphere they blow from the northeast, and in the southern hemisphere from the southeast. In some places they blow six months of the year in one direction and six months in the opposite direction.

trail arm, trailing arm *n.* The arm that the surfer extends to the rear while surfing. (MF)

trail foot, trailing foot *n.* In a normal stance, the foot toward the tail of the board.

trailing edge *n.* The rearmost edge of a surfboard or piece of water-riding equipment.

train surfing *n.* The very dangerous practice of riding on the rooftops of electric passenger trains in Rio de Janeiro, Brazil; what a **subway surfer** does in New York.

tram surfing *n.* Riding on top of a tram without falling off. (Grenoble, France; P)

transfer *n.* The act of exchanging boards on a wave, accidentally or on purpose.

transitional maneuvers *n.* A competitive surfing term used to describe moves that come in between minor maneuvers and major maneuvers; they have little influence on scoring potential. They are (in descending order of degree of difficulty): MID-FACE TURNS, PUMP TURNS, FOAM PUMP TURNS, FACE PUMP TURNS, TRIM, FOAM TRIM or GROVELING, STALLING, RECOVERY, and PRONE OUT. (L&L) Also see METHODS OF FINISH.

treacherous *adj.* **1)** Characteristic of hazardous waves or babes. **2)** Said of a potentially dangerous situation. Usage: "It's fully treacherous out there."

tri *n.* A TRI-FIN surfboard. (Australia)

Toadally Tubed
From the flipbook by John Iwerks (see pg. 192 for ordering information)

tri-fin
Photo: Bud Clark

tri-plane hull
Shaper Al Merrick
Photo: Don Balch

tropics
Art: Peter Spacek

tri-fin or **trifin** *n*. A three-fin surf-board. Often referred to as a THRUSTER.

tri-plane hull *n*. A double concave planing surface, which consists of a shallow concave on each side of the stringer that extends from the center of the board to the fin(s).

tribalism *n*. See LOCALISM. (MM)

trim *v*. **1**) To ride across the face of a wave laterally or almost parallel to the wave's line and to the shore. **2**) To steer the board so that it planes best across the face of a wave. **3**) To orient oneself on the surfboard so that it can go, or plane, as fast as possible. **Trimming** involves placing one's body weight so that the board sits correctly in the water (has the maximum practical area in use as a bearing surface on the wave face) and is able to exploit the wave's speed to the fullest. It is most relevant to riding a Malibu. **4**) To achieve the best speed and balance. **5**) *n*. The status of the surfboard when a surfer is trimming; the positioning of the board on a wave. Usage: "He was in trim." (MF)

trippin' *n*. A surf dance that sprang from Dick Dale's crowd at the Rendezvous Ballroom in Newport Beach in the early 1960s ("Let's Go Trippin'"). (PJN) See SURF STOMPS.

tropic tides *n*. Tides of maximum range, occurring twice a month when the moon is over the tropic of Cancer or the tropic of Capricorn. These tides are particularly large in summer and winter when the sun is respectively highest and lowest in the sky. (CCRG)

tropical cyclone *n*. HURRICANE.

tropical depression *n*. A storm grade below a tropical storm in strength, but stronger than a tropical wave.

tropical storm *n*. A storm grade below a hurricane, but stronger than a tropical depression.

tropical wave *n*. A storm grade below a tropical depression.

tropics *n*. **1**) The area of the globe between latitudes 22½ degrees north (the tropic of Cancer) and 22½ degrees south (the tropic of Capricorn). **2**) The home of many of the world's finest surf spots, including Hawaii, parts of Australia, Indonesia, and Fiji. Tropical waters are rich with potentially dangerous and poisonous marine life, more so than temperate waters.

"Toto, we're not in Kansas anymore." — Dorothy in *The Wizard of Oz*

troppo *adj*. **1**) Australian slang for too much time spent in the surf and sun. Usage: "You look a mite troppo, mate." (SFR, 6/87) Possibly derived from the Italian word *tropo*, meaning "too much." **2**) Having a bad sunburn or skin disorder (peeling, redness). See TOAST.

trough *n*. **1**) The low point between the crests of two waves. **2**) The bottom of the wave. (ORB) **3**) The space between two waves, two wives, or two paychecks. (JARR)

trough-to-crest transition *n*. Surfing from the bottom of the wave up to the top.

true foil *n*. The cross section of a fin, viewed straight on (or, in technical terms, 90 degrees to its height). See FOIL.

trunk it, trunkin' it *v*. Wearing only surf trunks while surfing — no wetsuit. (CSD) Same as SKIN IT, BARE BACK. Usage: "The water was so warm we were trunkin' it."

tsunami (sue-NAW-me) *n*. A series of waves (not a single wave) caused by a sudden movement along a large portion of the ocean floor. Means "tidal wave" in Japanese, although the waves it describes have nothing to do with tides. They should also not be confused with storm-surge waves. Same as SEISMIC SEA WAVE. See TIDAL WAVE.

A tsunami does not materialize as a wall of water on the horizon but is perceived as a rapid and drastic lowering of sea level, followed by an equally drastic elevation of sea level (sometimes twenty feet or more). Evidence suggests that one such wave in Indonesia reached a height of one thousand feet! Wave length may be several hundred miles, with periods ranging from fifteen minutes to an hour or more. Tsunamis travel very fast, up to four hundred miles per hour.

tube, tubing wave *n*. **1**) The tubular or barrel-shaped form of a breaking wave created by the plunging lip throwing out in front of the advancing wall. **2**) The hollow, cylinder-like tunnel formed by a wave curling forward as it breaks over itself. **3**) A perfect wave, one that encloses a surfer; the inside section of a hot wave. **4**) The space inside a tubing wave. **5**) A saltwater tunnel. (WLK) Same as PIPELINE, BARREL.

"[A tube is] the G-spot of surfing. Where the pleasure is. A tube is the product of wind, water and topography. A bit of ocean that rears up close to shore and spills over in a cylindrical motion. And just what is so special about it is known only to those who have experienced the view from the inside, which hasn't stopped hundreds of surf-stoked would-be Herman Melvilles from waxing lyrical about it." — Phil Jarratt, *The Surfing Dictionary* (1985)

tube chip *n*. Any tortilla chip that resembles a curling wave — usually encountered while dropping in to some *salsa picante* at a Mexican restaurant.

tube city *n*. A surf session with plenty of tubing waves. (BSM)

tube farting *n*. "Everyone knows that farting in bed is one of life's great pleasures. Who doesn't enjoy letting go with a real sheet stainer and then pulling the blankets over their head to inhale that concentrated personal aroma." —Brian Bile on "Tube Farting," 1/82 (TKS, 5/87)

tube normal *n*. A tube ride that often results in a wipeout because the wave collapses over the surfer; primarily a surf-contest term.

tube radical *n*. **1**) A ride during which the surfer is completely covered up and emerges out of the tunnel before the wave collapses. **2**) The highest-scoring ride in a surf contest.

tube rat *n*. A surfer who frequently gets tubed. (C&M)

tube ride, tube riding *n*. **1**) A ride during which the rider disappears behind the curtain of a breaking wave — the ultimate sensation in surfing. **2**) The highest-scoring ride in a surfing contest. The degree of difficulty is measured by the size and hollowness of the wave and by the length of time in the tube. Crumbling tubes score less than dry tubes, where the surfer is completely enclosed. (L&L)

tube spit *n*. Spray forced by pressure out of a hollow wave when it collapses, sometimes ejecting the surfer out of the tube onto the shoulder of the wave. (RO)

tube suit *n*. A wetsuit with short legs and no arms. (Australia; NAT, 1985)

tubed *v*. To be riding inside the hollow section of a wave. (MM) See GET TUBED.

Everyone has been tubed at least once in his or her life — inside either of a pair of slender ducts, called the fallopian tubes, that connect the ovaries to the uterus in the human female reproductive system; first described by Gabriello Fallopio (1523-1562).

tube ride
Photo: Woody Woodworth

tube spit
Art: Bob Penuelas

tube rider or **tuberider** *n.* **1**) A surfboard that has been tube ridden. (SFG, 2/90) Same as PIPE CLEANER. **2**) A surfer. **3**) "**Tube Rider**" A song by the Surf Punks.

Tubesteak, Tubesteak Tracey, Old Tubesteak The nickname of Malibu surfer Terry Tracey, whose character was portrayed in the *Gidget* movies as Kahoona, a self-described surf bum who lived in a grass shack on the beach.

tubeward *adv.* Refers to surfing toward the tube.

tubies *n.* TUBING WAVES. (Australia)

tubular *adj.* **1**) Used to describe a tube-shaped wave. **2**) Valleyspeak for cool, as in "totally tubular."

tuck *n.* A crouching position on the surfboard; used for shifting body weight and gaining speed. (A&M)

tuck dive *n.* A maneuver used to duck under an incoming wave; same as DUCK DIVE, PUSH THROUGH.

tucked away, tucked in the tube *v.* To be surfing deep in the tube. See COVERED.

tucked-in bow, tucked-in stern *n.* A surfboard designed with a narrow bow or stern.

tucked-under edge rail *n.* A surfboard design feature. See CHINE RAILS.

tunnel skeg *n.* A tubular fin designed to minimize spinouts.

tunneled *v.* TUBED; GET TUBED. **—tunneling wave**

tunnels *n.* Exploratory observation communicated between females at the beach to indicate when a male who is wearing shorts is sitting in such a way that he is exposing his private parts. (Huntington Beach; anonymous, 1989)

turbo fin *n.* A skeg that is curved through its entire height.

turn, turning *v.* To change a board's course on a wave. The surfer leans in the new direction, and the board follows beneath his or her feet. (A&M, MF)

turn turtle *v., n.* Flipping the board upside-down and hanging on underwater as the wave passes over. Usage: "I had to turn turtle." See ROLL.

turning radius *n.* The distance required for a surfboard to complete a turn; a performance characteristic. A shortboard has a much smaller turning radius than a longboard, allowing the surfer to go higher up on the wave, come screaming down, pull off a radical turn, climb back up, then shoot down again, etc. (CC)

turnpiked *v.* What happens when you get stuck on a wave and can't get off and are forced to take it all the way in or face a heinous paddle-out through tons of white water. Usage: "I just got turnpiked. It took me fifteen minutes to get back out here." (Ocean Beach, San Francisco; BTV)

tweeked *adv.* How you feel, for instance: **1**) Thrashed — if you get rumbled in a wave. **2**) High — after smoking a joint. **3**) Hyper — from drinking too much coffee. (PZ)

twin fin or **twinfin** *n.* **1**) Any board with two fins. (L&L) Mike Eaton is credited with the twin-fin breakthrough in 1976. (CC, WLK) **2**) A shortboard (5'8" to 6'8") with a wide tail for maneuverability and a fin near the rail for stability in radical turns. The wider tail provides more planing area and lift, which allows for more speed from less wave. This design is especially suited to smaller surf (under six feet).

twinnie *n.* TWIN FIN. (Australia; SFG 2/90)

twirlie *n.* SPINNER. (Australia; JPD)

typhoon *n.* A tropical cyclone, or hurricane, that originates east of the Philippines or in the China Sea.

twin fin
Mike Cundith's twin-fin design with dual concaves
Photo: Don Balch

twin fin
Mark Richards
Photo: Jeff Divine / Surfer Magazine

Ugh Boots *n*. A faintly ridiculous form of winter footwear favored by surfers, made from sheepskin and named for women's reaction to them when teamed with a formal suit. (Australia; JARR)

ule (OO-lee) *n*. **1**) Hawaiian for penis. **2**) A jerk, analogous to the usage of *dick* in "What a dick."

ultimate cannon *n*. A very fast big-wave board; the fastest of the gun class of surfboard. (JKMJ, 1965)

ultralight riders *n*. Surfers who ride today's superlight type of shortboard. (W&B)

Uluwatu *n*. **1**) The world-famous left-ride surf spot off the southern tip of Bali, Indonesia; **Ulu** for short. **2**) Balinese for "place of the living dead" (SFR, 6/87) or "evil waters" (SFG, 3/90).

unbroken wave *n*. A developing wave, one that hasn't begun to break. Also known as GREEN WAVE.

uncontrolled *adj*. **1**) Refers to any wipeout, fall, or ungainly exit resulting in loss of board control. **2**) Said of any maneuver where the surfer falls before completion; such unfinished maneuvers are considered wipeouts in surfing competitions, and they detract from the wave score. (L&L)

uncool *adj*. Not happening; not nice. Usage: "That's *so* uncool." "That's *totally* uncool."

under-the-lip snap *n*. **1**) A standard surfing maneuver. Same as SNAP. **2**) An intermediate bodyboarding maneuver. (BB, 12/90)

underboarded *adj*. Using a surfboard that is too small for the size of the waves. Usage: "He's way underboarded." (Santa Cruz)

underheel rail grab *n*. A move in which a surfer riding in a squatting position reaches behind his or her legs and grabs onto the rail.

undersea canyon *n*. SUBMARINE CANYON.

undertow *n*. **1**) A misnomer — there's no such thing; one of the most ubiquitous myths of the seashore. (WB) See BACKWASH. **2**) A subsurface current of water moving beneath and in a different direction from the surface water; said especially of a seaward current beneath breaking surf. Common in areas where incoming waves prevent the water's returning to the sea in a usual surface current.

unlocal *n*. NONLOCAL. As the slogan says, "No unlocals." See VALLEY.

unmakable section *n*. An area down the line from the surfer where the wave has already broken, making it impossible to get around or through the white water. See FLOATER.

unmakable takeoff *n*. A situation where the wave is too close to breaking for a reasonably safe departure to be made.

unreal *adj*. Absolutely wonderful; far out. (MVA) Or, if you're in Hawaii, **"Onreal,** brah."

unreal waves *n*. Big waves.

unsurfable *adj*. Unridable.

up *adj.* Said of the surf when it's big, or good for surfing. Usage: "Surf's up!"

Up and riding! An exclamation used by surf contest announcers, such as Lord Tally Ho Sanders on Hawaii's North Shore, to alert spectators that a surfer has caught a wave. (1982)

updraft *n.* A wind rising up the face of a wave, caused by the displacement of air by the moving wave.

upright bottom turn *n.* A turn that the surfer carves out of the bottom of a wave while standing straight up on the board.

upwelling *n.* A process by which surface waters that have been driven offshore by winds are replaced near shore by deeper, colder, nutrient-rich water; happens, for example, along the California coast in summer. Usage: "The upwelling near the submarine canyon makes it foggy and cold." See FOG.

urinophoria *n.* The deliciously warm sensation that comes when one's elimination process fills one's wetsuit with its product. (SFG, 1990) Same as INTERNAL HEATING, PETER HEATER.

uvana (oo-VA-na) *n.* Hawaiian for sea urchin.

Art: The Pizz

Hand Wave, 1989. Artwork: Jim Phillips

The Wedge. Photo: Woody Woodworth

White shark. Photo: Bob Barbour

DANGEROUS SHOREBREAK

Staghorn coral. Photo: Woody Woodworth

Waimea Bay warning. Photo: Dan Jenkin

Hey! **Artwork: Bob Penuelas**

The Endless Summer

TM & © Bruce Brown Films, 1966.
Artwork: John Van Hammersveld

Sharkman. **Artwork: Rick Rietveld**

1-2-Go. **Artwork: Rick Rietveld**

Background photo: Woody Woodworth

Surf check. Artwork: Jim Phillips

Evening Glassoff. Artwork: Bill Ogden, Gordon McClelland Collection

K-Point. Artwork: John Severson,
Gordon McClelland Collection

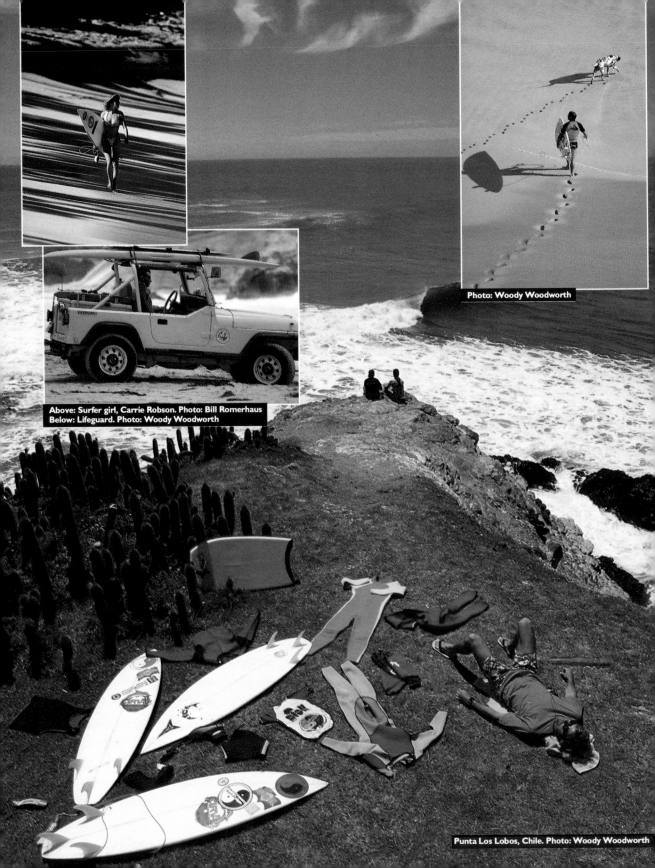

Photo: Woody Woodworth

Above: Surfer girl, Carrie Robson. Photo: Bill Romerhaus
Below: Lifeguard. Photo: Woody Woodworth

Punta Los Lobos, Chile. Photo: Woody Woodworth

V or **vee** *n*. **1**) The slight V-shaped configuration of a surfboard's bottom (often near the tail section) designed to minimize drag. **2**) A faceted planing surface. **3**) A bottom contour whose rear half is thicker on the stringer line than at the rails. (L&L)

VAIL Valleys Against Ignorant Locals — an organization formed in the early 1980s by surfers in the San Fernando Valley who "got pissed at local fags who think the ocean is only for people lucky enough to live by it." (Palmdale; SFG)

V-Land Short for Velzyland, a surf spot on the North Shore of Oahu, Hawaii, named by Bruce Brown in 1958 after Southern California surfboard builder Dale Velzy.

VW Bug *n*. A legendary surf vehicle. Surfmobile history was made when the first Volkswagens arrived in the U.S. in 1949. (SFG, 11/89) See BAJA BUG.

val 1) *n*. Short for VALLEY — a person who lives inland. **2**) **valish** *adj*. Having val characteristics. Usage: "That's so valish."

valley *n*. **1**) A derogatory term originally applied to the San Fernando Valley in Southern California and to anyone living there who came out to the beach; has come to mean any place inland or anybody living there. The perceived distance between the beach and the valley varies depending on the person you're talking to. **2**) A surfer or beachgoer who lives inland. (MCR) **3**) Outside two-mile limit and over the hill. (SP) **4**) **The Valley** The San Fernando Valley, just north of Los Angeles. See CAJON ZONE, LOCAL/VALLEY SWITCH, SAN JOSE. —**valley goons**, **valley boys**

valley cowboys *n*. A term for INLAND SURFERS in the late fifties and early sixties; the first use of *valley* in this context. Cowboy Phil Anderson was one of the first really good surfers to come out of The Valley. (MSO, A&M)

"Valley Girl" *n*. Frank Zappa's 1982 smash hit from the album *Ship Arriving Too Late to Save a Drowning Witch*. The lyrics consisted of words and dialogue heard by Zappa's daughter, Moon Unit, at the Sherman Oaks Galleria shopping mall in the San Fernando Valley, and included such expressions as "grody to the max," "Barf me out," and "Ohmigod, gag me with a spoon." Driven by the prominence of valspeak, surfing slang moved inland and burst onto the national — even international — scene.

"Okay, fine . . .
Fer sure, fer sure
She's a Valley Girl
In a clothing store."
—From "Valley Girl"

valley go home Common graffiti seen in Santa Cruz and other areas along the California coast.

valley lifeline *n*. A derogatory term for a SURF LEASH. (SP) Also called KOOK CORD.

valley
Valley voodoo doll
Art: The Pizz

valley sheep
Art: Rebecca Fish

valley sheep *n*. People from San Jose who say "du-u-u-u-de" (spoken like sheep). (Santa Cruz; SP)

valley surprise *n*. Since around 1980, the name of an infamous turn on the return trip from Santa Cruz to San Jose along Highway 17 — a major valley route to the ocean. There is some argument within the surfing community as to whether the actual turn is the first, second, or third hairpin turn encountered on the descent from the summit in the Santa Cruz Mountains into the Santa Clara Valley. (MPN, MCR)

valspeak, valleyspeak, valley-girl slang *n*. A special language that, according to the media, is confined to the San Fernando Valley — in other words, a media myth. In fact, many of the words and phrases associated with valspeak, for instance *gnarly, rad, radical to the max,* are surf terms that moved inland, transported by vals who were hanging out on the beach. The word *tubular,* for example, which surfers invented to describe a well-curved wave, was co-opted to mean "very good" in valspeak. (CC)

Van's The brand name of a canvas deck shoe popular with surfers; carries the slogan "off the wall" on the heel. Styles include Hawaiian print.

vee bottom *n*. **1)** The revolutionary 1960s concept of having two planing surfaces on the back third of a surfboard. Same as V or VEE.
2) Refers to a girl wearing a bikini that rides up at the sides. (JARR)

Velcro *n*. A nylon fabric that can be fastened to itself; invented by Switzerland's George de Mestral in 1948. Has many uses in the surfing industry, including in surfer's watchbands and in leash-strap "cuffs" used to secure a leash to the rider's ankle.

Jim Ganzer, artist, surfer, and founder of Jimmy Z. clothing company, introduced Velcro closures on surf clothing after experiencing the discomfort of hooks and snaps while lying on his surfboard. Mr. Ganzer describes the sound of ripping Velcro as "a modern mating call." The sound has been celebrated in the ZZ Top song "Velcro Fly." (DSL)

Ventures, the An instrumental surf band in the 1960s. Their hits included the theme of the TV series "Hawaii Five-0."

venturi effect *n*. The tendency of fluids to increase in speed as they flow from a larger area through a smaller one (ORB); an important concept in surfboard design.

vert *n*. Short for VERTICAL, as in "going beyond vert."

vertical *adj*. Refers to the perpendicular orientation of a surfboard relative to the ocean horizon, achieved while riding up to the top of a wave. **—getting vertical**

vertical takeoff *n*. A steep drop down the face of a wave. See NO-PADDLE TAKEOFF.

vibe *v*. A derogatory term for giving someone, usually a nonlocal, the silent treatment. Usage: "She vibed me out." See BAD AIR. **—getting vibed, bad vibes, cold vibes**

vibe of the day, vibe of the session *n*. The atmosphere created by how surfers react to each other — whether by sharing waves and taking turns or hogging waves; yelling at one another or not; sitting around and talking about girls or a party or making other small talk; long- and shortboarders getting along or not. The assortment of people in the water at any given time changes the vibe. One jerk in the water often ruins it for everyone; sometimes he's told off by the majority. The attitudes around surf contests always reduce the vibes, never enhance them.

victory-at-sea conditions *n.*
1) When the surf is big and stormy; derived from the title of the 1959 documentary *Victory at Sea* on the course of World War II at sea, which was adapted from the PBS TV series that always opened with a battleship pounding through some very mean seas. (W&B, EPZ) **2**) When the elements win. Go back to bed, go to work or school, or rent a surf movie video. There will be no surfing today. (JARR)

volcano *n.* A surf knob with an open wound that, because of constant knee paddling, is never allowed to heal; common to longboard riders in the 1960s. (DWK)

wahine
Alona
Art: I. B. Nelson

wag *n.* A jerk, loser, nonsurfer. (East Coast)

wahine (wah-HEE-nee) *n.* A Hawaiian girl or woman.

Waimea Bay *n.* A big-wave surf spot and contest site located on the North Shore of Oahu, Hawaii; first surfed by Greg Noll in November 1957 and later described by him as "Waimea's hang-on-to-your-balls super drop." The swell coming out of the very deep water creates high, wall-like waves. The **Waimea Shorebreak** is known for its pounding.

"The drop at Waimea feels as good as 20 ten-second tube rides put together. The feeling of conquering one drop there is better than anything, any wave, anywhere in my life." —Mark Richards, 1/84 (TKS, 5/87)

waiting room *n.* The area beyond the breakers where surfers wait for incoming waves. (MM) Same as LINEUP.

wake surfing or **wakesurfing** *n.* Riding the stern wave behind a boat — done standing on a surfboard, just as with an ordinary wave. See SKURFING.

walking *v., n.* Moving about on a surfboard. (MF)

walking the board *v., n.* Walking back and forth on the board to maintain control. Usage: "I was walking the board."

walking the dog *v., n.* Moving back and forth on a surfboard to alter speed. (MM)

walking the nose *v., n.* Moving foot over foot toward the bow of a board.

walking the plank *v., n.* **1**) Walking forward or backward on a surfboard while riding a wave. **2**) An old pirate term; referred to a method of executing unwanted visitors. (PZ)

wall *n.* **1**) The steep forward portion of a wave. **2**) The glassy face of a wave. **3**) The face of a wave before it has broken. **4**) The steep unbroken wave face extending along the shoulder. (L&L) See WALL UP.

wall-of-death *n.* A maneuver in which the surfer banks off the crest of the wave. (Australia; RA)

wall surf *n.* A wave face that seems to stand up vertically like a wall. (MF)

Waimea Bay
Photo: Woody Woodworth

walking the plank
Photo: Don Balch

wall up *v.* What happens when a wave is steep and not breaking from right to left or left to right. Usage: "The wave walls up on the inside." **—walled up** *adj.*

walled out *adj.* Used to describe large unridable waves that break evenly across the beach. (MM) Usage: "The place was walled out."

wallhangers *n.* Hand-shaped, wooden surfboards built primarily for display at surf shops and restaurants. (GN) Same as RESTAURANT BOARD.

wally *n.* Originally slang from England for a jerk or loser. BARNEY. (KSO)

wanker *n.* An individual displaying the classic symptoms of a complete lack of any common intelligence whatsoever. Windsurfers are sometimes referred to as **wind wankers**. (England; LJE) See GYRO WANKER.

wanks, wanketh *v.* Sucks. Usage: "It wanks." "It wanketh." (LH)

wannabee *n.* A neophyte or inexperienced surfer; a former hodad. (CVG) See WISH WAS.

warm-water wax *n.* A kind of wax made especially for use in warm water; has different properties from cold-water wax. Also called SUMMER WAX. See WINTER WAX.

warp *n.* Strands that run the length of fiberglass cloth. (ORB) See WELP.

washing machine *n.* An analogy for what it feels like to get held under and tumbled beneath a wave — like getting caught in the **rinse cycle** of a washing machine. Usage: "I was caught in the washing machine for the longest time." See HELD DOWN.

wasted *adj.* Screwed up, polluted, drunk. (A&M)

water *n.* The liquid that descends from the clouds as rain, forming streams, lakes, and seas, all of which provide some form of wave to surf on; a major constituent of all matter.

wave
Art: Jimbo Phillips

water bed *n.* A bed whose mattress is a plastic bag filled with water. (W9, 1853) Surfers are fond of water beds as places to rest or sleep close to their liquid medium.

waterlogged *adj.* A condition that may inflict a surfboard if its fiberglass skin is broken or cracked, allowing the foam to become saturated. A waterlogged board gets heavy. (ASKC) See FOAM ROT.

waterman *n.* A SURFER or anyone else who participates in water sports.

watery hollows *n.* Tubing waves. (MWV, 1990)

wave *n.* **1)** Undulating or rippling water, the three main natural causes of which are wind, earthquakes, and the gravitational pull of the moon and the sun. (WB) **2)** A moving pulse of energy; a horizontally moving ridge of water the particles of which move in closed curves. **3)** A requisite for surfing. (JRW) **—permanent wave, new wave, ultimate wave**

"Waves are an endless source of fascination for everyone, from scientists to surfers. Who, in watching, is not mesmerized by the ongoing cycles of surge and rush, flow and ebb, storm and calm?" —Drew Kampion, *The Book of Waves* (1989)

"Once more upon the water! Yet once more! And the waves bound beneath me as a steed that knows his rider." —Lord Byron, "Child Harlod's Pilgrimage," (c. 3, st. 2)

Wave A small coastal town just north of Rincon Point in Santa Barbara County, California.

wave action *n.* The continuous pounding of surf against the shore. See WAVE SHOCK.

wave attack *n.* A radical style of surfing. Usage: "Look at that dude's wave attack."

wave characteristics *n*. The multitude of possibilities exhibited by ever-changing ocean waves, which fluctuate from spot to spot in response to numerous variables (bottom topography, swell direction, tides, etc.). Wave descriptions are seemingly endless, and include pumping, gnarly, tubing, jacking, and so on.

wave collapse *n*. The action of a tubing wave that can no longer hold up. See TUBE SPIT.

wave crest *n*. See CREST.

wave-cut bench *n*. MARINE TERRACE.

wave face *n*. The unbroken surface of a wave. (L&L)

wave height *n*. The verticle distance measured from the trough to the crest of a wave. (WB) See WAVE SIZE, WAVE STEEPNESS.

wave knowledge, wave judgment *n*. A crucial aspect of surfing. It takes years to accumulate the experience needed to deal with the multitude of situations the sea presents — to know, for example, when to take off.

wave length *n*. The distance between two wave crests measured in seconds — the time it takes for one trough to pass a given point such as a buoy. (W&B)

wave lip *n*. The top part of a wave that throws out in front and over the wave face. Also called LIP.

wave period *n*. See PERIOD.

wave pool *n*. An artificial chlorinated surfing pool in which ridable waves are produced by a wave machine. (L&L) Located at inland water-theme parks, such as Allentown Wave Pool, Pennsylvania (site of the World Inland Surfing Championships in 1986) and Big Surf in Tempe, Arizona.

wave possession *n*. In competitive surfing, the issue of who has priority on a specific wave. Some associations still use the "first rider up" rule, but the majority have gone to "the rider on the inside" — the distinction is crucial! See INTERFERENCE RULE(S).

wave rebel *n*. SURF REBEL.

wave refraction *n*. A deflection from the path that waves are traveling, brought about by a number of factors. Refraction implies a change in both direction and speed — a common phenomenon at point breaks.

"On entering shallow water, incoming waveforms are increasingly influenced by the offshore submarine topography and are refracted such that the wave crests tend to parallel the depth contours. Waves arriving at straight coastlines with parallel depth contours and a sloping beach are slowed and experience a reduction in wavelength; the crests of the waves, however, remain parallel to the beach. Waves traveling obliquely toward a beach with parallel depth contours are refracted so that the crests become more aligned with the beach. Along an irregular coastline, waves are refracted toward promontories and away from indentions in the coast, a phenomenon that aids in selective erosion and a tendency toward a straight coastline, which explains why indentions can provide shelter from waves advancing toward the coast." (GRL) — *The New Grolier Electronic Encyclopedia* (Danbury, CT: Grolier Electronic Publishing, 1990)

wave rider or **waverider** *n*. A SURFER.

wave riding *n*. SURFING.

wave sailor *n*. WINDSURFER.

wave sailing *n*. WINDSURFING.

wave selection *n*. In competitive surfing, the waves you *want* to catch and the waves you *don't* want to catch. (L&L)

wave shape *n*. See SHAPE.

wave shock *n*. The force of waves as they strike the coast; measured by a seismograph.

wave pool
Photo: Rob Gilley

wave-size threshold
Art: Deano

wave size *n*. **1**) A measurement relative to a surfer's body height, made at the first opportunity to compare the standing height of the person against the wave face — generally at the first bottom turn. (L&L) The various wave sizes relative to body height are ankle slapper, knee slapper, waist high, shoulder high, head high, overhead, double overhead.   **2**) The height of a wave as measured from the back of the wave, calculated by doubling the height of the back to get the height of the face. See WAVE HEIGHT.

One theory about wave size has it that an imperial foot (twelve inches) is different from a surfer's foot, which supposedly is much larger. This means that in Hawaii, for instance, twenty-foot surf is called ten foot plus. At Hawaii's Banzai Pipeline, the roar of the wave helps surfers judge the size. Whatever the method of measurement, waves are always biggest in places where the coast faces into the swell. (ASL, 4/90; WLK; W&B)

"Ask ten surfers how to measure a wave and you'll get ten different explanations." —Corky Carroll (1989)

wave-size threshold *n*. A personal limit to the size of a wave that a surfer will attempt to ride. (L&L)

wave ski *n*. A cross between a kayak and a surfboard; used to ride breaking waves and unbroken swell. *Not* a surf ski.

A wave ski has a hand-held double-ended paddle for power, a seatbelt and foot strap for control and safety, and (usually) three adjustable fins. Wave skis range from 7 to 10 feet in length and 22 to 25 inches in width, and they weigh 20 to 30 pounds. The sport has been very popular in Australia for over fifteen years. The most popular types of wave skis are foam-filled fiberglass; foam-filled plastics are next in popularity, followed by hollow fiberglass. Fiberglass skis are slightly lighter and more performance oriented; plastic skis are a little heavier but very rugged.

wave ski
Photo: Rob Gilley

wave-ski surfer *n*. Someone who rides a wave ski.

wave speed *n*. The speed at which a wave travels in open water; swells travel at about thirty-five miles per hour before reaching shallow water. Over distance, waves die out and are replaced by following waves at such a rate that the group advances at just half the speed of the individual waves. (DKM)

wave spies *n*. A derogatory term for surf photographers because they expose little-known surf spots to the masses. (SP 3)

wave steepness *n*. The ratio of the height of a wave to its length; the limit is about 17. For example, a wave seven feet long can be no more than one foot high; when small steep waves exceed this limit they break. (WB)

wave train *n*. A succession of similar waves at equal intervals. (W9, 1897)

wave vehicle *n*. Any of various surf-riding crafts, such as a surfboard, surf mat, and bodyboard.

waveforms *n*. Waves.

wavelet *n*. A little wave; a ripple. (W9, 1810)

wax *n*. **1**) A mixture of paraffin, beeswax, incense, and coloring that is rubbed on the deck of surfboards to aid traction. By rubbing it on and building up a coarse, beaded surface, one neutralizes the inherent slipperiness of wet fiberglass. (NAT, 1985; SFG, 3/90) **2**) Another name for a sanding agent.

wax buildup *n*. Dirty old wax that has clumped together. See GUNGA.

wax comb *n*. **1**) A thin, plastic blade with one serrated edge that is used to score grooves into a fresh wax job or rough up an old wax coat, greatly increasing traction. (NAT, 1985)

Most wax combs have a sharp edge that can be used to scrape off wax buildup. Same as WAX SCRAPER. **2)** The only type of comb that many surfers use or own.

wax down *v.* Same as WAX UP. "We're waxing down our surfboards . . ." —The Beach Boys, *Surfin' USA* (1962)

wax job *n.* The end result of applying surf wax to the deck of a surfboard.

wax pocket *n.* A rear pocket on a pair of surf shorts designed expressly for carrying a bar of surf wax.

wax rash *n.* BOARD RASH.

wax scabs *n.* Old, dirty surf wax that has built up. (SFG 3/90) Same as WAX BUILDUP. See GUNGA.

wax scraper. *n.* A plastic scraper that can be used to scrape off wax scabs after a board has been left in the sun for a while to soften the wax. (SFG, 3/90)

wax substitutes *n.* Substances or materials used instead of paraffin or other surf waxes. Examples are aerosol spray-on waxes and stick-on grip strips or pads.

wax up, waxing up *v.* To apply wax to a surfboard. Same as WAX DOWN.

waxing off the top Sliding across the lip of a wave on a surfboard; a term coined by Peter Townend.

way *adv.* An intensifier commonly used in California to make adjectives way more cool sounding. (P) —**way cool, way rad, way stoked**

way back *adv.* In the tube. —**getting way back**

way upper crust *adv.* At the top of a wave. (MM)

weather radio *n.* An indispensable tool for all surfers — a surfer's best friend; provides continuous broadcasts of weather conditions and updated forecasts approximately every three hours. (WS)

webbed paddling gloves *n.* PADDLE GLOVES; first used in a pro competition by Glen Winton in 1986. (SFG, 11/89)

wedge *n.* **1)** A heavy, peaking wave. (NAT, 1985) **2)** A pie-shaped piece of foam or wood used in repairing a surfboard; it is forced into the damaged opening in the surfboard and glassed over. Also called PLUG. **3)** *v.* When two waves coming from somewhat different directions merge when they meet. The wedging part of the two waves usually breaks a great deal harder than the breaking part of either wave by itself. **4) the Wedge** The famous and dangerous surf spot, popular among bodysurfers and bodyboarders, located at the southern tip of the Balboa Peninsula, Newport Beach, California.

wedge
Photo: Woody Woodworth

wedging *adj.* A wave characteristic, as in "a wedging wave." See WEDGE, WEDGY.

wedgy *adj.* Used to describe how a swell refracts, or breaks up, and then stands up over a shallow bottom in a compact, peaky fashion. (Australian; MW)

weed *n.* **1)** A small person; a GROMMET. **2)** A large plant grown in a quiet corner of your garden and used under medical supervision to improve your surfing. (JARR)

weekly *n.* Refers to a "weekly chick" — a nonresident female who rents an apartment near the beach for a week or two and takes pictures of people she meets to show off at home as souvenirs. Usage: "I had about six or seven weeklies this summer." (Newport Beach)

weighting/unweighting, weight-on/weight-off *n.* Altering the amount of body weight acting downward on the board during a ride; can be accomplished for short periods by quickly flexing or extending the legs. (RA)

well-shaped wave *n*. Any wave that is suitable for surfing. (MF)

welp *n*. Strands that run the width of fiberglass cloth. Also referred to as *fill*. (ORB) See WARP.

west *n*. A wind or swell direction. Usage: "It's got way too much west in it."

west swell *n*. A swell that travels from west to east. (ORB)

west wind, westerly *n*. A wind that blows from west to east. (ORB)

wetsuit or **wet suit** *n*. A neoprene rubber suit used by surfers as insulation against cold water. Wetsuits are usually ⅛ inch thick (about 3 milimeters). The seams are glued together, or sometimes glued and stitched. The higher-quality suits are glued, stitched, and taped. They are designed to fit snugly but to allow a thin layer of water to enter, so that the water can be warmed by body heat and keep the user warm.

wetsuit
Jack O'Neill with prototype dry suit, Santa Cruz, early 1950s
Photo: O'Neill, Inc.

Wetsuits were pioneered by Jack O'Neill in the 1950s at Ocean Beach, San Francisco, where the water is cold year-round. He experimented by wearing sweaters from the Goodwill out in the ocean, then navy jackets sprayed with Thompson's water seal, and later, unicellular foam (PVC). (SCSM)

wettie *n*. An Australian term for wetsuit.

Westie loop *n*. A flip negotiated while holding onto a skimboard; named after Kurt Westgaard, who was the first person to do it. (TLH) Same as WIDDLEY.

whacks it off the top A common phrase used by surf contest announcers to describe various maneuvers performed on the wave lip or top of a wave.

whale *n*. BEACHED WHALE.

What up, bra? What up, bro? "Hey, what's happening?" (Topanga, California)

whine *n*. The sound of the skeg or tail of a surfboard cutting through the water at high speed. Also called SKEG HUM, WHISTLING SKEG.

whipturn or **whip turn** *n*. A maneuver in which a surfer taking off on a wave swiftly snaps the board into position.

whirlie *n*. A lesson taught to foul-mouthed young surfers. First the kid gets a warning, then if the bad words continue, an older surfer holds him by the feet, head-dips him into a public toilet, and flushes it to give his hairdo a whirlie. (La Jolla Shores; HJP)

whistling skeg *n*. A fin with a square afteredge that causes it to whistle at high speeds. Also called SKEG HUM, SKEG WHINE.

white-elephant break *n*. Really big surf on an outer reef. (GN)

white shark (*Carcharodon carcharias* — Latin for "having jagged teeth"): *n*. The world's largest predatory fish and the most feared species of shark. Popularly known as **great white shark**, they are also called *white* (in Australia) and *whitey* (in Santa Cruz).

White sharks are responsible for all shark attacks on humans between Santa Barbara in California and Washington State. They populate all the cool ocean waters of the world — for example, the colder waters off of southern Australia and Northern California. Averaging 5 feet long and 50 pounds at birth, they don't reach sexual maturity until they are around 14 feet long and weigh some 3,000 pounds. (Males grow to 14½ feet, females to 19½ feet.) White sharks never sleep; they simply swim and eat. Their average speed is three to four knots per hour; their favorite food seal or sea lion. They attack from below, take one bite, and retreat until their prey bleeds to death. In California, most white shark attacks occur between July and October; the slow months are February to April. (LMZ, MW, NHMLA) See RED TRIANGLE, SHARK, SHARK ATTACK.

white water or **whitewater** *n.*
1) The turbulent, foaming, bubbling water and froth created by the breaking of a wave. **2**) The broken part of a wave. Also called SOUP.

white-water surfing *n.* RIVER BODYBOARDING.

white-water takeoff *n.* When the surfer begins riding on a wave that has already broken.

whitecaps *n.* **1**) The tops of waves or swell blown off at sea, forming spume or spindrift. **2**) A wind-blown chop or wave with its crest broken into white foam; generally rolls a short distance and backs off.

widdley, double widdley *n.* WESTIE LOOP.

wide point or **widepoint** *n.* Refers to the widest part of a surfboard, which may be located anywhere from two inches behind center to eight inches ahead of center. The location influences the board's turning characteristics. The further ahead of center the wide point is placed, the longer and more drawn out the board's turns will be. A wide point in back of center makes the board turn more quckly and sharply.

wide turn *n.* Riding out in front of a wave and gradually making a wide arc to turn back up the wave face.

width *n.* A surfboard dimension measured at right angles to the length of the board, usually near the center at the widest point. Typically, boards are from nineteen to twenty-one inches wide. Wider boards contain more foam, providing more flotation and making it easier to paddle and to catch waves earlier. The increased planing area efficiently uses the energy from small and slow waves, providing more speed than a narrower board.

wiggle *n.* PUMP TURN. (Australia; L&L)

wild time *n.* A surf session with plenty of fast-breaking critical waves.

wilma *n.* A female DWEEB; from the character of the same name on "The Flintstones."

wind, wind force *n.* A prime factor in creating surf; can ruin good surf if it's blowing onshore, or make it even better if it's blowing offshore.

wind chill factor *n.* The effect of wind in lowering an already cold temperature even further. Tide books contain wind chill factor tables.

wind chop *n.* Waves produced by onshore winds blowing in the immediate vicinity of a surf spot; characterized by a bumpy-looking sea, whitecaps, and unhappy surfers. Wind chop can ruin the quality of excellent surf within minutes. See BLOW-OUT, BLOWN OUT. (S&C)

wind lift *n.* The strong updraft caused by an offshore wind blowing up the face of a wave. Wind lift can make it very difficult to drop in, and sometimes blows the surfer and board back over the top. (A&B)

wind line *n.* A distinct change in the appearance of the ocean surface at a certain place (for instance, ruffled on one side and smooth on the other), indicating that a stronger wind is outside the surf break or approaching it. —**advancing wind line**

wind peaks *n.* Waves with a short wave length caused by strong, local winds; very narrow and generally choppy.

wind speed *n.* The velocity of wind, as measured in miles per hour (mph) or knots per hour. A guide for measuring the speed of wind without instruments follows:

CALM — smoke rises vertically
1–12 mph — just feel wind on face,

leaves in motion
13–24 mph — raises dust or loose
paper, small branches move
25–30 mph — large branches move,
wires whistle
30–40 mph — whole trees in motion,
hard to walk against
—Adapted from the *"Easy Read" Tide
Book* (1989)

wind squall *n.* A gust of wind lasting only a short while — a common occurrence out on the ocean in the tropics. Also called PUFF. See SQUALL, RAIN SQUALL.

wind swell *n.* **1**) Waves created by local wind conditions. Such swell normally doesn't perform well at reef and point breaks because it is not influenced much by bottom formations. Because the waves have shorter intervals, they do not feel the bottom until they are in relatively shallow water. (W&B). See SEA STATE. **2**) Small, uneven peaky surf produced by prevailing winds within a few hundred miles offshore; the waves are four to five feet year-round, but most noticeable in the spring. Such winds are often a little stronger after the passage of a cold front. (S&C) —**west wind swell**

wind waves *n.* Waves caused by local winds. The three factors influencing the size of wind waves are wind velocity; the duration of time the wind blows; and the extent of open water across which it blows (the fetch). (WB)

Windansea A La Jolla surf break written about by Tom Wolfe in *The Pump House Gang* (1968).

windmill *v.* Paddling really hard and fast in an attempt to catch a wave. (GN) Usage: "I had to windmill to catch that wave." Jack London referred to the "windmill stroke" in 1907.

window *n.* See SWELL WINDOW.

windsurfing
Photo: Woody Woodworth

windsurfer *n.* **1**) Either a board or the rider who windsurfs. **2**) **Windsurfer** A trademark for a sailboard.

windsurfing *n.* The sport of wave riding and wave jumping using a surfboard mounted with a mast and sail, equipped with footstraps, and having a larger than normal fin area. Developed in 1969 by two Southern Californians, Hoyle Schweitzer and Jim Drake, windsurfing is popular on inland lakes as well as on bays and the open ocean. Also called SURFSAILING. See SAILBOARD.

windwankers *n.* A term used by keen surfers to describe wave sailors (windsurfers) whose egos are advanced beyond their skills. (Australian; MW)

windward *adj.* Refers to the side of the island that the wind and waves reach first; as distinct from LEEWARD.

wing, winger *n.* **1**) A design feature on the rail of a board. Same as BUMP WING. **2**) Small appendages on the rail of a surfboard, from three to fourteen inches from the tip of the tail. One, two, or three pairs of wings may be used. **3**) A protective edging of redwood or other wood along the bow and sides of an old-style surfboard.

wing tail, wing-tail board *n.* The predecessor to the sting, or stinger board; invented by Steve Walden in 1973.

winged keel, winged keel fin *n.* A fin invented by Cheyne Horan that is similar to Ben Lexcen's design of the America's Cup sailboat keel of the same name. See X-FIN.

winter break *n.* A break that occurs only in winter, when the beach profile changes and offshore sandbars shift. See SUMMER BREAK.

winter swell *n.* Swells generated by storms in the North Pacific from October to April; usually anywhere from 3 to 6 feet to 15 to 20 feet high. Some of these storms lie south of due west, others are farther north. The west swells are more common during the fall months. (S&C) —**west swell**, **north swell**

winter wax *n.* A type of surf wax designed especially for cold-water surfing conditions. See WARM-WEATHER WAX.

wipe out 1) *v.* To fall off one's board while taking off on or riding a wave. Same as TAKE GAS. **2)** To be knocked off a board by either a crashing wave or another surfer. **3)** In general, to fall off a surfboard. **4) wipe-out** or **wipe-out** *n.* Any situation where the forces of a wave overcome the skills of a surf rider; falling because of loss of control of the board. **5) "Wipe Out"** A song by the Surfaris (June 1963) that went to #2 nationally, making it the highest charting surf instrumental of all time. (PJN)

wired 1) *v.* Figured out; understood — to have a surf spot wired is to understand its individual nature, to know which swell, wind, and tide conditions suit the break best. Some spots are hard to wire. (MW) **2)** *adj.* Feeling great. (RO) Usage: "I was so wired after that tube ride."

WISA Women's International Surfing Association.

wish was *n.* Someone who wants to be a surfer. (PZ) Same as WANNABEE. Usage: "He's just a wish was."

witness *v.* To look, see, view, or watch over something. Usage: "Did you *witness* that wave, dude?" (LH) See SURF CRIMES.

womb *n.* The womb of the ocean — inside of a hollow breaking wave. Same as GREEN ROOM, GREEN WOMB.

woody or **woodie** *n.* **1)** A vintage wooden-paneled, surfboard-carrying

wipeout
Photos: Robert Brown

woody
Art: Jim Phillips

station wagon, for example, a 1934 Ford. **2**) The old car, usually a station wagon, that a surfer uses to haul boards to the beach. So named because of the wood paneling used on the sides of station wagons in the 1930s, 1940s, and early 1950s. (IDSM) **3**) An erection — morning timber. Usage: "I've got a total woody."

woofy *n*. Polluted water — and you can thank the antiquated Sydney sewage system for the introduction of this word. Same as ON THE NOSE, YUK, SURFING UNDER TURD. (Australia; MW)

work *v*. **1**) To attack or take on a wave. Usage: "He's really working the inside." **2**) To cause injury to a car or person. Usage: "That asshole totally worked me just because I took off in front of him." **3**) *n*. An activity for people who don't surf. (DS)

worked, getting worked *v*. Thrashed about in the soup. (MM) Usage: "I got worked on that wave."

World Tour *n*. In competitive surfing, the series of annual worldwide surf contests organized by the ASP, and culminating each December in the Hawaiian Triple Crown held on the North Shore of Oahu.

WSA Western Surfing Association. (U.S.)

X-fin *n*. A surfboard fin design described by inventor Scott Bucknell as a cross between a propeller and wings. The design was influenced by Australian guru Cheyne Horan's winged keel fin (which was inspired by Ben Lexcen's America's Cup sailboat keel), but instead of a single foil, it has two foils crossed over to form an X and requires two fin boxes. (SFG, 2/90)

Xmas Swell *n*. An Australian phenomenon that has created a cargo-cult mentality among surfers. Almost without fail, king (high) tides and other seasonal factors produce good waves for the festive season, which is just as well because few surfers will have been good enough during the year to expect anything from Santa. (JARR)

X-fin
Photo: John S. Callahan

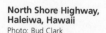

North Shore Highway, Haleiwa, Hawaii
Photo: Bud Clark

"Ya Shoulda Been Here Yesterday" *n.* A Surf Punks song implying "you missed some really great surf."

yabba-dabba-doo! A surfer's exultant cry, à la Hanna-Barbera cartoon character Fred Flintstone. (ASKC, 1965)

yarner 1) *n.* Someone who tells stories for hours on end, with basically no apparent objective or point. (ALN) Similar to RIGGIN. See FOSSIL.
2) yarn *v.* To spin yarns or talk forever.

yeah *adv.* What the surfer audience says at a surf flick during the projection of a hot ride, usually a tube ride, wipeout, or takeoff on a giant wave.

Yeeeooow! A surfer yell (upon taking off on a giant wave). (GN)

"You guys reeeally missed it" A phrase repeated throughout the movie *The Endless Summer* (1964), referring to surf that had been so good or big the day or week before.

You Should Have Been Here an Hour Ago: The Stoked Side of Surfing or How to Hang Ten Through Life and Stay Happy A great title for a book by Phil Edwards (1967) that has become a collector's item.

"There are uncounted millions of people right now who are going through life without any sort of real, vibrant kick. The legions of the unjazzed. But surfers have found one way. God knows, there are other ways. Each to his own special danger. Skiing is not enough. Sailing is near. Ski jumping is almost. Automobile racing has got it. Bullfighting makes you dead. The answer is surfing." —Phil Edwards

yowza! The orgasmic shriek of a surfer emerging from the green cathedral. There, we've got it all in one: surfing, sex, religion. (JARR)

yuk *n.* Surfing in polluted waters; same as ON THE NOSE, SURFING UNDER TURD, WOOFY. (Australia; MW)

yummy yellow *n.* A shark's favorite color of wetsuit. (1980) Some sharks seem to avoid dull-colored objects; they are attracted instead to bright colors, such as yellow or the orange often used for life jackets so that they can be easily seen by rescue crews. (NHMLA)

yuppie surfer *n.* An upwardly mobile surfer. (1980s)

Art: Karen T. Delgadillo

wall
Art: I. B. Nelson

Z

zero break *n.* **1**) The general area where the biggest waves break beyond the first break. **2**) The outermost line of breakers on a day of exceptionally large surf.

zigzag or **zig-zag** *v.* To change rails while dropping down the face of a wave. (MM) **—zigzagging**

zinc, zinc cream, zinc oxide *n.* **1**) A type of sun block that rays can't penetrate; applied to the nose and lips for maximum protection. White originally, but now available in fluorescent colors as well. **2**) A sun-protection ointment designed to make you look ridiculous while keeping your skin in place. (Australia; JARR)

zip board *n.* MALIBU BOARD.

ziplocked *adj.* Tucked inside a barreling wave. (W&B)

zipper, fast zipper *n.* A fast wave that breaks quickly and peels off like a zipper. See INSIDE ZIPPER.

zoners, zonies *n.* A semi-derogatory nickname for surfers from Arizona. (San Diego County)

zonked *adj.* **1**) Excited, as in "totally zonked." (CC) **2**) Exhausted. Usage: "I was completely zonked after that surf."

zoo 1) *n.* Used to describe a crowded surf or beach area, or too many surfers in the water. Usage: "Man, it's a zoo out there." **2**) **Zooport** An occasional name for Newport Beach, California, so called because of its crowded surfing conditions. **3**) **zooed** *adj.* Usage: "The beach was fully zooed with inland kooks." **—way zooed** (supercrowded), **zooed out** (crowded to the max)

zorries *n.* Inexpensive, stamped-out rubber sandals. Also called *sleepahs* (Hawaiian Pidgin) and *slaps*. Same as FLIP-FLOPS, GO-AHEADS, etc.

Zuma, Zuma Beach *n.* Named after a Chumash Indian tribe, Malibu's largest beach and popular surf spot, officially called Zuma County Beach; attracts hoards of crowds in the summer, hence the nickname **Zooma**.

zup "What's up?'

C'MON..!! FASTER FASTER!

ZZiiiiiiiiirrr!

zipper
Art: I. B. Nelson

zoo
Art: I. B. Nelson

APPENDIX A:
Ancient Hawaiian Surfing Terms

The earliest known surfing terms sprang from the Hawaiian people. Surfers of the kingdom of Hawaii had words for every aspect of the sport. Names for some of their favorite surfing locations illustrate this: *nuumehalani,* a surf site on Oahu, meaning "the heavenly site where you are alone"; *po'o,* a Kauai location for many ancient surf competitions, meaning "to hollow out"; *uo,* a Maui surf site that translates as "a nimble threading of a needle"; *hamakuapoko,* a well-surfed Oahu location that means "sky clouds of fragrance"; and *kahalaia,* the "site of four winds" at Hilo. Specific words detail specific surf situations. *Ahua* means a place close to shore where a broken wave rises and breaks again; *lauloa* is a wave crest that breaks from one end of the beach to the other; *kakala* is a swift, curling wave. (GFF) Also see Hawaiian and Hawaiian Pidgin English surfing terms in the main text.

ahua (ah-HOO-ah) *n.* A place close to shore where a broken wave rises and breaks again. Also known as KIPAPA or PUAO. (F&H)

alaia (ah-LAI-ah) *n.* A thin wooden surfboard, wide in the front and tapering toward the back, made of koa or breadfruit. Also called OMO. (F&H)

hamakuapoko (ha-ma-KOO-ah-PO-ko) *n.* A well-surfed Oahu location, literally "sky clouds of fragrance." (GFF)

he'e (Hay-ay) *v.* To slide, to surf (F&H); to slip or flee. (P&E)

he'e nalu (Hay-ay NA-lu) **1)** *v.* To ride a surfboard. **2)** *n.* Surfing; literally "wave sliding." (F&H) **3)** *n.* Surf rider. (P&E)

he'e pu'ewai (Hay-ay POO-e-wai) *v.* To ride toward the mouth of a stream or up a stream. (F&H)

he'e umauma (Hay-ay oo-MAU-ma) *n.* bodysurfing. (F&H)

hee (Hay-ay) *n.* **1)** A flowing, as of liquid. **2)** The menses. **3)**

A flight, as of a routed army. **4)** The squid, so-called because of its slippery qualities. (ADW, 1865)

hee (Hay-ay) *v.* **1)** To melt; to run or flow, as a liquid. **2)** To slip or glide along. **3)** To ride on a surfboard. **4)** To flee; to flee through fear. (ADW, 1865)

heenalu (HAY-ay NA-lu) *n.* Hee and nalu, the surf. (ADW, 1865)

heihei nalu (HAY-hay NA-lu) *n.* A surfboard race. (F&H)

honua nalu (ho-NU-ah NA-lu) *n.* The base of the breaker.

huia (hu-E-ah) *n.* An especially high wave formed by the meeting of two crests, said to characterize the surf of Kaipaloaoa, Hawaii. (F&H)

iki (E-key) *n.* The collision of a returning wave with an incoming wave; this phrase may have been coined on the west side of Oahu, where these situations are common. (SFR 1/90)

kaha (KAH-ha) *v.* To surf; to bodysurf. (F&H)

kaha nalu (kah-ha NA-lu) *n.* Bodysurfing. (F&H)

kahalaia (kah-ha-LAY-ah) *n.* The "site of four winds" at Hilo. (GFF)

kakala (kah-KAH-la) *n.* The surf in which an *alaia* board is used; a curling wave. (F&H)

kiko'o (key-CO-oo) *n.* A twelve-to eighteen-foot surfboard that is hard to handle but good for surf that breaks roughly. (F&H)

kioe (key-O-e) *n.* A small surfboard. (F&H)

kipapa (key-PAH-pah) *n.* **1)** The prone riding position. **2)** A place close to shore where a broken wave rises and breaks again. (F&H)

kulana nalu (ku-LAH-nah NA-lu) *n.* The place where a surfer paddles to catch a wave; usually the most distant line of breakers. (F&H)

lala (LAH-lah) **1)** *v.* To surf diagonally to the wave front. **2)** *n.* Diagonal surf. **3)** *n.* A wave front; a wave to the right.

lala muku (LAH-lah MOO-koo) *n.* **1**) A wave to the left. **2**) The seaward side of a cresting wave. (F&H)

lauloa (lah-oo-LO-ah) *n.* One of two kinds of surf ridden (the other is *'ohu*); a long wave that crests and breaks from one end of the beach to the other. (F&H)

lele wa'a (lay-lay WAH-ah) *n.* Canoe leaping — that is, leaping from a canoe with a surfboard in order to ride the wave. (F&H)

muku (MOO-koo) *n.* **1**) The side of a wave near the crest. **2**) The broken section of a wave. **3**) A wave to the left. See LALA MUKU. (F&H)

nala ha'i lala (NAH-lah HA-e LAH-lah) *n.* A wave that breaks diagonally. (F&H)

nala nui (NAH-lah NU-e) *n.* A big wave. (SCSM)

nalu (NA-lu) **1**) *v.* To form waves. **2**) *n.* A wave; surf. **3**) *adj.* Full of waves; wavy, as wood grain. (F&H) Usage: *"Ke naluo nei ka moana."* "The ocean is full of waves." (P&E)

nalu (NA-lu) *adj.* Roaring; surfing; rolling in, as the surf of the sea. (ADW, 1865)

nalu (NA-lu) *n.* **1**) The surf as it rolls in upon the beach; a sea; a wave; a billow. **2**) The slimy liquid on the body of a newborn infant. (ADW, 1865)

nalu (NA-lu) *v.* **1**) To be in doubt or suspense; to suspend one's judgment. **2**) To speak secretly, or to speak to oneself; to think within oneself. **3**) To talk together or confer concerning a thing. **4**) To think; to search after any truth or fact. (ADW, 1865)

nalu puki (NA-lu PU-key) *n.* A wave that shoots high. (F&H)

nalunalu (NA-lu NA-lu) *adj.* Rough; of sea with high waves; forming high waves. (F&H)

no ka pakaka ale (no ka pa-KAH-kah AH-la) *v.* Gliding on the surf; probably refers mainly to canoe surfing. (F&H)

nuumehalani (NU-oo-MA-ha-LA-ne) *n.* A surf site on Oahu; means "the heavenly site where you are alone." (GFF)

'ohu (O-hoo) *n.* One of two kinds of surf ridden (the other is *lauloa*); a low, small wave that rises without breaking but with enough strength to carry a board. Also called OPU'U. (F&H)

olo (O-lo) *n.* The long heavy surfboard reserved for chiefs. (F&H)

omo (O-mo) *n.* ALAIA. (F&H)

onaula-loa (o-na-OO-la LO-ah) *n.* A wave of great length and endurance. (F&H)

onini (o-NEE-nee) *n.* A surfboard used by experts, difficult to manage; a thick board made of *wiliwili*; perhaps the same as an *olo*. (F&H)

opu'u (o-POO-oo) *n.* A large surf, a swell. (F&H)

owili (o-WE-lee) *n.* A thick board of *wiliwili*; perhaps an *olo*. (F&H)

pa-ha (PAH-ha) *n.* A surfboard. (F&H)

papa he'e nalu (pa-pa HAY-ay NA-lu) *n.* A surfboard; literally, "a board for sliding waves." *Ha'awi papa he'e nalu:* To give a board with the understanding that it would be returned. Boards were apparently loaned rather than given. (F&H)

po'o (PO-o) *n.* A Kauai location for many ancient surf competitions; means "to hollow out." (GFF)

pu'ua (poo-OO-ah) *n.* A surfboard. (F&H)

uo (OO-o) *n.* A Maui surf site; translates as "a nimble threading of a needle." (GFF)

APPENDIX B:
Surfboard Construction Terms

Note: For definitions of terms, see dictionary.

Art: Bob Penuelas

accelerator
acetone
activator
air-inhibited resin
airbrush
belly
blank
blend, blended lines
blocky rails
bottom contour
bottom profile
boxy
breakaway edge or break-
    away edge
bump wing, bump
catalyst
cavitation
channel concave
channel hull
channels
chine rail
chopper gun
closed tail
cloth
cobalt, cobalt napthanate
composite
compression ding

concave
contour
crazing
crown
crowned deck
crowned rail
cup
cure
cure time
curve
custom surfboard
cutaway
deck
deck contour
deck line
deck patch
deck profile
delamination
diamond tail
ding
ding-ding
ding kit
ding repair
DMA
domed deck, slightly domed
    deck
double-glassed

dovetailed fin box
drag
E-glass
epoxy resin
exothermic heat
fairing
feather edge
fiberglass, fiberglass cloth
fiberglass dust
fin
fin area
fin base
fin box
fin canter
fin height
fin placement
fin rake
fin slot
fin toe in
flex
foam
foam blank, foam block
foil
free-lapping
full template
gel
glass

GREG NOLL SURFBOARDS

ALL GREG NOLL BOARDS ARE MADE FROM THE BEST QUALITY MATERIALS AND ARE GUARANTEED AGAINST TURNING YELLOW, FOAM EXPANDING, OR BREAKING IN TWO (UNDER NORMAL CONDITIONS) .....

BOARD PRICES

0' TO 9' FEET	$	100.00
9'1" TO 9'6" FEET	$	105.00
9'7" TO 10' FEET	$	110.00
10'1" TO 12' FEET	$	120.00
ISLAND BOARDS (OUR SPECIALTY)		
10' TO 12' FEET	$	130.00

INCLUDED IN ALL ABOVE **FREE** ARE : 1 REDWOOD CENTER STRIP / 1 EXTRA DURABLE GLASS FIN

(ALL BOARDS ARE GLASSED WITH **20** OZ. FIBERCLOTH)

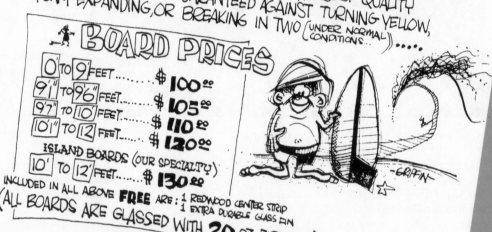

EXTRAS .... PIGMENT

PANELING 1 SIDE	$ 10.00
TWO COLOR PANEL	$ 15.00
SOLID COLOR	$ 10.00
SINGLE COLOR TAPE OFF	$ 10.00
TWO COLOR TAPE OFF	$ 15.00

CENTER STRIPS

1½ INCH BALSA	
2½ INCH BALSA	$ 5.00
MAHOGANY, TEKE, ASH	
⅛ INCH REDWOOD INLAY (CURVED OR STRAIGHT)	

LOCATED AT...
1402 PACIFIC COAST HWY., HERMOSA BEACH PHONE FRONTIER 6-4898

WHAT YOU SURF WITH

glass coat
glass itch
glass job
glass-on fin, glassed-on fin
gloss coat, gloss
gloss resin
gluing up
go off
goop
grind-down zone
grinder
grit cloth
hard planing edge
hard rail
hips
hot
hot coat
hot gooper
hydro hull
hydrofoil step, hydrofoil
  stepped
hydroplane step
injected molded fin
K-cloth, K-glass
kevlar
kick
kicked
kneeling patch
laminate
laminating resin
lap line
lay up
lift
lifted rail
line
melting lines
nose
nose guard
nose kick
nose tip
nose width

overlap
pigment
planer, power planer
planshape
plug
polyester resin
polyurethane foam, polyfoam
pressure ding
Pro Circuit Board (PCB)
pulled template
Q-cel
rail
rail apex
rail design
rail line
rail radius
rake
reshape
resin
resin fumes
respirator
rocker
routed skeg
routed stick
router
sand coat, sanding coat
sander
sanding agent
sanding block
sanding resin, surfacing resin
sandpaper
scoop
scratch-up zone
secret goo
set up
shape
shaper, surfboard shaper
sinker
skeg
skin
slot

speed bead
speed finish
spider ding
spoon
squeegee
standard foil
stick
stringer
stringer line
strip
stripes
styrene
surfboard stand
surform
tail
tail block or tailblock
tail corner
tail curve
tail design
tail kick
tail patch
tail planshape
tail width
tapered
template
textured deck
thickness flow, thickness foil
tint
true foil
tucked-under edge rail
V or vee
vee bottom
venturi effect
warp
wedge
welp
wide point or widepoint
width
wing, winger

left and right:
Circa early 1960s
Art: Rick Griffin, courtesy of Greg Noll

APPENDIX C:
Competitive Surfing Terms and Rules

Note: For definitions of terms, see dictionary.

ASP
competitive surfing
competitive surfing rules
controlled
drop-in rule, basic drop-in rule
eight ball
first rider up
functional distance
functional maneuvers
hassle, hassling
Huntington Hop
hustle

interference penalty
interference rule(s)
International Surfing
  Association (ISA)
major maneuvers
man-on-man
methods of finish
minor maneuvers
one man-one wave
priority
priority buoy
rider on the inside

right-of-way
scoring criteria
setting the scale
surfing criteria
transitional maneuvers
tube normal
tube radical
wave possession
wave selection
World Tour

thruster
Art: I. B. Nelson

APPENDIX D:
Surfing Medical Terms and Dangerous Marine Life

Note: For definitions of terms, see dictionary.

Surfing Medical Terms

all-timer's disease
board rash
bumps
common tit rash
coral cut
exostosis
haole feet
haole rot
kakios

knobs
knots
rash guard
reef rash
sea ulcer
skin
surf bumps
surf knobs, surf knots
surf fever

surfer's ear
surfer's eye
surfer's knee, surfer's knobs,
  surfer's knots
Surfer's Medical Association
  (SMA)
volcano
wax rash

Dangerous Marine Life

jellyfish
Portuguese man-of-war, man-
  o'-war
sea anemone

sea snake
sea urchin
sea wasp
shark

stingray
white shark

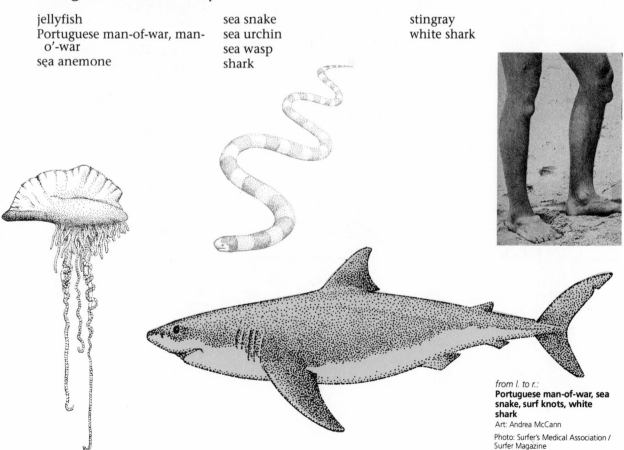

from l. to r.:
Portuguese man-of-war, sea snake, surf knots, white shark
Art: Andrea McCann

Photo: Surfer's Medical Association /
Surfer Magazine

APPENDIX E:
Wave Terms

Wave Characteristics or Conditions
bumpy
choppy
churning
clean
churly-churly
closed out
cranking
fair
flat
fast
glassy
good
disorganized
dredging
miragey
mushy
poor
punchy
shifty
slopey
slow
snappy
soft
solid
steep
suckey
tasty
thick
thin
top-to-bottom
treacherous
tubing
tubular
wedgy, wedging

Big Waves
behemoth
big smoker
billow
brown boardshorts material
hair ball
honker
huge monolith
loomer
macker
mondo
monster
mountain
quaker
rolling thunder
white elephant break

Kinds of Waves
A-frame barrel
ankle slapper
barrel
body whomper
bone crusher
bomber
boomer
burger
comber
cruncher
double bubble
double humper
double overhead
dribble
dumper
fringing wave
gnarler
grinder

humper
in-betweener
inside zipper
knee slapper
micro
mush doggie
mushburger
oatmeal
pipe, pipeline
plunging breaker
pounder
ripple
rodney wave
rogue wave
roller
shoaling wave
slab
shore pound
sleeper wave
slop
slot wave
smurph, smurphage
sneaker wave
spiller, spilling wave
square
stand-up tube
standing wave
stationary wave
storm surf
submerger
thunder crusher
tidal bore (tide wave)
tsunami
unbroken wave
wavelet

Things That Waves Do

acid drop
avalanche
backlash
back off
backwash
bowl
break
build
close out

collapse
curl
dissipate
double up
dredge
fat-out
feather
fire
flatten out

go off
hold up
hollow out
hydrocoffin
jack up
line up
max out
peak

Art: The Pizz

APPENDIX F:
Different Ways to Say the Same Thing

cool
bitchin'
guava
happening
hot
in thar
killer
live
rad
raw
sacred, sacy
stylin'
sweet

cool it
chill out
gel
mellow out

crowded surfing conditions
mob
plugged
too many guys out
zoo, zooed out

freezing-cold ocean water
arctic
brisk
burly
nip factor
nipple
nipson

goofy foot
dangle foot
goof, goofy footer
screw foot

grommet
beach grem
gremlin, gremmie, grem-
    mer
grom, grommet
helgi
surf mongrel
surf nazi
surf punk
surf rat
weed

heavy surfboard
barge
log, logger
plank
tank, tanker

hot
cool
filthy
killer
outrageous to the max
unreal

inland surfer
flatlander
inlander
smog monster
tourist
unlocal
val, valley, valley cowboy,
    valley sheep

skimboarding
Art: I. B. Nelson

kook

abb
barnacle
barney, barn, barnyard
darryl
dewey, duey
dip
dork
drip
dweeb (dweeby)
dwid
egg, eggroll
geek, geekster, geek-a-mo
gilligan
goob
goon
kahuna tuna
kak
kookster
quimby
rubberneck
spleet
squid
wally
wanker
wilma

leash

cord
ding string
leg rope
leggie
rope
shock cord
surf cord
surf leash

leash (derogatory)

dope rope
goon cord
kook cord
valley lifeline

lip (of the wave)

axe
guillotine
hammer

pseudo surfer

pseud
poser, pouser
wannabee
freeway surfer
highway surfer
dismo
wish was

really good surfing conditions

classic
epic
firing
foffing
going off
honing
insane
off its tits
off the Richter
pumping
raging
sano

ripping

lacerating
shralping
shredding
slashing
slicing
smashing
tearing it up
thrashing

runny nose (after surfing)

faucet nose
nasodrain
post-session nasal drip
(PSND)

someone who never takes a wave

buoy
decoy
duck

mallard
soaker

stealing another person's wave

dropping in
shoulder hopping
snaking waves

tube

barrel
churning cathedral
green room
glasshouse pipe
pipe or pipeline

in the tube

covered, covered up
in the tunnel
clocking in the green
room, room time
going to church
in the womb (the womb of
the ocean)
in the curl
in the Pope's living room
ziplocked

surfing in polluted waters

floaties
on the nose
surfing with poo
surfing under turd
woofy
yuk

urinating in a wetsuit

internal heating
peter heater
doing a sauna
urinophoria

vomiting

aqua boot
talking to the seals

wipeout

beef
biffing
bombing out
clam-shelled
creamed
down the mine
dump
eating it
face plant
gassed
hammered
launched
nailed
over the falls
pearling
pitched
prosecuted
quashed
rinse cycle
rumbled
splampted
stacked
sucking milk
taking gas
taking the whip
thrashed
turnpiked
tweeked
washing machine

Art: Karen T. Delgadillo

APPENDIX G:
Directory of Surfing Organizations

Surfing Associations

Association of Surfing Professionals (ASP)
P. O. Box 309
Huntington Beach, CA 92648
(714) 842-8826

Hawaiian Surfing Association
Reid Inouye c/o HOSP
P. O. Box 1707
Pearl City, Hawaii 96782

International Professional Surfers
P. O. Box 22521
Honolulu, Hawaii 96822

National Scholastic Surfing Association
(students and nonstudents)
P. O. Box 495
Huntington Beach, CA 92648
(714) 841-3254

Professional Surfing Association of America
530 6th St.
Hermosa Beach, CA 90254

Western Surfing Association
Ron Maxey
4 Laurel Lane
Laguna Hills, CA 92653

Women's International SurfingAssociation
Mary Lou Drummy
P. O. Box 512
San Juan Capistrano, CA 92693
(714) 493-2591

United States Surfing Federation
Dr. Colin Couture
11 Adamspoint Rd.
Barrington, Rhode Island 02806

Coastal Environment Protection:

The Surfrider Foundation
P. O. Box 2704 #86
Huntington Beach, CA 92647
(714) 960-8390

Longboard Clubs:

Blackie's Classic Longboard Association
P. O. Box 3148
Newport Beach, CA 92663

Breakers Surf Team
3740 Mission Blvd.
Mission Beach, CA 92109

Club Stewy
2102 So. El Camino Real
San Clemente, CA 92672

Del Mar Surf Club
P. O. Box 1114
Del Mar, CA 92014

Fog Dogs
P. O. Box 38
Loma Mar, CA 94021

Huntington Beach Longboard Crew
17106 Ash Street
Huntington Beach, CA 92647

Malibu Surfing Association
175 W. Linden Ave. Apt. #4
Burbank, CA 91502

Oceanside Longboard Surfing Club
P. O. Box 825
Oceanside, CA 92054

San Clemente Surfing Club
1403 S. Ola Vista
San Clemente, CA 92672

Santa Cruz Longboard Union
117 McMillan
Santa Cruz, CA 95060

South Coast Longboard Surfing Association
33122 Acapulco Drive
Dana Point, CA 92629

Swamis Surfing Association
P. O. Box 12
Encinitas, CA 92024

California Surfing Museums:

Santa Cruz Surfing Museum
Lighthouse Point
West Cliff Drive
Santa Cruz, CA 95060
(408) 429-3429
Open daily 12-5pm

Surfing Heritage
218 Pacific Street
Morro Bay, CA
Hours: 10-3 Saturday/Sunday
1st and 3rd weekends of the
month, plus major holidays

**California Surf Awareness
Center**
George's Restaurant
614 Hwy 101
Encinitas, CA
Hours: 7AM-2PM

Huntington Beach International Surfing Museum
(temporary location)
312 Walnut Street
Huntington Beach, CA

California Surf Museum
Promenade Shopping Center
4150 Mission Blvd.
Pacific Beach, CA
(619) 630-9313 or 942-9549
(Future location near
Ocenside Pier)

Hobie Sports
24825 Del Prado
Dana Point, CA

Encinitas Surfboards
107 North Hwy 101
Encinitas, CA

Hawaii:

Bishop Museum
Honolulu, Hawaii
(World's largest collection of
antique Hawaiian surfboards)

Photo: Bob Barbour

APPENDIX H:
Major Surf Spots Around the World

This is not an attempt to name every single surf spot on the face of the earth. Some of the places listed below may have several different breaks within the spot that have also been given individual names. Some of the place names in the list represent general areas or regions where there are numerous surf spots. Surf spots within a given country are generally listed from north to south.

Angola

Argentina

Australia
  East Coast
  Gold Coast, Queensland
    Burleigh Heads
  New South Wales
    Byron Bay
    Newcastle
    Sydney
      Narrabeen
      Dee Why
      Manly
  Victoria
    Torquay
      Point Danger
      Bells Beach
  Western Australia
  Margaret River

Bahamas

Barbados

Brazil
  Rio de Janeiro

Canada
  Vancouver Island

Canary Isands

Chile

China

Costa Rica

Dominican Republic

El Salvador

England
  Cornwall
    Newquay
    Porthleen
  Devon
  South Wales
  Porthcawl
  Gower Penninsula
  Freshwater

Easter Island

Ecuador

Fiji
  Tavarua

France
  Biarritz
    Anglet
    Grand Plage
    Cote de Basque
  Guethery
  Laffantania

Indonesia
  Bali
    Kuta Reef
    Nusa Dua
    Padang Padang
    Uluwatu
  Java
    Grajagan, "G-Land"

Ireland
  Northern Ireland
  Rossnowlagh

Israel
  Tel Aviv

Jamaica
  Boston Bay

Japan
  Tokyo

Kenya
  Malinda

Marquesas

Mauritius

Mexico
  Baja California
    K 35, K 38, K 39
    Todos Santos
    Scorpion Bay
  Mainland Mexico
    Mazatlán
    San Blas
    Mexican Pipeline

Morocco
  Hassan Surf

New Zealand
  North Island
    Piha Beach

Panama
  Gulf of Panama

Peru
  Punta Rocas

Philippines

Portugal
Ericeria
Figuera Da Foz
Lisbon
Peniche

Puerto Rico
Rincon del Mar

Reunion

Samoa

Seychelles

South Africa
Cape Town
Durban
  Bay of Plenty
  Dairy Beach
Cape St. Francis
Seal Point

Spain
El Duque
Mundacca

Sri Lanka

Tahiti

Tasmania

United States
California
Santa Cruz
  Steamer Lane
  Pleasure Point
Santa Barbara
Rincon
Zuma
Malibu
Huntington Beach
Newport Beach
Trestles
La Jolla Shores
Windansea
Pacific Beach
Ocean Beach
Imperial Beach
Tijuana Sloughs
East Coast
Massachusetts
  Cape Cod
Long Island
  Gilgo Beach
Virginia
  Virginia Beach
North Carolina
  Cape Hatteras
South Carolina
Florida
  Sebastian Inlet

Gulf Coast
Alabama
  Gulf Shores
Texas
  Galveston
  Corpus Cristi
  South Padre Is.
Hawaii
Oahu
  Makaha
  Waikiki
  Sandy Beach
  North Shore
    Pipeline
    Sunset
    Waimea
Maui
  Honolou Bay
  Maalaea

Uruguay

Vietnam

Art: The Pizz

Bibliography and Selected References

This section is divided into the following categories:

Books on Surfing
Coastal and Ocean Books
Books on Hawaiian Language
and Hawaiian Pidgin English
Surfing Periodicals
Articles in Other Periodicals

Newspaper Articles
Unpublished Surfing Research
Papers
Comics
Record Album Lyrics and
Liner Notes

Surf Punks
English Dictionaries
Books on Slang
Miscellaneous Books

Books on Surfing

Aaberg, Dennis, and John Milius. *Big Wednesday*. New York: Bantam Books, 1978. Glossary of Surfing Terms, pp. 208–214. "From bail out to wipe out: a unique guide to all great surfing terms."

Abbott, Rick. *The Science of Surfing*. Cardiff, England: John Jones Cardiff, July 1972.

Abbott, Rick, and Mike Baker. *Start Surfing*. Melbourne, Australia: Stanley Paul, 1980. Glossary, pp. 85–86.

Allen, Jim. *Locked In, Surfing for Life*. Everyday handbooks series; no. 316. Cranbury, N. J.: A. S. Barnes and Co., 1970. Glossary, pp. 193–196.

Anderson, Michael V. *The Bad, Rad, Not to Forget Way Cool Beach and Surf Discriptionary*. Oceanside, Calif.: Oceanside Printers, 1988. Southern California surfer talk.

Ball, Doc. *California Surfriders, 1946: A Scrapbook of Surfing and Beach Stuff*. 2nd ed. Redondo Beach, Calif.: Mountain and Sea Books, 1979. Originally published as Ball, John H. *Surf Riders of California*. Los Angeles: Norman Whale, 1947.

Blair, John. *The Illustrated Discography of Surf Music 1961–1965*. 2nd ed. Ann Arbor, Mich: Pierian Press, rev. 1985. "A Surfing Dictionary," pp. 123–125.

Blake, Tom. *Hawaiian Surfboard*. Honolulu, Hawaii: Paradise of the Pacific, 1935. Reprinted as *Hawaiian Surfriders 1935*. by Mountain and Sea in 1983.

_____*Hawaiian Surfriding, The Ancient and Royal Pastime*. Flagstaff, Ariz.,1961.

Bloomfield, John. *Know-how in the Surf*. Rutland, Vt.: Charles E. Tuttle Co., 1965. "Glossary of Surfing Terms," pp. 203–205. Originally published in Sydney, Australia, 1959.

Breaking Free. Available from Mountain and Sea Books, Redondo Beach, California.

Brennan, Joe. *Duke of Hawaii*. New York: Ballantine Books, 1968.

Burt, Rob. *Surf City, Drag City*. Dorset, England: Blandford Press, 1986. "Glossary of Surfing Terms," pp. 20–21.

Calisch, Rus. *Paumalu: A Story of Modern Hawaii*. San Clemente, Calif.: Paumalu Press, 1979.

Cameron, Kirk, and Zack Hanle. *The Surfer's Handbook*. New York: Dell Publishing Co., 1968.

Carroll, Corky, with Joel Engel. *Surf-Dog Days and Bitchin' Nights: Confessions of One Outrageous Surf Dude*. Chicago: Contemporary Books, 1989.

Channon, Bruce. *Surfing Wild Australia: Looking for Energy out on the Edge*. Mona Vale, New South Wales, Australia: Australian Surfing World, 1984.

Cleary, William. *Surfing: All the Young Wave Hunters*. Signet Book. New York: New American Library, 1967.

Colendich, George. *The Ding Repair Scriptures—The Complete Guide to Surfboard Repair*. Soquel, Calif.: Village Green Publications, 1986. "Glossary: A Few Key Terms," p. 88.

Conway, John. *Adventure Sports Surfing*. Harrisburg, Pa.: Stackpole Books, 1988. Glossary, pp. 120–121

Dalley, Robert J. *Surfin' Guitars—Instrumental Surf Bands of the Sixties*. Surf Publications, 1988. 6209 Oakbank Dr., Azusa, CA 91702.

Dewey, Nelson. *How to Body Surf*. Sidney, British Columbia, Canada: Saltaire Publishing Co., 1970.

Dixon, Peter L. *The Complete Book of Surfing*. New York: Ballantine Books, 1965. Glossary, pp. 212–216. Rev. ed. New York: Coward- McCann, [1967].

_____ *Men and Waves: A Treasury of Surfing*. New York: Coward-McCann, 1966.

_____ *Where the Surfers Are: A Guide to the World's Great Surfing Spots*. New York: Coward-McCann, 1968.

_____ *Men Who Ride Mountains*. New York: Bantam Books, 1969.

Drummond, Ronald Blake. *The Art of Wave Riding*. Hollywood, Calif.: Cloister Press, 1931.

Edwards, Phil, with Bob Ottum. *You Should Have Been Here an Hour Ago: The Stoked Side of Surfing or How to Hang Ten through Life and Stay Happy*. 1st ed. New York: Harper & Row, 1967.

Farrelly, Midget, as told to Craig McGregor. *The Surfing Life*. New York: Arco Publishing, 1967. "Glossary—Surfing Terms," pp. 19–92.

Filosa, Gary Fairmont R., II. *The Surfer's Almanac: An International Surfing Guide*. 1st ed. New York: E. P. Dutton, 1977. "Surfer's International Lexicon," pp. 180–198.

Finney, Ben, and James D. Houston. *Surfing—The Sport of Hawaiian Kings*. Rutland, Vt.: Charles E. Tuttle Co., 1966. "Ancient Hawaiian Surfing Terms," pp. 105–106.

Gardner, Robert. *The Art of Body Surfing*. 1st ed. Philadelphia: Chilton Book Co., 1972.

George, Sam. *Surfing: A Way of Life*. New York: Mallard Press, 1990.

Gleasner, Diana C. *Illustrated Swimming, Diving and Surfing Dictionary for Young People*. Englewood Cliffs, N. J.: Prentice-Hall, 1980.

Grigg, Ricky, and Ron Church. *Surfer in Hawaii*. Dana Point, Calif.: John Severson Publications, 1963. "Surf Jargon Glossary," pp. 64–65.

Grissim, John. *Pure Stoke*. New York: Harper and Row, 1982. Glossary, pp. 156–158.

Halacy, D. S., Jr. *Surfer!* New York: Macmillan, 1965. "Surfing Glossary," pp. 213–217.

Hemmings, Fred. *Surfing: Hawaii's Gift to the World of Sports*. New York: Grosset and Dunlap, 1977. "Illustrated Surfing Glossary," pp. 100–118.

Holmes, Paul. *Surfabout: The Complete Story of Professional Surfing and the World's Richest Contest*. Darlinghurst, New South Wales, Australia: Soundtracts Publishing, 1980.

Houston, James D. *A Native Son of the Golden West*. New York: Daily Press, 1971.

How to Surf for the Beginner. Honolulu: South Sea Sales, 1964.

Jamieson, Noel. *The Surfboard Riders Repair Manual.* Available from Perigian Beach Surf Shop, 1982.

Jarratt, Phil. *The Wave Game.* Broadway, New South Wales, Australia: Soundtracts Publishing, 1977. An inside look at professional surfing.

_____ *The Surfing Dictionary.* Sun Books. South Melbourne, Australia: Macmillian, 1985. An illustrated cartoon book.

Jenkins, Bruce. *North Shore Chronicles.* Berkeley: North Atlantic Books, 1990.

Jennar, Howard. *Making A Surfboard, The Complete Manual.* Darlinghurst, New South Wales, Australia: Mason Stewart Publishing, 1985. Glossary, pp. 93–94.

Jury, Mark. *Surfing in Southern Africa.* Struik Publishers, 1989. P. O. Box 1144, Cape Town 8000, South Africa.

Kahanamoku, Duke, with Joe Brennan. *Duke Kahanamoku's World of Surfing.* Cremorne, Sydney, Australia: Angus and Robertson, 1972. "Glossary of Surfing Terms," pp. 169–179. First published in New York: Grosset and Dunlap, 1968.

Kampion, Drew. *The Book of Waves.* Santa Barbara, Calif.: Arpel Graphics, 1989.

Kelly, John M., Jr. *Surf and Sea.* New York: A. S. Barnes and Co., 1965. Glossary, pp. 279–298.

Kinstle, James S. *Surfboard Design and Construction.* Long Beach, Calif.: Natural High Express Co., 1975.

Kirk, Cameron, and Zack Hanle. *The Surfer's Handbook.* New York: Dell Publishing, 1968.

Klein, Arthur H. *Surfing.* New York: J. B. Lippincott, 1965. "Words about some surfing words," p. 236. Reprinted in London: Kaye Ward, 1967.

Kuhns, Grant W. *On Surfing.* Rutland, Vt.: Charles E. Tuttle Co., 1963. Glossary, pp. 113–123.

London, Jack. *Learning Hawaiian Surfing: A Royal Sport at Waikiki Beach, Honolulu, 1907.* Hawaiian Memorial ed., Honolulu, Hawaii: Boom Enterprises, 1983. First published by Crowell Publishing Co., 1907.

Lorch, Carlos. *Lopez: The Classic Hawaiian Surfer.* 1982. Available from Mountain & Sea, Redondo Beach, Calif.

Loveridge, Richard. *A Guide to the Surf Beaches of Victoria.* Melbourne: Globe Press, 1987.

Lowdon, Brian J., and Margaret Lowdon, Ph.D., eds. *Competitive Surfing—A Dedicated Approach.* Torquay, Victoria, Australia: Movement Publications, 1988. Glossary, pp. 293–295; Appendix A, "Manoeuvre Definitions," pp. 296–298.

Lueras, Leonard. *Surfing: The Ultimate Pleasure.* An Emphasis International Book. New York: Workman Publishing Co., 1984. "A Surf Filmography," pp. 216–221.

Margan, Frank, and Ben R. Finney. *A Pictorial History of Surfing.* Dee Why West, New South Wales, Australia: Paul Hamlyn, 1970. Glossary: "A General Guide Is" pp. 313–319.

Masters, Ted. *Surfing Made Easy.* Van Nuys, Calif., 1962.

McGinness, Laurie. *Surfing Fundamentals.* Terry Hills, Sydney, Australia: A. H. and A. W. Reed, 1978.

McKissick, Mitch. *Surf Lingo—A Complete Guide to a Totally Rad Vocab!* Balboa, Calif.: Coastline Press, 1987. A cartoon book with glossary, pp. 81–86.

McClelland, Gordon. *Rick Griffin*. Surrey, Great Britain: Paper Tiger, 1980.

Morris, Vic, and Joe Nelson. *The Weather Surfer, A Guide to Oceanography and Meteorology for the World's Wave Hunters*. San Diego, Calif.: Grossmont Press, 1977.

Muirhead, Desmond. *Surfing in Hawaii: A Personal Memoir*. 1st ed. Flagstaff, Ariz. Northland Press, 1962. With notes on California, Australia, Peru, and other surfing countries.

Nelson, William Desmond. *Surfing: A Handbook*. Philadelphia: Auerbach Publishers, 1973. Glossary, pp. 219–227.

Nentl, Jerolyn Ann. *Surfing*. Mankato, Minn.: Crestwood House, 1978.

Noll, Greg, and Andrea Gabbard. *Da Bull—Life Over The Edge*. Bozeman, Mont.: Bangtail Press, 1989.

Olney, Ross. *The Young Sportsman's Guide to Surfing*. New York: Thomas Nelson and Sons, 1965. Chapter VIII, "Surf Talk," pp. 86–94.

Orbelian, George. *Essential Surfing*. 3rd ed. San Francisco: Orbelian Arts, 1987. First published in 1982. "Fiber Reinforced Plastics Glossary," pp. 231–238; "Essential Surfing Glossary," pp. 239–242.

Patterson, O. B. *Surf-riding: Its Thrills and Techniques*. Rutland, Vt.: Charles E. Tuttle Co., 1960.

Pearson, Kent. *Surfing Subcultures of Australia and New Zealand*. St. Lucia, Australia: University of Queensland Press; Hemel Hempstead, England: distributed by Prentice-Hall International, 1979. pp. 136–143.

Penuelas, Bob. *Wilbur Kookmeyer and Friends*. Del Mar, Calif.: Yipes Publishing, 1990.

Petersen's Surfing Yearbook Number Two. Petersen Publishing Co., Los Angeles, 1965. "Glossary of Surfing Terms," p. 224.

Petersen's Surfing Yearbook Number Three. Petersen Publishing Co., Los Angeles, 1966.

Petersen's Surfing Yearbook Number Four. Petersen Publishing Co., Los Angeles, 1969.

Pohl, Henry F. *Conquering the Surf: Lifesaving and Surfboarding*. New York: Hoffman-Harris, 1944.

Pollard, Jack. *The Surfrider*. New York: Taplinger Publishing Co., 1968. "The Surfer's Vocabulary," pp. 16–21. First published as *The Australian Surfrider*, by Sydney, Australia: K. G. Murray Publishing Co., 1963. "The Language of the Surfer," pp. 16–22.

_____ *How to Ride a Surfboard*. Wollstonecraft, New South Wales, Australia: Pollard Publishing Co., 1976.

Prytherch, Reginald J. *Surfing—A Modern Guide*. London: Faber and Faber, 1972. Glossary, pp. 129–133.

Severson, John Hugh, ed. *The Surfer — John Severson's First Annual Surf Photo Book*. Original ed. Dana Point, Calif.: Severson Studios, 1960. Reprinted in Dana Point, Calif.: Surfer Publications, 1973.

_____ *Modern Surfing around the World*. 1st ed. New York: Doubleday, 1964. "Surfing Terminology," pp. 162–186.

_____ *Great Surfing: Photos, Stories, Essays, Reminiscences and Poems*. New York: Doubleday, 1967.

Shackleton, Roger, and John Christensen. *All About Wave Skis*. Brookvale, New South Wales, Australia: Surfside Press, 1985.

Shaw, Stephen M., ed. *Surfboard*. Rev. ed. La Mesa, Calif.: Transmedia, 1983. Formerly published as *Surfboard Builders' Manual* (1963) and *Surfboard Builders' Yearbook* (1971).

St. Pierre, Brian. *The Fantastic Plastic Voyage: Across the South Pacific with Surfers and a Camera*. New York: Coward-McCann, 1969.

Stern, David H., and William S. Cleary. *Surfing Guide to Southern California*. Series title: International surfing guidebook series v. 1. Malibu, Calif.: Fitzpatrick Co., 1963. 2d ed. Los Angeles : Mountain and Sea Books, 1977.

Sufrin, Mark. *Surfing: How to Improve Your Technique*. New York: Franklin Watts, 1973. Glossary, pp. 59–61.

Surf, How To—The Complete Guide to Surfing. Darlinghurst, New South Wales, Australia: Mason Stewart Publishing, 1983.

Surfboard. La Mesa, Calif.: Aileen S. Brown, 1981.

Surfboard, How to Make Your Own. North Sydney, Australia: Australian Surfing Kit Co., 1965. "A Glossary of Surfers' Terms," p. 17–18.

Surfing the Big Wave. Available from Mountain And Sea Books, Los Angeles.

Surfing the Chain of Fire. Australian Surfing World. Available from Mountain And Sea Books, Los Angeles.

Thomson, Carl. *Surfing in Great Britain*. London: Constable, 1972.

Timmons, Grady. *Waikiki Beachboy*. Honolulu: Editions Limited, 1989.

Wardlaw, Lee. *Cowabunga! The Complete Book of Surfing*. New York: Avon Books, 1991.

Warren, Mark. *Mark Warren's Atlas of Australian Surfing*. North Ryde, New South Wales, Australia: Agnus and Robertson, 1988. Glossary, pp. 228–229. "An introduction to surf talk," p. 29.

Warwick, Wayne. *A Guide to Surfriding in New Zealand*. Wellington, New Zealand: Viking Seven Seas, 1978 Glossary. The third revised ed. does not have a glossary.

Wegener, Tom, and Bill Burke. *Southern California's Best Surf: A Guide to Finding, Predicting, and Understanding the Surf of Southern California*. Redondo Beach, Calif.: Green Room Press, 1989.

White, Graham. *Surfing*. Sydney, Australia: Paul Hamlyn, 1977.

Wright, Bank. *Surfing California: A Complete Guide to the California Coast*. Redondo Beach, Calif.: Manana , 1973.

_____ *Surfing Hawaii*. Redondo Beach, Calif: Mountain and Sea, 1972.

Young, Nat. *Nat Young's Book of Surfing*. Sydney, Australia: A. H. and A. W. Reed, 1979. Glossary p. 87.

_____ *Surfing Australia's East Coast*. Sydney, Australia: New Century Press, 1980.

_____ *The History of Surfing*. Palm Beach, New South Wales, Australia: Palm Beach Press, 1983.

_____ *Surfing & Sailboard Guide to Australia*. Palm Beach, New South Wales, Australia: Palm Beach Press, 1985.

_____ *Surfing Fundamentals*. Palm Beach, New South Wales, Australia: Palm Beach Press, 1985. Glossary pps. 126–128.

Coastal and Ocean Books

Bascom, Willard. *Waves and Beaches*. Garden City, N. Y.: Anchor Books, 1980.

California Coastal Access Guide. California Coastal Commission. Jo Ginsberg and Erin Caughman eds. Rev. ed. Berkeley: University of California Press, 1991.

California Coastal Resource Guide. California Coastal Commission. Joanne Ginsberg and Madge Caughman eds. Berkeley: University of California Press, 1987.

Dutton, Geoffrey. *Sun, Sea, Surf and Sand: The Myth of the Beach*. New York: Oxford University Press, 1985.

Gross, M. Grant. *Oceanography*. 4th ed. Columbus, Ohio: Charles E. Merrill Publishing Co., 1980.

Groves, Don. *The Oceans: A Book of Questions and Answers*. New York: John Wiley and Sons, 1989.

Hendrickson, Robert. *The Ocean Almanac*. New York: Doubleday, 1984.

Suiso, Ken, and Rell Sunn. *A Guide to Beach Survival*. Haleiwa, Hawaii: Honolulu Water Safety Consultants, 1986.

The Times Atlas of the Oceans. Alastair Couper, ed. New York: Van Nostrand Reinhold Co., 1983.

Books on Hawaiian Language and Hawaiian Pidgin English

Andrews, Lorrin . *A Dictionary of the Hawaiian Language*. Lahaina, Maui, Hawaii, 1865.

Carr, Elizabeth Ball. *Da Kine Talk: From Pidgin to Standard English in Hawaii*. Honolulu: University of Hawaii Press, 1972.

Pukui, Mary Kawena, and Samuel Elbert. *Hawaiian Dictionary*. Honolulu: University of Hawaii Press, 1971.

Pukui, Mary Kawena et al. *The Pocket Hawaiian Dictionary*. Honolulu: University of Hawaii Press, 1975.

Simonson, Douglas (Peppo) et al. *Pidgin to da Max*. Honolulu: Peppovision, 1981.

_____ *Pidgin to da Max Hana Hou!* Honolulu: Peppovision, 1982.

Speak Hawaiian. Honolulu: Paradise Products, 1973.

Surfing Periodicals

Action. Imperial Beach, California.

Australia's Surfing Life. Burleigh Heads, Queensland, Australia.

Beach Culture. Dana Point, California.

Beach Happy. San Clemente, California.

Beach 'n Waves. San Diego, California.

Body Boarding. San Clemente, California.

Breakout. Bimonthly. Carlsbad, California.

Groundswell. Honolulu, Hawaii.

International Surfing, Bimonthly. Hermosa Beach, California. See *Surfing*.

Kema. Dana Point, California.

Local. Santa Cruz, California.

Making Waves. Huntington Beach, California. Newsletter of the Surfrider Foundation.

Riptide. Burleigh Heads, Queensland, Australia.

Skimboard. South Laguna, California.

South Swell. Jacksonville, Fl.: South Swell Publishing.

Surf Guide. Monthly. Santa Monica, California.

Surfer. Monthly. Dana Point, California. See "Eastside Speak" in Sections (August 1990): 78.

Surfin' Life. Tokyo, Japan.

Surfing. Monthly. San Clemente, California. See "Surfspeak—Beach Blanket Babble." Vol. 17, no. 12 (December 1981): 19.

Surfing Illustrated, Quarterly. Hermosa Beach, California.

Surfing Medicine. Published by the Surfer's Medical Association, San Francisco.

Surfing World. Monthly. Sydney, Australia.

Tracks. Monthly. Darlinghurst, New South Wales, Australia: Mason Stewart Publishing. See McTavish, Bob. "Pods for Primates: A Personal History of Surfboard Design." In The Best of Tracks, 1976, pp. 120–132.

Tres 60. Santurce, Vizcaya, Spain.

Waves. Waterloo, New South Wales, Australia.

Wave Length. England.

Wave Rider. Bimonthly. Cocoa Beach, Florida.

Wind Surf. Paris, France. See "Do You Speak Surfer?" No. 18, 1990: pp. 16–17.

Articles in Other Periodicals

"Still Surfin' After All These Years" by Jonathan Kirsch, *New West* vol. 6, no. 5, (May 1981): 90–91.

"Surfin' Safari Revisited" by Laura Bernstein and Jill Johnson Keeney, *New West* vol. 6, no. 5, (May 1981): 92–99.

"Surf Wars" by Frank Bies, *New West* vol. 6, no. 5, (May 1981): 100–105.

Thrasher. San Francisco, California.

"Surfing on California Beach is a Favorite Summertime Sport." *Life.* vol. 9 (August 1940): 50–52.

"Waves & Thrills at Waikiki" *National Geographic.* vol. 67, no. 5, (May 1935): 597.

"Surfboarders Capture California" *National Geographic.* vol. 86, no. 3, (September 1944): 355.

"'Hey Man, My Wave!': The Authority of Private Language." *Poetics Journal*. no. 6, (1986): 3–5. Rep. from a talk given by Michael Davidson at New Langton Arts, San Francisco, March 22, 1984.

"*The Development and Diffusion of Modern Hawaiian Surfing.*" Finney, Ben. *The Journal of Polynesian Society*, vol. 69, no. 4., (December 1960).

"Hitch-hiking on the Big Waves" *Popular Mechanics*. vol. 77, no. 2, (February 1942): 72–75 + 166.

"*Surfboarding in Oceania: Its Pre-European Distribution.*" Finney, Ben. Sonderdruck aus Wiener Volkerkundliche Mittelungen VII. Jahrgang–Bd. II, Nr. 1–4.

"The Mechanics of Waves and the Art of Surfing." Wolkomir, Richard. *Oceans* (June 1988): pp. 36–41.

Newspaper Articles

Greth, Carlos Vidal. "Surfing in the City." *San Francisco Chronicle*, People Section, B3–B4, June 24, 1988. Glossary, "Official Argot of the Surf-Stoked."

Pine, Jon. "Surfing's developed a colorful language." *Contra Costa Times* Concord, CA p. 8B, Monday, June 12, 1989. Glossary.

Stillman, Deanne. "Surf's Up Again: On Screen, on Canvas, on the Radio." *New York Times*, Arts & Leisure, Section 2, September 2, 1990.

Zamora, Jim Herron. "Why Valley Girls and Mutant Turtles Sound Like Surfers." *The Wall Street Journal*, September 27, 1990.

Unpublished Surfing Research Papers

Digman, Debra. "Oral Testimonies of Santa Cruz Surfers: The Creation of a Culture." University of California, Santa Cruz, 1972. Special Collections GV840.S82M6 Santa Cruziana Archives.

Irwin, John Keith. "Surfers: A Study of the Growth of a Deviant Subculture." Master's Thesis, Department of Sociology, University of California, Berkeley, 1965.

Levine, Alice. "Stories of the Santa Cruz Surf Culture." University of California, Santa Cruz, 1972. Special Collections GV840.S82M654 Santa Cruziana Archives.

Lux, Anna Kathryn. "Surfing in Santa Cruz as Told through a Life History." University of California, Santa Cruz, 1987. Special Collections GV840.S8 L89 1987 Santa Cruziana Archives.

Spencer, C. Philip. "A Surfing Oral Tradition in Santa Cruz: 'Tales and Things.'" University of California, Santa Cruz, 1975. Special Collections GV840.S82S67 Santa Cruziana Archives.

Comics

Silver Surfer. New York: Marvel Comics.

Surf Crazed Comics. San Clemente, Calif.: Paskowitz.

Tales from the Tube. Art-directed by Rick Griffin, 1973.

Wave Warriors. San Clemente, Calif.: Herbie Fletcher and Astroboys Productions.

Record Album Lyrics and Liner Notes

The Beach Boys. *Surfing U.S.A*. Album glossary. Capitol Records. 1961.

The Belairs and "The Origins of Surf Music: 196–963," with a written historical perspective by Paul Johnson. Los Angeles, Calif.: Iloki Records. 1987.

Golden Summer. Los Angeles: United Artists Records, 1976.

Surf Punks

My Beach. Surf Punks Glossary 1. New York: Epic/CBS. 1980.

Locals Only. Surf Punks Glossary 2. Malibu, Calif.: Day-Glo Records. 1982

Oh, No! Not Them *Again!* Surf Punks Glossary 3. El Segundo, Calif.: Enigma Records. 1988.

Surf Punks Fan Club Info:
Send Self Addressed Stamped Envelope to: P. O. Box 374, Malibu, California 90265

English Dictionaries

The American Heritage Dictionary. 2nd College ed. Boston: Houghton Mifflin Co., 1985.

Oxford English Dictionary. New York: Oxford University Press, 1971.

Random House Dictionary. New York: Random House, 1987.

Webster's Ninth New Collegiate Dictionary. Springfield, Mass: Merriam-Webster Inc., 1989

Books on Slang

Blowdryer, Jennifer. *Modern English: A Trendy Slang Dictionary*. Berkeley: Last Gasp of San Francisco, 1985.

Munro, Pamela, ed. *U.C.L.A. Slang: A Dictionary of Slang Words and Expressions used at U.C.L.A.* U.C.L.A. Occasional Paper in Linguistics, #8, Dept. of Linguistics, University of California at Los Angeles, 1989.

_____ *Slang U*. New York: Harmony Books, 1989.

Partridge, Eric. *Smaller Slang Dictionary*. New York: Dorset Press, 1961.

Miscellaneous Books

Bragonier, Reginald, Jr., and David Fisher. *What's What in Sports—The Visual Glossary of the Sports World*. Maplewood, N. J.: Hammond, 1984. "Surfing," p. 161.

Hart, James D. *A Companion to California*. New York: Oxford University Press, 1978.

Javna, John. *The TV Theme Song Sing-Along Song Book Volume 2*. New York: St. Martin's Press, 1985.

Nicholson, Margaret. *The Little Aussie Fact Book*. Long Beach: Australia In Print, 1989.

The World Almanac and Book of Facts 1991. New York: Pharos Books, 1991.

A note about sources used in compiling this dictionary: Like all dictionaries, *The Surfin'ary* draws on many sources. Although every effort was made to give credit for specific material, this wasn't always possible. Some definitions combine information from several sources; some terms are so widespread in there use and meaning that it would be senseless to attribute them to a single source. Nevertheless, all sources that contributed (knowingly or unknowingly) to this book are listed in either the bibliography or one of the credits sections. Concerning the editorial policy followed in compiling this book, except for verbatim quotations (which are clearly indicated and attributed), all material in this book has been edited, even when a source is cited.

Art and Photography Credits

Artists and Illustrators

Glenn Bering
Karen T. Delgadillo
Jen Delyth
Rebecca Fish
Rick Griffin
Roy Gonzales
Keith Hunter
John Iwerks*
Jim Lucas
Andrea McCann

I. B. Nelson
Bill Ogden
Bob Penuelas
Jim Phillips
Jimbo Phillips
Gary L. Prettyman
The Pizz
Dean Rankine ("Deano")
Rick Rietveld
Robbie Quine

Peter Schroff
John Severson
Tim Smith
Peter Spacek
Rick Stover
Surfer Magazine
John Van Hammersveld
George Woodbridge

*To order your own copy of "Toadally Tubed" Surfing Flipbook by John Iwerks, send $9.00 plus $1.00 postage c/o John Iwerks, P. O. Box 1551, Santa Barbara, CA 93102. Toadally Tubed is printed in color, measures 3x5 inches, and contains 105 pages. Each book is personally hand assembled and hand bound.

Photographers

Nina Aldrich-Wolfe
Rolf Aurness
Don Balch
Bob Barbour
Bishop Museum
Robert Brown
John S. Callahan
Aaron Chang
Bud Clark
Judith Cralle
Trevor Cralle
Peter Crawford
Jeff Divine

Tom Dodd
Kirwan Fox
Rob Gilley
Philip Hellsten
Dan Jenkin
Dennis Junor/Creation Captured
Tai Sing Loo
I. B. Nelson
O'Neil, Inc.
Bob Richardson
Mac Reed
Bill Romerhaus
Bill Schwob

Tom Servais
T. Severin
John Severson
Ron Stoner
Surfer Magazine
Surfers Medical Association
Fred Swegels
John Witzig
Leslie Werner
Woody Woodworth/Creation
   Captured

plugged Art: George Woodbridge / MAD Magazine, 1965

Additional Credits

Major Contributors

Ad the Rad Lad
Bernie Baker
Tim Baker, *Tracks* magazine
Bruce Brown
Corky Carroll
Will Church, via speakerphone, Santa Cruz Surf Shop
Michael Davidson, Department of Literature, University of California, San Diego
Peter Dixon
Dr. Dume, *Surfer* Magazine
Eric Fairbanks, *Surfing* magazine
Nathan Fletcher
Chris Gallagher
Matt George
Sam George
Jay Gould
Tex and Lynn Haines, Victoria Skimboards
Harold Hawkins and Tony Ramarez, c/o Total Control Surfboards, Corpus Christi, Texas.

Greg "The Gardner" Histed, aka "Frank"
Lisa Hybarger
Hal Jepsen
Dave "The Wave" Kinstle, aka "Flaco"
Matt Kechele
Rich Maile and Felix Alfaro, O'Neill Surf Shop, Santa Cruz
Ben Marcus, *Surfer* Magazine
Paul "Mango" McEntyre
Gordon T. McClelland
Julie Moniz, Santa Cruz Surf Shop (also Tina George and Mike Courtney)
Bev Morgan
Michael Martin
Anthony James Misner
Ellen Nachtigall
I. B. Nelson
Paco (Dan Jenkin)
Greg Noll
Bob Penuelas
Mike Peterson

The Pizz
Laura Platt
Robbie Quine
Mac Reed
Lisa Roselli
Richard Schmidt
Ken Seino, Chairman of the Boards for Cowabunga Surfware
Tom Servais
Allan Seymour
Marcel Soros, Natural Progression
Ward Smith
Drew Steele
Michelle Anne Stevens
Santa Cruz Surfing Museum
Toby at Arrow Surf & Sport, Santa Cruz
Peter Townend
Greg Travers, Ocean Energy, Santa Cruz.
Matt Warshaw, *Surfer* Magazine

Additional Contributors

Sunny Abberton
Victor Abubo
Amy & Laura Michele, The Agigian Sisters
Matt Allen
Nicole Andlinger
Aqua Culture surf shop, Half Moon Bay, CA
Kevin Ascher
Lloyd Austin
Benjah
Brian Baird
Dick Banfield
Mark Barbour
Steve Barilotti, *Surfer* Magazine
Rich Bass
Maya Berger ("Earth Puddle")
Big Stick Surfing Association
Katherine Bishop
Jeff Braverman
Dan Bush
Anton Calderon

Tyler Campbell
Tom Carroll
Bob Carlson of Carlson Designs
Sherry Carlson
Ted Cassidy
Gerry Chalmers
Richard Chester and Verne McCall
Karen T. Delgadillo
Chris Denney
Damian Dhar
Dennis Dragon
Mary Duffy
Lawrence J. England
Paul Feldman
Mike Ferreira
Rebecca Fish
Marcy Fleming
Toni Francavilla
Noah Franzblau
Rob Gilley
David Gilovitch, *Surfing* magazine
Cork Golston

Michael Golston
M. Gonzalez
Lulie Haddad
Jim Halperin (Jimbo)
Kini Harvey
Bob Hasier and Co.
Philip Hellsten, President, Old Wave Surfing Association
Jared Hermann
Bob and Jennifer Hightower
Edwin A. Hoey
Keith Hunter
Todd Jacobs, Channel Islands National Marine Sanctuary
Dr. Scott Jenkins, The Surfrider Foundation
Jodster (Hollywood, Florida)
R. Jones
Val "Skate" Jones
Justin (Santa Cruz grommet) Gamino

Carlos Kende, Northern Mexico
Coordinator, Association
Mexicana de Surfing A.C.
Erik Larson
Dru Lewis
Tamara Lipper
Brock Little
Tony "Delgado" Litwak
Mike Locatelli
Toni Logan
Ariel Marks
Jorge MacFarland with Scorpio
Surfing Tours of Isla Natividad
(Chula Vista)
Gary MacVicar
Paul McHugh
Lee Micheaux
Ira Miller
Mickey Muñoz
Barney Q. Nietschmann,
Department of Geography,
University of California,
Berkeley
Margot O'Neill
Jill Ornstein
Ron Ortron

A. Paskowitz
M. Paskowitz
Eric Penzower
Steve Pezman, *Surfer* Magazine
Douglas Powell, Department of
Geography, University of
California, Berkeley
Denny Plyer
Rusty Preisendorfer
Rosemary Prem
R.C., Santa Monica, California
James D. Rawls
Rich & Dunc, Glenalta,
South Australia
Kelly Richardson
Dave Romyn
Joe Ryan
Tim Ryan
Santa Crucial posse
Dennis Salles
Aaron Santell
Michael Schutz
Adel Shephard
Ken Shirriff
Scott Shurtz
Brad Smith

Jason Smith
Lynn Smith
Butt Stains (Long Beach)
Kirk Steers
Steve, Surf Side Sports,
Newport Beach
Shaun Tomson
Jonathon Toste
Bob Travis
Non Travis
Two Hindu Surfers
A. D. Vernon
Rick D. T. Wilson
Jos Walton
Stuart and Devin Watson
Mark M. Wagner
Ernest Weekly
Steven White
Dave Williams
Todd Wolf and the Boca Surf
Cafe crew, Florida
Mike Worth (*Big Wednesday*)
Yo Skankin' Dub Masters
. . . and a few others.

We'd love to add your name to this list — see next page for details.

Art: Jimbo Phillips

A NOTE TO THE READER

A Call for Submissions

Every conceivable effort has gone into making this book as complete as possible, but undoubtedly some terms and definitions were not uncovered and, regrettably, have been left out. This book, like any dictionary, will forever be a "work in progress."

Perhaps this collection of surfing terminology will inspire individuals like yourself to dig up old glossaries and recall forgotten or obscure terms, and maybe even create and introduce new words and phrases. Please send all comments, criticisms, corrections, and of course, any new terms or expressions to the address below for inclusion in a future revised and updated edition.

A Note about Submissions

Send in anything — technical shaper's terms, wave descriptions, surfboard design features, derogatory slang, surfing maneuvers — whatever.

Ideally we'd like to get the following information, although anything that you send will be greatly appreciated:

1) Surfing term, phrase, or expression; a key to pronunciation (if not obvious).

2) A thorough and detailed definition or definitions; can be serious or funny or both.

3) Usage: give at least one example of how the word is used in a sentence (surfing context).

4) Source: name of person(s) or publication(s) to be credited. (Anonymous contributions are also welcome.)

All contributions should be sent to:

Trevor Cralle, Editor
The Surfin'ary
P. O. Box 30877
Walnut Creek, California 94598
USA

We are always looking for interesting photos or illustrations.

We want your feedback!

Art: Jimbo Phillips

The Surfrider Foundation

The Surfrider Foundation is a nonprofit organization established for the protection and enhancement of the world's coastal and ocean environment through conservation, research, and education. Surfrider is dedicated to preserving the natural state of our waves and beaches, improving recreational opportunities, and assuring a clean and healthy marine environment for all people.

Since its inception in 1984, Surfrider has been a leader in California environmental advocacy, and it is now having a significant impact in Hawaii, and on the East and Gulf coasts as well. Among its many achievements are the prevention of an Imperial Beach breakwater that would have eliminated surf along a three-mile stretch of beach, the establishment of public accessways at Hammonds Reef in Santa Barbara, and the initiation, under the Clean Water Act, of a citizen suit against two pulp mills in Humboldt County, the largest such suit to be brought to date.

Our beaches and waves are besieged by more complex problems than ever before. Our ocean is used as a dump. The Blue Water Task Force was established to combat this situation. It is a grass-roots program of water quality testing along our nation's shorelines. Designed to insure compliance with state and federal water-quality standards, it calls for harsh civil penalties against violators.

By joining the Surfrider Foundation, you are standing up for the waves that stand up for you. For more information, write the Surfrider Foundation at P.O. Box 2704#86, Huntington Beach, CA 92647, or call (714) 960-8390.

Rick Rietveld Print

500 signed lithographs of Rick Rietveld's *1-2-Go* print pictured below (also in color section) were created especially for the Surfrider Foundation, with proceeds going to the Blue Water Task Force. Limited Edition: $150.

About the author

Trevor Cralle (KRAWL-ee) is a native California surfer with a degree in cultural geography from the University of California, Berkeley. He has worked for the California Coastal Commission, where he was one of the principal writers of the *California Coastal Resource Guide* and the revised *California Coastal Access Guide*. Trevor is an all-American swimmer, a scuba diving instructor, and an underwater video cameraman. In addition to traveling in over forty countries, he has sailed through the South Pacific on a thirty-nine-foot sloop, co-led marine educational field trips to Mexico, and is a windsurfing and lifeguard instructor and the head counselor at a summer water sports camp on the island of Antigua in the Caribbean.

Trevor "Coconut" Cralle
Photo: Leslie Werner

BACK COVER BALLOON TRANSLATION How's it going? The waves were great today, big and powerful like a Mack truck, and over twice my height in size. The unbroken waves approaching the shore looked like ribbed ridges. The wind was blowing favorably from the land out to the sea and the surface of the ocean had a smooth mirror-like appearance. The waves were rolling in to shore at an accelerated rate. I rode my surfboard from the highest point of the wave, down its steep front, and through a whirling tunnel of water that was retreating rapidly beside a jutting piece of land. Now the surfing conditions have become poor — the waves are shapeless and uneven. I'm going to go get some Mexican food and something to drink. See you later, pal.

Art: Jim Phillips

Enjoy *The Surfin'ary* in the privacy of your own wave!
Art: Robbie Quine